An Economic History of Modern Ethiopia

Edited by
Shiferaw Bekele

CODESRIA BOOK SERIES

An Economic History of Modern Ethiopia

First published in 1995 by CODESRIA

Copyright © CODESRIA

CODESRIA is the Council for the Development of Social Science Research in Africa headquartered in Senegal. It is an independent organization whose principal objectives include facilitating research, promoting research-based publishing and creating multiple fora geared towards the exchange of views and information among African scholars.

		HC
ISBN	**2-86978-042-7 (Soft cover)**	845
	2-86978-043-5 (Hard cover)	.E257

Cover designed by Ousmane Ndiaye Dago
Typeset by Marie Therese Coron, CODESRIA
Production Consultants: Foster & Phillips
Printed by Antony Rowe Ltd.
Distributors: ABC, 27 Park End Street, Oxford OX1, IHU

CODESRIA would like to express its gratitude to the Swedish Agency for Research Cooperation (SAREC), the International Development Research Centre (IDRC), the Ford Foundation, the Rockefeller Foundation, the Norwegian Ministry of Foreign Affairs and the Danish Agency for International Development (DANIDA) for supporting its research and publication activities.

Contents

Contributors iv

Acronyms v

Preface vi

1. An Overview of the Economy, 1941-74 1
   Shiferaw Jammo

2. The Evolution of Land Tenure in the Imperial Era 72
   Shiferaw Bekele

3. Peasant Agriculture Under the Old Regime 143
   Dessalegn Rahmato

**4. Running to Keep in the Same Place: Industrialization,
1941-74** 194
   Eshetu Chole

**5. The Development of Money, Monetary Institutions
and Monetary Policy, 1941-75** 232
   Befekadu Degefe

**6. Demography, Migration and Urbanization in
Modern Ethiopia** 277
   Alula Abate

Index 328

Contributors

Alula Abate is an Associate Professor in the Department of Geography of Addis Ababa University. He has published many articles on urbanization, population, agricultural cooperatives.

Befekadu Degefe is an Associate Professor in the Department of Economics of Addis Ababa University and a Senior Research Fellow in the Institute of Development Research of the same university. He specializes in monetary economics and has done extensive research in this field. He has published many articles.

Dessalegn Rahmato is a senior research fellow at the Institute of Development Research, Addis Ababa University. He is the author of two books, *Agrarian Reform in Ethiopia* (1984), and *Famine and Survival Strategies: A Case Study from Northeast Ethiopia* (1992), and two monographs, *The Crisis of Livelihood in Ethiopia* (1988) and *The dynamics of Rural Poverty: Case Studies from a District in Southern Ethiopia* (1992). He has published numerous articles on land policy, food security and peasant agriculture. His current research interest is in environment and rural policy.

Eshetu Chole is an Associate Professor in the Department of Economics, Addis Ababa University. He is the co-author of a book, *Profiles of the Ethiopian Economy* (1969) and has edited many publications. He has widely published numerous articles on various aspects of the Ethiopian economy.

Shiferaw Bekele is an Associate Professor in the Department of History, Addis Ababa University. He specialises in the social and economic history of nineteenth and twentieth centuries Ethiopian history. He has co-edited a book, *Kasa and Kasa: Papers on the Times, Lives and Images of Tewodros II and Yohannes IV 1855-1889* (1990) and has published articles on various aspects of modern Ethiopian history.

Shiferaw Jammo is a senior expert in the Branch Office of the World Bank in Addis Ababa. He has served as a senior civil servant in the Planning Commission before the revolution of 1974 and in several other government agencies afterwards. He has done extensive studies of the various sectors of the Ethiopian economy.

Acronyms

AIDB	Agricultural and Industrial Bank
CADU	Chilalo Agricultural Development Unit
CSO	Central Statistical Office
DA	Demonstration Area (of MPP)
EPID	Extension and Project Implementation Department (MoA)
FAO	Food and Agriculture Organization
IDA	International Development Association (World Bank)
IECAMA	Imperial Ethiopian College of Agriculture and Mechanical Arts (Alemaya Agricultural College)
IEG	Imperial Ethiopian Government
ILCA	International Livestock Centre for Africa (Addis Ababa)
ILO	International Labour Office
MLRA	Ministry of Land Reform and Administration
MoA	Ministry of Agriculture
MPP	Minimum Package Programme
MT	Metric Tons
OA	Observation Area (of MPP)
PCO	Planning Commission Office
RRC	Relief and Rehabilitation Commission
SIDA	Swedish International Development Agency
SRI	Stanford Research Institute (Menlo Park, California)
UNDP	United Nations Development Programme
USAID	U.S. Agency for International Development
USDA	U.S. Department of Agriculture
USOM/E	U.S. Operations Mission to Ethiopia
WADU	Wollaita (formerly Wollamo) Agricultural Development Unit
WHO	World Health Organization

Preface

The economic history of modern Ethiopia has not attracted sufficient scholarly attention. This cannot be generally attributed to the dearth of Ethiopian economists or historians, though it was in the fading years of the imperial regime that the country's scholarly community came of age. Although outdated and inadequately analytical, Richard Pankhurst's *Economic History of Ethiopia,* (1968), still serves as a useful work of reference for the period before the Italian occupation. This work still covers almost all sectors of the economy and provides a wealth of bibliographic material. But it has not been followed up by another work covering the period after 1935. We should note that some aspects of the period of Italian colonial economic policy have been studied at some length, mostly by foreign Ethiopianists. In recent years, Ethiopian scholars have begun to invade this field as well, and Haile Mariam Larebo's *'Agriculture in Ethiopia during the Fascist Italian Occupation of Ethiopia 1936-1941'* (1989), which attempts to reconstruct the history of Ethiopian agriculture under Italian rule, is a case in point. Nevertheless, no serious research has yet produced any global picture of the state of the Ethiopian economy during the period under consideration and the two previous decades.

The economic history of the imperial regime (1941 to 1974; the significance of these two landmark dates is too obvious to warrant elaboration here) has not yet been the subject of a systematic historical investigation though synchronic studies on one or another aspect of the economy, which covered limited time spans, have been published. Cursory surveys of the economy have also been attempted in several books as part of a general treatment of the imperial regime. Assefa Bekele and Eshetu Chole did make laudable efforts with their *Profile of the Ethiopian Economy* (1969) which served the useful purpose of bringing analyses and considerable empirical data on various sectors of the economy under one cover. However, since their work is nearly a quarter of a century old, the absence of a comprehensive work still makes it difficult for one to fully understand the nature of the socio-economic transformations that took place in the country during the period under review. However - and this is significant from the standpoint of most of the contributors to this volume - a number of courses given at the College of Social Sciences and the Faculty of Business Studies and Economics of Addis Ababa University (AAU) deal in full or in part with the period on which there has been no adequate textbook or reference material.

It was for these reasons that we decided to jointly prepare a book on the Economic History of the Imperial Regime, though, ideally, it would have been best for a single author to tackle the subject. In the process of researching and writing these chapters, we realized that it would take a much shorter time to fill the gaps through interdisciplinary collaborative projects than it would have taken a single author to do so. Another advantage of such a collaborative effort was the fact that various specialists were brought together to tackle a broad subject for which a single author would either have lacked the necessary expertise or prepared a work of uneven quality.

Aware of the fact that a greater proportion of the scholarly literature on Ethiopia was produced by foreign scholars who inevitably handled the subject matter within an external frame of reference, we decided from the very outset that this project should be undertaken by Ethiopians alone in order to bring out the Ethiopian perspective in one book. It is up to the reader to judge whether or not we succeeded in doing so.

After the essays were written, we organized, from 31 January to 2 February, 1992, a workshop to which we invited experts in the various areas of the subjects covered, as well as interested academics and specialists, to discuss the drafts. This turned out to be a very stimulating and useful exercise which, we believe, did contribute greatly to the improvement of the essays in this volume.

The essays cover in considerable detail the major sectors of the economy, namely: land, agriculture, the manufacturing sector, macro-economics, the monetary sector as well as demography, migration and urbanization. We, more than anybody else, are aware of the fact that these essays do not constitute an exhaustive coverage of the subject. The whole issue of environment and environmental degradation, fiscal history, international trade, developments in transport and communication, all of which could not be covered, are subjects that are essential to the study of the modernization effort in the country. In spite of these shortcomings, however, we hope the work will be of use to students, instructors, researchers and the general reader concerned about Ethiopian history and its development record in the modern period.

A supplementary volume will be published soon with a comprehensive bibliography on the economy of the period. Moreover, this work will be followed up by a second volume which will examine, in considerable depth, the economic history of the 1975-91 period during which the military authorities, who overthrew the imperial regime, set themselves apart from their predecessors by instituting 'socialist' development policies, and restructuring the economy in line with these policies.

This project could not have been realized without the generous assistance of the Council for the Development of Economic and Social Research for Africa (CODESRIA) which funded the Workshop and also published this book. The Institute of Development Research of AAU provided logistic support and other assistance. We would like to extend our gratitude to these two institutions and to their staff who facilitated our work.

Shiferaw Bekele
Addis Ababa
July 1992

I. An Overview of the Economy 1941-74

Shiferaw Jammo

This chapter reviews the major trends in the Ethiopian economy during the period after independence from Italian occupation in 1941 up to the revolution of 1974 but, more specifically, after the integration of the economies of Eritrea and Ethiopia in 1952. In order to view developments in the Ethiopian economy in their proper historical context, it would be appropriate to highlight the most significant events during the period under review, marked by political and economic currents of considerable importance. These were: a) the federation of Eritrea and Ethiopia in 1952; b) the abortive military coup of 1960; and c) the oil crisis of 1973 and the drought and widespread famine of the same year. Those events will be examined in somewhat greater detail in the following paragraphs.

The federation of Eritrea and Ethiopia in September 1952 [1] in accordance with a decision of the United Nations (Fifth Session of the General Assembly, Resolution 390 (V) of 2 December, 1950), was perhaps the most profound event, for not only did it result in a considerable enlargement of the political boundaries of the Empire of Ethiopia, to use the parlance of the times; it also resulted in a significant expansion and modernization of the Ethiopian economy. Because of its exposure to Italian influence since colonization in the 1890s, Eritrea had a longer industrial tradition and therefore a head start in the development of its economy, compared to the rest of the country. The gross value of industrial production originating in the region immediately before the federation was estimated to have constituted a third of the combined gross value of the industrial production of both regions, whereas the value of foreign trade was just over one-quarter of the country's total value of international transactions. The integration of the economies of the two regions thus resulted in considerable expansion in the value particularly of industrial goods produced, in the volumes of saving, investment and consumption, in public revenue and expenditure as well as in the size of foreign trade, all of which are important macro-economic variables constituting components of this review.

The second momentous political development in Ethiopia was the attempted military coup of December 1960. The coup was the most significant of a long line of revolts, palace intrigues and plots, beginning with the Tigrai peasant (Woyane) revolt of 1943. It represented the first major attempt at toppling the aristocratic rule and was a dramatic political event during the post-war era. Among the proclaimed objectives of the coup leaders was the establishment of a democratic government that would be responsive to popular aspirations for economic and political reforms and improve the lot of the masses of the Ethiopian people. The coup was initially a success, at least in the capital Addis Ababa, where it apparently had popular support. However, it ended in failure but not before the coup makers had assassinated their captives of over 20 cabinet ministers and other prominent members of the aristocracy.

Although the coup was unsuccessful, it had considerable impact on the country's economic and political scene during subsequent years. Those who rose to positions of leadership after the coup included reform-minded technocrats with opportunities for introducing reforms within the existing system, partly as a result of the elimination of some of the arch-conservative elements of the aristocracy, but mainly because the ruling class became more predisposed to programmes of economic and political reforms as its only chance of clinging to power. Notwithstanding the influence of the new modernizing forces, the system remained essentially feudal. Nevertheless, the coup may be said to have set the stage for economic reform and radical political movements during the decade of the 1960s and up to the overthrow of the aristocracy in 1974.

The most immediate development after the coup was the introduction of measures for economic reform. In order to modernize the economy, the government issued a series of laws, beginning with the Income Tax Proclamation of 1961. According to the proclamation, existing and newly-established manufacturing enterprises were to be exempted from income tax for up to five years if the investment was more than 200,000 birr. This was followed by the Investment Decree of 1963 aimed at encouraging local and foreign investors. The Investment Proclamation of 1966, which superseded all previous investment laws, was hailed internationally as being the most liberal with the most attractive investment incentives. Partly as a result of these measures, foreign private investment increased substantially, rising from 86 million birr during the five years preceding the coup to 128 million birr between 1960-65, representing an increase of nearly 50%.

Another immediate post-coup development was the establishment of the Confederation of Ethiopian Labour Unions (CELU) barely two years later, under a labour relations decree issued in 1962. The decree was approved by parliament in 1963 as the Labour Relations Proclamation under which CELU was recognized and registered. Before then, no organized labour unions existed in Ethiopia, all attempts by workers to get organized being rebuffed by the government.[2] It should be pointed out that Ethiopian labour unions attained legal status only after a series of strikes organized, among others, by workers at the Wonji Sugar Estate, the Darmar Shoe Factory and the Indo-Ethiopian Textile Factory at Akaki, beginning in 1961. The proclamation was followed by a rapid formation of labour unions so that, by March 1970, no less than 120 unions with an estimated membership of over 55,000 were affiliated with CELU. In 1974, on the eve of the Revolution, CELU had an estimated membership of 80,000.

But the labour law also provided for the creation of a governmental machinery for overseeing labour union activities. Among other things, this took the form of a Labour Relations Board established under the Ministry of National Community Development and Social Affairs. As far as the government was concerned, strikes were tantamount to insurrection and stern measures were taken to put them down. CELU's leadership itself had close links with the government and was also closely associated with the International Confederation of Free Trade Unions (ICFTU) and the American Federation of Labour-Congress of Industrial Organizations (AFL-CIO),[3] so it was not known for its militancy. Although the Ethiopian labour movement lacked dynamic and militant leadership and had to operate under difficult conditions,[4] it played a significant role in bringing about the revolution of 1974. CELU called out a general strike in May 1974, the first ever in its history. The strike lasted four days, crippled the entire economy and contributed to the downfall of the aristocratic regime.

Another important consequence of the coup was the radicalization of Ethiopian students. The decade of the 1960s may be said to have witnessed the most intensive political activity among Ethiopian students, both at home and abroad. At the national level, the movement was spear-headed by the National Union of Ethiopian University Students. The Ethiopian student movements in Europe (ESUE) and in the United States of America (ESUNA) were amongst the most radical and militant student movements in the 1960s and early 1970s. Those movements were the embryos of the ensuing political organizations in the late 1960s, notably the All Ethiopia Socialist Movement (AESM), commonly known as Meison, and the Ethiopian Peoples' Revolutionary Party (EPRP) in the early 1970s. They played a crucial role in creating conditions for revolutionary changes and in shaping the character and ideological orientation of the revolution during its initial years.[5]

The last important economic occurrence that administered a *coup de grace* to the aristocratic rule was the economic crisis of the early 1970s. This crisis resulted from the internal political and economic ferment but was exacerbated by the global oil crisis of 1973.[6] The oil crisis led to an astronomical increase in oil prices and the country's oil import bill nearly tripled in one year. In January 1974, the government had to announce a 50%

increase in fuel prices in order to cope with the situation. This led to widespread increases in commodity prices, with merchants and landlords feverishly hiking the prices of basic goods, both manufactures and food grains. This aggravated the situation to a point where life for the urban and rural poor became unbearable and led to a chain of events which, as from February 1974, took the form of general strikes by workers, civil servants, taxi drivers, teachers and students, as well as co-ordinated mutinies in the armed forces and scattered revolts by the peasantry.

Although the 1974 revolution was triggered by rising fuel and commodity prices, there also were other issues, including an education sector review, whose unwelcome recommendations for educational reform were about to be implemented by the government, thus causing widespread disaffection among Ethiopian teachers. The cover-up, by the government, of the ravaging famine that resulted in the death of thousands of peasants in Wello and Tigrai as a result of the devastating drought of 1973,[7] aroused the wrath of peoples the world over and resulted in the isolation of the aristocratic regime.

In general, the situation immediately before the revolution was characterized by dire economic conditions with mass starvation and widespread pauperization of the peasant masses, massive unemployment and rising inflation in the urban areas resulting in total disaffection among the populace as a whole. Thus, drought and famine, the global oil shock that resulted in deteriorations in the country's general economic conditions precipitated the popular revolution of 1974. The revolution brought the aristocratic regime to its knees and ushered in the most radical change in the country's political and economic system since the restoration of monarchic rule in 1941.

The structure and development of the Ethiopian economy under the feudal system may be best understood if it is conceived of as comprising two parts: a very large subsistence sector characterized by extremely low levels of output and productivity, saving and investment, and a monetized, albeit small, sector. In contrast to the traditional or subsistence sector, where peasant masses eked out a miserable existence, there thrived, on the other hand, a fairly advanced sector which took the form of urban enclaves where commerce and manufacturing flourished and which was the seat of absentee landlords, bureaucrats and wealthy merchants. The subsistence sector accounted for over 50% of the gross domestic product (non-monetary) up to the mid-1960s. It was dependent on rain-fed cultivation of food crops as well as some cash crops with antiquated methods of cultivation. It remained vulnerable to the vagaries of nature, so that minor aberrations in climatic conditions easily tipped the delicate balance between food supply and demand, resulting in mass starvation and the death of thousands of peasants.[8]

Life in the subsistence sector moved, for a long time, within a vicious circle of cause and effect, with the subsistence economy trapped at the lowest equilibrium levels of production and consumption and with little exposure to the process of exchange.[9] Characteristic of the subsistence and monetized sectors were unfavourable terms of exchange against the former, enormous inequalities in the distribution of wealth and incomes, large disparities between regions and still larger discrepancies in the distribution of social and other services between the two sectors.

Like all economies specializing in primary production, the Ethiopian economy depended on the exports of a handful of primary products, mainly coffee, and on imports of capital and intermediate goods, industrial raw materials and consumer goods. The monetized sector formed an effective link with the global economic environment. It did not only thrive on the meagre surpluses generated in the subsistence sector but also acted as a conduit for funnelling such surpluses to the outside world. And since the economy was dependent on the exports of a few primary commodities, changes in global economic conditions taking the form, for example, of shifts in world coffee prices or in import prices had serious repercussions on its performance. Dependence on the international economy was accentuated by persistent deteriorations in the terms of trade resulting from inelasticity of demand for the country's primary exports as compared to increases in import prices of manufactures.[10] Therefore, not only was the Ethiopian economy vulnerable to climatic conditions; it also remained hostage to changes in the international economic environment.

Because of its fragmentation before the federation and lack of data, no meaningful macro-economic review of the Ethiopian economy can be made before the 1950s. Most economic aggregates which constitute the subject matter of this chapter did not even exist before then. The immediate preoccupation of the authorities after the war was to organize the bureaucracy the administrative machinery, the judiciary, defense and security and the little that existed of social and economic infrastructure with economic development receiving only minor attention. Therefore, a meaningful review of the Ethiopian economy can only begin in the 1950s on the basis of data obtained from the country's comprehensive five-year plans. Documents on the five-year plans, the first of which was prepared in 1957, contain comprehensive national accounts data which, though admittedly crude, have been a convenient source of data on the Ethiopian economy during the years under review. In the few instances where references are made to data prior to 1952, it should be noted that such data would be exclusive of Eritrea.

Finally, while making no pretensions about covering all the elements of the macro-economic universe in this chapter, the author has attempted to canvass as wide a range of topics as is feasible, so that the reader may get an exposure of a more complete picture of the economy. The chapter should only be viewed as a starting point for a more thorough study and as an attempt to provide a stimulus to students of economics for further inquiries into the development of the Ethiopian economy during the period under review. Such an exercise would be useful not only for filling the glaring gap in the country's economic history and for viewing Ethiopia's economic growth in its proper historical context, but also for designing appropriate policies and strategies as solutions to the country's seemingly intractable economic problems, and for a sustained growth of the economy which, measured by any standard, has remained the most backward.[11]

This chapter has been divided into six parts. Following this introduction and background, a general review of the country's economic development plans is presented. The next section examines the long-term record of the growth of the gross domestic product and per capita income along with the major sectors — agriculture, industry and services — followed by developments in saving, investment and consumption. Fiscal and monetary developments are presented after that, followed by a look at external economic relations. Finally, appropriate conclusions are drawn from the analyses set forth and on the basis of the author's observations.

Economic Development Plans: Synopses

Introduction

The decade after World War II was characterized by the revival of development economics which, like most special fields of economics, may be said to have had its ups and downs. It may be argued that the study of economic development emerged with the publication of Adam Smith's *Wealth of Nations* in 1776, which was pre-eminently a book on the economic development of England. Thereafter, economic development remained the main concern for several years, with leading western economists such as Thomas Robert Malthus, John Stuart Mill, David Ricardo, etc. devoting their attention to an explanation of the long-run course of the economy. For about a century after Mill's *Principles of Political Economy* published in 1848, however, the attention of economists shifted to the distribution of income, business cycles and other short-run problems of economic development.

After World War II, a study of economic development, particularly the economic problems of the less developed countries or the 'third world' as they came to be called, began to attract the attention of economists once again. Partly as an offshoot of the Marshall[12] Plan designed for the reconstruction of war-devastated Europe[13] but mainly due to the experience with planned development in the Soviet Union after the Bolshevik Revolution of 1917,[14] elaborate theories were constructed and models developed as solutions to the poverty and instability of the large number of countries, some of which were beginning to emerge from colonial rule. There was a new burst of interest in the theory of economic development and an enormous outpouring of literature on the subject.

Some of the major theories were 'balanced growth', or the synchronized application of capital to a wide range of industries (Rosenstein-Rodan, Nurkse, etc.), while others advocated exactly the opposite, unbalanced growth or 'the big push', arguing that a large and comprehensive package of investment in selected sectors of the economy in accordance with a pre-determined strategy would be the best way to achieve economic growth (Hirschman Singer). Other development theories included the 'theory of unlimited supplies of labour' according to which economic development should result from the transfer of surplus labour from the 'subsistence' to the 'capitalist' sector (Lewis 1951). In his *Stages of Economic Growth*, Rostow argued that countries pass through several phases of economic growth as they change from traditional societies to modern, consumer-oriented economies, given certain conditions such as an increase in the rate of saving and investment of 10% or more of the national income.[15]

Those theories implied that some kind of economic planning was necessary in order to promote economic growth. In his book, *Principles of Economic Planning*, Lewis (1951) defined six kinds of planning for use by less developed countries. In the same year, a United Nations group of experts recommended that '...the governments of underdeveloped countries should establish central economic units with the functions of surveying the economy, making development programmes, advising on the measures necessary for carrying out such plans and reporting on them periodically'.[16] The United Nations developed a standard system of national accounts as aid for the preparation of development plans, while economists worked out growth models as tools that could assist in plan formulation. Western economists who at first were skeptical about planned economic development and argued that the exercise was doomed to failure later concluded that less developed countries could only break out of the vicious circle of poverty and start on a path of sustained economic growth by means of planned development. Moreover, it became a condition for less developed countries to adopt some kind of planning in order to be eligible for economic and technical assistance. In due course, economic planning became so fashionable that for a country not to have a plan was considered as falling out of fashion. It was against this background that Ethiopia came to adopt comprehensive planning as from the mid-1950s.

The first steps taken towards the introduction of economic planning in Ethiopia took the form of sectoral programmes which included industry, agriculture and forestry, road construction and maintenance, education, transport and communications. The first sectoral programme to be elaborated was the ten-year industrial development programme of 1945. It was prepared with the assistance of the United States Technical Assistance Mission, the precursor of the United States heavy involvement in Ethiopia that was to last until the revolution of 1974.[17] Similarly, separate programmes were elaborated for agriculture and forestry in co-operation with the United Nations Food and Agriculture Organization. In transport and communications, a four-year programme (1952-56) was worked out for the rehabilitation and extension of the road network. A programme for the improvement of the country's telecommunications network was prepared early in the 1950s and a ten-year programme for the development of education was also elaborated during this period. According to the First Five-Year Plan, a number of surveys and studies were undertaken in different sectors of the economy in order to assess the country's natural resource base and development potentials. Those studies and surveys undoubtedly provided useful inputs to the First Five-Year Plan.

Although numerous sectoral programmes were developed during the decade after the war, they could not be implemented because existing conditions were not favourable. However, the programmes and studies helped to gradually prepare the ground for the formulation of comprehensive development plans. The task of drawing up a national plan was entrusted to the National Economic Council, set up in 1954, comprising a Planning Board, a policy-making body, and a Secretariat, the office of the Planning Board which was responsible for preparing the country's first and second five-year plans. It was upgraded to the Ministry of Planning and Development in 1966. The reorganization was the result of recommendations made by an Administrative Reform Committee set up towards the end of the first plan, the objective being to modernize the administrative machinery with a view to surmounting shortcomings in plan formulation and implementation.

Before the revolution of 1974, three five-year plans were prepared and the fourth was nearing completion but was overtaken by the events of 1974. The plans were conceived within the framework of a 20-year perspective plan covering the period up to 1982, with per capita incomes projected to rise (in current prices) from about 100 birr in 1962, the beginning of the second five-year plan, to 188 birr in 1982, the last year of the fifth five-year plan. Brief summaries of Ethiopia's development plans have been presented below as a background to the examination of trends in the overall economic growth during the period under review.

The First Five-Year Plan: 1958-62

The First Five-Year Plan was originally prepared to cover the period 1957-61. However, since the plan became effective only in 1958, it was extended for six months up to 1962. The major objectives of the plan were: a) to promote the development of physical infrastructure as a requisite for accelerating economic growth; b) to develop social infrastructure in the form of education and health, and to devote particular attention to the training of technical manpower to implement the plan; c) to accelerate the modernization of agriculture; d) to raise industrial production based on locally available raw materials and to meet requirements of the domestic market; and e) to direct economic policy, with focus on fiscal policy, for the mobilization of financial and human resources required for economic development. The macro-economic objective of the plan was to attain an average annual growth rate of 3.7% in national income.

By and large, the structure of investment was consistent with the objectives of the plan. Out of the total planned monetary investment of about 520 million birr,[18] 240 million birr, or about 46%, went to infrastructure. Industry, including manufacturing industry, electricity and mining, received 138 million birr, or about 26%, while agriculture received only 43 million birr, or about 8% of the planned monetary investment. About 57 million birr (11%) was allocated to education, health and community development. The remaining 10% of the investment went to such sectors as housing trade and tourism. Foreign sources constituted about 170 million birr, or 33% of the monetary investment.

The total investment of about 840 million birr (monetary and non-monetary), which was said to have been attained by the end of the plan, surpassed the anticipated investment of 674 million birr by about 25%. The bulk of the investment (about 60%) went into transport and communications, housing and construction. Agriculture, manufacturing and mining received 270 million birr, or about 32% of the total investment. The growth of imports averaged 3.5% annually while exports grew by 6.4%. Coffee exports were some 20% higher in 1962 than in 1957 and hides and skins were nearly 50% higher. Production of cereals fell short of target, however, such that, in 1960, about 45,000 tons of wheat had to be imported to meet shortfalls in domestic grain production and the growing demand on the part of the population. The gross value of industrial production rose from 73 million birr to 116 million birr over the plan period, mainly as a result of the completion of the Koka hydroelectric power plant which accounted for a substantial increase in the supply of electricity. Food and textile industries contributed about 80% of the total manufacturing output.

The national income registered an average annual increase of 3.2%, slightly lower than the targeted 3.7%, but higher than the estimated population growth of 1.5%. In general, except for social services and manufacturing industry, all the other sectors were said to have overshot their targets. Some of the shortcomings in the implementation of the plan included low levels of savings, shortage of skilled manpower, including administrative and managerial personnel, and the inexperience of the administrative machinery as a whole. The First Five-Year Plan could only be considered as the preparatory phase for more elaborate future plans. The plan was drawn up without the participation of concerned government departments and agencies; it lacked co-ordination between investment programmes and was devoid of bankable projects; it remained unpublished and even confidential.

The Second Five-year Plan: 1963-67

The Second Five-Year Plan constituted the first stage of a 20-year perspective plan stretching into the beginning of the 1980s. The overall objective was to bring about a structural transformation of the economy from a predominantly agricultural base to an industrial and agro-industrial one. The plan was designed to contribute to the fulfilment of this long-term goal by expanding the economy's productive capacity. It considered agriculture to be the 'leading economic activity' which would result in '...the largest contribution to the increase in national production' (Ethiopia 1963:69). Agriculture was to supply more food for the growing population, more raw materials for industry and goods for export. Therefore, unlike the first plan which placed emphasis on the development of infrastructure, the second plan shifted emphasis to agriculture. The macro-economic objective of the plan was to attain an average annual growth rate of 4.3% in gross domestic product, rising from about 2.1 billion birr in 1962, the base year of the plan, to 2.7 billion birr by the end of the plan. The total planned investment was 1.7 billion birr, almost double the actual investment said to have been realized during the first plan. Planned monetary investment amounted to about 1.5 billion birr, and non-monetary investment to 245 million birr, or about 14% of the total investment. Foreign sources amounted to 554 million birr.

Consistent with the plan's objective of raising agricultural output, the sector received the highest priority in the investment programme. Resources allocated to agriculture amounted to about 363 million birr, or 21% of the total investment. In terms of monetary investment, however, allocation to the sector was only 242 million birr (about 17%). Monetary investment in agriculture was mainly intended for general surveys of the country's river basins (Awash, Blue Nile, Wabe Shebelle, etc.) as well as for irrigation schemes. Manufacturing industry was next in the allocation of investment with about 320 million birr (19%). In terms of monetary investment, manufacturing industry ranked first with 22% of the total investment. Transport and communications also continued to receive high priority in the second plan with an allocation of 317 million birr. Most of the investment in transport and communications was for road construction(105 million birr) and air transport (89 million birr). As in the first plan, educationand health ranked low and received a mere 4.1% of the total investment. This was despite the plan's pronouncement that '...the fulfilment of the long-term development programme depends greatly on the availability of technical personnel, both of secondary school and university level' (Ethiopia 1963:74).

The total investment outlay of the second plan amounted to about 1.6 billion birr and the economy was said to have registered an average annual growth rate of 4.6%, resulting mainly from an increase in monetary gross domestic product. Investment in transport and communications and in electric power surpassed plan targets while investment in manufacturing industry and agriculture fell short of target (the latter by about 60%). In general, the implementation of the second plan continued to be hamstrung by the same factors that constrained the effectiveness of the first plan.

The Third Five-year Plan: 1969-74
Since the recommendations of the Administrative Reform Committee for improving the administrative capacity and inter-ministerial co-ordination were not acted upon until 1966, the government postponed the preparation of the third plan in order to allow more time for the committee's recommendations to be put in place. However, a one-year investment programme was prepared for 1968. The Third Five-Year Plan was drawn up under improved conditions and represented a refinement by comparison with its predecessors. As with earlier plans, foreign planning specialists continued to be involved in its preparation and, with improvements in the availability of statistical data, the techniques used for its preparation became more refined and sharpened. With the new administrative reforms in place, a large number of relevant government departments were involved in its preparation. The experience gained from the evaluation of the two previous plans also provided a valuable input toward the preparation of the plan. The third plan was originally drawn up to cover the period up to 1973 but because of shortfalls in implementation, it was later extended by one year.

The overall objective of the third plan was to attain a 6% average rate of growth in the gross domestic product which was projected to increase from about 3.6 billion birr to about 4.8 billion birr. This was expected to result in an annual per capita income growth of 3.7%. Other objectives included an enhanced standard of living for the population and the building of a stronger foundation for rapid and sustained economic growth. Agriculture was projected to grow at an average annual rate of 3% (1.9% for subsistence agriculture and 5.7% for commercial agriculture). The attainment of this target was considered vital to achieving the 6% rate of growth in the gross domestic product, with commercial agriculture expected to provide the dynamism required for achieving the projected rate of agricultural growth. Industry as a whole was to grow by 11% with manufacturing industry expected to grow more vigorously at an annual average rate of 15%. This was to be attained through a more efficient utilization of existing industries and the establishment of new ones, as well as improvements in productivity.

The plan's ambitious investment target clearly implied a high level of resources. The total planned investment outlay of about 3.4 billion birr was double the planned investment in the second plan. About 2.9 billion birr of the total investment was in monetary terms, the remaining 550 million birr being non-monetary investment. In order to attain the anticipated volume of investment, the plan assumed a growth rate of 12% annually in the saving ratio. Of the 2.9 billion birr in monetary investment, just over one billion birr was expected to be covered from foreign sources. Of the total monetary investment, the highest share (about 22%) went to transport and communications. Manufacturing industry came next with an allocation of 565 million birr, or about 20%. Although the plan recognized the importance of agriculture for the economy's overall growth, the sector was not given the priority it deserved, with an investment expenditure of only 312 million birr in the sector; this was about 11% of the total investment. As in earlier plans, education and health continued to be accorded the lowest priority in the third plan with an investment of only 150 million birr (5.2%).

Late in 1971, the government decided to extend the period of the plan by one year, that is up to 1974. A mid-term evaluation of the plan revealed that it would not be feasible to attain the targeted rate of growth. According to the evaluation, the rate of growth of the gross domestic product during the first two years of the plan averaged only about 4% per annum, which figure was well below target. The major reasons cited, according to the review, were: a) the closure of the Suez Canal and the fall in coffee prices; b) the institutional and policy reform measures recommended by the Administrative Reform Committee could not be fully implemented; and c) extension of the plan to allow more time for the completion of projects and programmes required for preparing the Fourth Five-Year Plan.

In the mid-plan review the gross domestic product was revised downwards and was projected to grow at an average rate of about 5% yearly. The target for agriculture was reduced from 3.1% to 2.5% yearly, with greater attention focussed on peasant agriculture. What was known as the Minimum Package Programme (MPP) was introduced in 1971 in place of comprehensive or intensive package programmes which incorporated improved inputs, conservation, credit extension and marketing services. The MPP was intended to provide peasant farmers with credit, improved seeds and fertilizer, feeder roads construction and marketing services at a much more rapid rate than the comprehensive programmes. The programme was to benefit some 400,000 peasant farmers, or about 10% of the 1971 peasant population. Non-agricultural sectors were projected to grow at an average rate of 8%.

As the revised Third Five-Year Plan was nearing completion, the government considered an outline strategy for the fourth plan. A large number of planning specialists and committees representing various government departments laboured tirelessly on alternative macro-economic growth paths and sectoral strategies and policies within the framework of a draft outline strategy worked out by the Planning Office. The fourth plan was to cover the period 1975-79 but it did not live to see the light of day. For, even as the government was embarking on its preparation, and before completion of the third plan, the revolution of 1974 erupted and swept away both the government and the plan into the dustbin of history.

In sum, starting with a number of sectoral programmes of medium and long-term duration during the decades after World War II, Ethiopia embarked on a series of integrated plans beginning in 1958. The first plan was drawn up in 1957 but became effective only in 1958, after a delay of six months. The plan focussed on the development of infrastructure. The second plan emphasized the development of the 'propulsive sectors' — mainly agriculture but also manufacturing industry. In the third plan, priority shifted to the optimization of growth, the objective being the attainment of a higher standard of living. Agricultural production continued to receive priority with focus on the development of commercial agriculture.

One striking feature of Ethiopia's development plans was their heavy reliance on foreign sources of finance. As shown in Table 1 below, in the first plan, 170 million birr was expected from foreign sources. This was about 33% of the planned monetary investment. In the second plan, reliance on foreign sources increased quite considerably and constituted 554 million birr, or about 38% of the planned monetary investment. Foreign sources to help implement the third plan were expected to provide a little over 1 billion birr, or about 37% of the planned monetary investment.

Table 1: Investment Outlays and Share of Foreign Capital (million birr)

Plan	Total monetary investment	Anticipated foreign capital	Foreign capital (%)
First Plan	520	170	33
Second Plan	1,500	554	38
Third Plan	2,900	1,050	37

Source: Compiled by author

The heavy reliance of Ethiopia's plans on foreign sources was due to low levels of domestic savings. The government's presumptions of high inflows of external resources turned out to be wrong, and since the inflow of foreign resources was generally lower than had been anticipated, it contributed to shortfalls in the package for implementation of the plans. There were a number of serious obstacles which frustrated the implementation of Ethiopia's plans. First, the prevalent feudal system within which the plans were prepared was clearly inimical to a system of planned development. Feudal rule was characterized by a pervasive system of an outmoded land-holding system that hampered all efforts at planned development. A half-hearted attempt was made to ameliorate the situation by establishing the Ministry of Land Reform and Administration in 1966 to work out a kind of legislation regarding land tenure. However, the Ministry continued to face formidable obstructions throughout its existence. The system remained feudal and the economy predominantly subsistence and pastoral, so that planning in Ethiopia may be said to have been little more than a futile attempt.

In addition to the feudal structure, there was a serious lack of data for planning purposes, with the degree of accuracy of data used ranging from low credibility to mere conjectures. For example, the size of the population a major parameter and the very object of all economic activities was based on dubious estimates, as were data pertaining to agricultural production. Economic planners faced serious problems because of the absence of reliable data and had to bemoan the fact that 'the collection and compilation of relevant statistical data presented a serious difficulty in the elaboration of the Second Five-Year Plan' (Ethiopia 1963:31).

The absence of well-formulated projects was yet another problem that hampered implementation of development plans in Ethiopia. In order for plans to be implemented efficiently they should contain well-prepared and co-ordinated projects and programmes. The absence of an institutional machinery for project planning, comprising identification, appraisal, implementation, follow-up and monitoring, posed a serious obstacle to implementation of plans.[19] This meant that resources, both domestic and external, could not be mobilized on a timely basis or that they were used inefficiently. This problem continued to be a serious stumbling block to the implementation of development plans in Ethiopia.

Even though economic planning in Ethiopia suffered from numerous shortcomings, it had its positive sides. The exercise succeeded in putting in place the institutional machinery, however inefficient, and in providing opportunities for training a cadre of Ethiopian planners. It established a high degree of consciousness regarding the need for planning as an instrument of economic growth. The surveys, studies and explorations undertaken towards establishing the country's natural resource base were also of enormous significance. The macro-economic data collected in the course of preparing the plans and the system of national accounts that was put together were certainly valuable and have enabled us to have a closer look at the growth trends of the Ethiopian economy.

Growth of Output and Demand

Introduction

This section examines the implications of the broad objectives of Ethiopia's five-year plans in terms of macro-economic performance. The general trends in the performance of an economy are measured by means of aggregate data on output and demand, such as the gross domestic product (GDP), savings, investment and consumption. The production of goods and services constitutes, in general, the basis of an economic activity, its two basic uses being consumption and capital accumulation. Generally, the structure and trends of output and the performance of an economy are best analyzed via a system of national accounts which provides a comprehensive framework for a systematic and integrated recording of the flows of transactions in an economy. First developed in the 1930s under the influence of John Maynard Keynes, national accounting practices became standardized by the United Nations after World War II.

The problems of accurately measuring economic flows and of constructing national accounts in backward countries such as Ethiopia are all too obvious. Poor statistical base, including statistics on population[20] and a large subsistence base render the task of putting together a meaningful national accounts system well-nigh impossible. It must, therefore, be recognized that data on aggregate output for the Ethiopian economy, particularly those of the 1950s, contain statistical flaws and are subject to wide margins of error. In addition, since the measurement of economic aggregates and comparisons of data become increasingly difficult and tend to lose meaning over a long period of time, the data should be interpreted only as broad orders of magnitude indicating the general trends of the Ethiopian economy, rather than accurate measurements or comparisons.

Growth of Output

The first attempts at estimating the Gross National Product (GNP) for the Ethiopian economy was made in the mid-1950s by the Planning Board during the preparation of the First Five-Year Plan. Earlier attempts had also been made by the State Bank of Ethiopia in 1952[21] on the basis of agricultural production data for that year and industrial production data for 1951. The State Bank estimated Ethiopia's GNP at 2.1 billion birr with agriculture accounting for about 85%. But its findings were considered crude, at best, by planners at the Planning Board who came up with their own estimate. No documentation has been found regarding the concepts and methodology used, but the planners probably based on the United Nations system of national accounts. GNP estimates made by the Planning Board for the 1950s were spotty and solely intended for 1950, 1954 and 1957.[22] In 1964, the Central Statistical Office, established in 1961 in response to the need for statistical data for national planning purposes, produced provisional estimates of national accounts for the period 1961-63. Measurements were made in terms of expenditure as well as by industrial origin, and were obviously rough owing to the rudimentary nature of the data.

The trend rate of growth of Ethiopia's GDP[23] for the 1950s probably averaged about 3% at 1980/81 constant factor cost. The estimate is based on time series for national accounts beginning in 1961 as prepared by the National Planning Office and as estimated by the author on the basis of GNP figures in the First Five-Year Plan document.[24] GDP increased at an average annual rate of 3% between 1950 and 1960 whereas its major components agriculture, industry and services averaged about 2%, 10.8% and 4.3%, respectively. Distributive services, comprising transport and communications, wholesale and retail trade, increased at about 5% whereas other services, including banking and insurance, public administration and defence, education, health, domestic services and housing increased at 4.6%.[25]

The increase in GDP was partly due to the integration of the economies of Ethiopia and Eritrea in 1952, but it was also due to increased investment in manufacturing industry which, however small, registered considerable expansion during the first half of the 1950s. Taking into account an estimated annual average population growth rate of 1.5% during the decade, which increased from an estimated 16.5 million in 1950 to about 20 million[26] in 1960, the annual rate of growth in per capita income could be said to have been in the order of 1.5%.

In 1950 agriculture contributed about 78% of GDP and employed an estimated 90% of the population. On the other hand, industry as a whole, comprising manufacturing, small-scale and handicraft industries, mining and construction, made up just over 5% of the total GDP, thus indicating that industrial development in Ethiopia by the start of the 1950s was very much in its infancy. Services as a whole, comprising transport and communications, wholesale and retail trade, general administration, defence and security, represented about 17% of the GDP and were more than three times as large as the industrial GDP.

In the 1960s, the Ethiopian economy continued to register steady growth. During the first half of the decade, the GDP grew at an average annual rate of about 5%. Although the trend rate of GDP growth rather slowed down during the second half of the sixties, averaging about 4%, the performance may be said to have been satisfactory, given a number of adverse conditions such as poor weather, the closure of the Suez Canal and a slump in coffee prices. After attaining a peak in the mid-1960s, the growth rate of GDP dropped to an average of 3% a year during the first half of the 1970s. Thus, the growth of the economy averaged about 3% in the 1950s, 4.5% in the 1960s and 3% between 1970 and 1974, thus averaging about 3.5% between 1950 and 1974. Figure 1 shows the trend rate of growth of GDP between 1950 and 1974.[27]

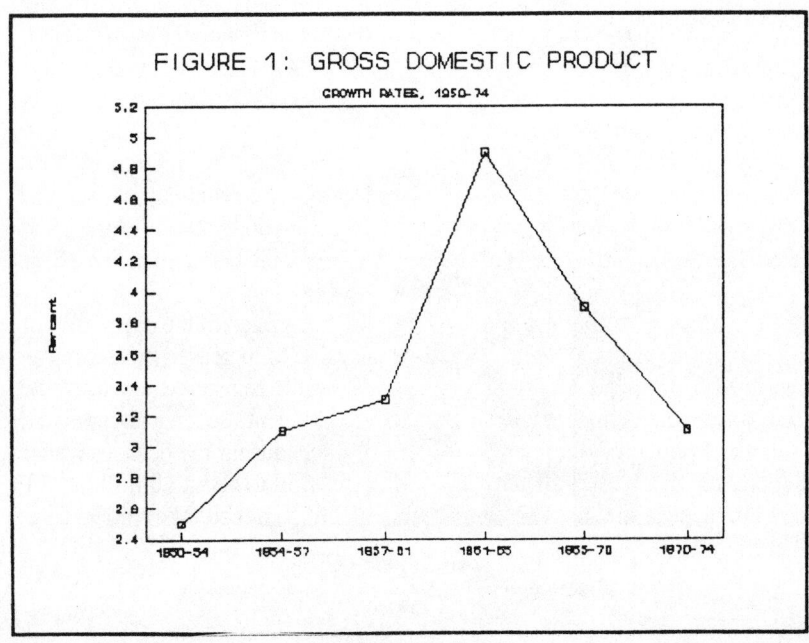

FIGURE 1: GROSS DOMESTIC PRODUCT GROWTH RATES, 1950-74

18 An Economic History of Modern Ethiopia

The performance of the Ethiopian economy during the period under review shows three distinct phases. The first phase covers the period from 1950 to 1959 and shows a steady rise in GDP, partly as a result of the federation of Eritrea and Ethiopia which led to an expansion in the size of the economy, but also because of an increase in investment, particularly during the second half of the decade. The second phase covers the period from 1960 to 1965 and shows an accelerating GDP growth rate, thereby reflecting a continuation of the economic expansion that began in the late 1950s.

The first half of the 1960s was characterized by a steady, albeit modest increase in per capita income, an increase in the level of private consumption averaging about 5.3% and an even higher rate of increase in public consumption of about 15.7%. The export of goods and non-factor services recorded a growth of 13.2% while the import of goods and non-factor services recorded about 12% growth yearly. Saving and investment showed considerable rates of growth of about 9.4% and 9.2% respectively. The third phase begins with the second half of the 1960s and marks the beginning of a slowdown in economic performance. Economic decline was accentuated, among other things, by a gradual decline in investment arising from an erosion in business confidence engendered by an atmosphere of political uncertainty and further exacerbated by the severe drought of 1973 that disrupted agricultural production, as well as the oil crisis of that year. In

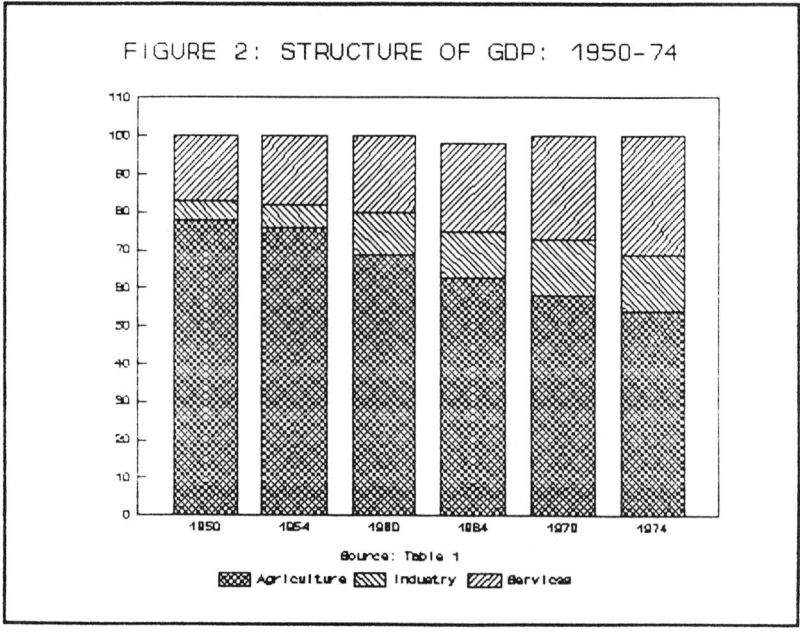

general, the Ethiopian economy registered a remarkable performance during the 1960s. In absolute terms, the size of the Ethiopian economy increased by about three and a half times between 1950 and 1974, rising from an estimated 1.5 billion birr in 1950 to 2.3 billion birr in 1960 and then to 5.2 billion birr in 1974 (current prices).

Historically, economic development involves changes in the structure of output. The share of agriculture in output and employment is high at the early stages of development but it begins to decline with an increase in the share of manufacturing industry. The logical next stage in structural transformation involves shifts towards the services industry. Figure 2 shows that there were apparent structural shifts within sectors of the economy between 1950 and 1974. As may be observed from Figure 2 and Annex 1 (see annexes at the end of this chapter), while the share of agriculture in total output declined from 78% in 1950 to 54% in 1974, the share of industry increased from just over 5% to about 15% during the same period. The share of services in total output rose much faster than the increase in industry, from an estimated 17% in 1950 to about 31% in 1974. These shifts do not have much meaning when one considers the fact that agriculture continued to hold a dominant place in the Ethiopian economy in terms of output, employment and exports and that there were no perceptible improvements in the welfare of the population.

Growth of Per Capita Income

In terms of per capita GNP (as measured conventionally),[28] Ethiopia's growth performance in the 1950s did not compare favourably with the performance records of other African countries. During the 1950s, the annual rate of increase in GNP for Ethiopia was estimated at 1.5% as compared to an average of 2.4% for Africa as a whole (Morawetz 1977:77). Annual per capita growth rates for individual African countries were: 0.9% for Egypt, 2.7% for Sudan, 1.9% for Ghana, 1.0% for Kenya, 1.6% for Malawi and 2.1% for Nigeria. Countries that did exceptionally well were: Somalia (10.6%), Angola (5.8%), Algeria (4.4%) and Senegal (4.4%). It should, however, be noted that while Ethiopia boasted 3,000 years of civilization and independence, almost all the countries cited here were colonial dependencies in the 1950s and had no independent existence of their own.

In the 1960s, however, Ethiopia's per capita income growth compared favourably to growths in other African countries. The annual per capita rate of growth during the period was about 2.5% as compared to an average of 2.2% for Africa as a whole. Per capita income growth also compared favourably with individual African countries such as Somalia (-1.1%), Senegal (-1.6%), Nigeria (0.4%) and Algeria (-0.7%). However, countries such as Tanzania (3.0%), Malawi (2.7%), Angola (3.7%) and Sudan (2.7%) performed much better. At least nine African countries for which data is available registered negative growths during the decade while seven others registered growths averaging less than 1%. Ethiopia's per capita income peaked in the 1960s but began to decline in the first half of the 1970s, averaging less than 1% as compared to an average of 2.8% for Africa as a whole.

Sectoral Performance

Agriculture

Agriculture has, for centuries, constituted Ethiopia's major resource base and occupied a pivotal position in the country's economic development during the period under review. However, because it remained basically traditional and pastoral, it made only limited contributions to the national economy. With favourable soil and climatic conditions, multiple river systems and sufficient rainfall over most parts of the country, as well as variations in altitude, the country can grow a wide range of crops and possesses enormous potential for sustained agricultural development. However, agricultural production and productivity have remained low, mainly because of an antiquated system of land tenure and backward technology. Agricultural development has also been hindered by other factors, including inadequate infrastructure, with the majority of peasants living in inaccessible areas far away from major roads and markets. Ethiopia's livestock was also large, indeed the largest in Africa, but the stock remained poor in quality such that its contribution to economic development also remained insignificant.

Agricultural technology remained backward, the most typical tools employed in cultivation being little more than the hoe, the sickle, other hand-tools and ox-drawn ploughs. There was little or no injection of external agents into the system in the form of modern technology for increasing output and productivity. Back in the 1950s, the use of fertilizers was nearly unknown, but even in the early 1970s fertilizer use per hectare of arable land was a mere 400 grams as compared, for example, to Tanzania (2,200 grams), Sudan (23,800 grams) and Malawi (5,200 grams). In 1960 there were only 1,000 tractors in the country. In 1974, irrigated land was less than 1% of the total cropped land. The use of fertilizers, improved seeds, credit and tractors remained almost unknown to Ethiopian peasants. Rain-fed agriculture was nearly the sole basis of agricultural production. As a result trends in agricultural production during the period under review show little increase in the total cropped area and almost static production of grains.

Grain production in the early 1950s probably averaged about 4 million tons and the area under cultivation about 4.5 million hectares. According to the

First Five-Year Plan, grain production increased from an estimated 4.1 million tons in 1958 to 4.5 million tons in 1963. It averaged about 4.7 million tons during the first half of the 1960s. The total area under production attained a peak at 6.4 million hectares in 1970-71 while grain production attained a peak at 6.2 million tons in 1969. In 1974 the total cropped area dropped to 4.6 million hectares (about the same as in the early 1950s) and total crop production to 3.8 million tons (considerably less than the production recorded in the early 1960s). This was due to the drought of that year which reflected the vulnerability of agricultural production in Ethiopia to changes in weather conditions. With an increase in the size of the population, there was a decline in the per capita production of grains, especially in the early 1960s. Per capita food production dropped substantially from an estimated 0.23 tons in 1954 to 0.14 tons in 1974.

That agriculture has played a dominant role in the Ethiopian economy is historically evidenced by the fact that it has remained a major contributor to GDP. According to available data, agriculture contributed about 78% of the GDP in 1950. Its contribution to GDP gradually declined to about 69% in 1960 and then to 58% in 1970. By 1974 its share in GDP dropped to about 54%. The trend should not be interpreted as reflecting meaningful transformations in the production structure of the economy. Rather, it shows the sluggish rate of economic growth and serious lags in output and productivity partly due to changes in climatic conditions. In general, the performance of the Ethiopian economy depended on the performance of agriculture, which was in turn dependent on weather conditions. Favourable weather conditions[29] guaranteed bountiful harvests and a rise in agricultural value added brought about improved economic performance while harsh climatic conditions resulting in poor harvests and lower GDP growth were harbingers of economic difficulties and hardship for the population. Therefore, agriculture remained a crucial barometer of economic performance and the well-being of the population as a whole.

During the decade of the 1950s, agricultural value added increased at an annual average rate of about 2%. This was only marginally higher than the estimated population growth rate of 1.6% a year. In the 1960s, agricultural value added increased at an annual average rate of about 2.2% and compared favourably with an estimated population growth rate of 2% during the decade. Thereafter, agricultural growth began to decelerate, averaging about 1.4% between 1970 and 1974 as compared to an estimated annual population growth rate of 2.2% during the period. Plunged in a quagmire of outmoded feudal production relations and backward technology, agricultural output and productivity stagnated with declining per capita food production in the face of a population which continued to grow unabated, increasingly becoming a burden on the sector and the fragile resource base.

Since agriculture will continue to be Ethiopia's major natural resource base in the foreseeable future, it is essential to increase the productivity of the sector so as to guarantee food security, further stimulate development in other sectors and raise the population's overall standard of living. The sector will continue to provide the domestic market for manufacturing industry, foodstuffs for a growing population, raw materials for industry, goods for the export market and the necessary foreign exchange for the acquisition of technology required for economic development. The strategy for agricultural development should focus on attaining increased output and productivity. A rapid growth of agriculture has historically been associated with policies such as the introduction of modern technology an essential means of raising the productivity of both land and labour provision of infrastructure and adoption of appropriate macro-economic policies.

Industry

The term industry is used generally and encompasses a wide range of activities. It includes small-scale and handicraft industries, mining and construction, electricity and water. With the exception of Eritrea, which had a longer industrial tradition as an Italian colonial dependency since 1896, industrial development in Ethiopia had to start virtually from scratch after World War II. According to available data, the gross value of industrial production amounted to a mere 22 million birr in 1950. In 1954, after the federation of Eritrea and Ethiopia, the value of industrial production rose to 62 million birr. In 1950, the number of establishments was put at 126 and the total number of salaried workers in the sector at about 10,000. Industrial growth was handicapped by, among other things, low savings, shortage of capital and skills, inadequate supply of power[30] and the poor state of the country's infrastructure.

In the 1950s, industrial enterprises were mainly small-scale and handicraft industries attracted to Addis Ababa and Asmara on account of the availability of infrastructure and other facilities. The concentration of industry in the environs of the two cities continued in later years as well. Following the traditional pattern of industrial development in less developed countries, industrial development mainly took the form of investment in leather goods, footwear and textile industries, flour and edible oil mills, beverage processing, construction materials and coffee cleaning plants. Of the 52 new enterprises established between 1952 and 1954, about 44 were for cleaning coffee and cereals.

Investment in manufacturing industry was almost exclusively in the hands of foreigners. In 1952, foreign investment in manufacturing industry amounted to 7.2 million birr but increased quite considerably in subsequent years. In the context of the ten-year industrial development programme drawn up in 1945, and as part of its industrial development policy, the government issued, in 1950, a policy statement with a wide range of incentives designed to improve the investment climate and to attract foreign capital. The law was issued in the form of a 'Notice', according to which the government would a) provide new enterprises with exemptions from the payment of income tax for a period of five years from the date of commencement of production; b) exempt new enterprises from customs duties for importation of machinery and equipment; c) permit foreign investors to remit annually, for the first ten years of production, ten per cent of the capital invested and fifteen per cent of the profit for an indefinite period; and d) refrain from imposing the participation of domestic capital on new foreign enterprises.

Spurred partly by the government's industrial development policy, the growth of manufacturing industry began to show certain dynamic tendencies. Several new enterprises were established in the early 1950s, the major investment being the Wonji sugar factory established by a Dutch sugar processing firm (the HVA of Amsterdam). Between 1951 and 1954, investment in new establishments amounted to 25 million birr, excluding Eritrea. The gross inflow of private foreign capital was, however, quite small and averaged about 11 million birr annually between 1950 and 1959. The inflow more than doubled to an average of 26 million birr during the first half of the 1960s. It slowed down to 24 million birr during the second half of the decade and averaged 25 million birr annually between 1960 and 1969. The inflow of private foreign capital began to peter out during the first half of the 1970s and ceased completely in 1973.

During the second half of the 1950s industrial expansion gained momentum and the country experienced an accelerated development of manufacturing industry. By the beginning of the First Five-Year Plan, the value of industrial production was no more than 83 million birr. It increased to about 108 million birr in 1960 and, although its contribution to national output continued to be negligible, the increase was nevertheless remarkable, averaging, as it did, about 10% annually. As compared to 1950, the index of industrial production rose to about 250 in 1955 and 455 in 1960. The supply of electric power, a significant indicator of the level of economic development, also increased substantially from about 17 million kwh in 1950 to over 100 million kwh in 1961.

Because of the favourable investment climate, industrial value added increased at an estimated annual rate of 11% between 1950 and 1959. In the 1960s the country continued to experience an accelerated development of manufacturing industry. It showed a remarkable growth of over 15% between 1961 and 1969, while small-scale and handicraft industries increased at a much slower rate of approximately 6%. The growth of manufacturing industry was even higher during the first half of the 1960s when it averaged just over 16% annually as compared to small-scale and handicraft industries (about 4.3%). Between 1970 and 1974 the growth of manufacturing industry slowed down to about 5.5% because of the general slump in economic growth, its contribution to GDP in 1974 being just over 15%. Between 1950 and 1974 the share of industry in total GDP increased nearly threefold.

The number of formal wage workers in manufacturing industry nearly doubled between 1950 and 1954, rising from about 10,000 to 18,000, partly as a result of the integration of the economies of Ethiopia and Eritrea Industrial employment rose from just over 25,000 workers in 1960 to about 50,000 in 1970. By 1974, on the eve of the revolution, the value of industrial production had risen to over 960 million birr and industrial employment to over 60,000. As in earlier years, the most important industrial establishments in terms of employment and gross value of production comprised food and beverages, textiles and construction materials. Mining and quarrying, electricity and water constituted negligible components of GDP, especially in the 1950s but even in later years. The combined contribution of these sectors to GDP was less than 5% in 1950. The country's mineral resources were far from being fully explored and therefore remained undeveloped. The share of mining and quarrying in total GDP was about 4 million birr in 1961. However, it more than doubled in 1965 to 9.5 million birr. It reached a peak at about 12 million birr in 1974, with gold leading the list of mineral output throughout.[31] Although gold accounted for much of mining output, there also were limited outputs of other minerals such as salt and platinum.

A major mineral finding in the 1960s was potash reserves in the Danakil Depression. Concession was given in the mid-1950s to Ralph M Parsons, an American company, for its exploitation and marketing. The company conducted detailed exploration and even erected a pilot plant for exploitation of the deposit which was estimated at 60 million tons. The project's investment cost was estimated at 180 million birr, but it never came to fruition, among other things, because of technical and marketing difficulties and the company eventually pulled out. In general, Ethiopia's mineral potential, including the extensive potash deposit, remained unexplored and locked up under the ground.

Ethiopia's large hydro-power resource, whose economic potentials were estimated at over 145 billion kwh, of which less than 2% was exploited, also remained untapped, partly as a result of lack of resources. The production of electricity was estimated at a mere 8.5 million kwh in 1945, but then rose to 17 million kwh in 1950, i.e. a twofold increase over a five-year period. The generation of electric power increased at the rapid rate of 18% as from 1956, however, with production rising from an estimated 73 million kwh in 1957 to over 100 million kwh in 1962, mainly because of the erection of the Koka hydro-power station in 1960 in the Awash Valley.[32]

As regards its share of the total GDP, electricity remained inconsequential in the 1950s and constituted a mere 0.4% of the GDP in 1961. It gradually rose to 0.7% in 1970 and then to 0.8% in 1974. In absolute terms, production of electricity increased from an estimated 17 million kwh in 1950 to about 390 million kwh in 1974. With consumption estimated at about 328 million kwh in 1974, there was an over-capacity of about 60 million kwh. As noted above, the development of industry in the 1950s was constrained, among other things, by shortages in the supply of electricity, so that investment in power generation helped remove one of the major hindrances to economic development. Nevertheless, the supply of electricity remained low when compared to other developing countries and in relation to the country's potential. Construction was another major component of industrial GDP, especially from the early 1960s. It included buildings and public works in general and represented a substantial proportion of economic activity comprising nearly 46% of GDP in 1961. It gradually declined, however, to 36% in 1970 and then to 27% in 1974. In absolute terms, it rose from an estimated 5 million birr in 1950 to 131 million birr in 1961 and then to 236 million birr in 1974. The decline in the share of construction in the total GDP resulted from an accelerated rise in the share of manufacturing and small-scale and handicraft industries rather than from an absolute decline in construction activity.

Services

The services sectors are very broad and encompass distributive services comprising transport and communications, wholesale and retail trade as well as other activities, such as public administration and defence, banking and insurance, education, health and medical services and housing. The distributive sectors play an important role in the movement of goods and services while services other than transport and trade are important in terms of building up the social infrastructure. Together, they accounted for an estimated 252 million birr in 1950, or about 16% of the GDP. In 1961 value added originating in these sectors more than doubled and amounted to about 540 million birr or 23% of the total GDP. It rose steadily to about 29% in 1969 and to about 34% in 1974.

Trade constituted the bulk of distributive services in the total GDP. In 1950, trade accounted for a mere 5% of the GDP, thus reflecting the low level of exchange attributed to lack of transport network for the movement of goods and services but also because of the subsistence nature of the economy. In 1961, the contribution of trade to GDP was still low (about 6%); it increased quite considerably to about 10% in 1974, with a trend rate of growth of 7.5% between 1961 and 1974. Transport and communications made up substantial components of the services GDP in the 1950s, averaging about 20%, according to available data. In 1961, the figure declined to about 14% of the total services GDP. It increased slightly to 16% in 1969 but stagnated at 15% up to 1974. The sector showed an average annual GDP growth of 10.4% between 1961 and 1969, but then declined to less than 7% during the second half of the 1970s.

Efforts to develop transport and communications began with the First Five-Year Plan as reflected in the high share of investment allocation to the sector. Subsequent development plans also continued to emphasize the importance of transport and communications. Between 1961 and 1965, large investments were made in road construction and maintenance, including loans and credits received from the World Bank totalling 82 million birr up to the mid-1960s. Efforts to expand transport and communications facilities were not only reflected in the national accounts. That large investments were made in the road sector was also reflected in the total length of all-weather and paved roads which respectively increased from 2,700 km and 800 km in 1957 to about 8,000 km and 3000 km in 1974. Arterial road transport radiated in all directions from Addis Ababa linking all provinces and journeys that took days shrank to hours. Although there was a significant expansion of the road network it was far from keeping up with demand so that it continued to be a serious obstacle to economic development. Major developments also took place in domestic air service with an extensive network of minor airports and landing strips. As from the 1960s, but particularly during the first half of the 1970s, the operations of the national air and shipping lines played a significant role in earning modest amounts of foreign exchange for the country.

The Imperial Highway Authority, established in 1951, was entrusted with the responsibility of developing and maintaining the country's road network while the Imperial Board of Telecommunications set up in 1952, had the responsibility of developing the country's telecommunication network. Considerable developments in telecommunication services took place between 1953 and 1966, partly on the basis of loans and credits advanced by the World Bank Group totalling 23 million birr up to the mid-1960s. There were major expansions in telecommunication services with telephone stations installed for all the principal towns. The number of telephones increased from a mere 5,000 in 1953 to over 66,000 in 1974; although it was admittedly small, this number showed a remarkable increase in absolute terms.

Services other than transport and trade grew at a much faster rate and more steadily. They represented only about 8% of the total GNP in 1950, but increased steadily from about 14% of the GDP in 1961 to 16.5% in 1970, and then to 20% in 1974. The major factors accounting for the rapid growth of the other services were expenditures on public administration and defence which rose substantially, particularly since the mid-1960s. The social services education, health and medical care also continued to grow steadily but remained significantly lower than the growth of other service sectors. Financial services, including banking and insurance, also experienced steady growth during the period. In terms of trend rates of growth, services grew by 7.6% between 1961 and 1974 (distributive services by 8% and other services by 7%).

Saving, Investment and Consumption

Saving

The mobilization of domestic resources is among the critical determinants for attaining desirable levels of investment and sustained economic growth. As a noted economist (Lewis 1951) put it, 'the central problem in the theory of economic development is to understand the process by which a community which was previously saving 4 or 5% of its income or less converts itself into an economy where voluntary saving is about 12 to 15% of national income or more'. Later on, other economists stressed constraints in foreign exchange. This so-called two-gap model of domestic saving and shortage of foreign exchange led developing countries to look increasingly to the flow of external resources to finance imports and investment. High rates of saving help maintain strong and sustainable growth by ensuring higher levels of investment. The level of national income is the most important determinant of saving, but also of levels of investment and consumption. The correlation between these variables has important long-run macro-economic implications. The rate of saving is directly correlated with the level of development, as measured by incomes per capita. The lower the per capita income, the lower the saving ratio, and vice versa.

Saving is generally influenced by fiscal policy measures. The most direct way to increase public sector saving is by restraining recurrent expenditures and increasing revenues. Higher rates of interest commensurate with the prevailing rate of inflation may also encourage private saving. In countries such as Ethiopia where consumption is at subsistence levels, saving may not respond to an increase in interest rates. What remains generally true is that saving does respond to the rate of inflation. A higher rate of inflation, if not accompanied by a commensurate increase in the nominal rate of interest, could be detrimental to private saving. Negative real rates of return on saving act as a disincentive to private saving. Given the prevailing rate of inflation, the rate of interest would have to be high enough in order that the real rate of return on saving remains positive.

Because of the preponderance of the subsistence economy and low incomes, saving in Ethiopia remained historically at low levels. But an expansionary budgetary policy which resulted in lower public saving was also an important contributory factor to a low saving ratio. From available data, the ratio of aggregate saving to GNP in 1950 amounted to an estimated 5.5%. It gradually increased to about 11% of GDP in 1960 and stabilized at around 11.3% during the decade. Domestic saving stagnated during the first half of the 1970s and remained at about the same level as in the 1960s but then dropped significantly to 7.5% in 1974. In absolute terms, gross saving rose from an estimated 85 million birr in 1950 to 272 million birr in 1960, representing more than a threefold increase. In 1970 it increased substantially to about 467 million birr. In 1973 the performance of gross domestic saving was at its highest historically and reached 722 million birr, or about 13% of the GDP. In 1974, however, it dropped to 415 million birr, thus reflecting the political and economic crisis of that year. Because of lack of data, particularly during the earlier years, no distinction could be made between saving in the public and private sectors.

In general, the case for increasing the saving rate is strengthened by the fact that both the level of investment and the long-run rate of growth of the economy are directly influenced by higher rates of saving. As pointed out above, the saving ratio in Ethiopia historically remained low because incomes were low and could barely exceed subsistence levels and public saving could not increase significantly because of expansionary budget reflecting, among other things, civil strife in the country, especially beginning in the mid-1960s. It may also be added that no vigorous efforts were made to fully exploit the saving potential of the Ethiopian economy. The subsistence sector effectively remained beyond the reach of financial institutions and had no opportunity for saving other than accumulation in kind, mainly in the form of livestock, and by investing in physical assets. Financial institutions did not adequately canvass the subsistence economy in order to tap the saving potentials of that sector. It should be noted that policy measures for the promotion of domestic saving for sustained economic growth will have little meaning if the saving thus generated is not channelled into productive investment.

Investment

As was pointed out earlier, the rate of growth of an economy is determined by the rate of capital accumulation which is in turn determined by the rate of saving. Gross domestic investment represents expenditures on the acquisition of capital goods and the value of physical changes in inventories. In order for growth to be sustained, new investments would have to be made in buildings, machinery and equipment and old and worn-out equipment would have to be replaced. The expansion of the economy's productive capacity would require substantial investments for the creation of new capacities, expansion of existing industries, and for replacement and maintenance. In addition to physical capital, human capital is also amongst the most critical factors in development. The experience of European countries earlier on and of countries in the Far East more recently that invested heavily in manpower development, shows a strong link between human capital accumulation and development. While investment in physical assets and human capital is important for economic growth, investment in such sectors as research and development, which indirectly contribute to higher productivity and enhance economic growth, is equally important. The question is how to optimally allocate limited resources amongst competing demands of various sectors, and within sectors, whether to create new capacities or maintain and operate existing activities efficiently.

Domestic investment in Ethiopia averaged less than 5% of the GNP in 1950. The gross investment ratio (gross investment as a ratio of GDP) for the period 1957-62 increased, on average, by 13% annually, rising from 5.4% in 1957 to 8.3% in 1962. The investment ratio rose from an average of 12.7% during the first half of the 1960s to 13.4% during the second half of the decade, averaging 13% for the decade as a whole. It dropped to about 11% during the period 1970-74. The bulk of the investment was made in transport and communications, manufacturing industry and power. During the period 1961-1965, investment in transport and communications absorbed about 40% of total monetary investment, while investment in manufacturing industry, mining and power increased significantly from 27% of the total monetary investment to 40% in 1965. Investment in agriculture remained low and relative to the importance of the sector in terms of its contribution to the national economy. In absolute terms, gross domestic investment rose from an estimated 62 million birr in 1950 to 295 million birr in 1960. In 1970 it increased to about 554 million birr but then dropped to 550 million birr in 1974.

Gross investment was not matched by sufficient domestic saving. This mismatch between saving and investment known as the resource gap was filled by an inflow of external resources. As discussed earlier, the country's three five-year plans depended rather heavily on external resources, the degree of dependence rising from 33% of planned monetary investment during the first plan to about 38% during the second and third plans. During the first half of the 1960s, gross domestic saving lagged behind gross domestic investment by an average of 39 million birr, or 1.4% of GDP. In the mid-1960s, the resource gap increased to over 110 million birr or about 3.2% of GDP. During the second half of the decade, however, it dropped significantly, averaging about 71 million birr, or about 1.7% of GDP. In 1972 and 1973 the situation was reversed and saving exceeded investment by a margin of 2% and 3.2% of GDP, respectively. In 1974, when saving dropped to a very low level, the gap between domestic saving and investment rose substantially to about 3% of GDP. In order to bridge the gap between saving and investment it would be necessary to strengthen the saving performance of the economy by introducing, among other things, appropriate fiscal policy measures and by tapping the saving potentials of the subsistence sector. This is among the necessary conditions for sustained economic growth.

Consumption

According to available data, the proportion of resources going to public and private consumption remained historically high in Ethiopia, leaving insufficient saving for attaining desirable levels of investment and growth. This was mainly due to the high propensity to consume, resulting from low incomes but also because of high levels of expenditures associated with administration and defence. In the 1960s expenditure on public consumption averaged about 10% of the GDP, rising from 7.6% in 1960 to 12.4% in 1964; it stabilized at around 10% for the rest of the decade. This pattern continued into the first half of the 1970s, though consumption increased to about 13% in 1974.

Public consumption is reflected mainly in recurrent budgetary expenditures, wages and salaries of public employees and military personnel, which accounted for the largest proportion of public consumption. Private consumer expenditures accounted for about 80% of GDP in the 1960s but declined slightly to about 78% during the first half of the 1970s. According to the Third Five-Year Plan, about one-half of the private consumer expenditure was on the subsistence sector. The third plan projected the rate of increase in consumption in the subsistence sector to grow in step with population growth in that sector. The plan also anticipated a decline in public consumption by cuts in recurrent expenditures (mainly general administration and defence). However, public consumer expenditures remained at about the same level and even increased quite considerably towards the end of the plan. Figure 3 shows the performance of investment, saving and consumption during the period 1950 to 1974.

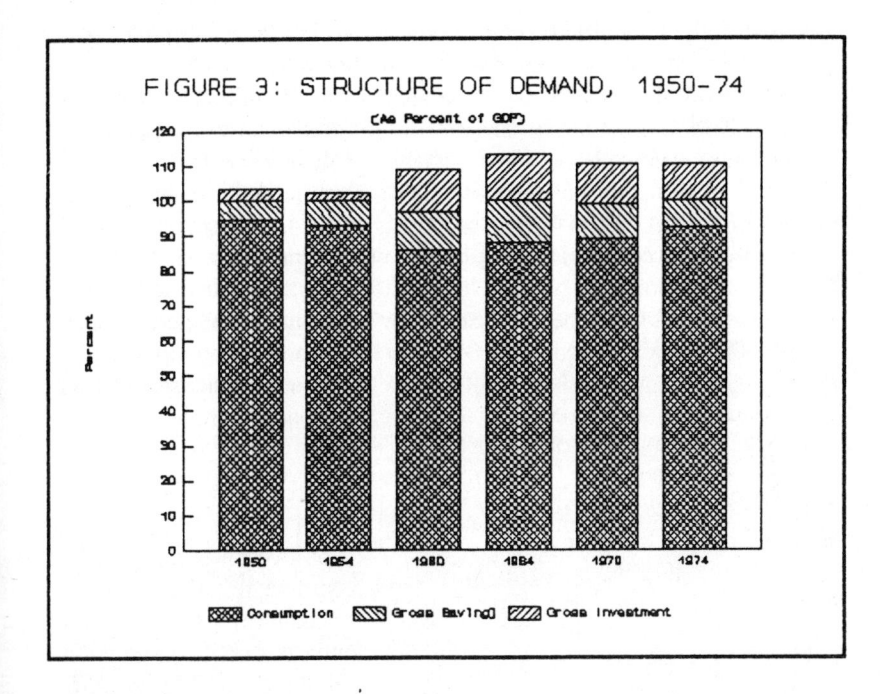

FIGURE 3: STRUCTURE OF DEMAND, 1950-74
(As Percent of GDP)

Consumption — Gross Savings — Gross Investment

Fiscal and Monetary Developments

Public Finance

Revenues and Expenditures

Trends in public revenues and expenditures may be examined in absolute terms or could be linked to macro-economic aggregates such as GDP. To a large extent, the fiscal performance of a country is influenced by overall economic growth, so that the growth of revenues and expenditures in Ethiopia during the period under review may be related to economic expansion, particularly the monetized sector. Immediately after independence, revenues and expenditures were low mainly because economic activities were low, but also because the bureaucratic machinery was still in its formative stages. After the liberation of the country in 1941, the authorities were faced with the immediate task of organizing the country's fiscal system, that is, the whole system of budgeting, taxation, customs and excise taxes. Because of the need to maintain and finance a standing army and a growing bureaucracy, increasingly larger revenues had to be raised and this provided the rationale for successive reforms of the tax laws.

As part of the reorganization of the fiscal system, tax laws were introduced in 1941 and taxes in kind were abolished and replaced by taxes payable in cash to the central government. In nomadic areas, a tax on livestock was collected in place of land tax. The system of tribute was replaced by a tax system on a cash basis. The system was revised in the Land Tax Proclamation of 1944, though it was not consistently applied throughout the country. A new land tax proclamation introduced in 1952 provided, among other things, for the collection of both forms of taxes, land tax and the tithe, on a cash basis. For the purposes of tax assessment, land was classified into three categories fertile, semi-fertile and poor with taxes imposed ranging from 65 birr per gasha (40 hectares) for fertile land, to 50 birr for semi-fertile land and 19.50 birr for marginal lands. In the lowlands, used mainly for pasture, a cattle tax was levied per head of cattle in lieu of land tax.

With the reorganization of the bureaucracy and reform of the tax system, revenues and expenditures began to show marked increases. Between 1943 and 1949, revenues averaged about 51 million birr,[33] rising from 28 million birr to 62 million birr at an average annual rate of 14.2%. During the same period, expenditures averaged 49 million birr increasing from 26.8 million birr to 69 million birr, rising at an average rate of about 18% annually.

Capital expenditure during the period averaged 2.5 million birr, thus reflecting that there hardly was much by way of investment. Current

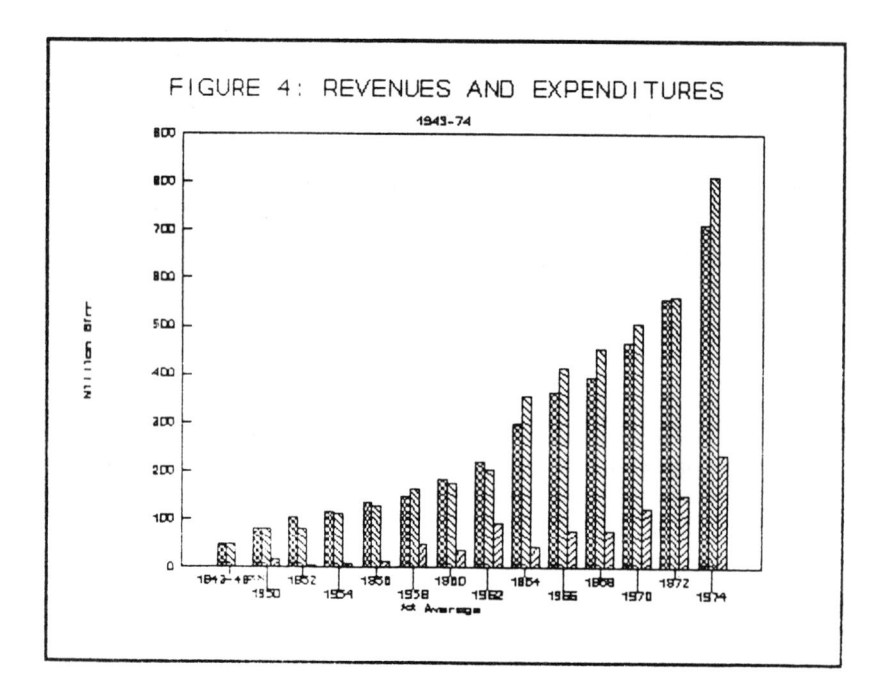

FIGURE 4: REVENUES AND EXPENDITURES 1943-74

revenues and expenditures grew steadily from about 80 million birr in 1950 to 134 million birr in 1959, growing at an average rate of about 6% yearly whereas current expenditures rose from 81 million birr to 137 million birr, growing at nearly the same rate as current revenues (about 7%).

The growth of revenues and expenditures during the period 1950 to 1974[34] is shown in Figure 4. It will be observed from the figure and Annex 4 (see annexes) that the growth of revenues and expenditures during the 1960s was fairly rapid. Revenues increased from about 185 million birr in 1960 to 429 million birr in 1969, rising at an average annual rate of about 10%. Revenues continued to rise steadily during the first half of the 1970s but at a considerably slower rate than in the 1960s. They increased from 466 million birr in 1970 to 711 million birr in 1974, rising at an average yearly rate of just over 8%. On the other hand, expenditures[35] rose from 176 million birr in 1960 to 474 million birr in 1969 and then to 811 million birr in 1974.

During the decade of the 1950s, current expenditures were kept well within revenues and there were even considerable budgetary surpluses with the exception of the latter half of the decade when a cumulative deficit of about 22 million birr was registered in the current account. Up to the mid-1960s, current revenues were adequate to cover expenditures. From 1966 onwards, however, revenues fell short of current expenditures, the only exception being 1973 when exceptionally high earnings from exports of oilseeds and pulses resulted in higher revenues. The degree to which current revenues were able to cover current expenditures between 1950 and 1974 is shown in Table 2.

Table 2: Current Revenues as Percentages of Current Expenditures 1950-74: Selected Years

Year	1950	1955	1960	1965	1970	1974
Revenues (million birr)	79.6	123	184.6	330.3	466	711.4
Expenditures (million birr)	81	115.7	176.5	394.4	507.1	811.2
Per cent	98.3	106.3	105.1	108.4	91.9	87.7

Source: Compiled by author

General services, defence and security absorbed significantly large proportions of the current budget and accounted for the rapid growth of public expenditure during the second half of the 1960s and in the early 1970s. A large part of public expenditures comprised wages and salaries as well as increasing outlays on defence and security. Defence expenditures typically made up over a quarter of total expenditures in the 1960s and early 1970s. The major factors accounting for high defence expenditures were external conflicts and internal civil strife. The conflict with Somalia over the Ogaden resulted in escalation of hostilities almost immediately after the attainment of independence by that country in 1960. Having fallen under the spell of the departing colonial powers, the Somali authorities were bent upon becoming a predator neighbour and a threat to neighbouring countries. This resulted in confrontations with Ethiopia taking the form of an armed conflict in 1964 along the entire length of the Ethio-Somali border. Hostilities were brought to an end through mediation by the Organization of the African Unity but the potential for further armed clashes remained high; this required continued vigilance and a relatively large and well-armed standing army.

The conflict in Eritrea also began to escalate upon the absorption of the region into the Ethiopian Empire in 1962, ten years after it was federated under a decision of a United Nations agreement. Expenditures on defence and security therefore made ever increasing claims on the country's meagre resources. Another reason for a steep rise in public expenditures was that development projects initiated in the context of the various plans entailed recurrent expenditures after they became operational. The first and second development plans were understandably biased in favour of economic and social infrastructure such as transport and communications, health and education, etc., and the budgetary implications of such schemes in subsequent years meant inevitable increases in the size of current expenditures.

Capital expenditures remained relatively low as compared to overall expenditures, especially in the 1950s, but then increased steadily from an average of 18.4 million birr in the 1950s to 73 million birr in the 1960s. Capital expenditures averaged about 169 million birr between 1970 and 1974 and concentrated, as in earlier years, on the development of physical and social infrastructure. Capital expenditures on agriculture, whose overwhelming importance in the economy was well recognized, as well as on health and education, remained pathetically low and were reflected, among other things, in backward agriculture and human resource development.[36] Capital expenditures comprised about 20% of total expenditure in 1970 but increased slightly to 23% in 1974.

It would be worthwhile, at this stage, to examine the relationship between economic expansion in terms of GDP and the growth of revenues and expenditures during the period under review. With the exception of two consecutive years, that is in 1952 and 1953 when there was an overall surplus averaging 20 million birr, Ethiopia always had overall budgetary deficits which rose gradually between 1950 and 1974. Deficits increased from an average of less than 2% of GDP during the decade of the 1950s to about 2.7% in the 1960s. During the first half of the 1970s, the fiscal deficit rose considerably, averaging about 4% of GDP. In the 1960s, the growth of current expenditures as a ratio of GDP averaged about 10% and was slightly lower than current revenues which increased at a slightly lower rate of 9.5%. Between 1970 and 1974, however, both revenues and expenditures averaged about 14% of the GDP, with revenues growing steadily from 9.8% to 13%, and expenditures from 10.7% to 14.6%. Current expenditures as a ratio of GDP in the 1960s increased at a faster rate than current revenues. Between 1970 and 1974, the ratio of current expenditures to GDP, as compared to current revenues, rose at a slightly faster rate. In 1974, current revenue as a ratio of GDP was 14%, as compared to current expenditure of about 15%. Growing budgetary deficits, which were indicative of the fact that the country was facing increasing difficulties in generating adequate revenues to cover rising expenditures, were financed partly domestically and partly from foreign borrowing. Figure 5 shows trends in current and overall deficits between 1950 and 1974.

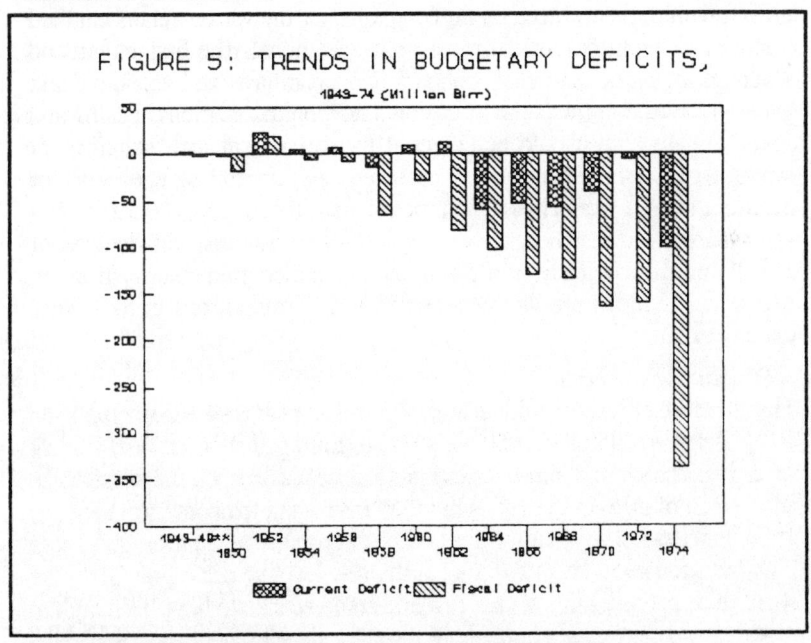

FIGURE 5: TRENDS IN BUDGETARY DEFICITS, 1943-74 (Million Birr)

While there is little that can be said about the appropriate size of a country's fiscal deficit, it would be true to say that the maximum sustainable debt would depend on a country's ability to service debts, both internal and external, consistent with the prevailing rate of inflation. Generally, and depending on the mode of financing used, a large fiscal deficit has negative impacts on one or more of the three macro-economic variables debt, inflation and the rate of growth of the economy. External borrowing leads to a greater debt burden while internal borrowing results in high interest rates and less private sector credit which leads to reductions in private sector investment and output. Fiscal deficits affect the rate of inflation if such deficits are financed through the creation of money. The higher the volume of money injected into the economy, the higher the rate of inflation. To a large extent, monetary expansion in developing countries is influenced by fiscal policy. Fiscal deficits also affect the balance of payments, higher levels of deficit being reflected in a more negative current account balance, and vice versa. Thus, fiscal policy has a direct impact on, among other things, external indebtedness, the rate of inflation and on the overall macro-economic balance.

In the context of the conventional rules of fiscal policy, it is argued that public revenue should exceed public expenditure or, failing that, revenues should at least be sufficient to cover expenditures. The argument is advanced in consideration of the need for higher public saving which would imply that it may not be sufficient to merely balance the current budget but that revenues should be increased, and current expenditures reduced, in order to generate investible funds for financing development programmes. While a sound fiscal policy would be essential for macro-economic stability and sustained growth, the orthodox balanced budget rule is, however, not desirable since it would have a contractionary effect on economic activities. It would result in an unnecessary reduction of expenditures with detrimental effects on the efficiency of the economy or indiscriminate cuts in public expenditures which are the most common and vulnerable targets in such exercises.

Structure of Revenue

The structure of revenues underwent significant changes between 1950 and 1974. Between 1950 and 1960, direct taxes averaged about 24% of current revenues. The share of direct taxes in total revenue dropped subsequently to an average of 20% in the 1960s but then rose again to about 25% between 1970 and 1974. The share of direct taxes in total revenue averaged about 23% between 1950 and 1974. Given the low level of per capita GDP, the share of direct taxes in total tax revenue could be said to have been high in relation to countries at comparable levels of development. In comparison with direct taxes, indirect taxes increased more rapidly because of the increasing monetization of the economy. Indirect taxes more than doubled from an average of 13.4% of total revenue during the decade of the 1950s to 27.5% during the decade of the 1960s. Between 1970 and 1974, revenue from indirect taxes increased slightly over the level of the 1960s and averaged 28.7% of total revenue. Between 1950 and 1974, indirect taxes averaged just over 23% and remained the second most important source of revenues after import and export duties. Taxes on foreign trade transactions continued to be the most important source of revenue yielding about one-third of total tax revenue between 1950 and 1974.

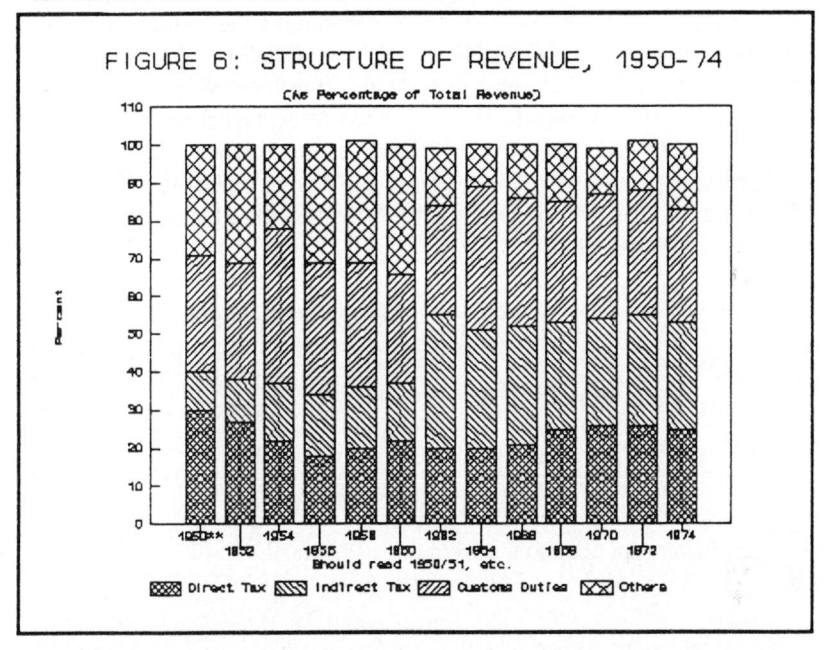

FIGURE 6: STRUCTURE OF REVENUE, 1950-74
(As Percentage of Total Revenue)

Should read 1950/51, etc.

Direct Tax — Indirect Tax — Customs Duties — Others

Altogether, the share of tax revenue averaged about 80% between 1950 and 1974, rising from about 73% in the 1950s to 77% in the 1960s and then to an average of 87.5% between 1970 and 1974. In absolute terms, total tax revenue rose from about 62 million birr in 1950 to about 540 million birr in 1974. The ratio of total tax revenue to GDP (measured at current factor cost) rose only slightly from 4% in 1950 to 5.2% in 1960 but nearly doubled to 10.5% in 1974. On the other hand, non-tax revenue, comprising charges and fees, pension fund, public sales of goods and services and profits, interests and rents, etc., declined steadily from an average of about 28% in the 1950s, to 23% in the 1960s and averaged 20% between 1970 and 1974. Figure 6 shows the structure of revenues between 1950 and 1974.

The dependence of public revenues on trade taxes arises mainly because of ease of tax administration and collection. Other taxes require more complex and costly systems of administration and are more prone to losses through evasion, bribery and corruption. However, with growth in GDP and improvements in institutional capacities, the tax system shifts away from taxes on trade towards other forms of taxes. This is evidenced by the structure of taxes in advanced economies where taxes on trade constitute a tiny share of total revenue, though the percentages were historically known to have been higher. The share of taxes on trade should therefore decline with the growth of GDP. The significance of a given tax system on the allocation of resources and economic growth is obvious. Unreasonably high levels of taxation will lead to widespread evasions and reductions in revenue, in addition to influencing investment decisions and economic growth. The tax system should periodically be reviewed and restructured with the objective not only of raising revenue but also reducing costs. A major objective should be to broaden the tax base rather than to simply increase the tax rate. This means a shift from taxes on trade to taxes on consumption.

Monetary and Price Developments

Money and Banking

After the defeat and expulsion of Fascist forces in 1941, the financial system in Ethiopia was in a state of turmoil and represented a microcosm of monetary chaos. During the years immediately after the war, there were three sorts of currencies that were circulating side by side: the Maria Theresa thaler[37] along with an assortment of coins, the East African shilling (introduced by the British military forces) and the Italian lira.[38] The lira, which had been proclaimed official currency of the country during the Italian rule, soon went out of circulation but the thaler and the shilling continued to function side by side as legal tenders. The government had little control over the supply of these currencies until they were outlawed, having been replaced by the birr as the only legal tender. The birr was issued, following the Currency and Legal Tender Proclamation of May 1945. The new currency was pegged to the US dollar at an exchange rate of 2.50 birr per US dollar or 2 shillings sterling.[39] However, because of its popularity and widespread use, the thaler continued to circulate in the countryside for several years even after it was outlawed.

Immediately after the war, the majority of the rural population remained outside the money economy, with barter as the major means of exchange. As a result, the volume of money in circulation was very low for a country of Ethiopia's size. Nearly a decade after the war, that is in 1950, the total supply of money was estimated at only 95 million birr. But since money had to finance the growing volume of production and credit in the monetized sector, it rose considerably over the years, thus showing the growing monetization of the economy. Total money supply, comprising notes and coins in circulation and non-governmental deposits, increased to about 187 million birr in 1959, rising at an average annual rate of about 11% between

1950 and 1959. The money supply stagnated at about 187 million birr between 1957 and 1959 after growing at an annual rate of 14% between 1950 and 1957. The stagnation in money supply was the result of falling coffee prices[40] and reduced earnings from exports.

During the 1960s, the money supply expanded vigorously as a result of the growing use of money, the expansion of domestic credit as well as increased earnings from exports, both of which have a strong impact on the expansion or contraction of the supply of money. Following favourable earnings from exports, the money supply increased steadily during the period from 237 million birr in 1960 to 422 million birr in 1965, rising at an annual average rate of 15.6%, and by 13.4% in 1965. This reflected larger volumes of coffee exports and higher export earnings, but it was also due to a sharp rise in credits, which amounted to 212 million birr in 1964.

Between 1965 and 1970, the growth of money supply slowed down, averaging about 9% annually, and again reflected a sluggish growth in coffee exports. In 1967, there was a near contraction in the supply of money which showed an increase of only 1.3%. This coincided with a decline in the price of Ethiopian coffee on the New York exchange which dropped by 13% between 1966 and 1967, thus influencing the country's export earnings and, consequently, the supply of money. During the first half of the 1970s, however, the money supply recorded a remarkable increase, growing from 615 million birr in 1970 to about 1.1 billion birr in 1974 an average yearly increase of 19% and nearly double the growth recorded between 1965 and 1970. This was again largely due to a substantial increase in earnings from exports which averaged over 21% annually, mainly due to unprecedented increases in earnings from the exports of pulses and oilseeds. Domestic credit also recorded a moderate growth of about 5%, increasing from 524 million birr in 1970 to 635 million birr in 1974.

In principle, monetary expansion would have to increase in tandem with economic growth. If the money supply grows at a lower rate, the shortage of credit and money in circulation would constrain economic growth. Conversely, if the volume of money in circulation grows at a faster rate than is justified by the rate of economic growth, inflationary pressures would endanger monetary stability that is necessary for a healthy economic growth. Because of the absence of capital markets, the instruments of monetary policy were limited to reserve requirements and ceilings on rates of interest; there seems to have been no direct credit control, the other instrument of monetary policy, by the monetary authorities. Because of low levels of inflation, interest rates were generally positive in real terms. The government's fiscal and financial policies were said to have been managed prudently, if not conservatively. Such a policy could not have been clearly supportive of higher rates of growth and may be said to have contributed to a slower growth of the Ethiopian economy during the years under review.

With regard to the development of financial institutions, Ethiopia's first post-war central bank was the State Bank of Ethiopia established by a proclamation in August 1942. Until 1963, when the Commercial Bank of Ethiopia was established, the State Bank handled both the usual regulatory functions of a central bank such as the regulation of money supply and credit, the management of gold and foreign exchange reserves, the issuance of currency as well as ordinary commercial banking functions. Since its establishment in 1963, the Commercial Bank of Ethiopia remained the most important publicly-owned commercial banking institution accounting for the bulk of all banking operations in the country. In later years, however, there were other foreign-owned banks, such as the Addis Ababa Bank (a subsidiary of the Barclays Bank of Britain), Banco di Roma and Banco di Napoli with limited commercial banking functions.

A development finance institution (the Development Bank of Ethiopia) was first established in 1951 with a loan of 5 million birr from the World Bank to provide long-term loans for agricultural and industrial development projects. The bank subsequently underwent several organizational changes until the establishment of the Agricultural and Industrial Development Bank in the early 1970s through the merger of the Development Bank of Ethiopia and the Ethiopian Investment Corporation. Other financial institutions included the Imperial Savings and Home Ownership Association, the Ethiopian Mortgage Share Company and the Ethiopian Tourism and Hotels Investment Corporation, a quasi-banking institution set up to finance development of the tourist industry and several insurance companies.

Notwithstanding the expansion of monetary institutions, banking services remained beyond the reach of the majority of the population who had limited or no access to formal credit. The rural population, especially peasants, had to depend on traditional sources of credit, the major suppliers of such credit being landlords, merchants and professional village money-lenders. Interest rates were usurious (one study made in the 1960s put interest rates on such informal sources of credit at 120%), so that debt remained a heavy burden for the masses of the rural population. Peasants remained in a vicious circle of debt with one loan succeeding another. Lack of access to financial institutions not only forced the rural population to depend on informal sources of credit, but also became a serious constraint on the mobilization of domestic saving. Therefore, banking services remained ineffective both as sources of rural credit and for mobilizing domestic resources for investment purposes. The banking system plays a major role in the economy of any country. The role of an efficiently functioning banking system becomes even more important in developing countries such as Ethiopia because of the absence of the capital market or because it is undeveloped, as well as low domestic saving relative to investment needs and limited access to external borrowing.

Prices

Despite the growing use of money, as evidenced by a steady monetary expansion, prices remained fairly stable during the period under review. During the decade spanning 1945-54, annual changes in price indices of imports remained more or less stable, ranging from about 78 points in 1945 (1949 = 100) to about 80 points in 1954. The only exception was 1948 when the index rose to about 118 points. On the other hand, the unit value of export price indices rose substantially during the same period from about 114 points (1949 = 100) to about 190 points. According to one study (Aredo, 1987) prices continued to be stable during the rest of the 1950s, with annual price changes averaging 2.4 points between 1953 and 1960 and 4.2 points between 1963 and 1974. Between 1970 and 1974, however, there was a major increase in the consumer price index for Addis Ababa (by 12%) mainly as a result of the drought of 1973-74. In February of 1974, the wholesale price index rose by about 35% as compared to a year earlier. Major increases were registered by items such as cereals (about 32%), oilseeds (about 40%), and pulses (about 200%). It should be noted that erratic trends in consumer prices, especially since the mid-1960s, after which the Central Statistical Office began to make available price indices for Addis Ababa, were more the result of weather conditions that resulted in bumper or poor harvests than fiscal or monetary policies.

External Economic Relations

Foreign Trade

Exports

Economic development in Ethiopia since the 1950s had a positive influence on the country's foreign trade, as reflected in an increase in levels of exports and imports, both in volume and value terms. Immediately after the war, that is in 1942, foreign trade was valued at 138 million birr with merchandise exports accounting for 66 million birr and imports for 72 million birr.[41] Between 1945 and 1950, merchandise exports averaged about 64 million birr with coffee accounting for 20 million birr. Hides and skins held the second place after coffee. In 1950, exports increased to 71 million birr with coffee accounting for 46% of the total.[42] During the decade of the 1950s, earnings from merchandise exports increased quite considerably and averaged about 143 million birr. During the first half of the 1950s, coffee averaged 55% of total exports, followed by foodstuffs, including cereals and pulses (23%) and hides and skins (16%). Oilseeds and pulses, and hides and skins, each constituted about 9% of total exports during the period.

Between 1960 and 1965, total exports increased at an average annual rate of about 10%, rising from 180 million birr to 290 million birr. For the decade as a whole, the rate of growth of exports averaged about 5.6% annually, while during the first half of the 1970s, exports picked up and continued to rise at an annual average rate of about 8%. Unlike other less developed countries Ethiopia's merchandise exports constituted only a small share of GDP. In 1950, exports were only about 4.6% of the GDP but rose steadily to about 9.5% in 1954 and 10.7% in 1957. During the decade of the 1960s exports almost stagnated at 7.4% of GDP, but then rose to about 9% in 1973 and nearly 10% in 1974, resulting mainly from substantial increases in non-coffee exports.

Coffee historically dominated Ethiopia's export trade a pattern that characterizes the export trade of less developed countries whose exports are dominated by primary commodities. Indeed, coffee remained the pillar of the country's export trade and the major determinant of economic activities. Receipts from coffee exports averaged about 30% of total exports between 1945 and 1949. The value of coffee exports averaged 55% of total exports during the 1950s and 56% in the 1960s. The volume of coffee exports averaged 71,400 tons during the decade and attained a peak in 1969 when 88,400 tons of coffee were exported. Earnings from coffee exports attained a peak in 1965 at about 188 million birr, partly as a result of an increase in world coffee prices (f.o.b. prices rose from 1,676 birr per ton in 1961 to 2,200 birr in 1965) and partly due to an increase in the volume of exports. Between 1970 and 1974, however, coffee exports dropped rather significantly to an average of about 51% of total exports, mainly because of higher earnings from non-coffee exports. The decline was accentuated in 1973 and 1974 when coffee exports dropped to a historic low of 38% and 28% respectively. In contrast, the share of oilseeds and pulses, in total exports rose to 26% in 1973 and 36% in 1974.[43] This did not imply that there was any shift towards a sustained diversification of exports, for coffee continued to dominate Ethiopia's export trade, averaging 54% of total earnings between 1950 and 1974, to the extent that earnings from coffee exports determined, among other things, budgetary revenues, public as well as private saving and investment; thus, the volume of imports and economic activities in Ethiopia remained at the mercy of fluctuations in world coffee prices.

Although coffee prices were regulated by the International Coffee Organization, of which Ethiopia was a member, the organization had little influence over developments in world coffee prices. Like the prices of most other primary commodities, world prices for this commodity not only fluctuated wildly but were also characterized by a persistent downward trend (in terms of constant prices).

Between 1950 and 1959 world coffee prices, measured in terms of current prices, averaged about 134 US cents per kg (spot, New York), whereas between 1960 and 1969 they averaged 0.98 cents per kg a decline of about 27% over the average price for the decade of the 1950s. Between 1970 and 1974, however, prices averaged about 138 US cents per kg, representing an increase of 41% as compared to the decade of the 1960s. This compared with a consistent rise in the unit value of export indices for manufactures during the period. Figure 7 depicts trends and fluctuations in world coffee prices between 1950 and 1974 both in real and current terms.

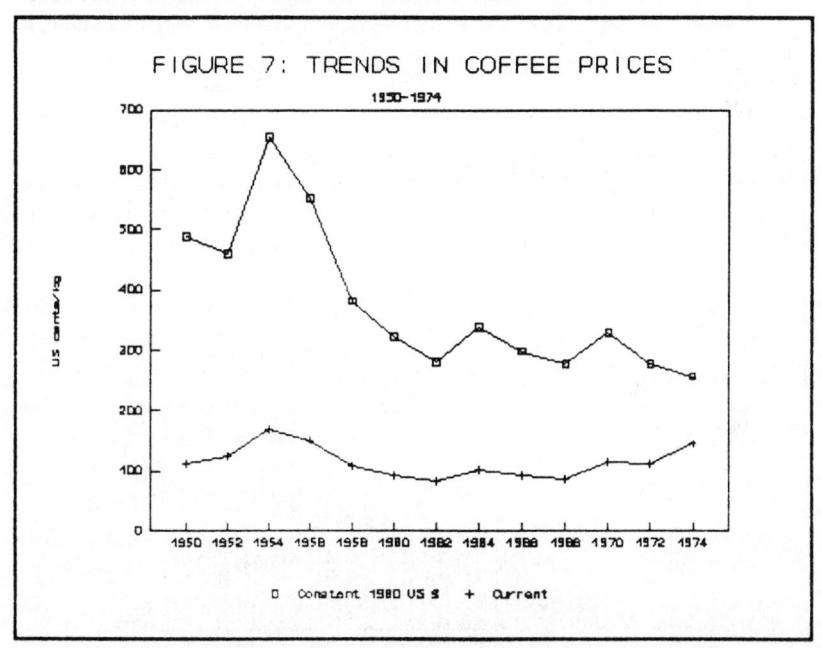

FIGURE 7: TRENDS IN COFFEE PRICES
1950-1974

In addition to coffee, non-coffee exports, mainly cereals (especially in the 1940s and early 1950s), hides and skins, oilseeds and pulses also featured prominently in Ethiopia's export trade. During the decade after World War II, Ethiopia was a surplus exporter of significant amounts of grains. Cereal exports were valued at 10 million birr in 1950, constituting some 13.4% of total exports and were nearly equal to earnings from hides and skins Earnings from cereal exports gradually declined to about 9 million birr in 1952 (about 8% of total exports). In 1954, earnings dropped to 2.4 million birr and accounted for about 1.4% of the total exports. Thereafter, and until nearly a decade later, cereals disappeared from the country's export trade.

In 1967, grain exports began to feature in the country's export trade. Cereal exports that year amounted to over 65,000 tons and were valued at 21 million birr. The following year, however, grain exports rose to 87,000 tons but dropped to 13 million birr in value.

Oilseeds and pulses, hides and skins exports increased until the mid-1960s after which they levelled off, presumably because of the closure of the Suez Canal in 1967 when the competitive edge of Ethiopian commodities diminished as a result of a much longer journey to Europe around the Cape via South Africa. However, both in volume and value terms, the export of these commodities remained insignificant until the 1970s when earnings attained record levels, rising from 44 million birr in 1970, to 129 million birr in 1973 and to 198 million birr in 1974. Earnings from oilseeds and pulses surpassed those from coffee exports (by about 30%) during the first half of the 1970s.

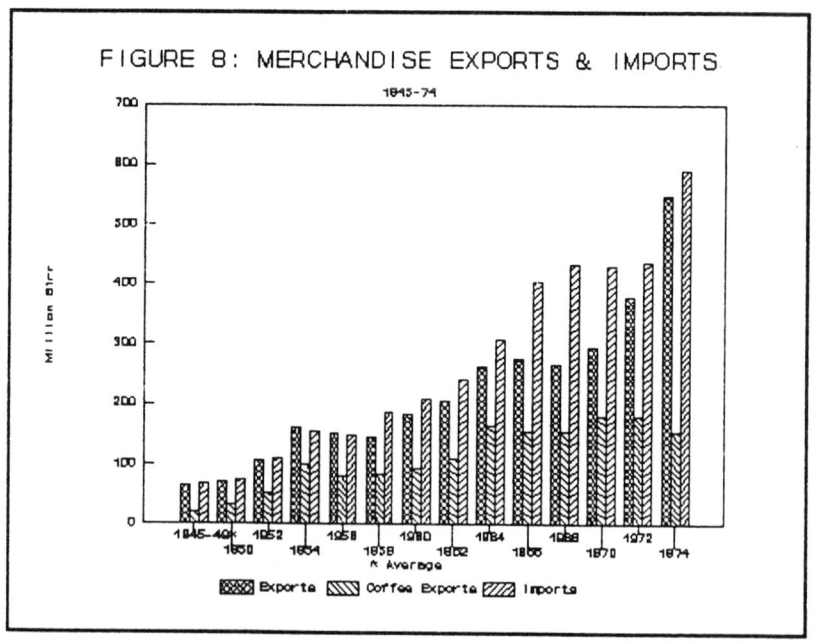

FIGURE 8: MERCHANDISE EXPORTS & IMPORTS 1945-74

In general, agricultural exports constituted the bulk of Ethiopia's export trade. Non-agricultural products still accounted for less than 10% of the total exports, thus showing that there were neither changes in the structure of exports nor in their diversification. Mineral exports were confined almost exclusively to gold which averaged about 7 million birr between 1950 and 1959. In 1974, earnings from exports of this metal were at about the same level as in the 1950s. Manufacture exports remained even less significant during the period under review. In absolute terms, exports rose from 71 million birr in 1950 to 547 million birr in 1974. Figure 8 shows the growth of merchandise exports and imports between 1945 and 1974.

Imports

While Ethiopia's exports were composed of a handful of primary products, the bulk of imports comprised finished goods including capital and intermediate goods for industry and consumer goods. Between 1945 and 1950 imports remained at low levels and averaged about 67 million birr. But even in the 1950s and 1960s, imports remained low, reflecting the low level of economic performance. However, as with exports, imports assumed increasing importance as from the 1960s. Imports began to grow more steadily with economic expansion, the growing demand for capital, raw materials and intermediate goods as well as the rising demand for consumer goods with rising incomes.

The value of merchandise imports increased from about 73 million birr in 1950 to 208 million birr in 1959, rising at an annual average rate of 11.6%. This was considerably higher than the rate of increase in exports (9.3%). Imports continued to rise in the 1960s more steadily and reached 388 million birr in 1970. Between 1960 and 1965, the growth rate of imports averaged 12% and was considerably higher than exports. The relatively high level of imports reflected higher economic growth and increased investment in the context of the country's second and third five-year plans. During the second half of the decade, however, imports slowed down considerably, averaging about 7.2% and continued into the first half of the 1970s with growth averaging 4.3%. This was partly a reflection of continued decline in economic growth during the period as compared to the high growth rates of earlier years. In absolute terms, imports increased from 73 million birr in 1950 to about 208 million birr in 1960. In 1974, merchandise imports stood at 590 million birr.

The growing importance of imports was reflected in a steady increase of imports as a proportion of national output. Imports accounted for a modest share of GNP in 1950, amounting to 4.7%. During the decade of the 1960s, however, imports averaged about 9.5% of GDP, and 9.2% between 1970 and 1974. Over 60% of the value of imports was made up of capital and intermediate goods as well as raw materials for industry; this shows the degree to which the country's industry remained dependent on imports. In 1950, raw materials and intermediate goods, machinery and equipment imports constituted about 30% of the total imports. In 1960, this figure almost exactly doubled to 61%, reached a peak in 1968 at 75% and then dropped to 61% in 1974.

There was a steady increase in the volume of capital goods in the composition of imports, from a mere 9% in 1950 to 30% in 1960, and from 39% in 1964 to 44% in 1974, thus showing a steady increase in investment. Fuel imports increased sharply[44] in 1974 and overshadowed almost all other imports. The volume of importation of consumer goods declined steadily from 69% of total imports in 1950, to 39% in 1960 and then to 24% in 1968. During the first half of the 1970s, however, there was an upswing in consumer goods imports which increased from 35% of the total imports in 1970 to 38% in 1974.[45] The composition of imports for selected years between 1950 and 1974 is shown in Figure 9.

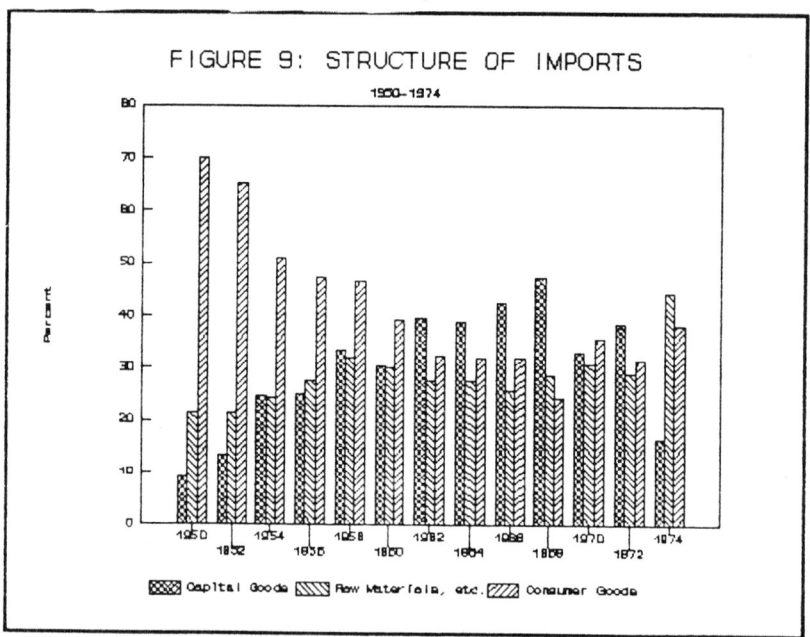

FIGURE 9: STRUCTURE OF IMPORTS 1950-1974

Two facts immediately become apparent in any analysis of Ethiopia's foreign trade. First, like many other less developed countries, Ethiopia's exports were composed of primary products, mainly coffee, which averaged 54% of the total export earnings between 1950 and 1974. There were no structural shifts in the composition of the export trade during the period under review. Secondly, imports comprised capital and intermediate goods as well as raw materials and consumer goods. In all cases, the fortunes of the Ethiopian economy remained entirely at the mercy of developments in the global economy. Lower prices for the country's exports and high prices for industrial manufactures, intermediate inputs and raw materials greatly affected economic activities.

The vulnerability of the Ethiopian economy to adverse developments in the international economy became more apparent in 1974 when, because of an unprecedented increase in world crude petroleum prices, the economy became exposed to a severe shock, resulting in the downfall of the government and sweeping changes in the political and economic system. A second factor that may be observed from the trend rate of growth of Ethiopia's foreign trade is that, while both exports and imports grew faster than GDP, imports rose more rapidly than both the rates of growth of exports and of GDP. Export earnings amounted to 97% of imports in 1950 but declined steadily to 88% in 1960 and to 69% in 1970. However, in 1974, earnings from exports rose to about 93% of imports.

Balance of Payments

Balance of payments is defined here as a record of international transactions comprising Ethiopia's goods and services exports in relation to imports and reflecting changes in the country's foreign exchange position. A credit entry in the balance of payments denotes a decrease, and a debit entry an increase in foreign exchange reserves.[46] The balance of payments has two parts, namely, the current account and capital account. The current account records the flow of goods and services and transfer payments between the country and the rest of the world. It is divided into visible trade and invisible trade; the former records the value of merchandise imports and exports while the latter records the value of intangible goods or services. The main items included in the current account are merchandise trade, exports of non-monetary gold, travel, transportation, investment, insurance and transfer payments. The main items in the capital account are official capital flows, private investment, amortization and reserves. A surplus on current account may be augmented or offset by net outflows on capital account.

Between 1950 and 1957, there was generally a surplus or only a small deficit in Ethiopia's trade balance. As from 1958, however, the deficit in trade balance began to widen, partly reflecting higher levels of growth and the needs of the economy for more imports. With imports rising faster than exports, the deficit in trade balance continued to rise steadily and averaged 113 million birr during the second half of the 1960s as compared to an average of 31 million birr during the first half of the decade. During the first half of the 1970s, the deficit in merchandise trade rose substantially to 148 million birr, except for the years 1973 and 1974 when there were surpluses averaging about 46 million birr. The surpluses resulted from exceptionally good export earnings from oilseeds and pulses, as noted earlier. During the period under review, the imbalance in merchandise trade rose from a small surplus of 0.2 million birr in the 1950s to a deficit of 72 million birr in the 1960s and 148 million birr during the first half of the 1970s (averages).

In contrast to the deficit in current account, Ethiopia generally enjoyed surpluses in its balance of payments. The surplus doubled between 1950 and 1954, rising from about 10 million to 20 million birr; it averaged about 12 million birr between 1950 and 1959. The surplus was earned on current account as a result of favourable world coffee prices which increased by 50% (in current prices) between 1950 and 1954. Surpluses in the country's balance of payments continued into the 1960s, the only exceptions being 1966 and 1967 when the country experienced deficits averaging about 26 million birr, partly as a result of a decline in exports attributed to lower coffee prices but also because of an increase in imports. Increases in imports in 1966 and 1967 were due to food imports resulting from adverse climatic conditions and poor harvests during those years.

For most years, receipts on capital inflows exceeded the deficits on current account. In the 1950s private and public capital inflows remained low and insignificant but, as from 1960, the inflow of private capital showed a moderate but steady increase. Public capital inflow, which took the form of official grants, technical assistance, loans and credits, also increased moderately from 1960 onwards. In general, Ethiopia's balance of payments showed continued improvements during the period under review, the overall surplus rising to an all-time high in 1974 when foreign reserves increased by 263 million birr. Foreign exchange holdings rose from 12 million birr in 1950 (able to finance about two months' imports) to 230 million birr in 1965 (able to finance 7 months' imports). Ethiopia's foreign exchange position was particularly strong during the first half of the 1970s with reserves rising from about 208 million birr in 1970 to 663 million birr in 1974. Trends in Ethiopia's balance of payments between 1950 and 1974 are shown in Figure 10.

No discussion of a country's external transactions will be complete without mentioning the terms of trade which refers to the relationship between the average unit value of exports and the average unit value of imports. A glance at commodity trade and price trends since World War II reveals that the prices of primary commodities exported by developing countries have generally fallen or risen less rapidly than the prices of manufactures imported by them. This leads to deteriorations for exporters of primary products and improvements in the terms of trade for exporters of manufactured goods. In other words, prices that developing countries receive by exporting primary commodities purchase, over time, less and less manufactured goods. If, for example, a vehicle could be purchased with the value of, say, 14 bags of coffee in 1954 (when coffee fetched 176.4 US cents/kg), it would require 39 bags of coffee in 1962 (when coffee fetched US cents 90/kg).

Countries that depend on the export of a single major commodity such as Ethiopia usually experience unfavourable terms of trade because of

FIGURE 10: BALANCE OF PAYMENTS
1950-1974

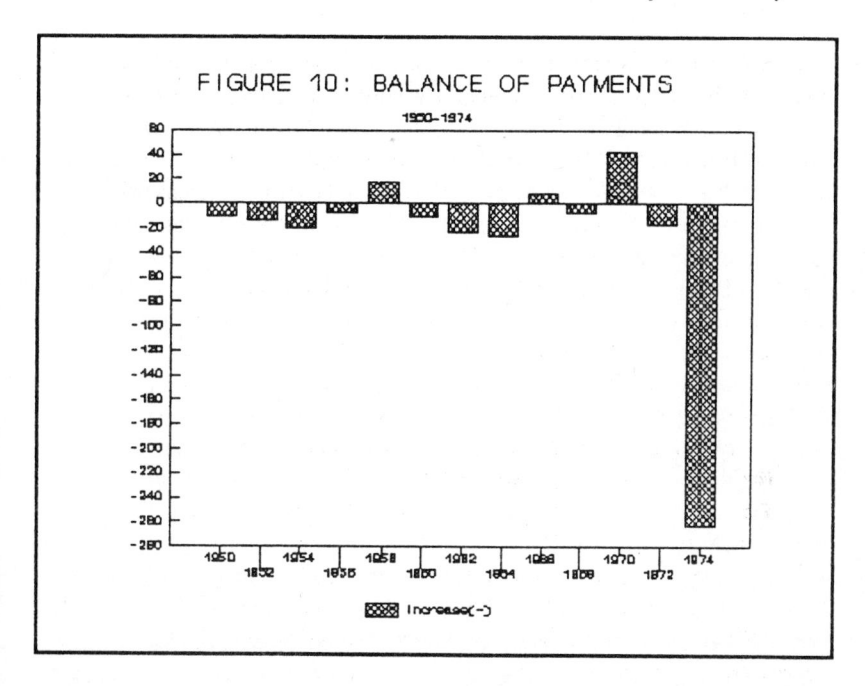

inelasticity of demand for their products and the downward trend in real prices in contrast to rising prices of manufactures. Although the terms of trade for Ethiopia cannot be examined because of lack of data, there had been a secular downward trend in world coffee prices (measured in constant prices) between 1950 and 1974.[47] Therefore, because of Ethiopia's dependence on coffee exports, there would be no doubt that the country had been experiencing unfavourable terms of trade accentuated in the 1960s when world coffee prices were depressed in the face of increases in imports.

Foreign Aid and Debt

Due mainly to the shortage of domestic resources, Ethiopia relied heavily on external loans and technical assistance from bilateral sources and multilateral agencies to finance its development programmes, especially beginning with the First Five-Year Plan in 1958. The country received considerable amounts of foreign aid, most of which took the form of loans and credits, but also significant amounts of technical assistance. Foreign aid could be traced back to the years immediately after independence when budgetary support was provided under the British budgetary subsidy programme beginning in 1942. Subsidies amounted to about 12 million birr in 1942 and averaged about 7.6 million birr thereafter until they were discontinued in 1945. The discontinuation of the subsidies was immediately followed by an inflow of official development assistance, mainly from

Sweden and the United States, which averaged about 2.8 million birr between 1945 and 1949. Official development assistance was estimated at 14 million birr in 1950, or about 0.75 cents in per capita terms.

The most important sources of economic and technical assistance to Ethiopia up to 1974 remained the United States and the World Bank Group. Ethiopia became a member of the World Bank soon after its establishment in 1945 and was amongst the first beneficiaries of loans and credits provided by the bank, after settling its subscription in gold equivalent to 100,000 birr in 1946. Between 1950 and 1955, Ethiopia received a total of three loans from the World Bank amounting to about 22 million birr, 12.5 million birr for road construction and maintenance, 5 million birr for the establishment of a development finance company (the Development Bank of Ethiopia) and about 4 million birr for the development of telecommunications.

In September 1951, a Treaty of Amity and Economic Relations was concluded between Ethiopia and the United States and became the basis for the subsequent flow of bilateral economic and technical aid to Ethiopia. The United States remained the largest bilateral source of loans to Ethiopia in the early 1950s. The bulk of the aid (35%) was for agricultural development, the next largest allocation being for health and education. The rest was used for the development of the country's civil aviation, the purchase of aircraft and airport construction and for the construction of highways. However, during the second half of the 1960s, United States aid became more oriented towards technical assistance. Out of the estimated 900 technical assistance personnel in Ethiopia in 1970 over 40% were Peace Corps volunteers from the United States. Towards the latter part of the decade an agreement was concluded with the Soviet Union for a loan amounting to 100 million rubles (about 250 million birr) during the visit to that country by Emperor Haile Selassie in July 1959.[48]

During the first half of the 1960s, the United States continued to be the largest bilateral donor with a share of 41%, followed by the International Development Association (IDA), an affiliate of the World Bank established in 1960 as its concessionary window (31%). During the second half of the decade, however, loans and credits from the World Bank Group rose considerably to 41% as compared to aid from the United States which amounted to 29%. In 1974, the share of loans and credits from the World Bank made up 44% of the total official development assistance, whereas the share of loans from the United States declined to 31%. Loans from Italy and the Federal Republic of Germany were nearly equal in amount and were about 7% of the total, while loans from Sweden amounted to 3.5%. Between 1962 and 1969, the combined aid from countries of Eastern Europe (the Soviet Union, Czechoslovakia and Yugoslavia) amounted to 12% of the total aid to Ethiopia. Much of the aid was used for the construction of physical and social infrastructure including land and air transport, power and telecommunications, health and education.

Loans and credits from the World Bank Group financed investments in physical and social infrastructure. Soviet aid covered the construction of a refinery at Aseb and a technical school at Bahar Dar, while loans from Yugoslavia were used mainly for the construction and expansion of the Aseb port and the Addis Ababa cement plant. Loans from Czechoslovakia financed the construction of the rubber and tyre factories at Addis Ababa and a tannery at Ejersa on the road to Awasa past the town of Mojo. Loans from the Federal Republic of Germany financed the construction of the road to Moyale on the Kenyan boarder as well as the Massawa cement plant. Italian loans were used mainly for the construction of the Lege Dadi reservoir which continues to be the major source of water supply to Addis Ababa. Swedish loans and grants were used for the installation of telephone facilities and for financing projects in agriculture, health and education, while loans from the Netherlands financed the acquisition of merchant ships for the country's fledgling shipping line.

According to official figures, the country's total foreign debt including undisbursed loans and credits, rose from an estimated 14 million birr in 1950 to 827 million birr in 1966. Foreign debt net of undisbursed loans rose from 77 million birr in 1960 to about 400 million birr in 1966. Between 1970 and 1974, total loans and credits (disbursed and undisbursed) increased from 1.3 billion birr to 1.8 billion birr. The conclusion of a loan agreement with the People's Republic of China in 1971, amounting to about 200 million birr, accounted for a substantial increase in commitments. Undisbursed loan balances rose from 440 million birr in 1966 (53% of commitments) to 654 million birr in 1970 (50% of commitments). Disbursements increased to 962 million birr, or about 52% of commitments, in 1974.

About 38% of loans and credits disbursed in 1970 was from the World Bank Group and 33% from the United States. The rest was from the Soviet Union (6.7%), Italy (12.6%), Germany (2.4%) and Sweden (1.4%). Nearly 70% of the outstanding debt was owed to the United States and the World Bank Group. Debts to Germany, Italy, Sweden, the Soviet Union and Czechoslovakia constituted the bulk of the remaining external debt. Total debt rose from 15.6% of GDP in 1970 to 17% in 1974, exclusive of undisbursed loans and credits. It averaged about 17% during the period from 1970 to 1974. Figure 11 shows the growth of external public debt between 1950 and 1974 in terms of total commitments. Although the rise in foreign debt was fairly rapid, the absolute volume of indebtness may be said to have been low in relation both to exports and the country's development needs and potentials. The debt service ratio (debt service as a percentage of export earnings) rose from about 5.5% in 1954 to 6% in 1965 and was considerably low when compared to other countries. It reached a high of 18% in 1970 but declined steadily to 9% in 1974. The debt service ratio, which averaged about 13.5% between 1970 and 1974, was, in part, a reflection of the primary nature of Ethiopia's exports and fluctuations in export earnings, resulting from cyclical changes in demand for the country's export commodities. It was high when export earnings were low, and low when earnings from exports were favourable. Despite the rapid increase in official development assistance which, in per capita terms, rose from the paltry figure of less than one birr in 1950 to about 58 birr in 1974, debt servicing remained relatively low. This means that the country possessed the potentials to borrow more and embark on bolder programmes of economic development.

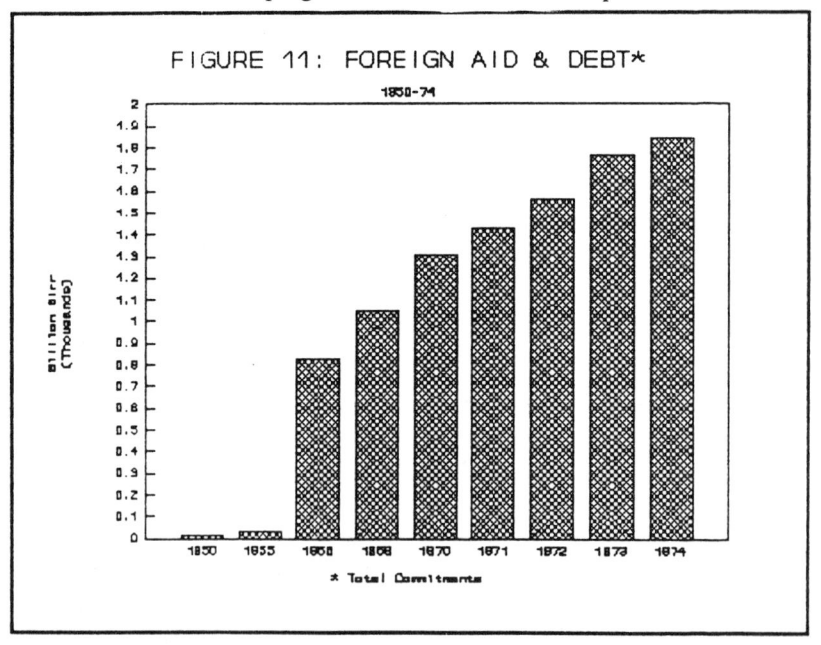

FIGURE 11: FOREIGN AID & DEBT*
1950-74

* Total Commitments

With the exception of loans from the Soviet Union and other centrally planned countries which bore interest rates of 2.5%, with grace periods of about two years and 12 years' maturity, the terms and conditions of most foreign loans were generally obtained on moderate terms and conditions with low interest rates and longer periods of maturity. Partly because of the low volume of debt but also because of the government's concern for donor sensibilities, the country maintained an impeccable record in the settlement of its international debt service obligations and a high degree of creditworthiness.

Observations and Conclusions

One cannot help but conclude that, in quantitative terms, there indeed had been considerable changes in several aspects of the Ethiopian economy during the period 1941-74. First, there were substantial changes in domestic output (an increase of nearly three and a half times between 1950 and 1974) with some changes in its structure. There was a twofold increase in agricultural value added and almost a fifteen-fold rise in value added in manufacturing. Secondly, there were important changes in the country's infrastructure. There were, for example, a 24-fold increase in the supply of electricity between 1950 and 1974, a rise of some 3.5 times in the mileage of all-weather roads, and an increase of over 13 times in the number of telephones.

Thirdly, there were considerable improvements in public finance with increases in revenues and expenditures. Between 1950 and 1974, public revenues rose by more than nine times while expenditures increased tenfold. Similarly, there were significant expansions in international economic relations. Although imports as a proportion of GDP did not show significant changes between 1950 and 1974, the absolute volume of merchandise imports rose by nearly eight times. There were also significant changes in the structure of imports, with the volume of capital goods imports rising from about 9% of total imports in 1950 to over 38% in 1974, and that of raw materials and intermediate goods, from 21% to over 44% during the same period. With regard to capital inflows, whereas the inflow of public foreign capital was insignificant in the early 1950s, and outflows for the service of foreign debt payments were negligible, by 1974 these elements had become significant items in the balance of payments. For example, total foreign debt (in terms of total commitments) rose from an estimated 14 million birr in 1950 to nearly 2 billion birr in 1974, whereas payments of foreign debt as a proportion of exports rose from an estimated 5.5% in 1954 to 9% in 1974. Annex 11 summarizes the major economic indicators of the Ethiopian economy between 1950 and 1974.

The question, however, remains whether these quantitative changes were reflected in perceptible improvements in the welfare of the masses of the Ethiopian people. At the highest level of generality, the major objective of economic development is a steady and sustainable improvement in the welfare of the population. There are three major, and perhaps equally important, means of achieving this objective along with mutually supportive policies: a) the attainment of high rates of economic growth and a sustained improvement in living standards, consistent with an efficient utilization of human and material resources; b) an equitable distribution of the benefits of growth among the population; and c) political freedom and civil liberties, in a broader sense. In the Ethiopian case, one may plausibly argue that these broad goals were far from being achieved for, when one looks at internationally accepted economic and social indicators of development, as well as degrees of political freedom, the evidence shows otherwise.

In 1974, the country was so backward that it was categorized amongst the world's least developed countries. Even among the 25 African countries categorized as least developed by the United Nations in 1974, Ethiopia was at the foot of the list. Indeed, in 1974, as before and immediately after independence, the masses of the Ethiopian people were still so wretched and poor as to be considered an epitome of poverty itself. There were numerous factors that accounted for the continued poverty of the Ethiopian people. Some of these were internal and were inherent in the social and political system; others were external and are beyond the scope of this chapter.

The first and most obvious constraint was the feudal mode of production and the antiquated system of land tenure. This was a serious obstacle to increasing output and productivity and to attaining desirable levels of economic growth. Although a comprehensive land reform programme was critical for attaining a breakthrough in output, all efforts towards introducing a workable land reform programme were vehemently opposed and resisted by the aristocracy and the Orthodox Church, even on the eve of the demise of the system.[49] The machinery of government remained archaic and conservative throughout, and fundamentally insensitive to the need for political and economic reforms. There was neither the political will nor an adequate machinery for implementing the various plans which were supposed to have brought about economic transformation.

The second factor was backward technology and lack of physical infrastructure, mainly in the form of access roads to rural areas, along with inadequate marketing arrangements and the low level of development of irrigated agriculture impeded agricultural output and productivity. During the First Five-Year Plan, the need to establish a network of roads penetration roads, farm-to-market and feeder roads was stressed but there hardly was any dent made in problems of internal transport and communications. The problems continued to present a serious obstacle to the movement of agricultural produce, but also to the introduction of new technologies and other vital services for increasing output and productivity. Paralleling the problems of physical infrastructure was the deficiency of social infrastructure with an extremely high level of illiteracy, disease and malnutrition which directly affected output and productivity.

In the context of a longer term perspective, the third major constraint that hampered economic growth in Ethiopia had to do with political conflicts of a violent nature that had been characteristic of its history. Although Ethiopian rulers boasted of independence and civilization stretching back into millenniums, what they bequeathed to succeeding generations was despicable poverty and wretchedness, and economic and technological backwardness, mainly because of unrelenting conflicts and rivalries amongst war lords for regional domination. Indeed, Ethiopia had always been either at war with itself or with other countries.[50] Writing in the early 1920s, a noted Ethiopian author, Gebrehiwot Baikedagn, tells us that Ethiopia's history was checkered by internal conflicts for several centuries. This is what he said:

The history of us Ethiopians was lamentable. For several centuries past, we enjoyed no peace whatsoever......Had we been able to live together in peace and with love for one another we could have, without doubt, attained wonders, for God has blessed us with his Grace. While wisdom and knowledge have lightened up the world, we continue to live in darkness. We are suspicious of one another and believe, wrongly, in internecine wars as heroism. We yet have to realize that we are brothers and that we belong to the same racial stock.[51]

The conflict continued during the post-independence years which were marked by palace intrigues and *Coups d'Etats*, spontaneous peasant uprisings and guerilla movements. The most significant of these were peasant revolts in Tigrai soon after independence in 1943, peasant revolts in Gojam and in Bale regions in later years, the struggle of the Somalis in the Ogaden and of other minority nationalities for the assertion of their rights, and the insurgent movement in Eritrea which intensified upon the repudiation of the federal status in 1962.[52] Such conflicts, which obviously had their roots in the repressive rules of tyrannical regimes, not only absorbed financial resources but also made claims on productive manpower, disrupted economic and social life and contributed to economic backwardness and a stagnant society. Democratic freedoms are essential preconditions for peace, political stability and economic growth. Given democratic freedoms and a state of peace and stability, able leadership and good governance, as well as appropriate social and economic policies, Ethiopia possesses considerable human and material resources to foster rapid and sustained growth. Among the noble goals of the revolution of 1974 and the aspirations of revolutionaries behind it precisely was the realization of those potentials. But, alas, events proved otherwise, for during the years after the revolution misery and poverty continued to be familiar, and indeed more intimate bed-fellows of the masses of the Ethiopian people. We will conclude this chapter by borrowing from the eloquent pen of Joseph Conrad who, of revolutions and revolutionaries, has this to say:

> *In a real revolution, the best characters do not come to the front. A violent revolution falls into the hands of narrow-minded fanatics and of tyrannical hypocrites at first. Afterwards come the turn of all the pretentious intellectual failures of the time. The scrupulous and the just, the noble, humane and devoted natures, the unselfish and the intelligent may begin a movement, but it passes away from them. They are not the leaders of a revolution. They are its victims: the victims of disgust, disenchantment often of remorse. Hopes grotesquely betrayed, ideals caricatured that is the definition of revolutionary success.*[53]

Notes

1. Eritrea was placed under British administration from 1941 until it was federated with Ethiopia in 1952. In contravention of the United Nations resolution, the federal arrangement was gradually weakened by the imperial government that transformed Eritrea into an ordinary province in 1962.
2. In Eritrea, labour unions existed separately but were disbanded in 1958 after a general strike in Asmara that year.
3. CELU was provided with financial and technical assistance by the AFL-CIO through the African-American Labour Center in New York.
4. The government exercised total control over labour union activities and even assumed the role of arbitrator by setting up a Council to decide on labour disputes. Leadership posts in CELU were filled by appointment rather than by election from among union ranks.
5. There was a brief spurt of political freedom, unprecedented in the country's history, in the initial years of the Revolution. Addis Ababa was awash with radical leaflets and tracts, the most conspicuous being the *Voice of the Masses*, organ of the AESM and *Democracia*, organ of the EPRP.
6. It would be of interest to note that the price of petroleum was only US$1.7 per barrel in the 1950s, remained steady at US$1.8 per barrel in the 1960s and early 1970s, but then increased sharply to US$9.6 per barrel in 1973 (an increase of over 430%) creating a wave of recession in the global economy.
7. Although the government later acknowledged the existence of famine in Wello and Tigrai, famine was, in fact, much more widespread than was acknowledged and also existed in at least four other regions, including Harerghe, Bale, Kefa and pockets of Shoa.
8. Drought and famine appear to have been permanent features of the life of Ethiopia's peasantry, with numerous occurrences being recorded in the country's history. Between 1900 and 1974, no less than 10 major occurrences were recorded, mostly in the northern regions. Major droughts in certain parts of the globe are said to coincide with sun spots or flares which, according to scientists, occur every eleven years. Given this hypothesis and on the basis of past records, it would be possible to make a near-accurate prediction of droughts in Ethiopia. A well-functioning early warning

system, food security, distribution and marketing systems, preparedness and prevention and other similar policies can help avert the disastrous consequences of the past years.
9. According to the First Five-Year Plan, only 18% of the total produce found its way to the market in the early 1950s, with 82% having subsistence, or non-monetary character.
10. In addition to commodity prices, other major elements of the international economic environment that are important determinants of the economic growth of developing countries include real interest rates, trade and industrial growth.
11. With a per capita income of less than 200 birr in 1974, Ethiopia was among the 25 countries classified as least developed by the United Nations.
12. The Marshall Plan for Europe involved large-scale economic and financial aid by the United States amounting to about US$10 billion in 1948/49 (more than 2.5% of the US gross national product at the time) and resulted in a successful recovery of European economies after World War II.
13. Contrary to the prevailing craze for privatization and market forces as conditions for economic and technical aid, John Maynard Keynes, a noted English economist, advocated state intervention for macro-economic stability and growth; the 'Keynesian Revolution' marked the end of the classical, *laissez-faire* economics. State intervention in economic activities in the West had its origin in the Great Depression of the 1930s.
14. As from the 1920s, the Soviet Union introduced planned economic development which resulted in rapid rates of economic growth and transformed a backward, agrarian country into an industrial giant. A dramatic development, since the completion of this chapter, was the break-up, in 1991, of the Soviet Union into 15 new sovereign nation states and the abandonment of a centrally-planned economy in favour of one driven by market forces. With a population of about 150 million (51% of what used to be the Soviet Union) and with a net output of about 61%, Russia is by far the largest of the new independent republics. Countries such as Czechoslovakia and Yugoslavia, mentioned later on in this chapter, have also disintegrated, each one of them into two or more sovereign states.
15. Growth theories have since taken tortuous twists and turns with little or no impact on the economies of most developing countries that, quite to the contrary, continued to backslide with pathetic growth performance and declining per capita income. They were postulated by armchair economists with little or no acquaintance with the economic and social milieu of countries they theorized about. Divorced as they were from political, sociological, cultural and psychological considerations and the influences of the external economic environment, all of which have critical roles in the process of social and economic transformation and, being universal rather than country-specific, the theories and models were little more than textbook solutions to the complex problems of social and economic development.
16. United Nations Department of Economic Affairs, Measures for the Economic Development of Developing Countries, 1951.
17. Dependence on the United States brought the imperial regime handsome rewards in the form of military aid (under a military agreement of 1953) amounting to about 475 million birr up to 1974 - a figure equal to almost half of all the military aid extended to African countries in that period - and economic aid (under an economic assistance agreement signed in 1951 and the Treaty of Amity and Economic Relations of October, 1953) amounting to about 800 million birr.

58 *An Economic History of Modern Ethiopia*

18. Total planned investment amounted to 674 million birr, including 'investment in kind' of 150 million birr. Investment in kind was assumed to include farmers' contributions in labour and material for the construction of rural houses and feeder roads with no financial implications.
19. In 1966 the government set up a 'Technical Agency' to help in the preparation and appraisal of projects. The establishment of this Agency and the Central Statistical Office helped improve conditions somewhat during the preparation of the third plan.
20. No population census was ever undertaken in Ethiopia during the period under review. Population figures for planning purposes were based on crude counts by the Ministry of Interior made early in the 1950s. So were population growth rates.
21. It appears that, in those days, computation of national and per capita incomes was a free-for-all exercise. In 1957, there were at least three estimates of per capita income that were floating around. Estimates were made by the State Bank of Ethiopia (95 birr) and the United States Operations Mission to Ethiopia (111 birr). The Planning Board came up with a figure of 91 birr and this became the official estimate.
22. GNP estimates of the Planning Board were put at 1,554 million birr in 1950; 1,687 million birr in 1954 and 1,801 million birr in 1957.
23. National accounts estimates for Ethiopia during the 1950s refer to GNP while those since 1961 refer to GDP. The author is of the opinion that, since net factor incomes from abroad were negligible in the 1950s, and even in later years, there would be no perceptible difference between GNP and GDP figures so that both may be used interchangeably.
24. For the purposes of long-term projection, GNP figures for the 1950s were calculated on the basis of 1980-81 GDP figures at constant factor cost. Average growth rates for the 1950s, worked out on the basis of data obtained from the first plan, were used for estimating GNP figures in the 1950s. Although admittedly crude, the method enables us to make rough projections of the growth rates of GDP and its components over a longer period.
25. Computations of growth rates in this chapter are done with the Lotus Spreadsheet formula.
26. Estimates of population growth and size, as reconstructed by the Central Statistical Office on the basis of the 1984 Census, are presented in Table A2.
27. This and subsequent figures are based on corresponding Annex Tables which, in turn, are compiled from such sources as the National Planning Office, the Ministry of Finance, the Central Statistical Office, the National Bank of Ethiopia and sundry publications.
28. The use of conventional gross national income statistics for intercountry comparisons may be of doubtful validity, particularly between rich and poor countries. Historical gross national product data in terms of purchasing-power parity may result in different figures.
29. In order to minimize dependence on climatic conditions, it would be necessary to strike an appropriate balance between rain-fed agriculture and irrigated agriculture in planning for agricultural development.
30. In 1950 the supply of electric power was estimated at only 17 million kwh. Because of supply shortages, it was typical for larger industrial enterprises to put up their own power plants.
31. Gold production was valued at less than 3 million birr up to 1973 when prices remained fixed at US$35/oz, or 3080 birr per kg. Thereafter, following sharp increases in world gold prices, the value of gold production went up to about 7 million birr in 1973, although production was only 621 kg and was much lower than the production for

An Overview of the Economy 59

1970 (849 kg). Gold production peaked in 1968 at 958 kg but was valued at 2.9 million birr.
32. The Koka hydro-power plant was put up at an estimated cost of 30 million birr with an initial design capacity of 36,000 kw. Financing was provided by the Italian Government under the war reparation agreement concluded between the governments of Ethiopia and Italy.
33. Includes British subsidy which averaged 7.6 million birr until it was discontinued in 1945.
34. Prior to 1960, revenue and expenditure data relate to the Ethiopian calendar year, i.e., from 12 September to 11 September. Since July 1960, however, the data relate to fiscal years beginning 8 July. Revenue and expenditure data before 1952 obviously do not include Eritrea.
35. Expenditures were classified functionally as 'ordinary' (current) and 'extraordinary' (capital) as well as by sectors. Current expenditures usually included some capital expenditure items, so that there was no clear-cut demarcation between capital and current expenditures. However, such items were very small and would make no significant difference regarding trends in current and capital expenditures.
36. Between 1950 and 1974, agricultural growth barely kept pace with population growth, whereas in 1974, adult literacy rate was estimated at 7%, primary school enrolment at 20%, population per physician at 74,000 and population per hospital at 3,000.
37. The thaler was a large silver coin and the origin of the word 'birr' which means silver in Amharic and subsequently used in conjunction with the new banknote. It had several denominations: 1 thaler = 2 alad(s) = 4 roob(s) = 16 temoon(s) or mehalek(s) = 32 besa(s) = 100 noos.
38. These were in addition to the use of barter which was widely practised throughout the country with lengths of cloth, bars of salt, etc. being used as the media of exchange.
39. This rate of exchange was to last until December 1971 when, following the realignment of international currencies, the birr appreciated against the US dollar at an exchange rate of 2.30 birr and maintained its old gold parity of 5.52 grams of fine gold. Since February, 1973, the birr was again revalued against the US dollar at a rate of 2.07 birr.
40. World coffee prices dropped rather sharply from 141 US cents/kg in 1957 to 99.7 US cents/kg in 1959, the decline averaging over 20% annually during the two-year period.
41. Like manufacturing industry, foreign trade was also almost entirely in the hands of expatriates. In 1951 there were about 200 registered exporters and importers, some of the major ones being Besse, A & Co. (Eth) Ltd., Gellatley, Hankey & Co. (Middle East) Ltd., Seferian & Co. (Eth) Ltd. and Sabean Utility Corp. Ltd.
42. The value of exports originating in Eritrea in 1950 was put at 20.4 million birr.
43. The volume of oilseeds and pulses exported in 1973 was about 238,000 tons. In 1974, however, it dropped to 230,400 tons, but earnings were higher than in 1973 because of booming prices.
44. Because of the phenomenal increase in world crude petroleum prices in 1974, Ethiopia's fuel imports rose from 42 million birr in 1973 to 101 million birr in 1974, an increase of 142%.
45. Food grains also featured in Ethiopia's import trade as from 1957 when some 45,000 tons of grains were imported into the country, partly as a result of crop failures that year. Food grain importation continued sporadically in subsequent years depending on variations in weather conditions. In 1965 and 1966, grain imports averaged 26 million birr. During the drought of 1973-74, commercial importation of grains amounted to 118,000 tons in addition to food and non-food aid totalling 934,000 tons.
46. Figure 10 should be seen in this context.

47. Exceptions were the years 1951-54 when the Korean War led to sharp increases in commodity prices and variations in the terms of trade.
48. Because of its non-concessional nature, the bulk of loans received from the Soviet Union remained unutilized for many years. In 1974, almost 15 years later, some 200 million birr of it was still undisbursed.
49. A so-called White Paper was hastily put together in April 1974 by a 'New Cabinet' of Prime Minister Endalkachew Mekonnen who was newly appointed by Emperor Haile Selassie. In order to stem the tide of the revolution, the Cabinet came up with a programme of reform among which was the imposition of ceilings on land holdings. This was immediately rebuffed by prominent members of the aristocracy who, barely four months later, had to face a firing squad.
50. According to one report, there were no less than thirteen wars or skirmishes between 1876 and 1904, i.e. over a space of two decades. These were mainly with Italy (six times) but also with the Dervishes (four times), Egypt (twice) and Britain (once).
51. In his reflections (in Amharic) accompanying a letter to his personal friend, a certain Paulos Menamno, while in exile.
52. The decision by the imperial government to break up the federation was as tragic as it was costly, for the hostilities that ensued were to last for decades afterwards, taking a devastating toll in human life and property and plunging the country ever deeper into the quagmire of economic backwardness.
53. Quoted in Johnson, 1983, p86.

Selected References

Assefa Bekele and Eshetu Chole, 1969, *A Profile of the Ethiopian Economy*, Oxford University Press, Addis Ababa.

Board of Trade, (UK), 1955, *Report of the United Kingdom Trade Mission to Egypt, the Sudan and Ethiopia*, Her Majesty's Stationery Office, London.

Boulding, Kenneth E, 1966, *Economic Analysis*, Vol. 2, Macroeconomics, Fourth Edition, Harper & Row, New York.

Central Statistical Office, 1963-78, *Statistical Abstracts*.

Dereje Aredo, 1987, 'Price Behaviour in Addis Ababa, 1953-1974', Paper Prepared for the Fourth Annual Seminar of the Department of History, Addis Ababa University.

Ethiopian Government, Ministry of Commerce and Industry, 1951, *Economic Progress of Ethiopia*, Berhanenna Selam Printing Press, Addis Ababa.

------------, 1952, *Final Report of the United Nations Commissioner in Eritrea*, Addis Ababa.

------------, 1955, *Economic Handbook of Ethiopia*, Addis Ababa.

Ethiopian Government, Ministry of Commerce and Industry, *Ethiopian Economic Review*, Nos. 1 & 2, December 1959, June 1960.

Gerard, J Gill (ed), 1974, *Readings on the Ethiopian Economy*, Haile Selassie University, Institute of Development Research, Addis Ababa.

Imperial Ethiopian Government, 1958, *First Five-Year Plan 1957-1961*, Addis Ababa.

------------, 1959, Office of the Planning Board, *Implementation of the First Five-Year Plan, Evaluation Report for the Period 1949-1951 EC*

------------, 1962t, *Second Five-Year Development Plan 1955-1959 E.C* (1962-1967), Addis Ababa.

------------, 1968, *Third Five-Year Development Plan 1961-1965 E.C* (1968-73), Addis Ababa.

------------, 1973, *The Third Five-Year Plan: An Assessment and Implementation Report*, Vol. I, Addis Ababa, 1973.

Jhingan, M, L, 1966, *The Economics of Development and Planning* Fifth Revised Edition, Vicas Publishing House, New Delhi.

Johnson, Paul, 1983, *Modern Times, From the Twenties to the Eighties*, Harper & Row, New York.

Kaplan, Irving, et al., 1971, *Area Handbook for Ethiopia*, US Government Printing Office, Washington.

Lewis, W Arthur, 1951, *Principles of Economic Planning*, Public Affairs Press, Washington.

------------, 1955, *The Theory of Economic Growth*, George Allen & Unwin Ltd, London.

------------, 1966, *Development Planning: The Essentials of Economic Policy*, Harper & Row, New York.

Meier, Gerald M, 1976, *Leading Issues in Economic Development*, Third Edition, Oxford University Press, New York.

Morawetz, David, 1977, *Twenty-five Years of Economic Development 1950-1975*, The John Hopkins University Press, Baltimore.

National Bank of Ethiopia, *Annual Report*, Various Issues.

------------, 1964-76, *Quarterly Bulletin*, Addis Ababa.

Nurkse, Ragnar, 1953, *Problems of Capital Formation in Underdeveloped Countries*, Oxford University Press, London.

Planning Commission Office, 1973, *Strategy Outline for the Fourth Five-Year Plan, 1974/75-1978/79*, Addis Ababa.

State Bank of Ethiopia, 1959-60, *Report on Economic Conditions and Market Trends*, Addis Ababa.

Syrquin, Moshe, et al., 1989, *Patterns of Development, 1950 to 1983*, The World Bank, Washington.

Tefferra Deguefe, 1959, *Capital Formation in Ethiopia*, University College Press, Addis Ababa.

United States Government, 1970, *United States Security Agreements and Commitments Abroad, Ethiopia*, Congressional Hearings, Ninety-First Congress, US Government Printing Office, Washington.

Annex 1: Gross Domestic Product by Origin, 1950-74
(At Constant 1980/81 Factor Cost - Million Birr)

Year	1950/51	1953/54	1956/57	1960/61	1962/63	1964/65	1966/67	1968/69	1969/70	1970/71	1971/72	1972/73	1973/74
Agriculture (Total)*	2416	2536	2735	2887	3013	3203	3331	3430	3510	3579	3705	3729	3707
Agriculture	-	-	-	2795	2908	3094	3210	3302	3376	3441	3558	3578	3550
Forestry	-	-	-	88	100	104	115	124	129	133	142	146	152
Fishing & Hunting	-	-	-	4	5	5	6	4	5	5	5	5	5
Industry (Total)	160	195	234	449	518	626	776	880	897	977	1020	1052	1045
Mining & Quarrying**	-	-	-	4	5	10	11	13	12	12	12	13	12
Manufacturing	36	48	69	99	127	180	224	284	315	356	369	394	390
Handicrafts & SSI	108	115	124	146	155	173	197	233	251	266	278	287	285
Construction	12	26	34	190	216	241	316	317	284	303	320	314	312
Electricity & Water	4	6	6	10	15	22	28	33	35	40	41	44	46
Services (Total)	524	616	696	838	981	1228	1368	1549	1646	1765	1888	2010	2121
Distributive Services	265	321	376	405	477	627	685	767	823	895	951	1004	1045
Other Services	259	291	320	433	504	601	683	782	823	870	937	1006	1076
GDP at Factor Cost	3100	3343	3665	4174	4512	5057	5475	5859	6053	6321	6613	6791	6873

Source: Figures from 1960-1974 are from the National Planning Office
Figures from 1950-1959 are author's estimates

* In the 1950s agriculture was classified into crop farming, animal husbandry, forestry and home processing

** Figures between 1950-59 are included in manufacturing

Annex 2: Estimated Population Growth Rates and Sizes

Period	Growth rate (%)	Year	Population (000's)
1940-1945	1.5	1940	16,281
1945-1950	1.8	1945	17,535
1950-1955	2.0	1950	19,183
1955-1960	2.1	1955	21,197
1960-1965	2.2	1960	23,550
1965-1970	2.3	1965	26,282
1970-1975	2.5	1970	29,488
		1974	32,225

Sources: Central Statistical Office

Annex 3: Structure of Aggregate Demand
(As Percent of GDP)
Selected Years, 1950-74

Year	Consumption	Gross Saving	Gross Investment
1950	94.5	5.5	3.5 *
1954	93.0	7.0	2.4 *
1960	85.7	11.0	12.0
1964	87.8	12.2	13.2
1970	89.2	9.8	11.6
1974	92.5	7.5	10.4

Sources: Central Statistical Office
* Net investment

Annex 4: Revenues and Expenditures, 1943-1974
(In Million Birr)

		Expenditure			Deficit	
Year	Current Revenues*	Current	Capital	Total	Current	Overall
1943-49**	51.0	49.9	2.5	51.5	2.0	- 0.5
1950	79.6	81.0	16.0	97.0	- 1.4	- 17.4
1952	105.2	81.1	4.3	85.4	24.1	19.8
1954	117.6	112.7	10.0	122.7	4.9	- 5.1
1956	137.7	130.0	15.0	145.0	7.7	- 7.3
1958	148.1	162.6	50.3	212.9	- 14.5	- 64.8
1960	184.6	176.5	36.6	213.1	8.1	- 28.5
1962	218.8	205.2	94.3	299.5	13.6	- 80.7
1964	297.8	356.5	44.3	400.8	- 58.7	- 103.0
1966	364.5	416.8	77.1	493.9	- 52.3	- 129.4
1968	396.7	454.5	75.9	530.4	- 57.8	- 133.7
1970	466.0	507.1	124.2	631.3	- 41.1	- 165.3
1972	556.8	563.1	153.1	716.2	- 6.3	- 159.4
1974	711.4	811.2	237.7	1048.9	- 99.8	- 337.5

Sources: Central Statistical Office

* Excludes grants

** Average

Note: Years up to 1959 begin on September 12
Years after 1960 begin on July 8.

Annex 5: Structure of Revenue, 1950-1974
(Million Birr)

Year	Total Revenues	Direct Tax	Indirect Tax	Customs Duties	Other*	Direct Tax	Indirect Tax	Customs Duties	Other
						\multicolumn{4}{c}{Percentage Distribution}
1950**	79.6	24.2	7.7	24.8	22.9	30.00	10.00	31.00	29.00
1952	105.2	28.1	11.3	33.1	32.7	27.00	11.00	31.00	31.000
1954	117.6	25.7	18.2	48.3	25.4	22.00	15.00	41.00	22.00
1956	137.7	25.4	21.7	47.7	41.9	18.00	16.00	35.00	31.00
1958	148.1	29.0	23.7	48.2	47.2	20.00	16.00	33.00	32.00
1960	184.6	40.4	28.5	52.7	63.0	22.00	15.00	29.00	34.00
1962	218.8	44.7	76.4	64.3	33.4	20.00	35.00	29.00	15.00
1964	297.8	59.1	93.2	113.2	32.3	20.00	31.00	38.00	11.00
1966	364.5	77.1	111.8	124.6	51.0	21.00	31.00	34.00	14.00
1968	396.7	97.7	111.1	128.3	59.6	25.00	28.00	32.00	15.00
1970	466.0	121.8	131.6	155.1	57.5	26.00	28.00	33.00	12.00
1972	556.8	142.1	160.7	184.3	69.7	26.00	29.00	33.00	13.00
1974	711.4	176.8	200.8	215.2	118.6	25.00	28.00	30.00	17.00

Source: Central Statistical Office
* Includes charges and fees, sales of goods and services, pension fund, profits, interests, rents, et.
** Should read 1950/51, etc.

Annex 6: Coffee Prices, 1950-1974
(US cents/kg, spot New York)

Year	Constant	Current
1950	488.9	110.5
1952	460.4	125.7
1954	654.6	170.2
1956	551.1	151.0
1958	381.4	108.7
1960	322.0	92.4
1962	280.5	83.3
1964	338.9	101.0
1966	298.4	92.8
1968	277.6	86.6
1970	328.4	114.6
1972	277.3	110.9
1974	256.8	145.1

(Prices)

Source: Central Statistical Office

Annex 7: Merchandise Exports and Imports, 1945-1974
(In Million Birr)

Year	Total Exports	Coffee Exports (value)	Coffee Exports (percent)	Total Imports	Trade Balance
1945-49*	64	19.2	30	67	- 3
1950**	71	32.7	46	73	- 2
1952	106	53.0	50	111	- 5
1954	160	99.2	62	153	7
1956	151	80.0	53	149	2
1958	144	85.0	59	187	- 43
1960	182	94.6	52	208	- 26
1962	205	110.7	54	242	- 37
1964	262	165.1	63	308	- 46
1966	277	155.1	56	404	- 127
1968	266	154.3	58	432	- 166
1970	295	180.0	61	429	- 134
1972	377	181.0	48	436	- 59
1974	547	153.2	28	590	- 43

Sources: Central Statistical Office

* Average
** 1950 should read 1950/51, etc.

Annex 8: Structure of Imports, 1950-1974
(In Million Bir)

Total	Capital Goods (a)	Raw Materials & Intermediate Goods (b)	Consumer Goods (c)	In Percent (a)	(b)	(c)
73.0	6.7	15.7	51.0	9.2	21.5	69.9
111.0	14.6	23.6	72.5	13.2	21.3	65.3
153.0	37.7	37.2	78.0	24.6	24.3	51.0
149.0	37.1	41.2	70.8	24.9	27.7	47.5
167.0	55.7	53.6	77.6	33.4	32.1	46.5
208.0	63.4	62.5	81.8	30.5	30.0	39.3
242.0	96.0	67.0	78.7	39.7	27.7	32.5
308.0	119.7	84.9	99.0	38.9	27.6	32.1
404.0	172.3	103.5	128.4	42.6	25.6	31.8
432.0	204.5	123.2	104.7	47.3	28.5	24.2
429.0	142.3	132.6	152.3	33.2	30.9	35.5
436.0	167.5	127.4	137.7	38.4	29.2	31.6
590.0	98.8	261.7	225.2	16.7	44.4	38.2

Source: Central Statistical Office

Annex 9: Balance of Payments 1950-1974, In Million Birr

Items	1950	1952	1954	1956	1958	1960	1962	1964	1966	1968	1970	1972	1974
Trade Balance	8.7	6.2	13.6	-0.1	-45.9	-9.4	-13.9	-44.6	-123.7	-157.5	-121.8	-144.3	76.0
Exports (f.o.b.)	81.7	117.2	168.3	157.6	151.2	195.6	205.1	263.1	280.7	274.9	307.3	323.9	598.8
Coffee Exports	32.6	50.3	99.5	80.1	84.1	94.4	98.2	166.4	156.0	153.3	181.3	164.7	166.1
Other Exports	49.1	66.9	68.8	77.5	67.1	101.2	106.9	96.7	124.7	121.6	126.0	159.2	432.7
Imports (c.i.f.)	73.0	111.0	154.7	157.7	197.1	205.0	219.0	307.7	404.4	432.4	429.1	468.2	522.8
Net Reserves	-1.3	-4.0	-4.8	-4.9	-8.1	-17.0	-52.2	-0.3	12.2	50.3	22.9	26.2	65.9
Net Goods & Services	7.4	10.2	8.8	-5.0	-54.0	-26.4	-66.1	-44.9	-111.5	-107.2	-98.9	-118.1	141.9
Private Transfers (net	0.2	-1.3	-2.4	-1.3	-4.1	-6.7	-7.7	-2.5	-0.3	-6.0	-6.6	3.2	34.3
Current Account Balance	7.6	8.9	6.4	-6.3	-58.1	-33.1	-73.8	-47.4	-111.2	-113.2	-105.5	-114.9	176.2
Public Transfers (net)	0.2	2.8	9.7	8.7	31.6	33.7	33.6	19.4	29.4	35.6	26.6	29.7	48.5
Non-Monetary Capital (net)	10.7	8.3	8.4	13.9	26.5	26.1	72.0	49.7	72.3	75.3	45.0	75.3	65.7
Long-term	2.2	3.9	-0.6	-0.3	13.3	18.3	58.7	8.9	56.3	59.2	16.9	89.7	119.5
Pv't long-term	8.5	9.4	7.1	8.6	3.1	13.0	13.3	40.8	16.0	16.1	28.1		
Short-term		-5.0	1.9	5.0	10.1	-5.2						-13.4	-53.8
Net Errors & Omissions	-8.1	-6.1	-3.8	-8.1	-17.7	-16.0	-8.9	4.5	1.6	10.1	-8.4	26.3	-27.3
Over Balance	10.4	13.9	20.7	8.2	-17.7	10.7	22.9	26.2	-7.9	7.8	-42.3	17.4	263.1
Net Monetary Movement	-10.4	-13.9	-20.7	-8.2	17.7	-10.7	-22.9	-26.2	7.9	-7.8	42.3	-17.4	-263.1

Source: Central Statistical Office

Note: Figures from 1950-69 refer to calender years
Figures from 1970-74 refer to fiscal years

Annex 10: Growth of Foreign Debt, 1952-1974
In Million Birr
(As of June 30)

Year	Total Commitments	External Debt Disbursed	Undisbursed
1950	14	n.a.*	n.a.*
1955	28	n.a.*	n.a.*
1966	827	387	440
1968	1051	508	543
1970	1309	655	654
1971	1431	716	715
1972	1562	782	780
1973	1763	821	942
1974	1843	881	962

Sources: Central Statistical Office

* not available

Annex 11: Selected Economic Indicators: 1950-74

Item	Unit	1950	1974	Index (1950=100)**
I. Population*	million	19.2	32.2	168
II. Gross Domestic Product (at current factor cost)				
Per capita	birr	>100	206	229
Total	mllion birr	1545	5167	334
III. Composition of GDP				
Agriculture	million birr	1211	2631	217
Manufacturing	*	>18	266	1478
Handicrafts	*	54	241	466
Services	*	524	2121	405
IV. Public Finance				
Revenues	million birr	80	711	889
Expenditures				
Current	*	81	811	100
Capital	*	16	238	1487
V. The External Sector				
Exports (of which)	million birr	54	547	101
Coffee Exports	*	19	153	805
Imports	*	67	590	880
Balance of Payments	*	8	189	2362
Public Capital Inflow	*	26 (1952)	1843	7088
Debt Payments (outflow)	as % of exports	5.5 (1955)	9	-

Sources: Central Statistical Office

* As revised by the Central Statistical Office

** For certain items base years are different

2. The Evolution of Land Tenure in the Imperial Era

Shiferaw Bekele

The land question is regarded as the central cause of the revolution of 1974. The complexity of this issue means that this chapter presents the broad outlines of the subject matter, some of the limitations of the existing literature on it and pointers to future research.[1]

Theories of Land Tenure

Before exploring the treatment of 'the already belaboured question of Ethiopian land tenure' (Bahru 1984:12), however, it is apposite to briefly review the prevalent theory on it. I will focus only on the fundamental assumptions underlying much of the literature and the basic organizing concepts of tenurial studies and then proceed to propose alternative concepts and approaches.

With the exception of R. Pankhurst and a couple of other writers, most of the scholars who have written on the tenurial system shared a similar paradigm. In 1966, Pankhurst published his monograph on *State and Land in Ethiopian History* in which he talked of land ownership not only by peasants but also by the church, the nobility, and even by the aristocracy in historic Ethiopia. Of course neither Pankhurst nor the others who discussed land were unaware of the widespread existence of *gult*; in fact they defined it as the grant of tributary rights over land by the state to the ruling class in return for service very often military and clerical. What makes this approach different from the dominant paradigm was the prominent place given to private large-cale land ownership.

In spite of the fact that they published their works when large-scale private ownership of land was declared absolutely non-existent in the long history of Christian Ethiopia by academic orthodoxy, Addis Hiwet and J. Mantel-Niecko accept it. In his small but very influential book, Addis writes that 'Abyssinian [Northern Ethiopian] feudal aristocracy... also had vast estates tilled by tenants' in addition to *gult*. He stresses the point by repeating that 'the ruling houses of Gojam, Tigray, and Wello were great landowners in their respective areas,' (Addis Hiwet 1975:29-30). Probably because he has not tried to document his admittedly large statement, Addis is not taken seriously.

That Mantel-Niecko's book, *The Role of Land Tenure in the System of Ethiopian Imperial Government in Modern Times* (1980) is an important and valuable work, has been pointed out by scholars (Bahru 1984:6). The work shows abundantly that the Polish scholar has carefully studied much of the *published* sources on land tenure.

And yet she writes:
> Among the estates which are covered by the term *rest* one can distinguish great lay and ecclesiastical properties and smaller ones. The former along with *gult* (in the original) were in past centuries granted by the emperors to churches and monasteries. These were at that time enormous tracts of land (for instance the *rest* which was granted to the Debre Bizen monastery in the fifteenth century went from the bottom of the valley to the mist line) (Mantel-Niecko 1980:109).

In spite of the fact that scholars (for example Crummey, Bahru, etc.) refer to this work, they do not seem to be convinced by this analysis. They prefer the paradigm substantiated by Hoben, later developed and refined by Aregay and Crummey.

Hoben developed his theory in one major and very influential book *Land Tenure Among the Amhara* (1973). His analysis of the system of land tenure is one of the best summaries of the fundamental theoretical presuppositions of much of that was written after the turn of the 1970s:

Traditionally, there were two basic principles of land tenure: *gult* and *rest*. *Gult* rights may be thought of as fief-holding rights, and *rest* rights as land-use rights. *Gult* (fief) rights provided economic and political support for the elite and in their territorial aspect constituted the framework for the administration of the peasantry. *Rest* (land-use) rights, on the other hand, played an important role in the social and economic organization of the local community.

> *Gult* rights over land were given to members of the ruling elite as a reward for loyal service to their lord, and to religious institutions as endowments. The individual or institution that held land as *gult* had the right to collect taxes from those who farmed it, and also had judicial and administrative authority over those who lived on it. *Gult* rights were thus far more than just a type of land tenure. They were an integral part of the Amharic feudal polity; they represented the granting away by a regional ruler of an important part of his taxing, judicial, and administrative authority.
>
> Virtually all arable and inhabited land was held by someone or some institution as *gult*. There was 'no land without a master' (Hoben 1973:5).

Thus, *gult* and *rest* were not only forms of property but fully overlapped with the two principal classes: *gult* for the *mekuanent* and *rest* for the *gebbar*.

Hoben predicates his theory on the postulate that there was a sharp division between lord and peasant. The other major emphasis of Hoben was, what he calls, rights. Over any piece of arable land, therefore, there were two layers of rights the land-use right (*rest*) of the *gebbar* and the tribute-right of the *mekuanent* and the church. 'It is of fundamental importance to remember that *rest* and *gult* are not different types of land but distinct and complementary types of land rights' (Hoben 1973:6).

While *rest* signified the small pieces of land tilled by peasants, *gult*s meant estates that extended:

From one to three or four square miles in area. A particular great lord or monastery might hold many estates of gult, and some of these might be contiguous. However, from an administrative standpoint, and in the eyes of the peasants, each estate of gult was a distinct unit with its own internal organization. Indeed these estates were the minimal and most enduring units of secular administrative organization(Hoben 1973:6).

Hoben further developed *rest* as communal ownership by ambilineal descent groups. Aregay, another scholar who has done work on the issue, is not however satisfied with the concept of 'communalism'. He rather prefers, what he terms, 'clan or lineage ownership'. He contends:

The people of Ethiopia, whether they belonged to the Christian empire or not, seem to have known only one form of land tenure: clan or lineage ownership. Research into Ethiopian land tenure has been complicated by the confusion of the rest or lineage ownership with the gult system. The latter has never been a form of land tenure. It was a system of defraying remuneration for services out of taxes and tributes which could have been collected in kind. Gult rights only conferred partial usufruct rights (Aregay 1986:118).

On these assumptions Aregay then proceeds to construct a theory to explain many aspects of the history of Ethiopian society and state. He does this because:

The rest system gave to the peasant the right to own in perpetuity through his lineage and descent group the imperishable land. The gult system, on the other hand, gave to the ruling classes the right to take from the peasant only portions of the grains which came out of the soil and some of the domestic animals that grazed on the fields. ... Rest rights were permanent, gult rights, even when intended to be permanent, were temporary and their enjoyment precarious. The temporariness and uncertainty of gult rights became a perennial source of political instability.

In other words, Ethiopian political systems were not based on the ownership of the means of production but on the right of appropriation of portions of the peasant produce. Hereditary ruling families could not evolve (Aregay 1986:121).

These *gults* being limited in number, the ruling classes would find it difficult to satisfy the demands of their offsprings, favorites, warriors and clergymen. This would lead to violent confrontations between those who demanded their share of *gults* and the State. 'The very members of the ruling classes who needed and created strong monarchs always became the ones to be dissatisfied with them and to try and weaken or depose them' (ibid:123). Thus, the *gult* system led to perennial political instability. 'Loyalties and political alliances became brief and unreliable because of intense competitions over *gult* rights. One can dare conclude that the political system which the *gult* could give rise to was feudal anarchy' (ibid). From this Professor Merid proceeds to explain the anarchy and wars that raged in Ethiopia from the Seventeenth through to the end of the Nineteenth Century (Aregay 1984; 1988; 1990).

Similarly, the *rest* system had much the same effect to begin with on the peasantry, and on the society as a whole, as it was essentially a peasant society. For instance, individualism could not develop within the society. Conformity in turn stifled initiatives, creativity and innovativeness. Suspiciousness became the hallmark of an Ethiopian. The society could be tension and conflict-ridden. The *gult* and *rest* systems, taken together, explain Ethiopia's technological backwardness and much else too.

If we accept this theory in its totality, then Stahl's application to Ethiopia of the tributary mode of production becomes a logical corollary. Aregay anchors himself, exactly like Merid, on the two concepts of *rest* and *gult* which he defines in much the same vein. Then he takes the concept of the tributary mode of production from the well-known African political economist, Samir Amin, who defines the concept thus:

The tributary mode of production is characterized by the separation of society into two essential classes: a peasantry organized in communities and a ruling class which monopolizes the political organization of the society and exacts non-commodity tributes from the rural communities (Stahl 1974:22).

Thus, it is an economic system somewhat different from the feudal mode of production because, in the former, the lord exploits the peasant primarily through rent while:

The tributary mode of production ... involves the persistent parallel existence of a village community and a social and political structure which exploits the farmer by exacting a tribute (Stahl 1974:22).

Stahl then concludes that 'the tributary mode of production was the dominant one in the Abyssinian Kingdom' (Ibid:23). This theory is accepted by a number of prominent scholars. (Dessalegn 1984:16-17; 1988:469).

The other prominent scholar, Crummey, who recognizes the tributary character of the mode of surplus appropriation nevertheless prefers the feudal concept as his nodal concept (Crummey 1983). Nevertheless, Crummey pleads for a further refinement of the concept of *gult* which, he argues, takes many more forms than has hitherto been recognized (Crummey and Shumet 1989). One of the features of Crummey's studies (1989, 1988b), is their comparative approach. He tries to compare the Ethiopian land tenure system with that of European feudalism, which he finds essentially similar to the Ethiopian system.

The application of the feudal paradigm to the system prevalent in Ethiopia has also been the subject of debate. Ellis, for instance, argues that the feudal paradigm is not only inapplicable to Ethiopia but is a hindrance to the understanding of Ethiopian society and history (Ellis 1976:275-95). He arrives at this conclusion after making a comparative analysis of the European feudal system and the Ethiopian system. Another scholar with a comparative bent, Donham, draws attention to the similarity of the Ethiopian system with those of African polities. In spite of having the same premise as Aregay, he concludes that the Ethiopian mode falls within the African system rather than within European feudalism (Donham 1986).

One can, therefore, see that sharply different theoretical conclusions are drawn from the basic assumptions of the land tenure system: *rest* and *gult*. Whatever the differences in the theories and hypotheses formulated from them, the fact remains that these two concepts occupy pivotal positions in the analysis of not only landed property, but also the whole politico-social system.

It is, however, generally agreed among scholars that the central position that *gult* and *rest* occupy starts to change after the end of the nineteenth century. With the advent of capitalist forces into the country in the twentieth century, privatization of land made its appearance into the newly incorporated provinces i.e. southern, eastern and western Ethiopia. Thus, a dichotomy developed in the land tenure system of the country. The northern provinces (Northern Shewa, Gojjam to Tegrai with the exception of Southern Wello) remained within the *rest-gult* system while in the newly incorporated provinces a totally new system of private ownership of land evolved, albeit gradually.

Bahru Zewde (1984) has come up with the theory of the absolutist state for the pre-revolutionary regime of the Twentieth Century. One of the stepping stones of this state was privatization of land. 'What we now see in the period under discussion [1916-1935] are steps towards greater privatization of land. In southern Ethiopia, for instance, the *naftagna-gebbar* relationship gradually fades into a landlord-tenant one' (1984:12). This interpretation seems to be widely accepted. Thus, the modern era up to 1975 was characterized by the prevalence of two separate tenurial systems (Dessalegn 1984, 1988).

The land reform of 1975 did, therefore, abolish not only the system of land ownership in the south, east and west of the country but also the *rest* system of the north as well as any remnants of the *gult* system.

Towards an Alternative Theory of Land Tenure

This review demonstrates that the land tenure studies share basic assumptions in spite of their different theoretical conclusions. These assumptions have also served as cornerstones of major theories intended to explain the entire social system. There is clearly no doubt that they are extremely important. For this reason, one has to question how far these assumptions are based on substantial grounds. This will further lead us to enquire into the validity of making *gult* and *rest* the organizing concepts.

In order to answer these questions, it will be useful to start out with the way the Ethiopians themselves arranged, categorized and explained the various terms connected with land tenure in historic Ethiopia. As they themselves lived through the system they described, they would have a much better approach than the theoretical constructs developed by modern-trained Ethiopian and expatriate scholars. Our initial sources are the two well-known traditional writers: Mahteme Sellasssie Wolde Meskel (1942); Meskel (1942) and Werk (1948) and Gebre Weld Engida Werk (1948).

Gebre Weld occupied very high positions in the pre-Italian and post-Italian states. Therefore, his book in a way reflected the perceptions of the rulers or, to put it another way, the state perspective. The same thing could be said of Mahteme Selassie's work, because the author was a high courtier of Haile Selassie. The top-down approach of these two authoritative sources could give us, if we look carefully, the place land occupies in the whole State. This is very important, for the obvious reason that land was the medium through which the state functioned as a state. Knowing exactly how it was used would furnish us a major insight into the dynamics of state and society.

The two works are very synchronic. On the whole they reflect realities that obtained before the Italo-Ethiopian war of 1935-36. For a diachronic analysis, one has to look for other sources from the earlier centuries.

78 *An Economic History of Modern Ethiopia*

Gebre Weld introduces his book thus:

« የኢትዮጵያ የመሬትና የግብር ስሪት » ተብሎ
የተሰየመውን ይህን መትሐፍ የጻፍሑበት ምክንያት፤
ግናቸውም ሰው ምንም እንኪ የየከፍለ አገሩን ሥሪት
ቢያውቀው በሙሉ አያውቀውምና ያንዲ አገር ሰው
የሌላውን አገር ስሪት በግወቅ እንዲጠቀም በግሰብ ነው·
(Gebreweld, 1944:5)

(Since people knew the serit of their province and not of the others, I wrote this book entitled, 'The Ethiopian Land and Tribute Serit' in order to enable [readers] to know the serit of the other provinces).

The key concept of his book is therefore *serit*. Before we go into a discussion of the definition of this master concept, we have to see what Gebre Weld has to say regarding land:

በጊሰ ዘመን በመሬት ግብር እንደገበርበት ሲደረግ ብዙ
ወርቅና ብር የማይገኝ በመሆኑ ለንጉሠ ነገሥቱ መንግሥት
ለምር ጊዜና ለሰለም ጊዜ የሚያስፈልገው አስተደደር ሁሉ
በመሬት ተደለደለ፡፡ ስለዚህ የግብሩም ዓይነት በልዩ ልዩ
ስም ይጠራል (Ibid.;)

[Sometime in the past] the government found out that they could not raise much revenue in the form of gold and cash when they imposed taxes on the land. Hence, the various units of the administration both military and civilian were allocated land [whose tribute would be service]. Therefore the type of tribute-service was given different labels.

If I may rephrase the quotation it will read like this. Because revenues from (arable) land were insufficient to run the state, the land itself was allocated to people who gave various services. In other words, the state was run by land rather than by money.

To figure out the mechanics, the term *serit* becomes very useful. What was the meaning attached to this concept? We are fortunate in this regard because there are two traditional highly authoritative dictionaries of Amharic Kesate Berhan Tesema (1951) and Desta Tekle Weld (1962). On the basis of these two sources we give the following definition of *serit*, the noun derivative of the verb *serra*. Basically, it had four meanings. The first denotes obligation On any piece of land one or another service or tribute obligation would be attached. There was therefore no land without some kind of obligation attached to it. The owner of the land would have to discharge those obligations in order to be able to continue to hold it as his/her own piece of land. For instance, a king, queen (etege) or lord or lady would earmark a certain piece of land for a given church. This grant is not as uncomplicated as the literature invariably makes it out to be, for it simply designates the whole process 'land or tribute grant to a church' and then labels the land 'church land' or *'samon maret'*. What rather happens is that very often it was a specific service that was attached to the land. Thus, priestly service could be imposed on a certain piece of land. What this means is that, first, anyone who owns or in one way or another uses the land must, as his tribute obligation, give priestly service or if, for one reason or another s/he cannot discharge this service, find a priest to do it in her/his name.

The land would be designated *ye-qes meret* (which means priestly land) or *samon maret*. Land on which *debtera* service is imposed is not called *ye-qes meret*. It is rather called *ye-debtera meret*. The owner must give *debter service* if s/he is one; if s/he is not one, s/he must find a substitute. The same logic applies for *diyaqon meret, ye-gebez meret* etc. On the other hand, there are terms that designate general service, like *ye-meskel meret*. In this case, one has to ask the individual church and owner of the land in order to find out exactly what is required from the owner of that piece of land as an obligation.

At the time the 'grant' is made, this is not very difficult to establish. Land given to priests, for instance, is automatically priest land. The case becomes confusing in the succeeding generations because the descendants become numerous and also may become lay persons, in which case they would have to employ a substitute.

This arrangement is further complicated by another type of land allocation. In this case, a certain amount of tribute, very often in kind but sometimes even in cash, would be imposed on the land to be given to a certain church. This land is also called church land in the literature. Even informants invariably call it church land but they, unlike the books, could give the details of the arrangement if pressed further.

Land could also be assigned for military service. It can be said that land was assigned for military service when particular pieces of land are given out in return for military service. The granting of a piece of land, say, to a soldier who gave service by transporting tents during campaigns and then taking part in the ensuing battles, meant that an obligation to give carrier and fighting service is imposed on that piece of land. After the grant, anyone who holds that land (male, female, minor or aged) would be in duty bound to give military service either in person or by proxy. This kind of land would then be called, depending on the kind of specific service attached to it, *ye-zemecha maret, ye-gendebel maret, ye-galla maret* (as in historic Wello) etc. The term 'military lands' can be given as a collective category.

When a person asks what the particular *serit* of a piece of land was, he was therefore referring to one or another of this kind of obligation. The literature invariably presents these terms as different forms of tenure. In actual fact, these and many other terms listed by Gebre Weld and Mahteme Selassie indicate this kind of obligation.

Imposing an obligation was the equivalent of tax waivers. The so-called church lands are the most privileged because they are free from most of the tributes and taxes imposed on land. This is what makes church lands so attractive. Military lands come next in line because some of the tributes are waived in return for the service. The most well-known were the tributes required from *gebbar*. Owners of military land (peasants as well as lords) did not have to suffer the numerous *gebbar* obligations so well listed in the literature. Put another way, the *gebbar* pays all those tributes because he does not give government service.

The *serit* of a particular land is not permanent. It is bound to change and it normally does. One of the main functions of the kings and the lords was to deal with cases of *serit* either failure to fulfill obligations or changing *serit*, for example, military land could be turned into church land. Crummey has published a document in which a *chagn maret* was transferred to church land in the eighteenth century in Begemder (1988b).

Attaching obligation to land was only the first meaning of *serit*. However, this meaning was most often used in the society, and elderly and knowledgeable informants from the Amharic provinces would invariably state that there was no land without *serit* by which they meant obligation. This sense of *serit* tends to overshadow the other meanings which are used rather less often, but used nevertheless in the sources. One has to know them in order to be able to understand and use the sources effectively.

The second meaning denotes ownership. A particular piece of land with the obligations could be given out in perpetuity (*rest*) or temporarily (*maderiya*). These decisions are made at the time when obligations are attached to the land, or even later. Invariably, there is in the literature a confusion between the status of land as property and the various names (i.e., obligations) attached to it. *Rest* is privately-owned land. It is heritable. Nevertheless, it does not follow from this that *rest* was inalienable and absolute property, as is widely defined in the literature.

On the contrary, *rest* is conditional ownership conditional on fulfilling service obligations. It is also liable for confiscation in the event of lese majeste or homicide or some such big crime. These restrictions do not obviously give it an absolute status; nor is it correct to describe it as inalienable.

As pointed out above, the *rest* system is said to be the peasant system *par excellence*. Nevertheless, Northern Shewa did not fit neatly into this pigeonhole because lords just as well as peasants owned land as *rest* in large quantities. We are not talking of post-41 Shewa but rather the pre-35 one. What perhaps creates the confusion is the various names given to the *rest* One individual could own several gashas of *samon maret*, *gendabal maret* and *gebbar maret*. When owners talk of the obligations attached to the land, i.e., the *serit*, they refer to these terms; and when on the other hand, the subject of discussion is ownership, they state that all those gashas are their *rest*.

Not all land is owned in the form of *rest*. There is also a temporary form of ownership, called *maderiya*. This is land that is given to a person as long as he gives some service. Upon termination of the service or upon death, the land reverts to the state. Again, like *rest*, *maderiya* lands have different names and, like *rest*, *maderiya* cuts across classes. It is given to people ranging from the lowly peasant and servant to an aristocrat, from the ordinary cleric to the *abun*. Another very important distinction of *maderiya* land is that, while it gives the grantee rights over land, it by no means gives judicial or administrative authority. What makes this term sometimes confusing is the fact that a temporary transfer of tributes (or a portion of tributes) of a certain, usually small, area could be made to individuals for which the sources use the same word. The context very often makes it quite clear, however.

The third meaning of *serit* is tribute imposition. A lord or king would impose on a district, or even a province or provinces tribute to be paid in, say, honey or clothes or horses or grain, etc. The fourth meaning of *serit* is billeting. Soldiers and lords are spread among the people of an area in accordance with their rank. A lord would be billeted in the house of a lord of his rank or someone closer to him, and so on until you reach the ordinary soldier who would be imposed on the poor peasant.

For this chapter the reader will have to identify the context in which *serit* is used in the text in order to know its meaning. Before the discussions, a word is in order regarding *gult*. *Gult* too is sometimes used as a form of *serit*. The concept of *gult* or *melkenet* requires more treatment than it is given so far. I will come back to it a little later. But, for the moment, let's focus on *serit*.

In any discussion of land tenure in Shewa the term *serit* is central. The first question that people ask regarding the status of land is ሥሪቱ ምንድ ነው.

(What is the *serit*?) This is important because land use, land ownership or land rights can be understood in most cases only in reference to its obligation.

If we agree on this description, then it follows that the starting point of the study of land tenure should not be ownership (*rest*) or tribute but rather *serit*. At any rate, that is the way Gebre Weld, a prominent traditional authority on land tenure, approached it.

Gebre Weld has only been used by scholars for the specific information he provides. Unfortunately, his approach and perspective have not been the subject of inquiry. Without a knowledge of his perspective and his unstated and yet fundamental assumptions, one cannot really make full use of the facts he offers.

Mahteme Selassie's approach to this question has not attracted the attention of scholars either. The very organization of his book *Zekre Neger* yields insights if it is carefully assessed. For our purposes, what is inter*est*ing is the fact that land tenure is subsumed in his book under provincial administration or Internal Administration. One would normally expect documents relating to land tenure to be brought together under agriculture or, even better, treated separately in a whole chapter.

Selassie's reason for this classification becomes clear when one reads article nine of the very first frame of reference given to the Ministry of *Ager gezat*:

አገር አገዛዝ (the Ministry) (Mahteme Selassie 1962:104).

በሰውነቱና በቤቱ ግብር የሚያቶም እሱ [the Ministry] ነው፡፡

(It is this Ministry that levies geber on his person and on his house and all of his property).

Thus, the responsibility of levying gebir was that of the Ministry of Ager gezat. Of the manifold forms of *gebir*, service is among the important ones. If for instance, the state needed people for a given service, for example a postal service, it would recruit them and then either give them land which it would call የፖስታ ማኝ መሬት (Mahteme Selassie 1962:115) or it would recruit them from among people who used to give military service and whose land was consequently called *gendabal maret*.

When we look at the table of contents of *Zekre Neger*, we see that in section 6.4, which deals with land tenure, Mahteme uses the concept of *serit* in exactly the same way Gebre Weld uses the term. Both Gebre Weld and Mahteme Selassie do, therefore, have a similar approach to the land question. They start out with the term *serit* and not with *rest* and *gult*. They also organize the typologies and analysis round *serit* rather than *rest* and *gult*.

Their terms are taken mostly from what obtained in Shewa, though they do give useful but brief descriptions of the system in the other northern provinces of the country. Because Northern and Eastern Shewa are classified with the other northern provinces, with the exception of historic Wello, I will focus precisely on this area. Then I will look into the question of how similar the structure was to the one that obtained in the northern provinces.

After defining the various terms used in Shewa for the manifold forms of obligations attached to arable land or *serit*, Mahteme Selassie gives us data by district. I have aggregated the figures for the whole of the region in Table 1.

Table 1: Breakdown of Serit in Northern Shewa, early 20th Century (gasha)

Gebbar (maret)	Gendabal (maret)	Wereda gendabal (maret)	Samon (maret)	Yemengist Metkeya (maret)	Yeshaleqa Metkeya
18,911	12,095	11	7,185	25	1

Source: Mahteme 1962:139-142.

In Table 1, I have left out the figures I felt are not so relevant to the point I am trying to make, e.g. *chisenna maret*. Before we analyze this data, it is important to define the terms and evaluate the sources.

Gebbar maret is better known than the others and refers to land with obligations which gave the well-known *gebbar* services to a lord or the state. *Gendabal maret* was land given to those who gave one or another form of military service. *Wereda gendabal* consisted of the privileged stratum of the *gendabal*, mostly cavalry soldiers. A *wereda gendabal* had 'a status equal to that of a Balabat and Melkena, (Mantel-Niecko, 1980:89). The meaning of *samon maret* is too well-known to merit repetition here. *Metkaya maret* is government (*ye-mengest*)-owned land which could be at the disposal of the state or specifically the governor (Shaelqa). A point must be stressed. These terms indicate various forms of *serit*. But at the same time, they do not tell us about ownership, whether a specific land (gendabal etc.) was *rest* (permanently owned) or *maderiya* (temporarily owned).[2]

How far are these figures reliable? It is difficult to give a definitive yes or no to this question. They were taken from registers kept in Menelik's palace and as such could be taken as approximating reality. A snag arises when it is known that a *gasha* of land assigned for the soldiers (*gendabal*) could very well retain its name but could have been transferred to samon or some other purpose. This happened very often. The issue becomes even more complicated when one realizes that an individual could own many *gashas* of, say, *gendabal* land. Therefore, the figures may not be all that accurate.

However, assuming that the figures are accurate and that one *gasha* of, say, *gendabal maret*, is strictly in the hands of a (gendabal) soldier (it was initially distributed on such a principle; see Bairu Tafla, 1987:502-504), then it can be seen that in Northern Shewa the state had under its control 12,095 *gendabal* soldiers. As pointed out above, this figure could be much lower than this. There was also another mechanism for raising the figures. Those individuals who had a greater number of *gendabal maret* usually showed up with a considerable number of retainers on mobilization day. The story about *samon maret* is similar. On the surface, there are no less than 7,185 *gashas* of land which maintain the church, no matter who owned them.

The first thing we notice in this arrangement is that it is not neatly divided along class lines, as the *rest/gult* paradigm dictates. *Gendabal maret* owners range from an ordinary peasant to members of the aristocracy. All have to discharge their *gendabal* obligations in one way or another. When it comes to *samon maret*, it is the same arrangement, ranging from an ordinary peasant all the way to the royals. The most interesting aspect of *gebbar maret* is that the *gebbar* obligations are attached to the land rather than to the person. Hence, even a lord could own *gebbar* maret and yet the obligations would be carried out by proxy. On the other hand, peasants who did not own *gebbar maret*, peasants who owned *samon* or *desta* or *gendabal* were not *gebbars* in the strict sense of the word and did not perceive themselves as such.

How did this kind of arrangement relate to the state system? To answer this question, I will give a description of an army on the march. If one observed an army on the march, one would see those who transported tents or other luggage. Most of these people were peasants who came from the fields because they owned land that had carrier service as obligation. Numerous soldiers would also be there because they owned 'military land', i.e., land whose obligation was to give military service. In the middle, surrounded by their retainers, would be the lords. Added to this were the priests and women. A major expedition, therefore, reflected a cross-section of the society.

The same thing could be said for peaceful times. The *ghebbi* of Menelik in Addis Ababa can be taken as a case in point. Let us start from the gate and proceed slowly into the innermost *elfegn*. At the gate, the guards were very often soldiers who had come from the countryside to give their service on what was called a *warterra* basis. These soldiers were very often owners of *gendabal maret*. For instance, peasants came from as far north as Merhabate to offer guard services on a shift system. If we went to the kitchen area we would possibly see peasants from the royal *weregenu* lands butchering oxen and preparing the meat for the *wat bet* on a *war tera* basis. Then there would be the full-time servants, the slaves, craftsmen, priests, courtiers, lords and ladies and the royals most of them supported by land.

In one imperial *gebbi*, therefore, a more or less accurate cross-section of the society was represented. What a contrast from a feudal spatial arrangement! Here, on a hill, would be the castle with its own sturdy and insurmountable wall. As if the formidable walls were not enough, the castle would be ringed by a moat. Then, at some distance from the castle, was the village with its parish church. Rather far away was the town often surrounded by a defensive wall. The three settlements at the same time constituted three distinct classes: the lord, the peasant and the burgher. The wall and the moat symbolize to me the sharp separation between the feudal class and peasants, a separation that did not exist in Ethiopia.

The residence pattern in Ethiopia reflected the nature of the class structure, which was based on the structure of land tenure. Unlike in Europe, the lords in Ethiopia were surrounded by peasants and the lower gentry in their day-to-day life, in war and even in the church. It was only for litigation purposes, if at all, that a peasant walked into a castle in Europe. Even Ethiopian towns were not neatly urban. If we take Gondar, for example, we see that a fair proportion of the town's dwellers in the 1920s were farmers (Bahru 1988).

One factor, among others, that will help explain this contrast is the very nature of land tenure itself. To say that land was given in return for service is not an adequate statement. The land itself would be designated after the service which means that any one who tilled that land must fulfill that service. (I have heard that somewhere in one of the northern provinces there used to exist *yedemet maret*, where the owner of the land had to provide for the maintenance of cats that were supposed to catch the mice in a certain big church. Even if this story sounds implausible, it can easily illustrate the central principle of the system).

This principle opens the door to the understanding and systematic categorization of the multiple terms used for land. Reading Gebre Weld or M. Selassie can be confusing because of the multiplicity of the terms. During the revolution, I remember discussions on the radio following the land decree in which the discussants complained that in Wello there were so many kinds of tenure it was difficult to understand. It was in this same Wello that Professor Taddesse Tamrat, during a research trip in the mid-1960s, saw that the key to the store of a certain important church was in the hands of a Moslem. To say that a Moslem served a Christian Church sounds a contradiction in terms until we understand that this particular person was working for the church because he owned land which had service obligations to the church. In other words, it is the *serit* of the person's land that makes us understand this anomaly.

To ask what the *serit* was would therefore help us make sense of the numerous terms used in the Ethiopian books and in the documentary sources. Let us, for instance, take Gebre Weld and Mahteme Selassie to illustrate this point. I have categorized the terms they used into the following typologies. First, obligations attached to land. The following are found: *gebbar maret, gendabal maret, samon maret, melmel maret, gala maret, Ye-ali zemach maret*. From *Zekre Neger*, we get additional terms: *desta maret, siso maret, ye-madfena ye-metreyes chagnoch maret, ye-posta chagn maret, ye-denkewan chagn maret, ye-wehni zebegna maret, Ya-tkelt tekay maret*.

The second category consisted of terms denoting ownership-in perpetuity or for temporary use *rest, maderiya, quami gala maret, tenekay gala maret, ye-metkeya maret* (*ye-shaleqa* or *ye-mengest*).

The third category consisted of particular tribute assignments imposed on districts: *madbet, ganegeb, wareganu* and *balderas*. In the first and second case, grains were provided for the court, in the third, cattle and in the fourth, horses were raised. Finally, we have the typology of *gult, riste-gult* and *melkenat* and *balabat*.

The analysis so far presented is drawn from the works of Gebre Weld and Mahteme Selassie. That is why we should ask whether or not the above structural analysis was peculiar to Shewa or the same everywhere. This comparative analysis is critically important because, as I have hopefully demonstrated above, data from Shewa do indeed challenge the *rest/gult* framework which had been imposed on the study of Ethiopian land tenure systems. With the limited evidence from the northern provinces available for analysis, the only way to substantiate this hypothesis is to draw a comparison with the Shewan system. If there are more similarities than differences, then the hypothesis is proved.

If we take Gojam and Begemder, the sources become rather scanty. For Gojam, Gebre Weld lays down the ground rules only at the very opening/beginning of his chapter (p. 61) by telling us that in the ancient past Gojam was divided into three. Two-thirds of the province was allocated as military land and one-third as church land.

That church lands in both Gojam and Begemder were allocated in the same way as in northern/eastern Shewa, I will demonstrate below. For the moment, let us focus on military lands. Gebre Weld lays down the principle as follows:

በዚሁ በገስጋሽ (የመንግሥት ድርሻ) መሬት ሁለት ዓይነት መደብ ተመድቧል። አንደኛው ክፍል ገመታ የተባለ በግምት የተወሰነለትን የጨው ግብር የሚገብር ባለርስት ነው።። ሁለተኛው ክፍል ለወታደር ግስትደረያ እርበውን ከአምስት አንድ እያወጣ የሚሰጥ ባለርስት ... (ነው)። በቀድሞ ዘመን ትገሬ ይዘምት በነበረው ትገሬ ዘግች ተብሎ የሚጠራ መሬት ይገኛል። እንደዚሁም ልጅ እያሱ ከትገሬ በመጡ ዘመን ራስ ኃይሉ ደሴ ድረስ ሂደው ስለነበረ ወሎ ዘመቾ የተባለ ይገኛል ይኸም በለመሬት የወታደርነት ሥራ የሚሠራ ግብሩን ያስፍቃል፣ የግይዘምትም ግብሩንና አሥራቱን ይከፍላል እንጂ ርስቱ ከተወለጄ አይወጣም።

The part given to soldiers ... was of two kinds with different types of tenure. The first type paid salt tax on the estimated produce of the holding. In the second type a fifth of the produce was paid to the soldier... In former times those who had gone to battle were given lands for their service. Similarly when Ras Hailu went to Dessie and received Lij Iyasu when he came from Tigre, there were lands given to soldiers in return for their going to meet him. The holders of such lands performed the duties of a soldier and only paid asrat. Those who were not soldiers paid asrat and tax.

This description is rather elliptical. Of the two-thirds of the lands of Gojam, half was designated for *gebbar*. The owners were expected to provide *gebbar* services. The other half was designated for soldiers. This could be done in two ways. Either the *bale-rist* would offer military services on his own, in which case his land would have a tax-free status. Or he would support a soldier by giving him a fifth of the produce from the land designated as military land. The system was more or less similar in Begemder as well:

[በቤገምድር] ድልድሉም ሁለት እጅ ለመንግሥት አንድ እጅ ለቤተ ክርስቲያን ነው። ከዚሁም ከመንግሥት ድርሻ ገግሹን ለጨዋ ልጅ ተብሎ ተሰይሞ ለመቾ ተመድቧል። ... ገግሹም ለበሊገ ልጅ መሬት ተብሎ ጨውም ግርም ለሚገብር ገበር ተደልድሏል።

Two-thirds of the land went to the state and one-third to the church. Of the two-thirds taken by the state, half was given to nobles and soldiers. This was considered as maderiya. *In some places gebbars were given land in return for payment of taxes in honey and salt.*

When we come to the *zemecha lands*, the mechanisms become a little complicated. The *bale-rist* had two choices he would himself offer the service or he would give one fifth (*amsho*) of his produce to a soldier (ibid.).

When Hoben refurbished his thesis for publication, he cut out what, in my opinion, is one of the juiciest sections which is relevant to this discussion. The major thrust of his research was to find out about property rights over land, but he did not ask questions related to *serit*. While it was only in connection with qes maret that he asked this question, his findings are fascinating. He first lays down the theoretical foundation of land tenure in Gojam:

According to the ideology of land-holding in Gojam, two-thirds of the land in common parishes belongs to the king and one third belong to the church. The rights which belong to the church and the king are gult rights, not rest, land-use rights.

This fundamental theoretical division of the land is supposed to be reflected in each parish by the fact that a certain identifiable land, commonly called priest land, equivalent to one-third of the total land in the parish proper ... has upon it an obligation to maintain the service in the church (Hoben 1963:85).

I will come later to his 'fundamental theory'. At this point, what we should pursue is the question of *qes maret*:

The land which bears an obligation to support the service in the church, the priest land, may be the land of one or more maximal houses or of one or more major sub-houses. ... The apical ancestors of houses which support the service are believed to have been priests who were originally given their land grants as payments for their work in the church (Hoben 1963:86).

Hoben's statement that the land was believed to have been given to a priest originally could not always be true. Massive data recently uncovered show that church land was given to lay persons just as well as to the clergy (Wudu Tafete 1988b; Tarekegn Yibabe 1988; Solomon Tena 1988; Crummey 1989b). Whatever the case may be, the question that arises is: how did so many households that held one priest land carry out their obligations? This is where Hoben's detailed discussion is valuable. They offered priestly service in either of these two ways: by proxy (employ someone) or by doing it themselves. In the latter case, a schedule would be worked out according to which households could be called upon to provide service in the church in turns for a given period of time. Those who failed to meet the obligations would be penalized. Hoben goes on to discuss the conflicts generated as a result of the fact that this was a very complicated affair (Hoben 1963:87-96).

The first thing that strikes the reader of Hoben is the similarity of operations between the systems in Gojam and in Shewa at the grassroots level. Three questions have to be answered: a) what would the case be for the bigger churches which had many gashas of land? b) was this system for priest land existent only in Shewa and Gojam? c) are there other service obligations? Hoben is not at all helpful in answering these questions because his focus is exclusively on a small area. We have to turn to other sources and piece together fragmentary evidence to reconstruct a country-wide picture.

A former student of the Department of History from Meqet, *awereda* near the *Bashilo-Chacheho* axis, told me that *ye-zemecha maret* existed in the district. His description of the way this obligation was fulfilled is like Hoben's for the church. Either all the owners of that land would do it in turns or they would pay a given sum (usually one-fifth) of their produce to a soldier, or a senior member of the descent group, who was called *aleqa*, would do the service in return for which he would have a larger share of the land and other privileges.

McCann (1987) gives a brief but relevant description of this system as operated in Lasta and Wag:

> *The process of mobilization [for war] in the countryside put a great deal of stress on the organization of production and distribution. Peasants in northern Wello underwent at least three calls to arms during the 1928-30 period. Orders to gather arms and provisions for a campaign originated with state officials and filtered down through the rural strata to the household level. Officers and titled officials gathered their retainers around them and called on those peasant soldiers who enjoyed tax-free status. Chiqa-shums organized the call-up at the local level and collected food from those not eligible for service. About one-third of rural males had military obligations, another third performed labor services and the remainder stayed on the land for agricultural work* (emphasis mine).

What McCann should have added is the fact that military obligations were attached to land. If it was so then the modality is similar to that of Shewa, Gojam and Begemder. That the system in Wello is exactly similar to Shewa is now well established (Fekadu Begna 1990). The problem is that we do not have as rich data as, for instance, we do for Shewa.

What about Tigray and Hamasen? It is very difficult to imagine that the system could be all that different here. In any case, we have a contemporary account of an incident that took place in Tigray in the Nineteenth Century which could shed some light on the issue. It was N. Pearce, the early nineteenth century traveller, who left us the account in an entry in his diary for 24 April 1818. Pearce was himself present. A lord, Gebre Michael, and the *Abun* were quarrelling over a few districts. The *Abun* was governing them but Gebre Michael wanted them. Nevertheless, the *Abun* was not ready to give in. So Gebre Michael:

> begged [the metropolitan] that he would permit Fit-awari Guebra Amlac [sic lieutenant of G.M.] to command those districts as done formerly; the income should be duly gathered through him, and paid ... [to] the Abuna, and if any deficiency should happen in the payment of these incomes, even to a quart of corn, he, Guebra Michael, would be answerable for it. He also said, bowing to the ground: If you deny all this which I have requested, let me at least have the soldiers belonging to those districts, which are more than three thousand, and some of them my best men, the loss of whom will weaken my army, and my enemies will find pleasure in oppressing me ... [emphasis mine] (Pearce 1980:220).

It sounds like a very desperate plea. Gebre Michael so desperately wanted these districts that he was willing to forego the tributary revenues from them. If these soldiers were *gult* owners or professionals paid in kind it would not have been very difficult for him to transfer them. Apparently, he could not do so. The logical assumption for this could only be that they were soldier-peasants of those districts and that transferring them would mean giving up their *rest* and villages, which of course they would not do.

This deduction is supported by a rather brief description given in almost identical language by Gebre Weld and Mahteme Selassie.

ትግሬ የርስት አገር ነው። በርስቱም ግር ወይም ጨው እንደገብር የተደለደለ ነው። በዚህም ላይ ፈሰስና አሥራት ይከፍላል። ወታደርና መኳንንቱ የሚተደረው ከበርስት በሚገኘው ዳኝነትና አሥራት ነው። ግብርም የተፈቀደለት ግብር እየበላ ወይም የራሱን መሬት ግብር እያስቀደደ ግዕሩንም ከፍ ያለ ሲሆን የገረቤተን ጥምር ያስገብራል። ... በሹም አጋዚ ወልደስ በደጃዝማች ሰባጋዲስ ዘመን በርስቱ ወታደር እንደሆን የተመደበለት ነበር። ይኸውም ግግሹ የወታደርነት ሥራ ስለሚሠራ ከአሥራት በቀር ለለ ግብር አይከፍልም ግግሹ የወታደርነት ሥራ ሲተው ግን ሙሉ ግብር ይገብራል እንጂ በለርስት ነው።

Tegre is a rest province. The balerest pays his tribute in honey and salt. In addition to this, he pays tithes. The mekwanent and the soldiery are maintained by revenues raised from tithe and judiciary fees. [A noble or soldier] who was allocated tributes [from given areas] would live off it or [he] could get a waiver from the tribute of his land and if he was of a higher rank he could be allowed to collect [for himself] the tribute from his neighbours... At the time of Shum Agame Weldu and Dejazmach Sebagadis [early 19th century] there were bale-rest who were made soldiers. This means that so long as the bale-rest gave military service, he paid all the tributes if he ceased to give military service. [In the latter case] he remained a bale-rest [i.e. would not be confiscated for failing to give military service] (Gebre Weld 1988).

Mahteme Selassie gives the same description in similar words, with the exception of the last sentence where he makes it general:

በለርስቱ ወታደር ሆኖ የተመደበለትን የወታደርነት ሥራ ስለሚሥራ ከአሥራት በቀር ሌላ ግብር አይከፍልም። የወታደርነት ሥራ ሲተው ግን ሙሉ ግብር የሚገብር ባለ ርስት ነው።

(The balerest who became a soldier and gave his services would not pay tributes except tithe. But when he went out of military service, he would pay all the tributes).

Shum Agame Weldu and his son *Dejazmach* Sebagadis were lords of Agame and Tegray in late eighteenth and early nineteenth centuries respectively. This tradition indicates that they instituted new *serit*.

These brief descriptions show that the system was similar in general terms in both places, though it is very difficult to work out its detailed mechanics. Moreover, the description supports the argument made above that those 3,000-odd soldiers must have been peasants who had land which enjoyed tax privileges in return for military service. In short, they must have owned military land. Another brief description is given by Gebre Weld and Mahteme Selassie for Wag, which also falls into the same pattern:

ግብሩ ባንድ ጧፍ አለፃ አንድ ጉንድ ግር ወይም አንድ ብር የሚከፍል። ጥራሽ የግይከፈልም ይገኛል። በግምት አንድ ሰው የሚከፍለው ከአንድ አለድ እስከ ስምንት ብር ነው። ለምሳሌ ባንዱ ወረዳ አጋር አምስት መቶ ሰው ደኖራል። አምስቱ መቶ ሰዎች አንድ ሺህ ብር እንዲከፍሉ ሲታዘዝ የሻለቃው ከዚሁ ውስጥ ሁለት መቶ ሰዎች የኔ አሽከሮች ናቸው ግብር እንደይነኩ የሚል ቃል ለወረዳው ምስለኔ ያስተላልፋል። በዚህ መሐል የነዚያን ወታደርች ድርሻ ጥምር ሌሎች ገባሮች ይከፍሉ።

It is estimated that dues ranged from half a thaler to eight thalers. If these were given to five hundred Gebbars in one district and they were asked to pay one thousand thalers, the Shaleqa of the district would order the mislene to exempt two hundred persons whom he called his personal servants. Their tax was redistributed among the remaining three hundred.

This again shows us that the system was on the whole similar because the *land* of the soldiers was exempted from taxes. If this assumption is accepted, then we can conclude that from Shewa to Tegray, a more or less similar *serit* structure existed. While the general principle thus remained the same, there were differences in detail. A detailed field investigation is needed to flesh out this rather skeletal picture.

In any case, it can be said that the state structure in these provinces drew on the services of peasants in the same way.[3] Did it apply exclusively to the peasantry or did it include the ruling classes as well? Data from the post-Italian period show that the nobility did not own land in large estates except as members of peasant lineage groups. They lived on *'gult'*. On the other hand, data from the Gondar region strongly suggest that the ruling classes owned land in large quantities in the same way as the lords did in Shewa and the newly incorporated provinces towards the last quarter of the Nineteenth Century.

The case of the land grants by Iyasu II (1730-1755) and Etege Mentwab, the dowager empress, to the Quesquam church of Gondar is relevant here. A sum of 755 *gasha* of land was given out to 260 'dabtera' i.e., to persons who had to carry out church services (most probably *debtera* services) either in person or by proxy.[4] The 260 grantees belonged to social groups ranging from the aristocracy to the ordinary priest. A breakdown of the grant is worked out by Crummey and Shumet (1988:13-14) as follows:

A total of 260 'dabtera' holding 755 gasha gives an average of 2.9 gasha per dabtera. However, holdings were less uniform than this. Over one-third (36.5%) held only one gasha of land, while the same proportion (36.9%) held three or more. ... Further inequality marked this distribution. One man, Blatten Geta Galawdewos, held 9 gasha consisting of at least 109 fields. Two others, the princesses Wayzaro Aster and Wayzaro Eleni, held 7 gasha each, with the former holding over 67 fields and the latter 61.20. Ashkar Al'tash held 6 gasha consisting of 59 fields; and six other people each held 5 gasha with total fields ranging from around 40 to about 66. Hayla Selasse held 4 gasha with at least 70 fields. The eleven people just mentioned held between them 73 gasha (an average of 6.6 each) and 687 fields (an average of 62.5 each). The 56 smallest holders held between them 56 gasha (one each) and a total of about 497 fields (an average of just under 9 each). The difference in average size of holdings by fields between the eleven largest and 56 smallest holders is seven times.

Crummey has collected data on land grants from Gondar and Gojam from the Eighteenth to the Twentieth Century. We can therefore take the picture given above as a representative example and draw major conclusions from it. The first conclusion is that this form of grant was very similar to the grants that Menelik and other lords made in the late Nineteenth and early Twentieth Century to the churches in Addis Ababa and its environs. Undergraduate history students of Addis Ababa University studied almost all of these churches as a partial requirement for their first degree.[5] All of these churches unanimously demonstrate an exactly similar kind of land grant.

I have selected five of the principal churches of Addis Ababa Raguel and Mariam from Entoto, Holy Trinity, Urael and Yeka Mikael from Addis Ababa proper. The five students who worked on the history of these churches (Wudu Tafete 1989; Mekonnen Berhane 1988; Tsegaye Berhe 1989; Demeke Seifu 1989; Solomon Tena 1988) copied the land registers of these churches and attached them as appendices to their essays. The registers contain the location of the land its *melkenet, mektel wereda* and *wereda*, the size of land granted in gashas and the name of the grantee. The grantees belonged to the two sexes and were lay and clerical. The aggregate figure of the grants is presented in Table 2.

Table 2: Grants of Land to Selected Churches in the Addis Ababa Area (late 19th to early 20th Century)

Name of Church	Nobility and Gentry No. of Grantee	Nobility and Gentry Size in Gasha	Clergy No. of Grantees	Clergy Size in Gasha
Raguel	220	251	73	68.5
Entoto Maryam	386	411	68	92
Holy Trinity	145	184.5	98	244
Urael	41	40	106	126
Yeka Mikael	24	15.25	132	79
Total	816	901.75	477	609.5

Source: Aggregated from Wudu Tafete, 1989; Mekonnen Berhane, 1988; Tsegaye Berhe, 1989; Demeke Seifu, 1989 and Solomon Tena, 1988.

The first similarity between the grants in Table 2 and those of Quesquam is that the lands are given in gashas. Most of the grantees received one gasha each. The lands were spread in the districts to the west and south of Addis Ababa, reaching as far as Nazareth and Arsi as well as Chebo. The class background of the grantees is remarkably similar, ranging from the aristocracy of both sexes to the gentry and from the top clergy (e.g., Tsehafi Te'ezaz Gebre Selassie) to the ordinary cleric. Etege Menen, Princess Yeshashe Werk (the niece of the emperor) and Princess Tenagne Werk were involved.

There are other interesting facts in these documents. For instance, the following six distinct Moslem names appear in the register of Entoto

Maryam church as *bale-rist*: no. 232, Sheh Ahmed; no. 235 Mustefa Mohammed; no. 237 Mohammed Karoki; no. 240 Mohammed Nurgelatu; no. 241, Hasane' Nur; and no. 269, Haji Umar Sheh Ali. The type of *serit* for one gasha of the first person was *qesnna*, which meant that one *gasha* must support a priest. Since a Moslem could not obviously be a priest, he would employ a substitute. The obligation of the lands of Mustefa Mohammed, Mohammed Karoki, Mohammed Nurgelatu, Hasene Nur and Haji Umar was *debternat* again to act as a *debtera* or to employ one. Obviously they would opt for the latter choice.

Of the five Addis Ababa churches, three (Entoto Maryam, 503 *gashas*; Holy Trinity, 428.5 *gashas* and Raguel, 319.5) were extremely well-endowed rich churches. The holders of their land belonged not only to the gentry but also to the aristocracy and the royal family (Etege Menen, Tenagne Werk, Yeshashe Werk, *Ras* Beru, the emperor himself etc.) which was a sure guarantee of influence and wealth for the church.

These grants were also similar to the Quesquam church in another sense they were given out in one gasha in several places to individuals far apart from each other. This striking similarity leads us to raise a number of very important issues. First and foremost, this grant demonstrates the manner in which *serit* was imposed. Because the documents do not give us the obligations attached to and rights over these lands prior to their grant to a church, we are unable to trace the transformation from one form of *serit* to another. As it were, therefore, we have to start from the grants themselves.

In actual fact the grant meant that a new *serit* was now imposed on these lands. The grants were a variant of *ye-samon meret* or *ye-mesqel meret* or simply church lands. They were granted to the church in perpetuity, which means that they could not be transferred to another institution. Put another way, their *serit* could not be changed to any other, say military *serit*.

To say that these grants were given to a church was, in actual fact, to say that they were given out to individuals who could carry out the functions of the church and otherwise support it. In the socio-political system of the time, institutions did not have any mechanism of collecting tributes in kind or cash and redistributing them to their staff in turn. What was done was to parcel out the land and give it to individuals who would keep the institution going.

Therefore, we see that the lay nobility were also given land. Out of the 260 grantees of Quesquam, 146 (56.2%) were lay and 114 (43.8%) were members of the clergy. The picture was the same for the Addis Ababa churches though the specific proportions varied from case to case.

For the first two major churches, the lay nobility had a preponderant role, while for the latter three the case was reversed. We should not be misled into thinking that the clergy would continue to have the upper hand because, as the first generation of clerics dies out, the next might not necessarily go into priesthood or the inheritor could be a woman. In other words, the likelihood of the land passing on into lay hands was very great.

Table 3: Size of Holdings of Lay and Clerics for Five Addis Ababa Churches

Name of Church	Lay Holdings In Gasha	In %	Clerical Holdings In Gasha	In %
Raguel	251	78.6	68.5	21.4
Entoto Maryam	411	81.7	92	18.3
Holy Trinity	184.5	43.1	244	60
Urael	40	24.1	126	75.9
Yeka	15.25	16.2	79	8.38

Source: As above.

Crummey and Shumet (1988:24) conclude from their findings:

Thus, the Quesquam charter was as much a device for supporting the lay nobility and the social hierarchy in general as it was a device for the support of the church and its serving priests. In a more extended sense, the charter also legitimated the social order by incorporating it into the structure of the church.

I believe that this analysis misses the whole point of *serit*. The charter was indeed a device for the support of the church but this was done by attaching the obligation of supporting the church to a particular land. What was central to the system was not so much the individual as the land with the obligations (*serit*). Individuals come and go but the land with its *serit* would always be there and whoever owned it would be duty bound to support the church in one way or another. This is the logic.

Secondly, the lay nobility were involved in this church and in all of the Addis Ababa ones because these were major churches. At the grassroots level, the large lay peasantry were involved in the parish church in exactly the same way as Hoben demonstrated in his study area in Gojam (1963:87-98). It is not, therefore, a particular class that is involved in the church but the entire range of society from the king and the Etege down to the ordinary peasant. The Ethiopian church was not an institution separate from the State. It was a church within the State and had no separate administration. It was run by members of the society, whether lay or clerical. The difference was that, if the person was lay, the job was done by a proxy.

The other issue that emerges from the data above is that of ownership. Crummey argues that these grants were *gult* grants (1988:24). In all of his other studies of land documents he uses the concept of *gult* for these lands. He argues that what was granted was the tribute and not the land. Crummey's approach focussed on the specific documents only. It would be valuable if a comparative perspective were adopted and one tried to look at the charters of the late nineteenth and early twentieth centuries. The procedure for granting the latter is so similar to the eighteenth century system that one wonders whether there could be a difference in the sphere of ownership.

In the charters of the late nineteenth and early twentieth centuries, the land was given to individuals as *rest*. The lands were therefore privately owned. This ownership was nevertheless conditional on supporting the church. In the 1840s, King Sahle Selassie of Shewa distributed land to the church and the soldiery in the same manner as documented by Mariam and McCann for the Addis Ababa, Becho and Ada districts. The unit of grant and measurement was gasha and land was given either as *maderiya* or *rest*. The ordinary soldiers/priests got a gasha each while the officers got more. It was the land that was given and not tributes. If there was private, conditional, large-scale ownership of land in mid-nineteenth century Shewa, then all other factors remaining equal, one can hypothesize that, in the Gonderine era, what was granted was the land rather than tributes only.

This hypothesis is based on two points. First, it should be stressed that, in terms of political economy, there was no fundamental difference between the mid-eighteenth century Gonderine society and mid-nineteenth century Shewa. Capitalist forces had not yet encroached upon the political economy of Shewa. Secondly, the whole conception of *gult* itself is ambiguous. It is used by scholars to mean all kinds of tributes collected by lords as well as a specific number of villages given out to lords from which they would exact tributes. These kinds of villages were essentially different from, say, one *gasha* of land alone given to a lord. In the latter case, the lord could not be an administrator, judge, etc. over the gasha. These functions were carried out by the *gult-gazh* and not by the holder of the *gasha*. This was made clear in the grants for the Addis Ababa churches in which the *mekenenet* where the land was allocated was mentioned by the name of the melkena. For instance, in the Entoto Maryam register, the list goes downwards province, *awraja*, *wereda*, *meketel wereda* and the last, *melkegnaw*, indicating clearly that the *melkenet* was the last unit of territorial organization and administration. And *melkegna* was the exact equivalent of *gult*. Applying the term *gult* for both of them is therefore confusing and even misleading.

It is thus important to conceptualize precisely this term. We are fortunate in this context to have a book written most probably in the first decade of this century entitled *Handbook of Abyssinia*, Vol. I (1917). The time of writing is very important as the institutions of old Ethiopia had not yet been diluted by capitalist incursions. The anonymous authors collected their information from 'the field', which gives their book a great deal of solidity. They gave particular attention to the administrative and military structure of the state. They looked into institutions in Tigray and Hamasen. One of these institutions was the *gulti*, a Tigregna version of the Amharic term described as follows:

> *The country is divided into provinces, each ruled by a governor (said to rank as Bal-nagarit) who depends directly on the Emperor; a province into districts, to rank as Bal-qamis; a district into Gulti, or groups of villages, each group ruled by a Shum-gulti or Gultegna, or Melkana; a Gulti into Addi, or small groups of villages, each ruled by a Shum or Shum-Addi; and an Addi into villages, each ruled by a Chiqa or Chiqa-shum* (Handbook, I, 1917:264).

This description might just as well have been written about the administrative structure of Shewa. The *shum-gulti* was a good Tigregna version of the *melkena* or *balabat* in the Shewan administrative structure. Both of them had similar functions. The following job description from the same contemporary source of a *shum-gulti* can just as well serve for his Shewan counterpart of the same age:

> *The shum-gulti, assisted by the shum-addi, fixes the proportion of the state dues which each addi must pay; he also acts as a court of appeal in civil and criminal matters from judgements of the Shum-addi; he is responsible for order in his gulti and is, of course, the military chief of the district. In return for this he (a) has his land cultivated free of charge by the resetnyatat; (b) receives all of the fines (demnab) which he may impose in his judicial capacity; keeps a part, generally one-tenth, of the tribute collected by him; and (c) receives certain presents, eg. a sheep from each Addi at Easter (emphasis mine)* (Handbook, I, 1917:274).

Thus, *gult* denoted a certain institution, that of the local governor which is indicated in some regions (e.g. Gojam) by the use of the term *gult gezh*. The use of *gult* as a generic term for all kinds of tribute rights therefore leads to confusion.

My contention is that we should *rest*rict the term *gult* to the office of the local governor only. We should *rest*rict it to this meaning so long as we use it as a concept. On the other hand, we should always be aware of the ways the term and its verb form have been used, particularly in the Ge'ez sources. Golete has also been used in the sense of the Amharic *tekele* to mean 'to give land permanently'. *Gult* signifies, in this context, land given to individuals permanently and a *gultegna* in this sense becomes a synonym for the Amharic *teklegna* (Huntingford and Beckingham 1965). While therefore being careful of its various usages in the sources, we should try to stick to the word's territorial and administrative meaning when we use it in our writings to avoid confusion.

Gult was indeed an office of governor a little above the soil or the *chiqa-shum*. The governor was entitled to part of the tribute that was due to the state. In other words, they would keep to themselves a proportion of the tribute collected for the state. In the case of Tegray the share of the *shum-gulti* was one-tenth which would be topped up by other mechanisms. Two conclusions can easily be deduced from this: first, the office of the *gult* governor ensured a certain revenue; and second, because *gult* was one of the lowest administrative territorial offices of the system, there were so many *gults* in the kingdom.

Hence, *gult* governorships were given out to all kinds of individuals ranging from members of the royal family to low-level retainers of both sexes. There is plenty of data to show that individual lords could be governors of many *gults*.

Two questions must be answered in order to understand this phenomenon. First, how could an individual discharge duties as a governor if given so many *gults*?. Secondly, since an integral obligation of a *gult* governor was to establish law and order, how many soldiers could be raised from the *gult* in times of war to discharge military duties along with the *gult* governors whose office equally obliged them to perform military duties?

To answer these questions, we have to turn to the institution of proxy. For the Ethiopian socio-political system, this institution was its bloodline. One of the major beneficiaries of this institution was *gult* governorship. An individual could be governor of as many *gults* as they could be granted because all these *gults* could be run by a proxy. This proxy carried out all the functions of a *gult* governor and sent the revenues from it to the latter in return for a share of it.

Because of the ubiquitous proxy institution, the office of the *gult* governor could be made a device of ruling class support. But the proxy institution was not restricted to this office only. The entire *serit* arrangement was very much contingent on this institution. For instance, the whole structure of church and military lands cannot be understood without taking into account the proxy institution. Much of church land was in the hands of the laity who ran the church by employing substitutes. An individual who owned *gashas* and *gashas* of *debtera* land would employ several *debtera* to do the job. In this way, the church could be assured of perennial services.

Military lands were run in the same way. There were innumerable ways of discharging the military obligations attached to one's land, which, incidentally, was at the root of much of the confusion on land tenure. The easiest to understand was the arrangement according to which an individual peasant or lord who owned military land discharged the duties himself. But there were innumerable other ways of doing the same thing by proxy. One way was by a shift system among descendants of the 'founding father' the person who was first given the land as military land. The other mechanism was simply to support or employ a soldier. Sometimes a lord would also impose on the land a soldier who would be given a fixed proportion (one-fifth in Begemder and Gojam) of the produce. There are other ways as well. For instance, I discovered that two brothers who used to live in Addis Ababa before 1935 inherited two *gashas* of military land. When mobilization was declared in 1935, they did not want to answer the call. So they found an adventurer who was willing to go. The two brothers agreed that they would give him half a *gasha* upon his return which he would use for his lifetime. They signed a contract to this effect and he went to war.

The proxy institution is a source of confusion in understanding the essential elements of the system. For instance, the different forms of *samon maret* (*Ye-debtera, Ye-qes, Ye-mesqel, Ye-gedam, rim,* etc.) are generally translated as 'church land'. In some ways, this is an inaccurate translation because the Ethiopian church did not actually own the land. The English expression also leads to confusion as to why the laity owned or at least controlled so much of 'church land'. The term '*samon maret*' or many of its other forms (except *gedam maret*) can best be translated as 'lands set aside or given to those who had to offer services to the church themselves or by proxy'. The 'ownership' was individual.

This question of ownership of land is said to have been 'settled' by academic orthodoxy a long time ago. The orthodox interpretation is that land was owned as *rest* by peasants communally. The lords had the right over the tributes only, which were given the generic term '*gult*'. This orthodoxy must be questioned in its entirety. For instance, Princess Aster was given seven *gashas* which were made up of over 67 fields. One can give hundreds of examples of this kind from the sources of the eighteenth century alone. The question is what right did she have over the field and over the *gasha*? First, this *gasha* was located in a particular *gult*, the governor of which exercised judicial and administrative duties for which he charged fees. Princess Aster did not have those rights. On the other hand, she had the right to sell, bequeath or offer that particular land as a gift to another individual, as Crummey has demonstrated (1983). If she had all these rights over a particular land, that land was her property. The tricky question arises when the status of the *gebbar* comes in. Was he a tenant? I suggest that the whole notion of a tenant be used carefully in Ethiopia. In the Amharic language, its equivalent, *tekeray*, made its appearance rather late.

Let us look at the issue from a different angle. What were the obligations of the *gebbar* to Princess Aster? First and foremost, he had to give her a portion of the produce, and then follow other obligations. If he did not do so, she would *give* the land to another *gebbar*. Thus, she really was the owner. On the other hand, he inherited the land from his father and he could use the land so long as he fulfilled his obligations. He could not, for instance, sell his land to another lord, though he could 'sell' it to another *gebbar*. Hence, he had a right, but a limited right, to the land while Princess Aster could pass as an owner by many of the criteria of ownership but with a qualification that it was conditional ownership. Hence, those seven gashas of land given to her were her *rest*. The concept of ownership in a pre-capitalist Ethiopian tradition did not have the same meaning as in a capitalist one, where it denotes absolute possession. If we agree on this caveat, then we can accept Bahrey's definition of *Shemageles* as: 'lords and hereditary landowners who share their land with their [*gebbars*] labourers' (Pankhurst 1966:34).

The academic orthodoxy of *rest/gult* should therefore be revised. The discussion so far hopefully demonstrates the inadequacy of these terms as pivotal organizing concepts. We should replace them with a concept that will serve as a more useful theoretical tool.

Abolition of Serit in the Twentieth Century

The Twentieth Century saw structural transformations in many aspects of state and society, one of the most important being land tenure. The central figure of this period was Teferi Haile Selassie who was in the forefront of those who championed the abolition of the *serit* system.

This section traces the changes in *serit* that led to its gradual abolition in the second half of this century.

Separation of Land and State Institutions

While in exile in London, Haile Selassie looked back on his years of leadership and listed among his major achievements the attempt to abolish the *serit* as he himself put it:

በኢትዮጵያ እንደቀየውና እንደተለመደው አገረገኙዎች የጦር ሹሞች ናቸው እንጂ የሲቪል ሹሞች አልነበሩም ፡፡ ስለዚህ ለወታደሮች በየአለቃቸው እየከፈሉ ከዚያው ከገዞታቸው ውስጥ ግደሪያ እያሉ ይስጧቸዋል እንጂ አገሩ ሁሉ በመንግሥት እጅ ሆኖ በሲቪል ሹሞች ግብሩ እየተሰበሰበ ለወታደሮችም ለሌላም ለመንግሥት ጉዳይ ወጪ ግደረግ አልተለመደም ነበር፡፡

ይህንም ከብዙ ዘመን ጀምር የቆየውን ልግድ በንድ ጊዜ
ለማፍረስ ያገር ውስጥ ሁከት ያስነሳል በማለት ስለሰጋን
አደራረጉን ለማሳየትና በጥቂቱ ለማስለመድ ጅጅጋ ጠርጠር
ባሌ ወለጋ ሰዩ ጀማ የሚባሉትን አውራጃች በመንግሥት
እጅ አድርገን ገቢዉ ገንዘብ ለወታደርችና ለሌላም
ለመንግሥት ጉዳይ ወጪ እንዲሆን ግስለግጀ ምስሌ
አድርገናል። (ሀይለ ሥለሴ፣ 1965:54)

It had remained customary in Ethiopia for all provincial governors to be military chiefs, but there were no civilian rulers. Therefore it was not the custom for the whole country to be under the authority of the government and to allocate taxes, collected by civilian officials, to the army and for other government business, but the governors used to pay the soldiers through their own officers and to give them quarters in their governorate.

As we were uneasy about abolishing all at once this custom which had persisted for a long time, thinking that it might provoke disturbances in the country, we arranged to demonstrate this mode of procedure and to make it acceptable in slow stages by placing under the authority of the (central) government the districts of Jijiga, Tchartcher, Bale, Wellega, Sayo and Jimma; and we also saw to it, as an instructive example, that revenues be applied to the expenditure on the army and other government business.

This quotation gives us an insight into the fundamental contradiction of the period: centralized taxation versus *serit*. It also gives us an insight into the gradualist and moderate approach of Haile Selassie. When he came to power the modernizers who rallied around him had one common platform abolition of *serit*. While Teferi also fully shared this position, the difference was one of tempo.

The literature on changes in land tenure in the era of Haile Selassie primarily focus on the concept of 'privatization'. It is argued that from the turn of the twentieth century, the concept of private ownership of land made its appearance with the advent of capitalism. Because the newly incorporated provinces had been conquered, large-scale private ownership of land was gradually introduced in these regions where land had been communally owned before. This communal land was confiscated by Menelik's forces and then distributed in the form of *gult*. Later, with the expansion of the market economy, *gult*s were privatized and a new *gebbar* system established.

McLellan's book, *State Transformation and National Integration: Gedeo and the Ethiopian Empire, 1895-1935* (1988) is taken as the standard reference work to demonstrate this gradual privatization of land. In fact, what

102 An Economic History of Modern Ethiopia

the book shows is what would normally happen in such situations in Northern Ethiopia.

When Shewan forces first arrived in Gedeo, *gebbar* was allocated to the soldiers according to their ranks. A common soldier who was a member of the Barud Bet regiment was allocated 21 *gebbar*s and a junior officer, 37 *gebbar*s. The number would go up to hundreds as the ranks rose up. Priests were also allocated *gebbar* (McLellan 1988:65). This was not, by any means, an introduction of a novel practice but something that had existed before.

As the new rulers consolidated their power, land was measured out and distributed to individual settlers more or less on principles similar to those applied in the North. Before we comment on these principles, we will present some very interesting facts. There was a well-established tradition of land distribution at the close of the Seventeenth Century in northern Shewa, collected and transmitted to us by the famous historian, Asme. Negase Kristos, the governor of Menz, expanded his domain in the direction of Yifat and Tarma Ber by conquering the adjoining districts. He then distributed land to his people as follows:

... ነጋሲ መሬት ወይም ሪም መትከል ጀመሩ። ያንድ ቤተ ክርስቲያን አገልጋዮች ገጠር ብትሆን ስድስት ሰሞነኛ ስድስት አወደሽ ነው ደብር ስትሆን አሥር ሰሞነኛ አወደሽ ገን ልክ የለም።... አገር ሲያቀኑ መጀመሪያ ለነዚህ አንድ አንድ ጋሽ ይነሰል መሬት ሲተርፍ አንድ ጋሽ የገንደባል። ገንደበል ዘግቾ ነው በጎንደር ጨዋ ይሉታል። አንድ ጋሽ የገባር እርሱም የግድ ቤት ነው። በለይ መልከኛ ይሸግል። የተረፈውን መሬት እየከፈለ ለጭሰኛ ይሰግል። ከዚያ ዘመን ጀምር እስከ ዛሬ ደንቡ ይህ ነው።

Thus, Nagasi began to allot plots of land or Rim. Those who celebrate the mass in a church are six Samonanna [and] six Awaddas in the case of a Gatar, and eight Samonanna and an unlimited number of Awaddas in the case of a Debr. ... On the occasion of the pacification of a region, a Gassa is allotted to each of these [groups]. If there is an extra plot of land, one Gassa is for the Gendabal; Gendabal is a contingent of campaigners, [and] it is called Cawa in Gondar; one Gassa is for the Gabbar that is the madbet. A malkanna would be appointed above them. The rest of the land is distributed among tenants. Since that time the tradition has remained the same.

These grants were made at the close of the Seventeenth Century. Though this tradition does not specify the status of the ownership (*rest* or *maderiya*), it is quite clear that it was the land that was given, not a tribute. At about the same time, land measurement was carried out in the Gonder region on the orders of Emperor Iyasu I (1682-1706). Basing on D'Abbadie, Pankhurst writes that in the course of the measurement, the land was distributed. The original 'owners were allowed one-third of the area they were occupying, the other two-thirds returning to the state. Of this amount, one-half was given to the churches and the other half was retained by the state. Provincial tradition refers to this as a triple division' (Pankhurst 1966:54-5).

This information is fully corroborated by the oral tradition recorded by Gebre Weld Engeda Werk (p. 57). It is interesting to note that the unit of measurement was the *gasha*. One can observe that this kind of land measurement and (re)distribution was not unique for the periods mentioned above and that the practice must have a long history behind it. It is also interesting to note continuity in the ground rules that governed the operation. I am not implying that they were implemented to the letter. Far from that. But the spirit of the principle provided the general framework. As per this framework, one-third of the land would be put aside for the original owners. Of the remaining two-thirds, one-third would first be put aside as church land and the remaining one-third as military land. The land was given in small plots to private individuals.

It should therefore not come as a surprise if the same ground rules governed Negus Sahle Selassie's distribution of land in central and western Shewa in the 1840s. It should not be surprising either that the same principles guided the process in the 1870s in the newly incorporated regions. What made the difference for the latter era was the opening up of the country to the capitalist world, which considerably distorted the system and profoundly altered its historic course.

The first important point to be made is the fact that *not all* the land was confiscated following the conquest in the era of Menelik. It was discriminatory confiscation that was practised. The lands of the rebels (rebel communities, ethnic groups etc.) were alienated and the rebels turned into tenants. Those that peacefully accepted the Shewan forces were not touched. The most successful among these were Leqa Neqemt (Wellega), Leqa Qelem (Wellega), the kingdom of Jimma, Assosa and Beni Shanguel. The other provinces were subjected to a considerable degree of confiscation. Pankhurst has published information from travellers' sources in the first half of this century which shows that, in many of the districts, it was the land of the rebels that was confiscated (Pankhurst 1966:135-148). Detailed local work needs to be done to test this picture.

Land obtained in such a fashion was apportioned on a three-thirds or four-quarters basis. One-third or one-fourth would be set aside for the local chiefs. It was called sisso. A considerable amount of data has been gathered to show that the sisso principle was not always kept and that the share was much lower than that, going as far down as one-sixth (Mahteme Selassie 1962:108; Pankhurst 1966:13d ff.; Tessema Ta'a 1984:186). Obligations of military service were attached to these lands and had the effect of integrating the local chiefs into the system (Mahteme Selassie 1962:108). Moreover, the *sisso* arrangement paved the way for the emergence of a landed class from among the local people.

The *rest* of the land was shared out between the church and the military on these same principles for Shewa, Gojam and Begemder. The military land was apportioned to individuals theoretically at the following rate: 1 to 3 *gasha* for a soldier, 10 *gasha*s for an *hamsa aleqa*, 20 *gasha*s for a *meto aleqa* and 30 *gasha*s for a *shambel* (Gebre Weld 1948:34; MahtemeSelassie 1962:114). One should note that this was only the guiding principle and was not by any means strictly implemented. The lands were given names which indicated their *serit gandabal*, *gebbar*, *desta*, *samon*, etc. In many of the southern provinces measurements of some kind were carried out after the distribution. Mahteme Selassie has compiled data on stretches of land for many of the newly incorporated provinces (see pp. 133143) under two headings *kelad*-measured lands and *non-kelad*-measured lands. He gives estimates for 28 districts in the latter category.

All of our sources (Gebre Weld, Mahteme Selassie, Pankhurst) agree that the lands were given in two forms: *rest* and *maderiya*. Land was given as *rest* in many places in the newly-incorporated areas from the very outset. The problem is to prepare an inventory to give us an insight into the regional and ethnic background of the new class of landlords.

McLellan has looked into this issue by giving us the percentage of the origin of a sample of his settler informants broken down into officer and ordinary soldiers, as well as civilians. Let us look at the total percentages: Shewa (69%), Gojam (12.05%), Wello (5.0%), Tigre' (4.0%), Begemder (2.03%) and 'Other' (7.5%) (McLellan 1988:51). The figure for Shewa gives a misleading ethnic picture Shewa having Amhara, Oromo as well as Gurage. For instance, a good proportion of the settlers in Sidamo were the retainers and soldiers of *Dejach* Balcha which meant that the majority of them were Oromo and Gurage. Hence, the percentage for Shewan Amhara would be less than what the estimate here suggests.

The new landlord class had a heterogeneous character, in terms of both ethnic and regional background, though it was dominated by the Amhara. The famous 'Gondare' regiments (a generic term used for all regiments made up of soldiers recruited from the northern Amharic provinces of Wadla-Delanta, Begemder, Lasta and Semen) were spread out in large numbers in Arjo (Wellega), Illubabor, Kefa, Hararghe. The Oromo of Selale were garrisoned in Arsi. The Gulele and Finfine Oromo of the Addis Ababa region were relocated in the same province. The Oromo of Chabo and Mecha and the Gurage were settled in Sidamo and in many other provinces in the south. In addition to these were the Shewan Amhara. Wello and Gojam and Tegray had their share too. We should also add the local landlords for whom the *sisso* served as an entry ticket into the national landed class. Moreover, in some of the rich coffee districts of Wellega and Jimma (Jimma itself, Leqa-Neqemt, Leqa Qellem, most of the districts in Gimbi) land confiscation was not carried out on a significant scale, which opened the way for the rise of a class made up of a considerable number of rich Oromo landowners in these areas.

Whatever its structure, the fact that it was a landlord class from the very beginning should not be contested. A source of confusion might very well be the use of the term *maderiya*. The *maderiya* holder was just as good a landlord as the *rest* holder, the difference consisting in ownership rights only, as long as his/her *maderiya* was not abrogated. In both cases the grantees were landlords as far as the peasant was concerned. They had absolutely the same privileges over the *gebbar*. Tesema Ta'a, who wrote on the process in Wellega has, unlike McLellan, understood the relationship between peasant and lord very well:

The peasants who lived on maderiiya maret given to the members of the local or non-local feudal hierarchy or to the church had no claims on the land. They worked the land only on the sufferance of the owner who could impose difficult conditions or even evict them (Tesema Ta'a 1984:188).

It could be because he did not ask himself this question that McLellan draws from his data a misleading conclusion:

... *[Before 1935] neftenga-gabbar ... was being transformed into a kind of proto-tenancy. A definitive landlord system would emerge only after the Italian war, when soldiers were permitted to convert part of their maderiaya into rest...* (McLellan 1988:9).

He stressed his thesis again when he wrote: 'The landlord-tenant relationship did not fully develop until after the Italian war' (McLellan 1988:93). This theory totally blurs the actual relationship that the *gebbar* was the tenant of the *bale-maderiya*.

The process of conversion of *maderiya* into *rest* was not a post-Italian phenomenon, as McLellan asserts. It was something that continued side-by-side from the very beginning. The other interpretation that emerges from McLellan's book is that the process he described for Gedeo (and by extension, for all the incorporated areas) was a phenomenon unique to our era as well as to the conquered provinces. This is a misunderstanding of the nature of the system. In traditional technical terms what was done in Gedeo can be expressed as a total change of the *seritserit* changes of. Changes in *serit* frequently occurred in the northern provinces as well. A common occasion for change of *serit* in the north was major rebellions, punished by the confiscation of the land of the rebels or other penalties such as execution, etc. For instance, in Wello, following *Negus* Mikael's campaign to Shewa after the coup d'etat of 1916 which toppled his son, Iyasu, a large army marched to Wello. Initially, the peasants were given to the soldiers in more or less the way *gebbar*s were distributed to neftegna in Gedeo which McLellan describes. But later, during the governorship of Ras Kebede Mengesha (1918-1925), a considerable area of land was confiscated and given to troops from the southern provinces (Asnake Ali 1986:1).

Following the Weyane revolt of 1941-43, the same thing was done in Raya Azebo (Fekadu Begna 1990). A considerable proportion of the land of the rebels was confiscated and distributed to some members of the nobility on the basis of rank using *gasha* as a unit of measurement. This practice has an old history. Basing on the chronicle of Iyasu I (1682-1706), Pankhurst writes that in 1689, Iyasu, 'when faced by a refusal by the people of Wag to pay their annual tax, sent a garrison of *chewa* to the area, allotting them two-thirds of the land, and leaving the rebels only a third' (Pankhurst 1966:56). A few years later a similar punishment was meted out to the people of Shire. In short, rebellions led to changes of *serit* in the north, just like in the south.

This change of *serit* was not a mere transfer of land. It involved setting up institutions which would be supported by the new *serit* arrangement. Hence, giving land to a certain regiment in the south meant that regiment was made permanent. So long as the land was military land, the holders would be there to serve in the army. In short, Menelik built up his huge politico-military and administrative structure on the basis of the *serit* of the land of the newly incorporated provinces.

One of the major ambitions of Haile Selassie and the Westernizers around him was to change precisely the *serit* foundation of the system into money in order to create a modern army and bureaucracy. In the years between 1916-35, they were not able to do much, as Haile Selassie himself admitted.

One major upshot of the Halian invasion and the subsequent occupation was the total dismantling of these political-military and administrative institutions. The same institutions in the North and the leading members of the big regional ruling houses of the North were either in disarray or were compromised by the Italians (Seyoum, Hailu) or were killed.

Haile Selassie took advantage of this situation upon liberation by taking gradual measures to abolish the *serit* system and did not attempt to restore the old politico-military institutions. With the introduction of money, a civilian bureaucracy, and a professional salaried army, *serit* outlived its *raison d'etre*. The liberation force under Haile Selassie was received by patriotic bands scattered and disorganized. It was not very difficult for him to absorb as many of the patriotic leaders as possible into the bureaucracy and some of the ordinary patriots were recruited into the army and the police. Thus, abolishing *serit* and making land a property subject to tax only was started in earnest from the very beginning.

In an *awaj* that was issued only five months after Haile Selassie's entry into Addis Ababa (on November 3, 1941), the following was laid down:

በለፋት በምስት ዓመቶችም የደረሰብህን መከራና ችግር ተመልክተን ቀድሞ ትገብረው የነበረውን እኩሌታውን አስቀርቼልሀለሁ። ይኸውም የምትከፈለው በብር እየተገመተ ነው። የብሩም ግምት ተቆርጦልሀል። የጉልበት ሥራ የገዴታ የእንጨት የሣር ያመት በዓል መዋያI የጢስ፤ ሌሎም ይህን የመሰሉውን ሁሉ በፍጹም ፍቄልሀለሁ።

ነገር ግን በጉልበት ብቻ የሚገበርበት እንደደስታ ግንደበል ያለ መሬት እንደሌለው በለርስት ይገብራል። እንደ እዲሱ አስተደደር ደንብ እገር ገዢዎችና የመንግሥት ሠራተኞች ሁሉ ደሞዝ አደሪ ስለሆኑ ከዚህ በለይ የተወሰነውን ግብር የምትከፍለው ለመንግሥት ግምጃ ቤት ነው።
(ገብረወልድ፤ 1984:70)

Whereas we have understood the difficulties that befell you during the past five years, we are permitting you to pay only half the taxes you paid before. Henceforward the payment of tax will be in money. The amount to be paid will be announced later.

Manual labour, firewood, grass, contribution for annual feast days and miscellaneous dues and taxes are abolished. However, desta, gindabal and such other lands which give a tax of manual labour will be entitled to pay tax in the same way as other landowners. The new administration entitles all governors and government officials to salaries; and the above-mentioned taxes will be paid to the government treasury.

The abolition of *serit* was a gradual process, however. It took over two decades to disappear completely.

Initially, a series of laws were issued to systematize taxation and to terminate obligations attached to land as well as any form of tribute payment. The very creation of a separate civilian and military structure paid in cash was a blow to the system. For instance, as the police and the modern professional army grew and expanded their services, the usefulness of peasants who owned land with military obligations attached to it first diminished and then ceased (Fekadu Begna 1990). The police took over such peacetime chores as guarding prisons and ensuring law and order, while the professional army assumed the responsibility of fighting national or civil wars.

The State also took gradual steps to abolish the institution of *gult*. Proclamation No. 90 of 1947 went one step further by creating local judges or *atbiya dagna* which further reduced the powers of the *gult-gezh*. Finally, in a proclamation issued in March 1966 *gult* was abolished in all its forms. By then, it had no place in the new provincial bureaucratic structure maintained by money and run by professional civil servants and police. The functions of the *gult-gezh* had already been bureaucratized their tribute-collecting functions had been taken over by the Ministry of Finance, adjudication by the newly-established district courts and by the *atbiya dagnas* at the grassroots level, military service by the national army and law enforcement by the police. Though the transformation was far from complete in remote districts, the advances had gone so far ahead by 1966 that the State felt confident enough to abolish it without creating any vacuum.

Gult was an institution that was abolished without generating a relatively strong social resentment leading to rebellions or any other form of powerful protest. This is a process that should have been explained by those scholars who put it up as a major device of ruling class support and wealth.

The Abolition of Tribute Exactions

The significance of the change, even if gradual, from tribute and other exactions to systematic taxation has not been entirely appreciated by scholars, particularly radicals who wrote on the subject. As they researched and wrote in an era of Haile Selassie-bashing, it was perhaps difficult for them to make a sober assessment of the subject matter.

The dues and tributes on peasants had been manifold. All the people who had claims over arable land paid *tithe* or *asrat* (one-tenth of the produce). This affected the ordinary peasant as well as the lords. Only the church was exempted. There were also other exactions like offering gifts to lords. In addition, *gebbar* peasants had *gebbar* obligations sundry labour services, which are well known. Taking tithe and other tributes together and, considering the estimates of other scholars, Crummey quite rightly concluded that 'overall one might hazard the guess that the normal level of surplus extraction amounted to about one-third of peasant production' (Crummey 1989a:128).

As if this was not enough, there were other exactions which were irregular and yet extremely onerous. Travellers who came to the country before the Twentieth Century pointed out that it was these irregular exactions much more than the regular tributes that did the most damage to the peasant (Crummey 1983). In the period after 1941, however, these had disappeared. The effect this change had on the 'quality' of peasant life had not at all been investigated. In a country where the percentage of owned holdings was greater than tenant holdings, such instances of surplus extraction must be examined carefully in conjunction with population growth and the subsequent increasing fragmentation of land. The question I am driving at is this: is it only exploitation that was at the root of so much rural poverty, or were there other additional and equally important factors that could explain it (like population explosion and environmental degradation)? Though this question cannot be answered here, the other question how the changes affected government revenue? can be.

In terms of taxes only, government revenues from land were not considerable. 'The land tax was not destined to be an important source of revenue. For the period 1964-65 to 1970-71, for example, it represented less than 2% of the total tax revenue', wrote Eshetu Chole in an interesting study (Eshetu Chole 1987:93). The agricultural income tax which replaced the tax in lieu of tithes did not generate much revenue either. In the considered judgement of Eshetu Chole, 'there is no doubt that, as a revenue source, the tax on agricultural income fared better than the tax in lieu of tithe (which it replaced) and the land tax proper. This is evident from its rising relative share in government revenue. It represented 3% of the total tax revenue between 1969-70 and 1973-74' (Eshetu Chole 1987:96). Other taxes (Education Tax and Health Tax) were also 'insignificant in the country's revenue structure'.

While this is generally the story when looked at from the government point of view, the issue has not been the same when viewed from the perspectives of the peasant. Haile Selassie issued a series of decrees to systematize taxation. Not long after liberation (in 1942) a major tax proclamation was issued. The taxes were fixed as follows: per *gasha*-E$15 for fertile, E$10 for semi-fertile and $5 for poor land. Laws intended to amend or elaborate this proclamation were issued in 1944, 1947, 1958 and 1967. These laws show that the taxes were not very high not compared to the taxes imposed by the People's Government of the Mengistu regime. That this tax was in the best interests of the big landlords goes without saying. Unfortunately, this has attracted greater attention from students rather than the question of why it did not bring about significant changes.

This leads me back to two points raised above. First, things were much better for the peasant, as far as surplus extraction was concerned, in the era 1941 to 1974 than ever before. Secondly, the perspectives from which land tenure has been viewed have inhibited a full understanding of the problem.

Absolutization of Rest

Significant changes have indeed taken place over the first three quarters of this century in terms of land tenure proper. Much of the focus of study has been on the 'process of privatization'. However, in the first place, *gult*s and *riste-gult*s as mechanisms of surplus extraction were abolished rather than being transformed into private ownership. And these mechanisms were prevalent in the north rather than in the incorporated provinces. In so far as *gult*s were at the same time administrative units within the State structure, they were not replicated everywhere in the south because the structure of local rule was also maintained. For instance, *balabats* were retained in a great number of the districts in the south. Retaining a *balabat* of course left no room for the imposition of *gult* if we agree on the definition given above.

If we are talking of 'privatization' then, I think we should focus on *maderiya* land and *ye-mengist maret*. *Maderiya* land would be said to have been 'privatized' if we use this term to mean land that is being transferred from temporary to permanent and absolute ownership. I prefer the term *restization*, though there is no need to squabble over terms. What makes the notion of privatization confusing is the fact that it was said to have altered the relationship between lord and peasant from the *neftegna-gebbar* relationship into a landlord-tenant one. Indeed, we have to be careful about the notion of privatization and at least qualify it to avoid confusion.

If, however, we shift our focus and look at the whole issue of land ownership, we will be able to make sense of a whole process that has not been recognized for what it was even by the best students of the subject. What kind of ownership was the *rest* form of ownership? As I have tried to demonstrate above, *rest* meant permanent, heritable and conditional ownership of land. *Rest* was subject to *alienation* alienation in the legal sense of the word (transfer of ownership of property from one person to another) in the event of failure to fulfill the obligations attached to it and in cases of *lese majeste* and homicide.

If we therefore agree that the *rest* form of ownership was conditional, then we can easily trace a process of 'absolutization' of *rest* which started in the Menelik era and was completed in that of Haile Selassie. The first document I have been able to discover in this regard is the *awaj* of Menelik in January 1891:

ንጉሥ ነገሥት ምኒልክ የፍትሀ ነገሥት ሥራት
ተመልክተው በጥር 1883 ከዋያት [የወሎ ሸዋ ወሰን] መልስ
እዋጅ እድርጌልሃለሁ። ምንም ብታጠፉ ገንዘብሀ ይወረስ
እንጂ መሬትህ አይነቀል ብለው እዋጅ ነገሩ። በዚህ ነገር
መኳንንቱም ሠራዊቱም እጅግ ደስ አለው። (ገብረሥላሴ፣

After consulting the Feteha Negest, Emperor Menelik proclaimed that all the gasha maret from Wayat [Wello-Shewa border] to Awash should be rest as in Menz. He decreed that whatever the crimes you commit, your money should be confiscated and not your land. This pleased very much the nobility and the army (Gebre Selassie 1959:179).

This document has to be carefully assessed. To begin with, *ye-gasha* maret in this context means land given to soldiers. Secondly, the land was given as *maderiya*. Now it was made *rest* like the system in Menz. The *awaj* demonstrates first that the *rest* form of ownership was conditional, and that the *rest* owners had not all along been happy with it. We should also note that it was only one condition that was removed.

In 1907, this same question was raised all over again as a top agenda item in the very first session of the first Council of Ministers:

ሚኒስትሮች ሥራ ሲጀምሩ በመጀመሪያ ምክራቸው
የሠሩትን ሥራ ከዚህ ላይ እንጽፋለን። ቃሉም ይህ ነው።
ሰው በተጣላ ጊዜ ከባላጋራው ጋር ተቂቀል ሲነጋገር እልፍ
ጆራፍ እሰጥ እያለ ውርርድ የሚተከለው ሁሉ ይቅር።..
በወንጀልም ቢገኝበት በከብቱ በሰውነቱ ይቀጣ እንጂ
መሬቱን አይነቀል። ነገር ግን ነፍስ ገድሎ የሄደ
በመንግሥት ክፉ ሥራ የሠራ ይነቀል ርስትም ግላት ያበት
የናት መሬት ደግሞ በወርቁ የገዛው መሬት ነው እንጂ
የመንግሥት መትከያ የሆነ አይደለም። ደግሞ የመትከያም
መሬት ቢሆን መንግሥት ርስት ያደርገለት ይረጋል።
(ገብረሥላሴ፣ 1959: 335 - 336)

We will write down below the first law they instituted when the Ministers started work. This is the text. Whenever a person quarrelled with another person and took his enemy to court, he should not henceforth lay down a wered of thousands of whip lashings. If he committed crime, his land should not be confiscated, rather he should pay in money or in cattle. But if he committed homicide or lese majeste his rest and maret should be confiscated. Rest meant inherited land while maret meant land he bought.

Ye-metkeya maret is not included. But if it is a metkeya maret given as a rest then it would be included (Gebre Selassie 1959: 335-336).
The decree does not stop here, and it goes on to regulate inheritance of land. This quotation speaks for itself. This same principle was enshrined in article 75 of the Annex to the Constitution of 1931:

መሣፍንቶችና አገረ ገዢዎች ሴሳም የኢትዮጵያ ተወሳጅ የሆነ ሁሉ ማናቸውንም ዓይነት ወንጀል ከሥራ በሕግ እንደተጻፈው ይቀጣል እንጂ አስከሁን በጄ የነበረውን ወደፊትም በገንዘቡ የሚገዛውን ርስቱን እንዳይነቀል በሕግ ተወስኗል። (ማሕተመ ሥሳሴ ፤ 1962:789)

It is provided by law that the mesafent, governors and any other Ethiopian would not have their rest which they own or which they will buy confiscated. They would be punished by the law (Mahteme Selassie 1962:789).

This provision removed a major condition of *rest* which made the *rest* form of ownership very close to absolute, private ownership. All this shows that in the past, the Ethiopian polity used *rest* as a mechanism for ensuring loyalty and obedience to the law, as well as getting a certain service (military or otherwise). Whether or not this was an effective mechanism is beside the point in the context of our theme. What should be stressed here is the fact that its conditionality was maintained by the State. But, with changing times, that mechanism became a hindrance. I have already cited the *awaj* of 1941 in which service obligations attached to land (like *gendabal*) were abolished. The owner was simply required to pay taxes. The institution of *gebbar maret* was abolished in Article 4 of *awaj* No. 70 of 1944. The *gebbar* obligations attached to *gebbar maret* were annulled and in their place the owner was required to pay taxes to the government in cash.

Thus, a process that was started in 1891 (as far as I could establish) was consummated in 1944, with the exception of church lands. Refinements of the same law continued afterwards. This process coincides with, and is a reflection of, a parallel process the increasing Westernization of the Ethiopian State and the penetration of capitalism into the country. This was a progressive development which Haile Selassie and the men around him pioneered and guided. It was progressive in the sense that it guaranteed absolute, private ownership of land which has always been a prerequisite for capitalist development in the rural areas.

The process of absolutization of *rest* changed the status of ownership in the rural areas, particularly arable land. What was the situation in urban centres? The question of the nature of land tenure in pre-Twentieth Century urban centres has not been tackled seriously as yet. It is a theme that will open up a fresh perspective on a number of social issues, including *serit*. For the purpose of this chapter, I will briefly comment on developments in Addis Ababa after its foundation in 1886.

When Addis Ababa was founded, land was allotted to the lords, to mercantile communities and expatriates. The lords in turn distributed it to their retainers, craftsmen and merchants attached to their court, to the clergy of their church and so forth. But we do not know the nature of the grant. Was it given as inalienable, private property or for temporary use? This and many other features of the settlement of Addis Ababa need to be looked into.

This kind of research would enable us to know the background against which Menelik issued a decree in 1907 which provided for absolute, private ownership of land. It was instituted that owners must have title deeds. These title deeds must have been introduced for the first time. The person who had title deeds must pay taxes to the municipality. Land could also be sold (Mahteme Selassie 1962 E.C.). The expatriate community could own, buy and sell land with the proviso that they should obtain prior government authorization. Thus, *rest* in Addis Ababa acquired an absolute status as early as 1907 while the process took a much longer time for arable land.

Land Tenure from Liberation to Revolution

What did land tenure look like in the period 1941-74? What were its essential features?

The process of transfer of *maderiya* land to *rest* has already been discussed. The trend moved steadily upwards from the early 1940s onwards. The expansion of grants of government lands to individuals has also been noted. These two processes must be seen in conjunction with the extensive grants of land in the form of *rest* that had been carried out from the 1880s onwards. We also notice during 1941-74 increasing land transactions, particularly in coffee and tea-producing provinces. The general impression that we have is of a considerable number of sales, though we should note that no detailed study has been undertaken on this aspect of land accumulation. In any case, the sum total of these processes was the emergence of a big landed ruling class and its corollary, a sizeable tenant population.

No census of the landed class has been done. For this reason, one is forced to talk on the basis of impressions. For one thing, it is true that this class was big in terms of both number and wealth. For another, landlordism was a phenomenon of the southern, south-eastern and south-western provinces. In the north, it was found in southern Wello and Raya Azebo as well as in Shewa. This disparity needs to be explained.

My contention is that in the north as well the tenure system allowed and had landlordism in the past. The challenge is to explain why we do not have it in our era. I suggest that fragmentation explains its disappearance. Ownership of land large-scale and noble just as much as small-scale and peasant holdings, was subject to fragmentation. This was due to the inheritance system which did not have a law of primogeniture. Therefore, as time passes and new generations come forward, the *rest* lands of nobles would be divided and redivided and eventually become small-scale holdings.

To take one example of land grants given by Crummey (1983), Princess *Weyzero* Aster was given seven *gasha*s in one grant alone. It would be quite logical to assume that she owned many other *gasha*s as well. This was in the mid-Eighteenth Century. At that time, the land fund was limited and compounded by the fact that the State could not confiscate the land given as a *rest* (unless upon rebellion etc.). Moreover, the economy being more or less a non-monetary one, no large-scale and widespread land transactions, could be conducted. Even if the land sales that were discovered for Gondar and Gojam indicate transactions one should not conclude from this that it was easy to accumulate land. Thus, looked at from various angles, the descendants of Princess Aster had less and less land to share as time passed. If this was the case, one may wonder how the State could support the newly emerging nobility. One may hazard the hypothesis that it would give out only *gult*s to the governors and their retainers. Thus, by the Twentieth Century, we are left with only *gult* as the device of ruling class support and with the peasantry as owner-cultivators.

In the south, however, that process had just started. In fact as it unfolded, the market economy came into the picture and the very status of *rest* was changed and land became a commodity. With an increasing volume of money in the society, moneyed groups bought large portions of land and thus became landlords. In the 1960s there was a big scramble to buy coffee land in Kefa, Sidamo and Hararghe. The price of land accordingly went steadily up. This is a subject worthy of investigation in its own right. Suffice it to say that this process added a new variable into the equation.

All these factors led to the emergence of a big landlord class having land in certain areas of the country only. In general terms, this has been well known. The problem arises when we start looking for hard facts. The most widely-used data are those generated by the famous surveys of the Ministry of Land Reform towards the end of the 1960s and the early 70s. These surveys have been subjected to strong criticism and their data declared suspect and by no means reliable (Mesfin Wolde Mariam 1991). One of the major criticisms is that the data are not sufficiently reflective of reality and that the sample was not very representative. Moreover, the way the data were gathered has not been accepted as the best methodology.

Fully cognizant of these criticisms, I nevertheless feel that they are of considerable value if only as indicators of the general pattern. The reader must constantly keep in mind this cautionary remark. The researchers did not try to collect figures from landlords. They were rather more interested in the extent of tenancy for which they collected information by asking questions on holdings (rented or owned). Given the nature of our data, we can arrive at the extent of landlordism through the estimates on tenancy.

The percentage distribution of holdings by tenure of eight provinces in 1969 is shown in Table 4. Among the eight provinces given in the table, tenancy was prevalent in three of them (Keffa, Wellega and Shewa). If we take the data for the next year (1970) we see that Illubabor (63%) and Hararghe (49%) would also be added to this group. Arussi, Sidamo and Gemu-Gofa also had large numbers of tenants. These figures show that it was in the newly incorporated areas that landlordism was prevalent, and that in the northern provinces there was very little tenancy.

Table 4: Percentage of Holdings by Tenure (1969)

Province	Owned	Rented	Partly Owned Partly Rented	Total
Shewa	33	51	16	100
Arussi	48	45	7	100
Wellega	41	54	5	100
Gemu-Gofa	53	43	4	100
Wello	60	17	23	100
Sidamo	61	37	2	100
Tigre	75	7	18	100
Keffa	38	59	2	100

Source: MLR, Land Tenure Survey of Keffa Province, 1969, p45.

The estimates for the whole nation, excluding Eritrea and Bale, are shown in Table 5. We can see that nearly 7 million peasants (36%) were fully tenants and about 2 million (10%) were partially tenants.

These data must further be scrutinized. To begin with, the recent census has shown us that the population must have been much higher than these estimates suggest. Moreover, and much more importantly, the whole idea of tenancy was rather ambiguous. How many of the tenants were tenants of landlords and tenants of other peasants? This is a difficult question to answer and the above data hide this situation. An opinion can be hazarded that tenancy to peasants must have been considerable, which means that the percentages given would have to be lower when one talked of landlordism. When, for instance, we take the provinces which had no landlordism to talk of (Begemdir, Gojam, Tigre) the figure, though not overwhelming, is still high enough to caution us when the discussion focusses on landlordism. The introduction of new technology (mechanized agriculture) gave a new and ugly feature to landlordism and large-scale eviction. This was first observed on a big scale in the middle Awash Valley and in the Arsi region.

Table 5: Distribution of Tenants (late 1960s)

Province	Rural Population	Wholly Rental	Partly Owned Partly Rented	Total Rentals
Arussi	690,600	307,764	50,724	358,488
Begemder	1,087,200	97,848	62,232	160,080
Gemu Gofa	583,300	249,412	21,633	271,045
Gojam	1,344,500	172,785	95,024	267,809
Hararghe	1,435,570	703,429	71,778	775,207
Illubabor	515,375	376,224	10,307	386,531
Keffa	969,100	571,769	29,073	600,842
Shewa	3,585,000	1,828,350	573,600	2,401,950
Sidamo	1,987,590	735,408	39,751	775,159
Tigre	1,410,800	988,848	257,218	356,066
Wollega	1,064,100	574,738	49,715	624,453
Wollo	2,061,800	360,552	474,214	834,766
Totals	16,734,935	6,076,927	1,735,269	7,812,396
		36%	10%	46%

Source: Ministry of Land Reform Surveys.

Eviction has aroused a great deal of opposition and condemnation, mainly from radical intellectuals and students (both Ethiopian and foreign Ethiopicists), giving the impression that it was a major feature of the country. Yet, the data show the contrary. Dessalegn Rahmato has written a very interesting paper on mechanized agriculture in this period. He gives data on the location and size of farms (Dessalegn 1986:73). Of the four major areas he lists (Arsi, Rift Valley, Awash Valley and Humera), only one was located on the highlands where peasant agriculture was practised. The *rest* were found in nomadic areas.

Apart from Arsi, there were a few farms in Ada, Bale, Kefa, Harar, Wollega etc. The total farm area covered was 57,000 hectares, which was not a very impressive figure at the national level. Dessalegn also gives the estimated evicted tenant population for Arsi (1986:85):

> *The most serious criticism of rural capitalism was that it led to large scale evictions of peasants. The evidence for this comes mainly from Chilalo in Arsi province ... A study prepared for CADU later reports that the number of farm holdings in the awraja had been reduced by 6,500, or roughly by*

21,000 hectares due to evictions by mechanized agriculture. Another official study has estimated that if the rate of eviction seen in Chilalo had been repeated in other parts of the country, namely 3.5% per year, about 5% of the tenant population of the country, some 55,000 households... would have been driven off the land by the early 1980s.

Looked at from the perspective of the country as a whole these estimates of mechanized eviction are not very large. The kind of eviction that was dangerous to the tenant was rather the eviction because the landlord wanted it. Landlords had full powers to evict their tenants, though tradition very often militated against that practice. The fact remained, however, that the tenant was under a certain insecurity as a result of this, as fully recognized by critics and the government. Hence, the tenancy bills drafted were designed, *inter alia*, to define, regulate and restrict this power of the landlord and give security to tenants. These bills were rejected by Parliament, which indicated that there was an awareness of the problem even in government circles.

Insecurity was one of the main worries of the tenant. His greater worry was rent payment. Rents were paid in a number of ways, the most common being payment in kind and in services. Cash payment became more and more important though its rate of growth could not be estimated. Dessalegn compiled data on the various modes of rent payment prevalent in the 1960s and early 1970s from the surveys of the Ministry of Land Reform (Table 6).

Table 6: Mode of Rent Payment for Rental Holdings (late 1960s, %)

Province	In Kind	In Cash	Crop & Cash	Services
Shewa	78.0	15.0	3.0	4.0
Arussi	92.0	7.0	1.0	-
Wollega	36.8	48.6	11.9	2.7
Gemu Gofa	17.8	66.0	6.0	10.2
Wollo	84.2	8.5	6.0	1.3
Sidamo	12.3	84.6	3.1	-
Tigre	89.0	5.0	5.0	1.0
Keffa	31.2	63.9	4.9	-
Illubabor	25.1	65.8	19.1	-

Source: Dessalegn, 1970: 29.

The two forms of payment (kind and cash) were evenly distributed. In Shewa, Arsi, Wollo and Tigre, payment in kind was most predominant. In Gemu Gofa, Illubabor, Sidamo and Keffa cash payment was the principal form, while it was significant in Wollega. Normally a tenant would pay 50%

of the gross produce to the landlord. Since the law put the maximum at 75% the landlord might even charge higher than 50%. I still find it difficult to accept the verdict that the rent was about 75% of the gross produce (Dessalegn 1970:33) for the simple reason that this would not make economic sense to the tenant given the small size of his holdings and his primitive technology.

In addition to rent payment, the tenant had other obligations One of the most common was taking the landlord's grain either to his/her residence or to the market. The tenant was also obliged to give sundry labour services like building houses, fetching water, giving a hand during parties, etc. These were onerous obligations varying from place to place and from lord to lord.(For a detailed discussion of peasant experiences, especially tenant hardship, see the next chapter and the works of Dessalegn listed in the bibliography).

In much of the critique of rural Ethiopia, the blame for the poverty and backwardness of the rural world has been placed on the shoulders of landlordism. This is only partially correct, however, it constitutes just one side of the story. The obverse story is that the small size of holdings and increasing fragmentation of farms debilitated all peasants regardless of the status of their holdings From the available data it is difficult to trace increasing fragmentation from 1941 to 1974. But the estimates that we have for the end of the 1960s give a very gloomy picture. Gilkes summarizes the data as follows:

The Ethiopian small farmer, whether he is tenant or small freeholder, also suffers from the size and fragmentation of his holdings. In any analysis of the agricultural scene the small size of the holdings is immediately striking. 95 per cent [of all the holdings except in Eritrea and Bale] are three hectares or less. This probably gives an exaggerated picture for the calculations were based upon measured fields and would certainly involve underestimation of the unmeasured ones. The pattern however appears to agree with other sources. The Third Five-Year Plan made the point that 90 per cent of the peasant farmers had less than five hectares. On top of these small farms there is an enormous amount of fragmentation, and although the amount does vary from province to province, the majority of holdings are held in two, three or four parcels (Gilks 1975:120).

Looking at farm size without taking into account the peasant mode of production would not give us the full picture In the Ethiopian setting, agricultural technology had not yet reached the level of high productivity per unit of farmland. With the exception of the onset complex provinces, agriculture was space-intensive (Gill 1974:45-47). In other words, to produce more, greater farm size was required, all other factors remaining equal. Viewed from this angle, the above figures do give a dismal picture. When, however, the rate of population growth (2.5% to 3%) is included in the equation, one can see the resulting poverty and underdevelopment.

The northern provinces were fortunate in terms of tenancy. When it comes to the size of holdings, the picture looks grim (Table 7). What is striking is the fact that in the zero to 0.5 hectare bracket, the estimate for the large province of Begemdir and Simen was about 50% and for Tigray 45%; and when this is added to the second category (0.5-1) 69% and 68% respectively, one can see that the predominant proportion of the peasantry in the northern provinces were doomed to deepening poverty. Compared with tenancy, fragmentation seems to have been no less a pernicious feature of the rural scene. In fact, in the long run, it was an even more dangerous trend.

Table 7: Percentage of Operated Holdings by Size

Province	Percentages of Holdings			
Hectares	0 - 0.5	0 - 5.1	1 - 2	2 - 5
Tigre	45%	23%	21%	11%
Begemdir and Simen	49%	20%	22%	8%

Source: Markakis, 1974: 81.

It is therefore legitimate to point to fragmentation as a major problem of the agricultural sector. This conclusion strikes us with explosive power when we realize that, in terms of land productivity (or yield) Ethiopia's record was one of the lowest in the world. As one specialist put it: 'yields for most crops are very much lower in developing countries than elsewhere, and yields in Ethiopia ... are rather below the average for the developing world as a whole' (Gill 1974:46). Increasing land fragmentation due to increasing population growth therefore brought about the deepening of the poverty of the peasantry. This phenomenon also made the peasant vulnerable when natural catastrophes (drought being on top of the list, as well as others such as locust invasion) struck. This led in the end to a kind of chronic involution in the countryside, long after 'land to the tiller' (the putative panacea for many of the ills of the agricultural sector) was proclaimed and implemented (Dessalegn 1984). Radical as it was, the land reform proclamation, was not formulated with this process in mind; it should therefore not be surprising if it aggravated the problem rather than ameliorating it.

The land reform decree was designed to bring to an end landlordism and exploitation, regarded as being responsible for most of the ills and poverty of the countryside. This kind of perception overlooked or downplayed the fact that landlordism, just as peasant holdings, was based on fragmentation in most cases. Landlords very often had their lands scattered over large areas of the country a *gasha* or two in this district, a few in that one and a few others in still a third place and so forth. It was quite common to find *gashas* scattered in small parcels in several villages. Rarely did big landlords have their lands concentrated in one piece or estate in one district or *awraja* alone. Moreover, the *gashas* were further subdivided into small parcels and given out to as many as 20 or even more tenants per *gasha*. This assumption must be seen in the light of the population dynamics of the country. In half a decade or so, the same *gasha* would be parcelled out to 25 or more households. This could be done by the tenants themselves (the father sharing his plots with his sons) or with the knowledge and guidance of the landlord or his/her agent. One can confidently generalize that this was the picture of the provinces where large-scale landlordism obtained.

Assuming that this statement could serve as a valid generalization for the country as a whole (without forgetting to underline the need for detailed field investigation and collection of data), we can deduce the following conclusions about the structural weaknesses of landlordism in Ethiopia when viewed from the angle of development economics. First, fragmented landlordism makes it difficult, if not impossible, for the landlord to play the role of organizer of production. This was especially difficult for the big landlords who had their 'estates' spread out over several districts and even provinces. At the very least, fragmented landlordism made 'absenteeism' an inevitable feature of the system.

Secondly, given the prevalent agricultural technology in the framework of this kind of fragmented landlordism, it perfectly made economic sense to leave the task of production to individual peasants and free oneself for the task of searching for profitable ventures of investment in the towns. For instance, Ras Abebe Aregay used all his free time and quite a substantial portion of the time he should have been in his office as Minister of Interior in the 1950s to develop a whole neighbourhood in Abuare (a section in Addis Ababa) in what used to be Ras Mulugeta Sefer, where he built many villas. He supervised the construction of all the individual villas. Abebe was not the only dignitary to diligently pursue his investment in areas where he expected quick and high returns. The emperor himself, Ras Mesfen Sileshi, Ras Andargatchew Mesay, his spouse, Princess Tenagne Werk and many of the descendants of the Taytu and Zewditu clans, etc., did precisely the same.

Critics of absentee landowners of the time were at best being naive, and at worst silly, if they expected Ethiopian landlords to display extreme altruism. It would indeed have been altruistic for a big lord to live in the mud and dust of rural Ethiopia when he had within his easy reach all the glamour and luxury of the big cities. It was not only a simple desire to lead a good life that pushed all the big lords into the cities, particularly Addis Ababa, but also the pursuit of self-interest. A lord could promote his interests much better by living in the big cities than in far-off mountains, which had no infrastructure to speak of. In rationally pursuing his self-interests the big lord was just like any other social class in any society.

In much of the literature (whether radical or liberal) absentee landlordship was diagnosed as the worst feature of landlordism. The 'feudal lord' was ceaselessly blamed for not living with the peasants and organizing production. In my opinion, both the portrait and critique of absentee landlordship reflected a rather Eurocentric perception of a non-European reality.

Thirdly, it should be remembered that this kind of fragmentation made the task of collecting rent a cumbersome and wasteful process. It is a well-known fact that there was a whole group of intermediaries between the big landlord and the tenant. At the village level, there was the *mislene* responsible for all the land affairs, the most important of which was collection of grain, storage and other chores. Very often there would be a co-ordinator at the provincial level. These agents dealt with the household of the lord in Addis Ababa, or in the provincial capital, with transportation of the produce and its marketing. This was no easy task and it involved a lot of movement to and fro. The whole process would cost the big landlord quite a bit as it left considerable room for 'embezzlement' and opportunities for pilfering. Complaints about being 'fleeced' by one or another agent were often heard in the 1960s from the big lords and ladies. This phenomenon needs to be studied in its own right, but tentatively it can be suggested that the whole process would somewhat reduce the amount that would end up in the hands of the lord, which leads to the hypothesis that fragmented landlordism was not all that convenient to accumulation of capital.

Finally, the landlords (absentee or not) were invariably blamed for failure to invest in agriculture. This could have been dismissed as a rather superficial criticism were it not for its rather well-camouflaged Eurocentricism. In Europe, particularly in the epoch of the industrial revolution in Britain, landlords played a big role because they invested in their farms. It perfectly made sense for them to do so, as the urban economic activities were in the hands of a fast-rising bourgeois class and, even more important, it was economically expedient to invest in the agricultural sector (the inclosure movement for instance). Since then, European landlords have taken good care of their estates, which gave rise to the common assumption that a landlord was someone who invested in his estate where he resided as a matter of course. The assumption followed that Ethiopia was particularly archaic because the landlords did not invest in their estates. It seems to have occurred to nobody to raise the question of whether it really made economic sense for big landlords to plough their money into their fragmented holdings when they could channel it into sectors (real estate, manufacturing, services, import-export trade, etc.) that would bring them quicker and much higher returns.

This point is supported in a roundabout way when we see the attractions that mechanized farming came to have for the moneyed sectors of the population, including landlords, when it started to bring in considerable returns in a fairly short period. As can be seen in the next chapter, the landed class went into commercial agriculture in the late 1960s and 1970s. Nevertheless, as the author points out, the fact that 'among the landed classes the local gentry were by far the largest group' of investors is itself an indication that this sub-class had earlier been left behind in its investment in the urban areas which were now being crowded, therefore it made good economic sense to invest in commercial agriculture. This development demonstrates that even if landlords were ready to invest in agriculture, they did it in other areas of the economy which relegated this sector to the backwater.

To conclude, therefore, one among many of the structural deficiencies of landlordism in Ethiopia was the fact that the movement was itself too was shackled by fragmentation. Indeed, fragmentation coupled with population growth, natural disasters, an indifferent State, and the relentless forces of the market turned out to be a major nemesis of the peasant class, and also hampered the landlord class. To what extent were critiques and observers aware of this complicated nature of landlordism in the period?

Perceptions of the Land Question

Three broad schools of thought on the land question can be identified: the radical, liberal and conservative schools. These three lines of thought were not in themselves homogeneous and in fact different approaches can be detected within each one of them. The radical school argued for 'land to the tiller' as a solution to the land question. This group was spear-headed by radicals of the Ethiopian Student Movement (ESM), both inside the country and abroad. In the liberal school, there were various, rather ineffective, groups who advocated land reform of some kind in which private landownership would be recognized and some sort of ceiling imposed, while tenancy would be legally defined. The conservatives could further be subdivided into two those who recognized the need for some sort of reform to legally define and regulate tenancy and those who totally refused to accept the need for any change in the tenurial system.

Of these three groups, the most vociferous and successful were the radicals Because their programme 'land to the tiller' was more or less implemented by the Derg, and because a section of them took an active part in its design and implementation, the radicals left the deepest impact on the country and people. For this reason, this section focuses on them.

It is quite possible to link the genesis of the radical movement to the critical intellectual effervescence that made its appearance on the national scene from 1955 when the first post-war generation of university-trained young men came from abroad or graduated from Addis Ababa University College. Radicalism in the true sense of the word (struggling for sweeping, revolutionary social changes as opposed to introducing reforms) made its appearance in about 1963-64 in the then Haile Selassie I University when a clandestine Marxist-Leninist student group was formed. In a matter of a year (1964-65 academic year) they popularized their 'programme' for the agrarian sector so well that they were able to stage a big demonstration. 'Land to the tiller' was both a slogan and a programme for reform. From the 1965-66 academic year onwards, the programme gained increasing speed, rising to a crescendo in 1974. By this time, it had acquired the status of an article of faith among radical intellectuals and the educated youth so that even the liberal, reformist school could not seriously challenge it, let alone the conservatives.

What was the intellectual foundation of this 'land to the tiller'? How much knowledge of the land question of Ethiopia in general and of the tenurial structure in particular did its advocates have? These questions cannot be thoroughly answered in this chapter, which is confined to sketching out a general picture of the intellectual perception of the whole issue of land.

Not a lot of material has been produced by the radicals in the form of scientific articles, monographs and books based on empirical research. For the most part rhetorical pieces aimed at converting readers, rather than building up arguments on the basis of empirical data, were written.

Among the young radicals, Dessalegn, in an article entitled 'Conditions of the Ethiopian Peasantry' published in 1970, comes to grips with the whole issue of the agrarian question. Judging from the numerous references to it in many serious publications on modern Ethiopia and from my own observations, this was a leading and influential article. Rereading it two decades after its publication, I cannot but be impressed by its seriousness, high standard, theoretical framework and the wealth of information it contains. It does not have the marks of a student author but rather that of a serious and mature scholar. I will therefore concentrate on it as a reflective work of the highest level of radical thinking on the land question. This is even more justifiable by the fact that this seminal work was not followed up by other radical intellectuals. This was partly due to the fact that soon after its publication, although not connected with it, a serious rift transpired within the Ethiopian Student Movement to impact future developments. The issue of contention was what was called 'the national question' (i.e. the ethnic question) and the 'form of struggle'. The interests, attentions and energies of radical intellectuals were taken up by these issues, on which a great deal of literature was produced. It should also be noted that the land question was the least controversial of all the issues students grappled with. Dessalegn's writing was accepted by rival factions and groups.

Dessalegn obviously uses the Marxist paradigm and places Ethiopia within the feudal formation. He states that 'the structure of Ethiopian feudalism is, in many respects, almost identical with that of medieval Europe. The key figure in the system is of course the Ethiopian peasant' (Dessalegn 1970:28). Dessalegn and other radicals saw serfdom in peasant tenancy. Throughout his article, he simply equates tenancy with serfdom and uses the two terms alternatively.

Dessalegn devoted over nine pages to 'the economic subjugation of the peasant'. He mentions only in passing the other very serious problems of the rural world (such as small size of holdings and fragmentation). The neglect of these burning issues is in a way understandable because the Ethiopian peasant was indeed, or he perceived him as a serf.

Dessalegn looked at the class structure. 'Rural Ethiopia is composed of three major classes: a) the aristocracy, or large land owners, b) what, for lack of a better term, I shall call the petty or local gentry, and c) the peasantry'. While the first two were propertied, the latter class was 'propertyless' and 'authority-less'.

How could the miserable conditions of the peasants be changed? Dessalegn's ideas were shared by his fellow travellers (1970:48-49):

How can the peasant change his conditions? Will it be through better laws, clearer definitions of tenancy rights, or improved land registration and cadastral surveys? Can it be done by granting ownership rights to tenants over government-owned land? Or will land reform, but of a kind which does not disturb the equilibrium of the feudal system, provide the antidote?

The peasant problem is too fundamental to be resolved with such facile measures. It is not the deficiencies of the system that create rural misery, but the system itself. Peasant servitude and deprivation will not be eliminated so long as the land-less are under the economic subjection of the landlord. Only when the direct producers toil for no other but themselves will they be able to attain emancipation, and to raise their standard of living to a level consistent with human dignity. In this connection, the slogan LAND TO THE TILLER [in the original] is indeed subversive.

Serfdom that fundamental relationship that binds the producer to the appropriator of the produce must be destroyed in order to liberate the serf. Ultimately, this act of liberation will have to be performed by the serf himself.

It would have been much better if Dessalegn had commented on what exactly he meant by 'land to the tiller'. Other publications do not attempt to clarify the slogan either. We are therefore left with no means of gauging the depth of radical understanding of the issue. It can be said that most of them did not bother to think about it. They rather took it for granted that it would be implemented in a socialist setting.

It was with these remarks that Dessalegn concluded his essay. Underlying his thought is the belief that, with the landlords gone, many of the problems of the countryside would go. None of the prominent radicals followed up the work that Dessalegn so well pioneered. This does not mean that they did not write on this issue. On the contrary, much was produced, but it was propaganda rather than serious work. Resolutions of student congresses both in the country and abroad always contained a section on land which was described as a 'burning question'. In student speeches (for instance, during elections for offices in student organizations) the land question was invariably included because the student had to express his/her 'stand on the land question'.

The radicals' approach was dominated by a crudely understood Marxist paradigm which concentrated on the evils associated with exploitation to the exclusion of all other features of the system. The belief that removal of the exploitation was a panacea that would open the way for a glorious future informed the entire literature. Abolition of landlordism and the restoration of land to the tiller were envisaged within the general scenario of a communist revolution.

In this connection, Dessalegn's paper published in 1986 a decade and a half later entitled 'Moral Crusaders and Incipient Capitalists: Mechanized Agriculture and Its Critics in Ethiopia', is interesting to note. In this paper he castigates the Marxist writers of the early 1970s who condemned mechanized agriculture on the grounds that it led to large-scale eviction and displacement of peasants as well as alienation of their land:

We believe however that the criticism of mechanized agriculture in this case was at bottom a moral one, for under the existing conditions in rural Ethiopia the modernization and technological advancement of agriculture could not have taken place without evictions and peasant displacement. It is the government's indifference to rural unemployment, and its inability to provide alternative sources of income that should have been criticized. This is not an endorsement of the injustice done to the peasantry by the landed classes, but a recognition of reality, however unsavoury it may appear (1986:85-6).

He tried to explain the moral basis of the Marxist condemnations of incipient rural capitalism:

It is curious but true that commercial agriculture aroused a feeling of hostility or suspicion among many observers right from its very inception, and we believe the underlying basis of antipathy was a moral one. The idea of the brutal machine threatening the lives of thousands of destitute peasants ... could not fail to arouse deep moral outrage, which led eventually to the rejection in whole or in part of modernization as a means of rural development (1986:69).

Dessalegn is absolutely right in his views. But he arrived at this conclusion after years of research and reflection on the peasantry. History was not so generous to his youthful fellow travellers of the 1970s who were overtaken by events in which many of them either lost their lives or languished for years in prison. Hence, 'land to the tiller' was decreed and implemented long before its radical authors matured and reflected on it much more deeply than they did in their youthful days.

Apart from and in addition to exploitation, ethnic domination made the land question a central issue. In the newly incorporated provinces, the landlords were predominantly 'Shewan Amhara' who exhibited extreme chauvinism. The aristocracy, drawn mainly from the Shewa region, owned extensive areas of land in these provinces. The people were therefore subjected to double injustice economic exploitation and ethnic domination. 'Land to the tiller', by getting rid of the landlord and giving it back to its original owner, was designed to destroy the very basis of this ethnic domination.

One of the attractions of Marxism-Leninism was its promise to resolve the problem of ethnic domination. Stalin's tract on the national question, treated with reverence, announced with the panache of a religious work, that the 'national question' would be resolved once and for all and in the best of ways if its doctrines were accepted and implemented. The programme of 'land to the tiller' fitted perfectly into this doctrine as it was seen as one of the expressions of 'self-determination by nation/nationalities'.

'Land to the tiller' was therefore an integral element of a much more complex programme for restructuring State and society. Giving land to the peasantry was just the first step. Following that, it would be organized into co-operatives which would then develop into collectives. Collectives would transform the peasant into a worker and complete the agricultural revolution. Radicals were not overly concerned with the other problems of agriculture (fragmentation, primitive technology, etc.) because they would be taken care of in the course of the revolution. As the ideology was so confident about this, and also because it was believed that it had already been successfully implemented (Soviet Union under Stalin, China, Korea), radicals took the programme as an article of faith.

The liberal group, on the other hand, lacked dry, clearly-defined programmes. For instance, in 1970, a major conference was organized by the Ministry of Land Reform and Administration in Addis Ababa during which over 35 papers were read. With the exception of the radicals (Eshetu Chole) who more or less knew what they wanted, most of the other papers took up agrarian reform as a topic but did not propose recommendations or tentative solutions to the problem. At the end of the session, the conference recommended that something be done about landlord-tenant relations:

It was observed that the problems of agricultural tenancy are so acute that a remedy must be provided promptly. In this connection, it was indicated that a large proportion of the farming population works and lives on the land of landlords paying high rents and receiving low yields. Similarly it was pointed out that tenants under existing landlord-tenant agreements have no security of tenure (MLRA Seminar 1970:480).

The remedy the conference recommended was legislation and the creation of various agencies to implement it.

Tenancy was not the only problem but the first among many in the perception of the liberals. Cadastral surveys, registration of land, settlement of peasants on new or government land, systematization and reform of agricultural taxation were singled out as possible areas of reform. Expansion of extension services, infrastructure and education were always raised. The problem of ceiling of ownership was mentioned but never discussed seriously.

The foreigners in this group came up with specific recommendations although these were never implemented by the government. Two experts, H.S. Mann and J.D.C. Lawrence, sent by FAO for this purpose, must be singled out. They carried out a good number of field surveys and submitted recommendations for land reform, tenancy reform, reforms in what they called 'communal land tenure' and in the system of taxation. In order to implement these reforms, they proposed that a specialized government agency be set up. Not much came out of the liberal recommendations, except perhaps a faster establishment of the Ministry of Land Reform in 1966.

The conservatives fell into two sub-groups: those who believed in some sort of reform and those who did not. The Emperor and Aklilu Habte Wold, the Prime Minister, clearly belonged to the former group. In a speech he delivered before the Parliament and the nation at large on 2 November 1961, on the occasion of the anniversary of his coronation, the Emperor stated that:

The fundamental obstacle to the realization of the full measures of Ethiopia's agricultural potential has been simply stated: lack of security in the land. The fruits of the farmer's labour must be enjoyed by him whose toil has produced the crop. The essence of land reform, while fully respecting the principle of private ownership, is that landless people must have the opportunity to possess their own land, that the position of tenant farmers must be improved, and that the system of taxation applying to land holdings must be the same for all (Bezuwork 1992).

The quotation speaks for itself. Only one elaboration is called for. When the Emperor proposed that 'landless people must have the opportunity to posses their own land' he meant three things. First, the government must give out in the form of *rest* the land it held as *ye-mengest maret*. Secondly, the term 'landless people' did not necessarily mean landless peasants but all those, including high officials and members of the clergy, who did not own land. There is conclusive evidence that no less a person than Aklilu Habte Wold was given land to the tune of nine *gashas* in Arsi province because he was 'landless' (Bezuwork 1992). Many other high-ranking officials were granted land in large proportions. Thirdly, the Emperor was also suggesting that the government would encourage the opening up of unoccupied land.

Prime Minister Aklilu Habte Wold also emphasized the need for land reform in a speech delivered on 11 April 1966 on the occasion of the establishment of the Ministry of Land Reform:

To give greater emphasis to land reform, the Land Reform Agency, created several months ago, pursuant to the recommendation of the land reform committee, has been transformed into a Ministry. The Minister of Land Reform, seated in the Council of Ministers, will present and debate his proposal at the highest executive level of the Government. The increased status thus given to the body charged with the preparation and implementation of programmes in this field is only a proper recognition of the high priority attached to this fundamental reform (Bezuwork 1992).

In line with this position, both the Emperor and the Prime Minister took measures to bring about 'land reform'. Yet, their commitment to change was rather half-hearted. Hence, they did not stand up against the other wing of the conservative class which did not want to see any change in the tenurial structure. This was clearly demonstrated in both houses of Parliament (the Senate and the Chamber of Deputies) when three tenancy bills tabled in 1963, 1970 and 1972 were rejected (for a detailed discussion of these bills see Bezuwork, 1992). These bills were highly watered-down laws designed to legalize, more than anything else, the relationship between the tenant and landlord.

Liberal reformists within the government were frustrated, for example Ato Belay Abay, the Minister of Land Reform, who was eventually dismissed. Their apprehension of the dangers of failure to institute reform was perceived as doom forecasting.

Was landlordism all evil? Or, put in a different way, did landlordism have any positive effects? It is curious that this very important question was not raised as an issue for debate even by economists because capitalist industrialization was achieved through the help of landlords.

There are certain interesting indicators that show that the answer to this question was yes. The manufacturing sector grew at an impressive speed in the 1960s. There were two groups of investors the expatriate community (Greeks, Armenians etc.) and the landed class, particularly the aristocracy. The Emperor, Princess Tenagne Werk, Ras Mesfin Sileshi (to mention only a few) were among the major investors. One can argue that the aristocracy got some of its funds from the agricultural sector.

The 1960s also witnessed an impressive expansion of urban centres. Addis Ababa took on its modern appearance (high-rise buildings, double lane avenues, four-star hotels, etc.) mainly in this decade. Again, we see the landed class being active in this expansion. Much of the investment in real estate and small house construction was by this class. *Ras* Mesfin and *Ato* Gebre Weld Eengda Werk could be cited as typical cases. Again, one can argue that the capital for this extensive investment came partly from agriculture through the agency of this same class.

The landed class was ceaselessly faulted for conspicuous consumption, resource wastage and so forth. This criticism was, on the whole, correct. Unfortunately, however, this led to the other extreme of totally denying the fact that it ploughed back at least part of the surplus in its hands into the economy.

The landed class was also viewed by most foreign observers, ranging in political persuasion from the extreme left to the extreme right, as archaic. By labelling it 'feudal' the Ethiopian left used a loaded expression that signified not only outdated modes of exploitation but also an archaic and extremely backward class that had not changed for ages. This widely-held perception of this class unfortunately led to the blurring of a very interesting process of transformation that went on right under the eyes of otherwise perceptive observers.

The landed class, at any rate the top cream, found itself in an unprecedented position in the 1920s. The country was being opened up faster than ever. An increasing number of expatriate (Indian, European and Arab) merchants started coming into the country bringing with them an endless number of consumer goods never seen before. The Bank of Abyssinia opened in 1905 and was slowly beginning to have an effect. The only railway line in the country reached Addis Ababa in 1916 bringing with it not only a vast opportunity of easy travel from Ethiopia abroad but also facilitated a flow of goods in unheard-of quantities.

The country was coming into contact with the outside world and this offered both challenges and opportunities. The focus in the historical literature so far has been on the challenges this opening-up brought in its wake. But the opportunities are of equal importance and, in terms of consequences, perhaps of greater significance than the challenges. Many members of the ruling elite travelled abroad, including women. Menen, with a large entourage of women, went as far as Jerusalem, visiting Egypt along the way. Aristocratic ladies like Princess Yeshash-Werk and even her mother, the rather old Weyzero Aselefech, Princess Tenagne Werk, Weyzero Aster, and several others travelled to Europe and not only visited but also shopped in Paris and London before 1935! In the decade and a half before the Italian invasion of 1935 the top ruling class was considerably transformed in its way of living as well as in its mentality (i.e. its attitudes, values and norms).

To this scenario one should add the Italian invasion and subsequent occupation which, if anything, further accelerated the ruling classes transmutation. Moreover, the introduction of new technology (for example, new modes of transportation) further deepened the process. Take as an example the automobile. A major by-product of this machine was that it made redundant the large number of retainers that lords maintained.(Remember that this retainer force could be automatically transformed into a military force should the need arise). By the 1950s, not only was travelling on mule back considered by a large group of retainers as a thing of the past; it was also a subject of ridicule by the other lords and ladies who by then had already become extremely conscious of being 'civilized' i.e. westernized.

The automobile was not the only novelty that led to the disappearance of the retainer class. Changes in the State structure meant there was no longer any need for lords and ladies to render military and other services to the State. On top of this, it now became increasingly expensive to maintain a large retainer force which not only had to be fed and supported but also armed. The story of Ras Demissew Nesibu who went into heavy debt in order to arm his large number of followers and feed them as far back as 1910 is well known. It is for this reason that competition among the lords of Menelik to outnumber each other in the number of their retainers and in the quality of firearms with which they were equipped was not followed up by their sons and daughters at the time of Haile Selassie. The competition was now in the quality of the limousine one owned, in the size of one's mansion, in the extent of one's wealth in terms of real estate or enterprises and in the domain of where one spent one's 'vacation', so to speak (in France, or Italy or inside the country in one or another of the newly emerging resorts of Ambo, Debre Zeit, Langano or Wendo Genet). What we see now is the slow rise of conflicts over land between the children of the one-time retainers of the lords of Menelik and the latter's descendants. The latter-day lords tended to claim as theirs the lands given out by their fathers to retainers.

The lords of the post-1941 era were more than glad to be rid of a large retainer force. That the idea of having a large number of followers as a status symbol had become old-fashioned by the 1950s is a reflection of the socio-economic realities and of the changed mentalities of the era. These changes were enthusiastically adopted by the class itself, which makes us wonder from where the scholars got their notions of Haile Selassie 'disarming the nobility', of 'the decline of the nobility' and of the 'nobility's opposition to these trends' about which they talked with so much confidence dressed up in attractive Marxist or liberal theories. Other questions still need to be seriously looked into. To take just one example: none of the *rases* and *dejazmatches* and other highly titled lords really needed their tenants to come and work for them (build their fences, grind their grains, cut wood for them and serve them in other ways) as the *gebbars* used to do for the lords of earlier eras. It is true that these labour exactions were practised by the small rural-based landlords but to say that the big lords required them is simply nonsense. The latter did not even want to see the *gebbars*, let alone demand their services, for which the peasants no longer had the requisite expertise. They would only soil the well-trimmed compound and the beautiful villas. Yet these chores are still routinely listed in the literature (even in works by otherwise respectable scholars) without any qualification whatsoever!

By the 1950s, we have a much transformed landed ruling class (at least the higher segment of it) living in Addis Ababa and the other big provincial cities in big modern villas furnished with European furniture. For the first time in the country's history, lords started to live separately from even their erstwhile urbanized followers, a phenomenon new to the country. In the past, rulers lived with their people, in the sense that they were surrounded by their retainers ranging from their highest retainer (who could be a lord in his own right) to their lowliest servant. Thus, Addis Ababa acquired a peculiar feature among major African colonial cities in that the residences of the rulers were surrounded with the shanties of their followers which frequently had their share of prostitutes, criminal elements, beggars, idlers and the like, whereas colonial cities were neatly divided into the native quarter and the European quarter, with their own distinctive characteristics.

This feature, nevertheless, slowly started to change from the 1950s, the period under consideration. The descendants of the lords started migrating to the Old Airport neighbourhoods as early as the 1950s, and later to the Bole neighbourhoods. Some moved out (like Ras Mesfin, Ras Andargachew, Ras Abebe Aregay) into the north-western suburbs of the city (Gulele) where they walled themselves off in spacious villas from their surrounding lower-class neighbours. The descendants of Afa-Negus Nesibu, for example, one of the senior lords of the Menelik era, turned the area around his old mansion into a villa-studded neighbourhood, somehow managing to push further down into the valley the descendants of the retainers of the old grandee. By coincidence, the emperor also relocated in 1961 into the Jubilee Palace, which had been built rather away from the servant quarters that used to constitute an intrinsic part of the *gebbi* of the past. Thus, from the 1950s, the ruling class was truly cut off from the lower orders of the society (including the peasantry) spatially, physically and culturally. The retainer class, which had been an intermediate social force in the pre-Twentieth Century Ethiopian socio-political system, and a continuum (without break, it should be underlined) between the top members and the lowliest subjects of the society, gradually ceased to exist, killed by the very class for which it must have been created.

This process of metamorphosis also involved a change in the structure of the ruling class societal functions, one of which was to serve as an instrument of (at least partial) redistribution of social wealth. There used to be innumerable ways of channelling a considerable proportion of the wealth collected from the labouring classes back into the society in the socio-political system of pre-Twentieth Century Ethiopia. The most frequently cited was the large, perennial banquets (*geber*) that were thrown by the lords to their retainers and to their subjects. There were other even more institutionalized forms, the most significant of which was supporting a large number of people in the form of regular rations of grains or butter. In this system, the biggest redistributors were the king and the queen themselves.

This role was gradually abandoned. The focus now was on accumulating wealth for themselves and themselves alone. Along with this change in their societal role, coupled with the enormous opportunities for self-indulgence that western capitalism made available to them, and to which they subscribed with passionate enthusiasm, they developed an attitude of indifference, even contempt, to the conditions of their compatriots and a sense of irresponsibility in their duties to their country. The massive tragedies of famine that afflicted their countrymen, not to mention the other chronic problems of Ethiopia, did not generate passionate responses among them.

No wonder that the ruling class were widely viewed as greedy by the common people from the 1950s to the 1970s. The execution of the top officials and dignitaries of Haile-Selassie's court by the Neway brothers at the end of their abortive coup, in December 1960 was understood by the ordinary folk, as far as I could establish, not in terms of corruption but in terms of their greediness. A widely circulating story about the refusal of the famous Debre Libanos monastery to accept the body of Ras Abebe Aregay for burial was told and retold in the days soon after the abortive coup, explaining the refusal by the sins he had allegedly committed, which had in turn mainly emanated from his greediness. Greed was a charge that the Derg also successfully levelled against the ruling class, successful in the sense that it was widely accepted.

Thus, for the big landed class, the new times threw up an insatiable need for cash more than ever. And it was required immediately and in large quantities. The question of how the class satisfied this hunger for money has never been seriously asked before in the literature. And yet it is an important question that gives insight into many aspects of the nature of Ethiopian transformation in the first three quarters of this century.

There is no reason why we should deny the Ethiopian ruling class the rationality that economists have given to homo oeconomicus What economic opportunities did they have and did they make a rational choice from among them? These questions should guide us. Indeed, the big lords and ladies found out very early that investing in what we call real estate, i.e. building houses for renting, was one of the best mechanisms of acquiring quick money and a lot of it too (by the standards of the time). With the opening in Addis Ababa of the headquarters of the Economic Commission for Africa (1958), the Organization of African Unity (1963), and the numerous embassies all through the 1950s and the early 1960s as well as the flow into the country of Americans and West Europeans as peace corps, expert missionaries, agents of one or another enterprise, the market for modern houses, particularly villas could not be any better. So they built them in large numbers (it should be noted, though, that by the late 1960s, the market showed signs of glut). They had also discovered even before the Italian invasion that investing in the modern sector (like in import-export trade and in the manufacturing sector) was another way of acquiring new wealth.

For the ruling class, the agricultural sector was the last place for investment for the simple reason that it paid off slowly, not to mention the fact that it required a great deal of prior investment in infrastructure. The exceptions prove the case. For example, Ras Mesfin ploughed much of his money into real estate and into the modern enterprises. But when it paid he did not hesitate from putting his money into agriculture he built a relatively large vine farm in Guder, about 150 km from Addis Ababa. The Emperor also set up a farm in Yerer in Harar and in Ada near Debre Zeit. The case of haricot beans demonstrates dramatically that if investment in agriculture paid off and quickly, then lords as well as other moneyed groups were ready to rush in.

Thus, the landed class, especially its top segment, was far from the other classes not only in its very visible way of life, in appearance, its mentalities and its tastes, but also in the nature of its relationships with other social groups as well as in the character of its role in the society and, last but by no means least, in its absolutely new sources of wealth.

Yet social-scientific analysis has always presented the ruling class as if it dropped out of the Nineteenth or earlier Century like a *deus ex machina* into the second half of the Twentieth Century. Indeed, the views of the radical and even liberal critics lack historical depth, partly as a result of their own weaknesses but also, and even more significantly, a reflection of the underdevelopment of Ethiopian studies. Ethiopian studies had yet to take up the theme of Ethiopia's Westernization, a process that had started in earnest by about the third decade of this century and one that still continues to roll.

This process of westernization involved a profound overhauling of cultural values and norms, as well as metamorphoses, mutations and transmutations of social and political structures and not just mere introduction of technologies. For example, the sociological concepts we work with, like 'feudal lord', were fashioned out of European material. Hence, they do not signify the fact that we are dealing here with social groups that are either so profoundly metamorphosed or are in the process of being so completely transmuted or are already new mutants out of earlier social groups as to be unrecognizable. The process is further complicated by the fact that Westernization had not been a smooth process; rather, it had been a painful one that generated more than its due share of social conflicts, convulsions, upheavals and revolutions. For this reason, the process requires rethinking of the many assumptions taken over from Eurocentric approaches, as well as fresh conceptualizations and theories. In short, Ethiopian studies must develop its own sociology of Westernization in order to come to grips with its subject matter.

Nomadic Lands

In much of the literature on the land question, the issue of nomadic lands has been curiously overlooked, or has not been given as much attention as it deserves. Yet, as a study report prepared in 1983 put it:

The Ethiopian nomads inhabit the low-lying areas generally below 1500 m elevation which often correspond to the rangelands receiving an average rainfall of below 700 mm. The area that they utilize is around

769,000 km^2 which is about 61% of the total area of the country (UNDP/RRC 1983: 3).

Nomads as a whole occupy by far the larger size of the country's territory. All the major rivers pass through nomadic lands where they actually become accessible for settlement, irrigation farming and large-scale fishing. Two of the country's major natural parks are located in these areas. There is, therefore, no doubt that nomadic lands are very important, especially for the future of the country. Any study of the land question would not be complete without including the vast nomadic lands.

A discussion of land tenure in nomadic areas can be properly understood when placed within the context of nomadism. The UNDP/RRC study report, already cited, defines nomadism as:

The way of life of a community of people for whom constant mobility is an integral part of making a livelihood in areas where there are not enough resources to stay in one place. Nomadism in its classical sense i.e. continuous mobility with total dependence on hunting gathering does not exist anywhere today. Nomads now keep different kinds of domestic livestock and are acquiring and using items such as grain, craft and manufactured goods through symbiosis and trade with sedentary agricultural people and city dwellers. Their mobility has also been reduced because of various interventions affecting the size of their territory. Hence, today, nomadism is viewed as a continuum that can take any combination of economic possibilities falling between agricultural life with no movement at one extreme to pure nomadism having no need for or use of agricultural products at the other (UNDP/RRC 1983:3).

We can deduce a number of conclusions from this definition. First, nomadism was a good adaptation to the dictates of the environment until modern technology outdated it and made it archaic. Secondly, nomadic areas should not be seen in isolation from the adjacent highlands because their respective peoples have adopted a meaningful and ecologically dictated division of labour. The lowlanders depend for all kinds of agricultural produce on the highlanders and vice versa.

The nomads in Ethiopia do not have homogeneity. They can be divided into two groups: pastoral nomads and nomadic hunter-cultivators. The pastoral nomads are by far the greater of the two in number and occupy much larger territory. They are found in the Eritrean lowlands, in much of the Rift, in the Ogaden, in the river basins of the lower Omo and lower Baro as well as in the lowlands of Asosa, western Gojam and western Gondar. Various authorities have estimated their population at about 1.4 million (UNDP/RRC, Part III, 1984:6). Pastoral nomadism can be defined as:

A type of livelihood which is based on a livestock production system that is ecologically adjusted within a given level of technology to the utilization of the marginal land resources of the area and semi-arid regions of the country that are not suitable for rain-fed agriculture (UNDP/RRC 1983:6).

In this definition, two elements livestock and land are the key or most critical factors in pastoral nomadism. Forage and water are spotty and seasonal in this region, which requires a wider space to move around. This factor also explains why the river basins (Shebele, Genale, Awash etc.) become so valuable for pastoral nomadism.

The nomadic hunter-cultivators are much fewer in number than the pastoralists. Bender offers the estimate in the region of 189,600 to 200,100 not at all an impressive figure (UNDP/RRC, Part III, 1984:6). They are found in two areas lower Omo Basin and lower Abay Basin. From the basin of the lower Abay extending up to Quara in the north are found the Gumuz, who are the only hunter-cultivators in that region, while in lower Omo are found the Tirma, Chai, Bale, Me'en and Kwegen ethnic groups. They live by hunting, gathering and a slash-and-burn system of cultivation (UNDP/RRC 1983:3-4).

What kind of land tenure do all these pastoralists and hunter-cultivators practise? A general answer could be given to this question if detailed local studies were made. There are studies on one or another of these groups, as part of larger ethnographic research by anthropologists, particularly for the people of the lower Omo Basin, but the data are not complete over the whole range of nomadic areas. Generalizations, such as the one below, made by the UNDP/RRC research group, nevertheless abound in the literature:

There is a communal system of landownership among the nomads. But the limits of territoriality, usufructuary right and level of organization of the ownership vary. Each social unit, which is also the unit of production, has territorial delimitation. Other similar units may have access to grazing rights on reciprocal principle or are excluded from such rights (UNDP/RRC 1983:10).

This quotation, though one of the common ones, does not say much. For instance, what is the strength of a 'social unit' in terms of households? What exactly does 'communal' mean? Does it refer to a clan or a small fraction of a clan consisting of closely inter-related families? Is there any inheritance system? How about exchange (like sales, gifts, barter) of land? Above all, do chiefs, especially the more powerful ones (e.g., 'sultans') have privileged access to land? The above definition by no means gives a clue to all these questions. It is curious but true that as yet we do not have a standard synthesis on this theme.

This is all the more striking because land tenure is at least as important (if not more) to nomadic peoples as it was to a highland society. After all, it has been one of the key causes of the interminable feuds and conflicts between sub-clans, clans and tribes which characterize all pastoralist societies. Whenever attempts are made to explain these interminable conflicts in the literature, competition for pastureland and water is invariably offered as the decisive factor. Or the rather general statement competition for and conflict over resources is given as the cause. These interpretations, though correct in themselves, nevertheless hide the important fact that all these conflicts have been conflicts over ownership or, to put it another way, control of the land where these resources are found. So the land tenure system cannot but be regarded as a key element in the nomadic political and social system just as much as, say, in a feudal political system.

This fact was proved in a dramatic way with the expansion of mechanized agriculture in the Awash Valley in the late 1960s. By the close of the decade about 33,870 ha. were under modern cultivation in that part of the valley inhabited by the Afars (calculated from Dessalegn, 1986:76). This is by no means a small figure when it is realized that this is choice land found on the banks of the river. The question of the fate of the original inhabitants and owners of these lands inevitably arises. Dessalegn states that 'more than half the available land in the lower Valley was considered the property of the Awssa fiefdom, the Sultan of which had long exercised *de facto* jurisdiction over all land within what he believed was his jurisdiction' (Dessalegn 1986:77). Dessalegn compiled an inventory of the modern farms controlled by Ali Mirra, the Sultan at the time (Table 8).

Table 8: Cultivated Land Controlled by Ali Mirra

Type of Holding	Area in Hectares	% of Total
Land for sultan's private use	4,085	21.2
Land used by sultan's tenants	10,720	55.5
Land used by sultan's relatives, agents, etc.	1,150	6.0
Land used by small Afar farmers and obtained through sultan	2,550	13.2
Berga Estate (mechanized, non-Afar)	800	4.1
Total	19,305	100

Source: Dessalegn, 1986:77.

Even if, with considerable caution, we can use the term 'Ali Mira's fiefdom' for Awsa, the fact remains that he was a chief in a much bigger political system headed by a monarch who had considerable authority over him. If he had confiscated all these lands from its rightful owners, they indeed had the option of petitioning the emperor, as so many people used to do, or of rebellion. I have not come across any evidence to demonstrate that either of these two courses of action happened. The possibility that he had confiscated all this land from the clans who had supposedly owned it 'communally', either by fraud or by force, should therefore be received with considerable scepticism. This point reinforces all the more the validity of a previous issue i.e. that the structure of nomadic land tenure and its transformation through time is a subject worthy of investigation. Through what process of transition did Awsa arrive at a stage where 'more than half the available land' became 'property of the Awsa fiefdom'? We leave this question to a future researcher with a note that only when it is taken up, not only for Awsa but also for the whole of the nomadic areas, can a truly comprehensive and synthesized account of the history of land tenure in Ethiopia be written.

Conclusion

The land question requires a much more extensive treatment than it is given here. But this treatment must be framed out of a fresh perspective and should try to avoid the straightjacket that the prevalent *rest/gult* paradigm offers. I have tried to submit an alternative approach by proposing another organizing concept *serit*.

It is my contention that if we organize our studies on the basis of *serit*, we can trace an evolution in the form of *rest* ownership as well as sketch out the dynamics and mechanics of the political system.

With the changes in the political economy of the country the *serit* system was gradually abolished. The land tenure structure of the post-liberation era was therefore the result of a long process of evolution. It was seen as an archaic system and opposition against it gradually acquired support in the early 1960s, picked up momentum in the late 1960s and early 1970s, and arrived at a crescendo in 1974. The land question was consequently regarded as one of the major causes of the revolution. But how correct is this widespread perception? There is clearly a need for rethinking.

The imperial regime did not face serious peasant opposition. There were peasant revolts, or revolts in which peasants took a leading role, like the Weyane revolt of 1941-43 and the rebellions in Yeju (1948), Bale (1963-70), Gedeo (1960) and Gojam (1968). But the government was able to suppress them without much trouble, with the exception, perhaps, of the Weyane and Bale rebellions. Be that as it may, the countryside was quiescent, particularly in the years immediately before 1974. Even during the turbulent early months of the revolution, the peasantry was law-abiding.

It was in the urban centres that the storm had been brewing for several years, to finally explode in the face of the Emperor in the fateful month of February. In the words of J. McCann[6] a leading scholar in the historical studies of Ethiopian peasants:

> Though rural imagery 'land to the tiller' and the 1972-74 famine dominates much of the literature on the 1974 revolution, that upheaval was fundamentally an urban phenomenon. The unrest which brought Haile Selassie's government down was the cumulative disaffection of teachers, taxi drivers, bus drivers, high school students, and ultimately, young military officers. The rural metaphor 'land to the tiller' championed by university students disguised the wide, more entrenched urban class interests involved in the revolution.

McCann is right in the sense that the land question did disguise urban interests which brought about the revolution. On the other hand, we should not overlook the fact that the high degree of popularization of 'land to the tiller' also led to the dominant (though flawed) perception among so-called 'petty bourgeois' circles (junior army officers, professionals, teachers etc.) that the landed class, particularly the aristocracy, were responsible for all the problems of the country, and that their removal was a sine qua non. If 'land to the tiller' did not cause the revolution, at least it helped to shape subsequent events.

When the Derg stole the idea from the radicals and decreed the agrarian reform and 'land to the tiller', it was primarily to hit at the aristocracy. Ideas in history have their own curious ways of impacting society and 'land to the tiller' is no exception.

Notes

1. This brief review does not cover the publications before the turn of 1960. Earlier studies such as those by Conti Rossini (1909-10, 1916), I Guidi (1906), M. de Coppet (1930, 1931) are not reviewed because their basic assumptions and interpretations are incorporated into the works published after 1960 onwards.
2. Readers interested in the meanings of the many Ethiopian terms used in land tenure may refer to the solid works of Mantel-Niecko (1970) and Berhanu Abebe (1971) who have compiled and defined, with the help of Ethiopian authorities, a big set of lexicons used in land documents. The reader should nonetheless be aware that the majority of the terms were drawn from Shewa, followed by Wello and Yejju. They were not necessarily used in the other northern provinces; and when they were used, they could possibly have a different meaning.

3. I have left out Hamasen, Seraye and Akele Guzai because academic orthodoxy assumes that, in these *awrajas*, land tenure was communal on the whole. The data collected by scholars and observers such as Perini, Conti Rossini and Nadel provided the evidence for this theory which has given it the aura of absolute truth. But the student will have to be sceptical of this orthodoxy on two counts. First a perceptive observer of Eritrean society in the 1940s has come up with a very intriguing hypothesis regarding the genesis of 'communal' ownership of land:

There is, however, a strange contrast between the forms of evolution obtaining in English and plateau [Hamasen etc.] land tenure concepts for, whereas in England society had developed individualism at the expense of its early collectivist organization, the plateau communities moved from the individual principle towards collectivism (Trevaskis Papers: 11).

Trevaskis argues at some length how the village communities in highland Eritrea 'approached collective land tenure', an earlier individual ownership (pp. 11 ff.). This is an approach worth investigating in greater depth.

Secondly, the whole notion of 'communal' ownership of land has been abandoned on the basis of solid evidence for other African societies with far less or even no complicated class structure (Cheater 1990; Bohannan 1968:77-92). One can raise the question as to why highland Eritrea could be an exception.

I am grateful to Professor Irma Taddia of the University of Bologna (Italy) who enabled me to consult herxerox copy of some of the Trevaski's papers which are kept in the Brdleian Library of Oxford University.

4. The gasha was a unit of measurement of land, exactly as it was used in the Twentieth Century up to the Land Decree of 1975. A fraction of a *gasha* in that era was a *meder*. A *gasha* ranged from about 7 or 9-10 to 56 *meder* depending on the area and topography (Crummey 1988a).
5. For a representative example see Wudu Tafete Kaso, 1989; Mekonnen Berhane, 1988; Tsegaye Berhane, 1989; Demeke Seifu, 1989; Solomon Tena, 1988.
6. I am grateful to Professor Jim McCann for letting me quote from the last chapter of his book on Agrarian History of Ethiopia which is in press.

References

Addis Hiwet, 1975, (p.2) - *Ethiopia: From Autocracy to Revolution,* Merlin, London.
Asnake Ali, 1986, 'The Conditions of the Peasantry in Wello, 1917-1935. A Review of the Traditions', *Proceedings of the Third Annual Seminar of the Department of History*, Addis Ababa.
Bahru Zewde, 1984, 'Economic Origin of the Absolutist State (1916-35)',*Journal of Ethiopian Studies,* XVII.
------------, 1986, 'A Bibliographical Prelude to the Agrarian History of Pre-Revolution Ethiopia', *Proceedings of the Third Annual Seminar of the Department of History* Addis Ababa.
Bairu Tafla (ed.), 1987, *Asma Giyorgis and His Work: History of the Galla and the Kingdom of Shewa,* Stuttgart.
Balsvik, R R, 1985,*Haile Selassie's Students: The Intellectual and Social Background to Revolution 1952-1977,* East Lansing.
Berhanu Abebe, 1971,*Evolution de la Propriete Fonciere au Chov a, (Ethiopie) du regne de Menelik a la Constitution de 1931,* Paris.
Bezuwork Zewde, 1992, 'The Problem of Tenancy and Tenancy Bills (With Particular Reference to Arssi)', MA Thesis Submitted to the History Department of AAU.

Bohannan, P & L, 1988, *Tiv Economy*, Longmans.
Cheater, A, 1990, 'The Ideology of 'Communal' Land Tenure in Zimbabwe: Mythogenesis enacted?' *AFRICA*, London, Vol. 60, No. 2.
Conti Rossini, C, 1916, *Princippi di Dirito Consuetudinario dell' Eritrea*, Roma.
Crummey, D, 1980, 'Abyssinian Feudalism', *Past and Present*, 89.
----------, 1983, 'Family and Property Amongst the Amhara Nobility', *Journal of African History*, XXIV, 2.
Crummey, D and Shumet Sishagne, 'The Lands of Dabra Sahay Quesquam, Gondar', *A Paper Presented to the Xth International Conference of Ethiopian Studies (Paris 1988)* (Revised March 1989).
Crummey, D and Shumet Sishagne, 'Land Tenure and the Social Accumulation of Wealth in Eighteenth Century Ethiopia: Evidence from the Quesquam Land Register', *A Paper Prepared for the Symposium on Land in African Agrarian systems, Urbana, April 1988* (1988a). (unpublished)
Crummey, D, 'Theology and Political Conflict During the Zamana Masafint: The case of Este' in Bagemdar', *Proceedings of the Ninth International Conference of Ethiopian Studies*, Volume V (Moscow, 1988b).
De Coppet, *Chronique du règne de Me'ne'lik II, Roi des Rois d'Ethiopie* (t.I-II), Paris, 1930-1932.
Demeke Seifu, 1989, 'The Addis Ababa Urael Church (c. 1885 to 1974)', (BA Essay Submitted to the History Department of AAU.
Dessalegn Rahmato, 1984, *Agrarian Reform in Ethiopia*, Trenton, N.J.
Dessalegn Rahmato, 1970, 'Condition of the Ethiopian Peasantry', *Challenge* X, 2.
------------, 1986, 'Moral Crusaders and Incipient Capitalists: Mechanized Agriculture and Its Critics in Ethiopia', *Proceedings of the Third Annual Seminar of the Department of History*, Addis Ababa.
------------, 'Political Power and Social Formation in Ethiopia Under the Old Regime: Notes on Marxist Theory', in Tadesse Beyene (ed.), *Proceedings of the Eighth International Conference of Ethiopian Studies*, Vol. 1 (Frankfurt and Addis Ababa, 1988).
Desta Tekle Weld, 1962, p.10.
Donham, D, 1986, 'Old Abyssinia and the new Ethiopian Empire: Themes in Social History', in D. Donham and W. James (eds.), *The Southern Marches of Imperial Ethiopia: Essays in History and Social Anthropology*, Cambridge.
Ellis, Gene, 1976, 'The Feudal Paradigm as a Hindrance to Understanding Ethiopia', Canadian *Journal of African Studies*, 14.
Eshetu Chole, 1987, 'Towards a History of the Fiscal Policy of the Pre-Revolutionary Ethiopian State: 1941-74', *Journal of Ethiopian Studies*, XVII.
Fekadu Begna, 'Land and Peasantry in Northern Wello, 194--1974: Yajju and Rayya & Qobbo Awrajjas', (MA Thesis Submitted to the Department of History, 1990).
Gebre Selasse, *Tarike Zemen Ze-Dagmawi Menelik* (Addis Ababa, 1959 E.C.).
Gebre Weld Engdawerk, *Ye-Etopia Maretenna Gebre Sem*, Addis Ababa, 1948 E.C.
Gilks, P, 1975, *The Dying Lion*, Publisher London.
Gill, G.J, *Readings on the Ethiopian Economy*, Addis Ababa, 1974 (A bound teaching material of the Economics Department of AAU).
Guidi, I, 1916, *Gli Archivi in Abyssinia*, Roma.
Haile Selassie (Emperor), *Hiywotena Ya-Etiopia Ermja*, Vol. I (Addis Ababa, 1965 E.C.).
Hoben, Allan, 1973, *Land Tenure Among the Amhara of Ethiopia: The Dynamics of Cognatic Descent*, Chicago: The University of Chicago Press, 272pp.

------------, 'The Role of Ambilined Descent Groups in Gojam Amhara Social Organization', (PhD Thesis Submitted to the University of California at Berkley, 1963).

McCann, J, 1987, *From Poverty to Famine in North-east Ethiopia: A Rural History 1900-1935*, Philadelphia.

Kesate Berhan Tesema, 1951, (p.10).

McLellan, C, 1988, *State Transformation and National Integration: Gedeo and the Ethiopian Empire*, East Lansing (Michigan).

Mahteme Selassie, W.Meskel, *Zekre Neger*, Addis Ababa, 2nd. ed., 1962 E.C.

Mantel-Niecko, J, 1980, *The Role of Land Tenure in the System of Ethiopian Imperial Government in Modern Times*, Warsaw.

Markakis, J, 1974, *Ethiopia: Anatomy of a Traditional Polity*, Oxford.

Mekonnen Berhane, 'Entoto Maryam Church (c. 1884 to 1974)' (BA Essay Submitted to the History Department of AAU, 1988).

Merid Wolde Aregay, 1988, 'Alula, Dogali and Ethiopian Unity', *The Centenary of Dogali: Proceedings of the International Symposium*, Addis Ababa.

------------, 1986, 'Land Tenure and Agricultural Productivity, 1500-1859', *Proceedings of the Third Annual Seminar of the Department of History*, Addis Ababa.

------------, 1988, 'Literary Origins of Ethiopian Millenarianism', *Proceedings of the Ninth International Conference of Ethiopian Studies*, Vol. VI, Moscow.

------------, 1984, 'Society and Technology in Ethiopia, 1500-1800', *Journal of Ethiopian Studies*, XVII.

------------, 1900, 'Ye-tewodros alamawoch Ke-yet endemenchu', in Tadesse Beyene, et al (eds.), *Kasa and Kasa: Papers on the Lives, Times and Images of Tewodros II and Yohannes IV (1855-1889)*, Addis Ababa.

Mesfin Wolde-Mariam, 1991, *Suffering Under God's Environment: A Vertical Study of the Predicament of Peasants in North Central Ethiopia*, Berne.

MLRA, 1970, *Seminar Proceedings on Agrarian Reform, 25th November - 5th December, 1970*, Addis Ababa.

Pankhurst, R.K.P, 1966, *State and Land in Ethiopian History*, Addis Ababa.

Pearce, N, 1863, *The Life and Times of Nathaniel Pearce Written by Himself During a Residence in Abyssinia from 1810 to 1819*, London.

Solomon Tena, 'Yeka Mikael Church: A Brief History, 1846-1974' (BA Essay Submitted to the History Department, AAU, 1988).

Stahl, M, 1974, *Political Contradictions in Agricultural Development*, Stockholm.

Taddesse Tamrat, 1972, *Church and State in Ethiopia, 1270-1527*, Oxford.

Taye Gulilat, 1968, 'The Tax in Lieu of Tithe and the New Agricultural Income Tax: A Preliminary Evaluation', *Dialogue II*, 1, December.

Tsegaye Berhane, 'The Holy Trinity Cathedral, AA. (C. 1930 to 1974)', (BA Essay Submitted to the Department of History of AAU, 1989).

Wudu Tafete Kasu, 1989, 'The Twin Churches of Raguel (1887 to 1985)', (BA Essay Submitted to the History Department of AAU.

UNDP/RRC, *A Study of Nomadic Areas for Settlement - Study Report Part III - The Socio-Economic Aspects (Socio-Anthropology, Economy and Livestock Production)* (Project No. UNDP/RRC/81/001, 1983).

------------, *The Nomadic Areas of Ethiopia - Study Report Part III - The Socio-Economic Aspects, A Socio-Anthropology* UNDP/RRC - ETH/81/001, Addis Ababa, 1984).

------------, 1984, *The Nomadic Areas of Ethiopia - Study Report I - Major Findings and Recommendations* (UNDP/RRC - ETH/81/001, Addis Ababa.

3. Peasant Agriculture Under the Old Regime

Dessalegn Rahmato

Agrarian history is often written on a broad canvas. It reaches into the distant past, tracing critical moments of change in production and property, in agricultural techniques and practices. Except on few occasions, the pace of agrarian progress is slow, and the advances made by one social element and the gains lost by another become manifest only over long stretches of time. In this chapter however, we are limited by two principal constraints. First, the period covered, from the post-Italian period of the early 1940s to the fall of the Old Regime in the early 1970s, is too short to detect significant breaks or discontinuities in the agrarian order. The changes that did occur and the advances that were made during this period did not overtly disturb the social fabric, so that to the casual observer peasant society appears outwardly static. Secondly, peasant agriculture constitutes only part of the agrarian order of the Old Regime. The other, equally significant elements, namely, the system of land holding (covered elsewhere in this volume) and the class relations dependent on it, the physical and human environment, and the legal and political framework underpining agrarian relations are all outside the scope of this chapter.[1]

The rural history of this period is marked by significant agricultural trends and policy initiatives. In parts of the cereal-growing regions of the north and the *ensete* complex of the south-which together support some two-thirds of the country's rural population-peasant agriculture underwent a slow but steady process of involution. This was evidenced by diminishing resources, increasing vulnerability, and growing rural poverty. Having reached the limits of its development potential and failed to transform itself, peasant agriculture persisted with reduced vitality by the sheer strength of its inherited techniques and accumulated experience. Access to land and other means of production became more difficult and more complicated, the subordination of the rural producer to the landed classes and subsequently the imperial State grew more pronounced, and the subsistence ethos and survival-orientation of the peasantry, a growing number of which was threatened with marginalization, became all the more reinforced (Geertz 1963). On the other hand, there were areas showing promising prospects in the central, south-eastern, and south-western regions of the country, where attempts were being made to invigorate smallholder production by means of what were called the package programmes.

Moreover, in this same period, peasant agriculture became the object of State policy. This is perhaps what sets the agrarian history of the Old Regime apart from its predecessors. Through its successive Five-Year Development Plans, State policy sought to stimulate agricultural growth and to promote changes in peasant agronomy. As we shall see however, these policies had limited impact, and part of the blame lies in State perceptions of the peasant economy and in the orientation of development planning itself. Development policies had a clear class bias: they favoured the landlord and (except in the last quarter of the Old Regime) the emerging capitalist farmer. Even when they occasionally sought to provide support to the peasant sector, they were handicapped by the decision-makers' ideological bias which considered smallholder agriculture as backward and primitive (the word 'primitive' occurs frequently in policy documents) and upheld Western-style, technology-driven, large-scale agriculture as the only alternative.

The pitfalls of discussing peasant agriculture in this period have to do with the diversity of the country and the paucity of reliable data. The diversity of the country in terms of agricultural ecology and resource potential has been noted by agronomists and geographers but the significance of this diversity to the rural economy, and to the potential for agrarian change, remains insufficiently explored even to this day. The dearth of scientific knowledge about the country's natural endowments, and of reliable data on many aspects of rural production a problem relatively more limiting at the time than at present inhibits theorization or sustained analysis. The first 'census' of agriculture based on a more reliable field survey was carried out by the Ministry of Agriculture (MoA) in 1974-75, but even this offers only basic data on limited aspects of agriculture.

Research on Agriculture

Opinion is divided about the agro-ecological profile of the country. In the early 1960s, a visiting agronomist, using no better evidence than old physical maps, identified eight broad agro-ecological regions in the country (Bunting 1963). Westphal, writing about a decade later, accepted Bunting's judgment but added three more regions of his own, making a total of 11 (1974, 1975). A recent study, based on more modern scientific techniques, identifies 15 agro-ecological regions which are then subdivided into 140 agro-ecological zones. An ecological zone is a micro-region which is sufficiently uniform in climate, physiography and soil patterns (FAO 1988:88). The final verdict of the agronomists and ecologists has probably not yet been made; be that as it may, what is worthy of note is the diverse ecology of the country, and the complex variety of agricultural endeavour and material life this involves. In traditional agriculture such as ours, natural conditions and endowments determine the range of crops that can be grown, farming practices, responses to the environment, and, in direct or indirect ways, consumption patterns and household dynamics.

MAP 1: ETHIOPIA: ADMINISTRATIVE DIVISIONS (Circa 1974)

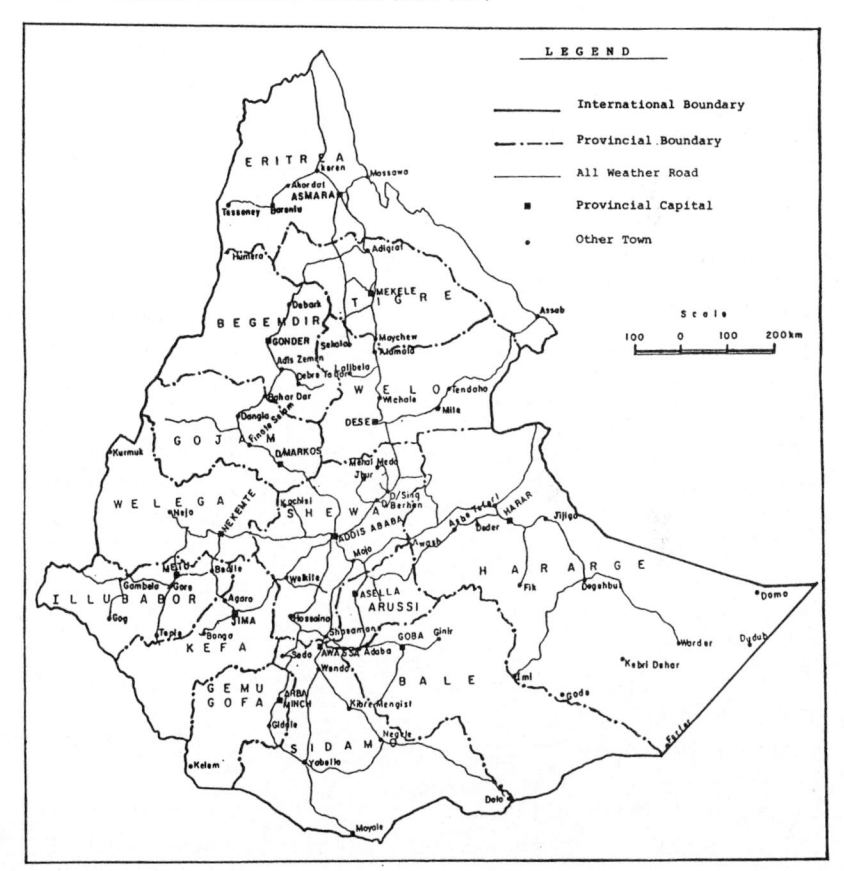

The diversity of natural conditions are almost matched by the diversity of agricultural systems. Westphal has identified four *major* agricultural systems. He calls these the seed-farming complex (corresponding basically to the food-grain producing regions of northern, eastern and western

Ethiopia), the *ensete* planting complex, shifting agriculture (practised mostly by minorities living along the full length of the western border of the country), and pastoral production. While it is neither exhaustive nor perfect, the merit of this approach is that the distinguishing elements are productive practices and environmental adaptation, rather than agro-climate and land potential as has been emphasized in recent studies [such as those conducted by the Ministry of Agriculture (MoA) and the Food and Agriculture Organization (FAO)]. In this study, we shall focus mainly on the two principal agricultural systems, namely the seed-farming and *ensete* planting systems.

MAP 2: ETHIOPIA: PACKAGE PROGRAMME AREAS 1974

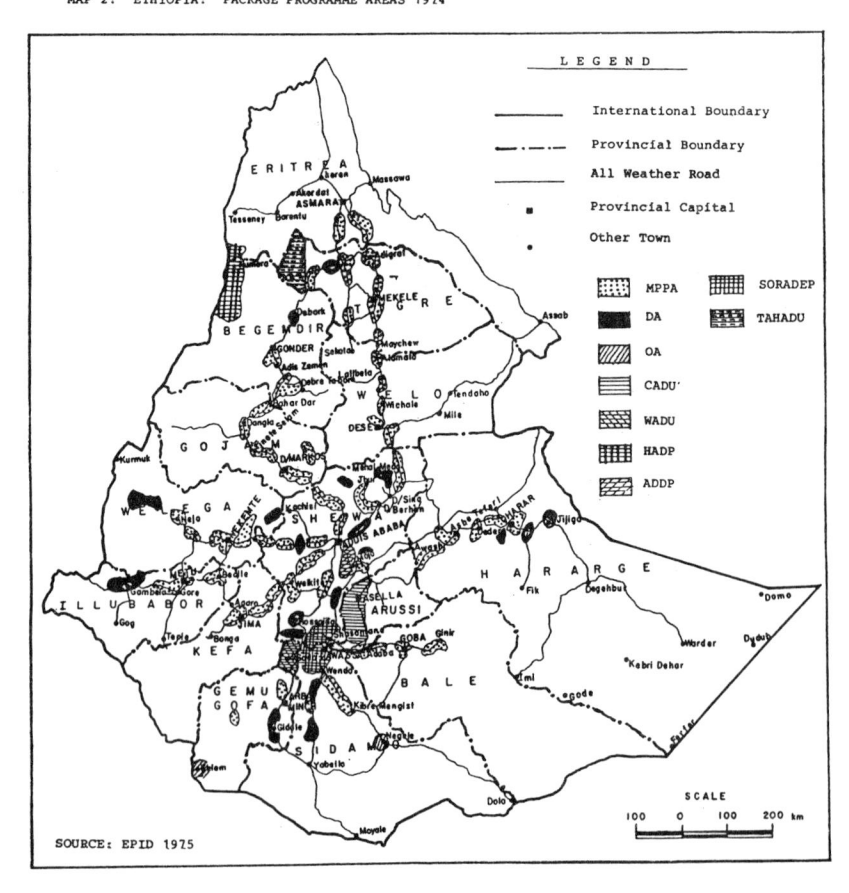

SOURCE: EPID 1975

As noted above, it was not until the fall of the Old Regime that useful information on peasant agriculture became available. The main written sources before then came from in-house or commissioned government reports, and reports prepared by or for donor agencies. Surprisingly enough, there were only a few works done by independent researchers. In the 1950s and early 1960s, decision-makers had to make do with information which, on the whole, was no better than intelligent guess work. From time to time limited micro-surveys (often in two or three kebbeles in one woreda) were carried out to provide a benchmark. Between the mid-1960s and early 1970, it was the Committee of Agricultural Experts working outside the Ministry of Agriculture, which issued serial information on agricultural performance. The Committee set annual figures for crop production, crop yield, land use, etc., sometimes on the basis of available estimates by agencies, but frequently by guess work or arbitrary decisions.[2]

The donor agencies which supported the government's development effort (mainly the World Bank and USAID) were equally close-minded with respect to development strategies and priorities. The 1950s and 1960s were the heyday of Modernization Theory in the West and the principal objective of development was believed to be to replace 'tradition' with 'modernity'. This was also the time when the idea 'big is better' was unquestionably accepted among economists and the donor community. The road to prosperity was seen to lie in large-scale enterprises employing modern technology and modern methods of management. Up until 1973 or thereabouts, when it quickly reversed itself and began to loudly advocate peasant-based green revolution programmes, the World Bank's 'agricultural modernization' strategy for the country placed high hopes on mechanization and large-scale commercial farms. This position was shared by USAID, whose advisors were impressed with the prospects of commercial agriculture expanding rapidly at the time (World Bank 1972; SRI 1969d; USDA 1969).

It is probably safe to say that the US was one of the key influences in agricultural policy-making during the Old Regime. The others, which also strongly influenced policy formulation and government thinking in general, were the World Bank, Sweden, through its CADU and EPID projects, and FAO, through its fertilizer promotion programmes. American influence on Ethiopian thinking on agricultural development and planning prevailed through its training programme in Alemaya and Jimma, its design of the country's extension services and its support of a few high-profile agricultural projects. It was, however, the two teaching institutions, Alemaya Agricultural College (founded in 1954) and Jimma Agricultural School (1952), which left behind the most significant legacy; the ideas they bequeathed to a generation of students, and the objectives which they promoted, have had considerable impact on the thinking of local specialists and policy planners.[3] A few words on US involvement in Ethiopian agriculture is thus in order.

US Involvement

The earliest technical co-operation agreement between the US and Ethiopia goes back to 1951, and from roughly this time to about 1965, US support to the country went mostly to agricultural education and training of extension personnel. In the period between 1965 and 1970, on the other hand, USAID placed more emphasis on strengthening institutional capacity for agricultural development, and a good deal of financial and technical support was provided to the Ministry of Agriculture (MoA) with this aim in mind. After 1970, however, the USAID became involved in financing large-scale regional development schemes, such as those at Ada, Shashemene and Borkena (Adams, 1970). Despite its shift of emphasis, agricultural education remained an important priority and USAID continued to support the two teaching institutions, Alemaya and Jimma, both of which were staffed by instructors recruited from American universities.

The American instructors who came to teach at the schools strongly believed that what Ethiopia needed was high technology and scientific techniques of cultivation and farm management. The model they had in mind, and which they placed before their students, was American agriculture. They were naive enough to believe that a transformation along this line was quite possible. Alemaya College in particular, which was set up in 1954, was for its time a high-tech marvel, with the most advanced equipment and the most modern teaching and service facilities. It was the goal of the college to prepare agricultural agents 'in the higher technical and scientific branches of agriculture' (Pankhurst 1957) as is done in the developed countries.

There was hardly any two-way interaction between the teaching units and the surrounding peasantry, and for this and other reasons the American staff had many unfounded views about the peasantry and peasant enterprise. They earnestly believed that experience had not taught the peasant much about agronomy or the environment. The 'problem of soil erosion in Ethiopia', states their first report, written before any of them had had the chance to examine existing agricultural practices seriously, 'is easily recognized by soil scientists but the average farmer either does not understand what erosion is, or else refuses to believe that it can and does exist in this country' (IECAMA 1953:153). As we shall see below, soil protection forms an essential element of peasant farming practices. Because of their ignorance of smallholder agriculture, they tended to think that anything that was not large-scale and worked by high technology was a throwback to pre-historic times. 'We see in Ethiopia today', one of the instructors wrote, 'a stone-age agriculture very similar to the kind of agriculture which existed in Mesopotamia at least 10,000 years ago ...' (Damon 1962:11). On occasions, their view of the peasant borders on the bizarre. They earnestly believed that the Ethiopian peasant was the most conscientious person in the world. 'The fact that there are purchase taxes on some products', explains one of the reports of the college staff, 'may be an additional reason why the farmer insists on going to the market place; that is where the tax collector is found' (Vol. III:89). The teaching staff found it hard to understand why the Ethiopian 'farmer' did not behave like the American farmer and sell his harvest, in the silo, to the grain dealer without going to the market himself. In the end, though Alemaya College graduates may have been well equipped to manage large-scale farms, their training nevertheless placed them at odds with peasant agriculture.

Writing about a decade after the US training programme had been established, Bunting saw considerable shortcomings in both Alemaya and Jimma. The American staff, he pointed out, had neither research experience nor even research ability; none of the teachers brought to either of the institutions experience in tropical agriculture, which would have been more relevant to the country (Bunting 1963:17-18). Indeed, according to documentary evidence (see Endnote 2 below), many of the research endeavours consisted for the most part of demonstrations of technical innovations scaled down ostensibly to Ethiopian conditions but hardly marketable in the rural areas. One significant research effort, however, was in soils, the classification and inventory of which was carried out over many years (Murphy 1963, 1968).

To round off the discussion a few words about the state of independent research on peasant agriculture is in order. Despite the fact that this country is, and has always been, a land of peasants, and agriculture continues to be the dominant form of economic life, neither the peasantry nor agrarian history attracted the interest of Ethiopian researchers. While in South Asia, in contrast, 'native' intellectuals returned to the countryside in droves in search of their own political and cultural heritage, and in the process 'brought' the peasant back into Asian history (Stokes 1978), Ethiopian intellectuals remained disdainfully distant from the muddy fields and hungry villages.[4] This says a lot about the values and ideological preferences of the country's intellectual community. One area which aroused some interest and may be cited as an exception was land, land taxation and land reform. A number of papers and monographs, mostly case-studies, were produced by Ethiopians but the quality of the works is quite uninspiring (Mesfin Kinfu 1974; Bahru 1986).

The first comprehensive study of modern Ethiopian agriculture was made by Huffnagel, working under contract for FAO (FAO/Huffnagel 1961). This work is a landmark, for, in contrast to earlier custom, it provided an extended discussion of peasant farm practices, crop regimes and animal husbandry. Here, we have, perhaps for the first time, peasant agronomy as the focus of interest in its own right, and peasant labour as a conscious endeavour informed by practical experience. While Huffnagel never lets us forget the numerous shortcomings of peasant production, he nonetheless offers us a relatively detailed examination of the rationale of peasant enterprise and the quality of cultivation and soil management techniques. It took over a decade before another work of similar scope and detail appeared. Westphal (1974, 1975) focused on the complex agronomic and ecological conditions of the country and examined peasant production in its many environmental settings. Both works, it should be noted, show considerable appreciation the latter more so than the former for peasant endeavour and technical competence.

There were a number of specialized studies with a regional focus which appeared between 1941-75,[5] some of which are worthy of note for their perceptive observations, and for breaking ranks with the 'peasant is backward' outlook prevalent at the time. Simoon's book (1960), a work of cultural geography focusing on rural life in what was then Begemdir and Semien province, falls midway in between: it is highly informative but defective in its analytical approach and conclusions. The author examined the rural economy and agricultural regime of the people of the province in the framework of their belief systems and argued that cultural attitudes have a strong bearing on environmental consciousness and such consciousness inhibits agricultural progress. His approach is really a variation of the 'cultural backwardness' theme dominant at the time and his conclusions are far from convincing.

On the other hand, the work of Jackson and his associates (1969) demonstrates how peasant adaptive skills respond to the challenge of unfavourable human and environmental conditions such as high population density, scarcity of resources, rugged topography, etc. The study focuses on the eastern highlands of Gamo Goffa and the minority nationalities who live there. Peasants here practice intensive cultivation combining root crops with cereals, and employ sophisticated and environmentally-responsible agricultural techniques which have enabled them to maintain themselves in food balance in the face of immense difficulties. The work is a tribute to the resilience of *ensete*-based smallholder enterprise and the resourcefulness of peasant cultivators.

Another work of a similar nature is that of Noel Cossins (1974). His monograph is about the central highlands, specifically northern Shoa, western Wollo, central Tigrai and south-eastern Gondar provinces-areas of rugged physiography, a fiercely independent peasantry and endemic environmental disasters. The focus is on the hardy nature of the peasantry and the precarious nature of survival, both of which have combined to shape agricultural practices and environmental consciousness. This is a work of environmental economy centred around the ceaseless struggle between man and nature, in which the latter is frequently victorious but the former refuses to give up. Here, we have an inhospitable natural setting, a fragile ecology and a tenacious peasantry whose adaptive skills have been stretched to the limits if not altogether exhausted in the face of colossal difficulties (Bauer 1977).

These works make up the documentary evidence on peasant agriculture in the period. Except for the literature produced by independent researchers, the written evidence is in the main neither rich nor stimulating, exhaustive nor reliable. Much of this latter evidence was not based on field surveys, primary investigation nor even on a healthy dialogue with the main agents of agricultural production, namely, the peasants themselves.

Peasant Agriculture: The Realities

The Dynamics of Peasant Agronomy

So often has peasant agriculture been condemned for its backwardness and for having held back the country's progress, that the view has come to be accepted as an article of faith, without doubt or question. The peasantry, it is claimed, is strongly attached to its traditional ways, and sticks tenaciously to customary practices even when these are shown to be less effective and less productive; change, in other words, is fiercely resisted and even considered immoral. This view would have been easily dismissed as just another urban, petty bourgeois prejudice against rural society but for the fact that it informs public policy and influences the distribution of investment resources and social services. Up until the closing years of the Old Regime, development planning was grounded on the proposition that very little growth potential was to be expected from the peasant sector, and that priority ought to be given to those sectors that promised accelerated rates of growth and a good return on investment.[6]

It is therefore essential to briefly look at the condition of peasant agriculture, its inherent dynamic and the potential it did or did not hold. It is, of course, true to say that, compared with say Swedish or Japanese agriculture, peasant production in this country was and continues to be backward, but so are a lot of rural enterprises in Europe or Asia. Measured in terms of land or labour productivity, many small-scale farms in Europe are more efficient than the giant farm enterprises in the United States. More fruitful, therefore, for our purposes, is an examination of the practical effort of the peasantry to determine the level of practical knowledge it has attained. This is a wide subject and we will have to content ourselves with a summary of the key points.

Indigenous agricultural technology in Ethiopia is superior to that used by peasants in the rest of Sub-Saharan Africa. Farming techniques incorporate considerable knowledge of soil management, environmental protection, and regeneration of soil fertility. Contour ploughing and ploughing to control run-off, mulching, ratooning, soil bunding and terracing are widely practised in many parts of the country. Water control and management techniques range from the sophisticated irrigation networks of the Gamo Goffa peasantry to the simple spring canal schemes found in Wollo and Begemdir.[7] The fertility of the soil is maintained through a complex system of crop rotation on the one hand, and bare fallowing on the other, which also provides pasturage for livestock (FAO/Huffnagel n.d.:14344; Westphal 1974:26-27).

All peasants know that manuring is good for the soil and contributes to higher yield and, in parts of the south, this and other forms of organic fertilization are widely used. Indeed, without organic fertilization and considerable knowledge of soil management, the densely populated regions of the *ensete*-planting complex would not have been able to survive. Here, a population density of 300 to 400 persons per km^2 is not uncommon, and average holding per household is often below half a hectare. Such is the dynamic of the intensive farming system of the region that peasants have for centuries managed to squeeze out of tiny plots of land enough food to sustain themselves and to remain free of the scourge of famine (Dessalegn 1992; Jackson 1970). It is worth noting that European agriculture relied on organic rather than chemical fertilizers (i.e. mainly animal manure), crop rotation and other biological methods of soil regeneration well into the mid-Nineteenth Century.

There is considerable evidence of peasant adaptability in cropping strategies as well. In the last four to five decades, long-stem crops such as sorghum and maize have grown in importance and in some instances displaced short-stem crops such as teff and barley in many parts of the highlands. These crops require comparatively less labour, are more stress resistant, and easier to store, thus reducing the risk of post-harvest losses. This indicates that the pattern of rural consumption is also undergoing change. There is evidence too that, since the latter part of the 1960s peasants have been switching from the traditional barley to oats cultivation which is spreading in northern Shoa, south-western Wollo and parts of Gojam. Oats are much hardier than barley, require very little labour, and have higher yield and greater forage value. According to two ILCA agronomists well acquainted with Ethiopian agriculture, the rapid adoption of oats, often against the advice of MoA extension agents, 'reveals a high degree of willingness to innovate on the part of [Ethiopian] farmers' when the comparative advantage of a crop or a farming method is clearly apparent (Jutzi and Gryseels 1984; Gryseels and Anderson 1983).

Cultivation techniques aimed at improving output and yield include multiple ploughing (which also minimizes weed growth); inter-cropping, i.e., the planting of different crops in the same field in the same season, a practice which also helps maximize land use and protects against crop disease and pests; sequencing of particular crops to benefit from the special advantages of the crops in question; and, in the *ensete* zone, combining cereals with root crops in a dynamic way so as to ensure food security.

These are what I call the 'discreet innovations' that peasants have pioneered on their own and practised for generations. In fact, the highland areas of the country have been farmed without interruption for over one thousand years; they have also been the sole source of sustenance for an ever-growing population in this same period. It is a tribute to peasant agronomy and 'traditional' techniques of soil management and environmental protection that these same lands (or at least the great portion of them) still have good farming potential today. There is another equally important point we need to remember, namely, that far from primitive or archaic, peasant agriculture had in fact reached a level of development comparable in many respects to European agriculture on the eve of what is known as the agricultural revolution of the Seventeenth and Eighteenth Centuries.

This revolution, which had such a decisive impact on the course of European economic history, was initiated not by sophisticated technology but rather by *new methods* of crop farming (employing the traditional tools of the peasantry), and by raising *new crops* which had the dual advantage of regenerating the soil and serving as nutritious fodder for livestock. It was only later, when the momentous changes were already under way, that large capital investments and advanced technology began to propel the revolution forward. The new farming methods which revolutionized agriculture involved what Marc Bloch, one of the most distinguished agrarian historians of pre-modern Europe, called 'man's liberation from fallow farming'. This consisted in the simple abolition of bare fallowing and the switch from a three to a four-field system on the one hand, and the cultivation of forage crops in place of fallow on the other a practice which made the dynamic integration of crop cultivation and animal husbandry possible (Bloch

1966:Ch. VI; Jones and Woolf 1969:7-11). A brief examination of some aspects of this momentous event in the development of capitalism provides a useful comparative perspective at this point.

The European Agricultural Revolution

There is no consensus among historians as to when the agricultural revolution in Europe began, but it is widely accepted that while the seeds of the revolution may have been planted in the Low Countries earlier, its dynamic results came to be observed on a large-scale first in England. It has been argued by some that the critical period of agricultural transformation was between 1660 and 1750 (Jones 1965; Braudel 1985), but others place it much later and in the next century, i.e., from 1750 to 1880 (Chambers and Mingay). The difference here may be a matter of differences in conceptualization and methodology. A third school contends that there were in fact three revolutions, the first starting in the latter part of the Seventeenth Century, and the third in the last decades of the Nineteenth Century (Thompson). Thompson goes on to argue that it was only in the third stage, i.e., from 1880 onwards, that the technical changes involved machinery, which replaced human labour, and chemical fertilizers, which replaced animal manure, crushed bone and other organic fertilizers. Previous to this, progressive husbandry, as it was then called, relied on human and animal labour, natural or organic inputs and improvements in crop rotation and livestock breeding. Even after the last quarter of the Nineteenth Century, there were low levels of mechanization in Europe partly because European farms, unlike those in America at the time, were mostly small-scale operations. As Braudel has succinctly described it, 'the real take-off in the progress of English agriculture before the industrial revolution' came not so much from machines or wonder crops as from new methods of land use, new timetables for ploughing, new forms of crop rotation which eliminated fallow and encouraged grazing, a useful source of [organic] fertilizer and therefore a remedy for soil exhaustion, attention to new strains of crops; [and] selective breeding of sheep and cattle' (Braudel 1985:559).

The sickle, the scythe (which was mostly used for mowing hay, not for reaping crops), and the wooden flail remained the basic implements in European agriculture up to roughly the middle of the Nineteenth Century (for this and what follows see Collins 1969a, 1969b). The humble sickle in fact continued to be the main hand tool much longer. In Italy and Austria, it was still widely used even in the 1930s. In parts of the US and Canada, it was not replaced until the mid-1840s. Earlier, in the Eighteenth Century, the harrow, which was widely used, was nothing more than bushes and twigs tied to a crude wooden frame. The European moldboard plough, in use since the Middle Ages, if not earlier, was heavier, cut deeper and turned the soil, hence simultaneously making furrows, while in contrast, the Ethiopian single-tine plough is lighter and only scratches the surface of the soil.

Turning to farming methods, it is worth noting that there are a great many similarities in practices between farmers in Europe, at the time of the agricultural revolution, and peasants in Ethiopia. In both cases, sowing was done by the broadcast method, and harvesting with the serrated sickle. Reaping was done in Europe from a stooping position whereas, in Ethiopia, it requires squatting, and the former practice is slightly more effective than the latter. In so far as threshing was concerned, the Ethiopian practice of trampling the harvest using farm animals is probably much better than the European custom of beating the crops with the unwieldy flail. The flail was time-consuming, and, according to some observers, up to 30% of the labourer's time was wasted rearranging the straws in position. Both here and in Europe, cultivators relied on organic fertilizers. The major advantage the European farmer at this time had over the Ethiopian peasant was that the former succeeded in achieving a closer integration of crop farming and livestock breeding. The biological innovations noted above enabled the European cultivator to raise more livestock per unit of land than is possible in this country even today, and this made it possible to obtain and use animal manure on a much larger scale (Thompson 1968).

In brief, the innovations which, according to Bloch, sparked off an unprecedented transformation, without which there would not have been an industrial revolution, were small, cheap and suitable for wide diffusion. In comparative perspective, it is clear that Ethiopian agriculture had made considerable progress, had in fact reached a critical turning point but, for reasons that are too involved to discuss here, failed to make that turn and carry out a revolution of its own.

All this is not to deny that peasant agriculture suffers from numerous limitations, including poor technology, and inefficient farming methods, which have become increasingly inadequate to provide food security to the growing rural population. Even when the peasant has made considerable investment in soil management and conservation he has not always been successful in minimizing the damage to the environment and, on occasions the competition for resources has led to destructive farming practices. However, the limitations of peasant agriculture should be viewed in the proper social and economic context.

Technology and Social Change

The question of technological change should not be viewed as a technical problem but as a social and economic one, and should be examined in the context of the existing social and property relations and economic system. As far as the Ethiopian peasant was concerned, the need for improved technology did not arise; besides, given the prevailing property relations, more production would have meant more of the surplus going to the landed classes and the State. Moreover, the landed classes themselves showed very little interest in technical change and improved farming methods (although a few exceptions may be cited). The agricultural revolution of pre-modern Europe, it should be noted, was poineered not by the peasants themselves but by enterprising elements from the 'middle' classes and the landed gentry who sought to profit from the new changes, and who were dissatisfied with the existing agrarian order. Further, a subsistence economy such as ours, which is geared primarily to the reproduction of the family and the satisfaction of basic needs as traditionally given, creates its own stable environment and shuns periodic social or economic disturbances. Thus, the reasons for the technological stagnation of agriculture must be sought not in the lack of the inventive spirit among the peasantry, but rather in the stagnation of the social environment, and the enfeeblement of economic life.

Another point is also significant. The successes of the agricultural programmes in some Third World countries today, notably in South Asia where the green revolution was tried on a large scale, were achieved by means of immense public investment. The countries concerned supported their agricultural sector, particularly the peasant sector, with large-scale financial and material investment which was raised either locally or was acquired as external assistance. This support went to finance and develop improved technology, improved farming practices, environmental protection schemes, land reform and rural infrastructure. Large subsidies or price support schemes went to agricultural produce, particularly for food grain which was mostly grown in peasant farms. In some of these countries, food price support to the peasantry still continues today, even when the peasant sector is no longer vulnerable and at the mercy of the elements. Similarly, it is well known that both the US and other advanced countries provided massive support in the order of billions of dollars annually to their farmers, who often are the most pampered elements in society. As we shall see, peasant agriculture benefited the least from public investment throughout the life of the Old Regime. For example, of the total of US$352 million of foreign loans which the country was able to utilize up to 1974, less than 8% went to agricultural development and spending on all the other major sectors was higher (CSO 1975).

Peasant Agriculture: The Record

When the full economic history of the Old Regime is finally written, it will reveal that its most damaging failure was in the area of agricultural development. While considerable effort was made to build up the modern sector of the economy, with some significant successes particularly in transport, communications and energy, agriculture continued to decline and the rural population became ever more vulnerable to periodic food crises.

The decline of agriculture is evident from the latter part of the 1950s. This may be because information on economic matters began to be available from this time on. Actually, the evidence suggests that the problem in some of the rural areas where the population pressure had long been acute areas in what Cossins called the central highlands, and in the *ensete* zone may have begun three or more decades earlier. This decline is characterized not just by insufficient agricultural output but by the ensemble of the processes I have called agricultural involution.

Before we discuss the dynamic of the involutionary process, let us briefly look at the agricultural resource base of the country. It was common for government officials and policy planners in this period (and at the time of the military regime) to wax eloquent about the immense potential of the country, and the vast resources that had yet to be utilized. This view was often echoed by the country's foreign backers, particularly the World Bank, which on more than one occasion prepared for the government reports purporting to show (largely on untenable evidence) that the untapped potential of the country was indeed staggering.[8] But the peasants knew better and, except for certain areas which offered farming and employment opportunities and attracted migrants, there was no large-scale out-migration of peasants in search of greener pastures. As I have argued elsewhere the agricultural resources in much of the highlands were fully (often over) utilized, and those lands which seemed to be underutilized were ones which either could not be brought under cultivation using existing peasant technology, or required massive investment in infrastructure and social services. The agrarian regime was increasingly under pressure from insufficiency of resources and a rapidly growing population. It is significant that when commercial agriculture emerged it did not, in many cases, bring new land into cultivation but rather displaced peasants on a large scale.

Up until the mid-1980s, when, with more accurate means of measurement, a more realistic assessment of the country's land potential was made, natural resource inventory was essentially guess-work, often revealing the optimism of the assessors themselves. The earliest land assessment was carried out by an FAO consultant at the beginning of the 1950s (MoA 1953); the most recent inventory, based on modern satellite imagery, was published in 1984 (FAO/UNDP 1984). Between the first and the last are considerable differences, but even with the aid of advanced technology, the accuracy of the latest inventory is still in question. Be that as it may, the last assessment clearly shows that more than half the area of the country is grazing and browsing land, about a third is not suitable for cultivation and only about

15% is under utilization. Significantly, the findings reveal that the chances of expanding the resource base for peasant agriculture are severely limited, and of doing the same for modern agriculture, only slightly better.

Smallholder Agriculture

How small was smallholder agriculture in the period under discussion? Household plots varied in size regionally. The reasons for this were not always population pressure alone, though this was a significant factor, but included the inheritance system, the marriage contract, or environmental limitations. In what were known as the rist areas, the system of partible inheritance was a cause of fragmentation of holdings, diminution of plots, insecurity, interminable litigation and household conflict. In the *ensete* zone, the limitations of the ecology and the requirements of root-crop cultivation confined populations to small areas whose carrying capacity had long been surpassed. Moreover, due to technological limitations few peasants were capable of operating on more than five hectares of land, which meant that even a small owner with five or six hectares was more likely to rent part of the land to a tenant operator. On the basis of a variety of regional studies, I estimate that by the end of the 1960s average per capita holdings in Arssi were between two-and-half to three hectares, in Gojam about two hectares, in north Wollo and parts of Tigrai one to one-and-half hectares, and in the *ensete* zone, half a hectare or less. I should note here that the Central Statistical Office (CSO) first and second round national surveys give much lower figures. Contemporary oral tradition suggests that family holdings in many of these regions were much larger a generation or so earlier, though we do not know how much larger they were.

Alongside petty holdings there was landlessness, which is both an indicator of poverty and of growing competition for resources. CSO surveys, for example, show that in Tigrai, Gojam and Wollo provinces landless households made up 20%, 18%, and 14% respectively of the estimated rural population there; the figures are a bit on the high side, but even if we reduce the magnitude by one-third, the extent of land shortage is quite considerable. Added to this was the fact that some 30% of farming households had no plough oxen at all and 33% had only one ox each in the early 1970s (MoA 1975, Vol. I:50). It is not hard to imagine what a debilitating handicap the shortage of farm oxen can be, especially in the predominantly plough-based, seed farming zones of the country.

One of the few government documents to paint a rather uncomplimentary picture of agricultural prospects in the country warns of increasing food scarcity in those regions where a majority of the population live. The report, prepared for the Ministry of Planning (1967A), shows that only a few areas in the country were food-surplus areas, and that, in contrast, 60% of the crop producing awrajas had permanent food deficits. The surplus areas were Arssi, Gojjam and Wollega provinces only; parts of Shoa and more than half of Begemdir province were considered weak in food balance (pp.:34-36; SRI 1969c: 44).

In the area of food consumption, the picture was even weaker. The government's estimate of between 175 and 190 kg. of cereal consumption per person per year (or 2,000 calories of daily energy intake) was questioned by a number of expert advisors (Ministry of Planning 1967a; Eichberger 1968; Abraham 1972). Abraham was of the opinion that average annual food grain consumption in the late 1960s was 150 kg. per person; this is about 411 gms. per person per day, less than the daily ration (500 gms.) set by RRC for famine victims during the tragedy of 1984-85. More recently, Watt (1988) has estimated that consumption was even lower and declining in the period 1966-1975. On the basis of a minimum daily requirement of 2,400 calories per person, a standard accepted by FAO and the World Health Organization (WHO), a moderately healthy peasant family of five would have to consume 13 quintals of food grain annually. Only the well-to-do peasants, perhaps less than one-third of the rural population, were capable of providing themselves with so much food grain in any given year. The available evidence in the 1960s, defective though it may be, indicated in fact that the country would face food shortage for over a decade, and that greater food imports would be necessary. The view of some specialists was that any increase in food production that may be achieved through improvements in peasant farming would go to feed the rural population and very little of it would be available for export (SRI 1968).

Food imports in fact grew in importance in the 1960s, and reached their highest level in the early 1970s. In the period 1945 to 1954, the country was a significant exporter of food. Indeed, stimulated by high world grain prices and shortage of food grain in the world market after World War II, the country boosted its grain exports in the second half of the 1940s (SRI 1969d). In 1946, Ethiopia exported 135,000 metric tons of grain; by 1947 the figure had reached 154,000. In the early 1950s annual exports averaged 84,000 metric tons; in contrast, in the late 1960s they were 72,000 (excluding coffee). While exports in the 1945-55 period were mostly cereals, those of the 1960s and early 1970s were dominated by pulses (horse and haricot beans and lentils). In the second half of the 1950s, the situation was reversed: cereal exports steadily declined while other food imports steadily grew in importance. Wheat imports in fact became significant as from 1952, reversing a seven-year export record. Food imports, which reached 83,000 metric tons in 1970, consisted of wheat, rice, sorghum, maize, oats, flour of all kinds and barley malt (Experience Inc, 1972, Report II, Annex C for all figures given here). Food import figures for the 1960s and 1970s do not include food aid, which became significant in the mid-1960s and in 1974-75.

There is insufficient documentation on the history of food aid in this country, though we know that the World Food Programme (WFP), which serves as the main conduit of multilateral food aid to Third World countries, began its operations here in 1965. In the next few years, due to famine and recurrent food shortages in various parts of the country, WFP as well as individual donors shipped in emergency food aid. Food-for-Work schemes using food aid may have been initiated towards the end of 1970 when food grain was used to pay for conservation activities in Tigrai and Eritrea provinces. While statistical data on food aid deliveries to the country in the 1960s are hard to come by, FAO sources indicate that food aid increased substantially in the last half decade of the Old Regime. From a modest figure in 1970-71, food aid deliveries reached 25,000 metric tons in 1972, rose to 96,000 two years later in 1973-74, and stood at 54,000 in 1975 (FAO 1983:20).

Information on crop output and productivity over many years or decades is not available, hence we cannot measure accurately the performance of agriculture and the state of the peasant economy. The best we have are estimates of output and yield made in different periods, by different sources, and using different methods, which makes comparative analysis virtually impossible. The figures in Table 1 are provided with this proviso, and while they may indicate a rough order of magnitude, they do not allow close comparison. They may perhaps suggest that the performance of peasant production over the three decades was far from outstanding; this conclusion is supported by circumstantial evidence and some reports which will be discussed later. The optimistic assessment of the government, contained in the first and second development plans, which claimed that steady progress had been made in food production in the 1950s and 1960s, cannot be sustained.

Perhaps the most telling evidence of the poor condition of peasant agriculture was the periodic food crises and famines that ravaged the country. Such disasters were not peculiar to the Old Regime; they were part of the peasant life experience in all earlier periods and centuries. What made the tragedies particularly deplorable was that they occurred in the Twentieth Century, under conditions of improved transport and communication, and in the face of considerable opportunities for assistance from the world community. The following were years of localized and large-scale famine in the country: 1953-54, 1957-58, 1962-66, and 1973-74, of which the last two were the most devastating to the peasantry, and the most damaging to the Old Regime (Dessalegn 1990a).

Table 1: Crop Yield for Selected Years
(quintals per hectare)

Crops	1956	1965-66	1974-75
Barley	3.0	8.3	7.5
Teff	6.9	6.0	7.0
Sorghum	6.6	8.2	8.8
Maize	5.0	10.0	10.9
Wheat	3.7	7.3	8.2

Source: FAO/Huffnagel for 1956 figures (selected years, excluding Eritrea); CSO, 1967 for 1965-66 figures; MoA, 1975 for 1974-75 figures.

The subject of famine, its causes and consequences, is beyond the scope of this chapter; besides, the last two famines have been covered extensively in several works which are easily accessible (Mesfin Wolde Mariam 1984; Shepherd 1975). The first two famines are relatively localized affairs; they are confined to Wollo and Tigrai, and parts of Eritrea. These areas, together with part of northern Shoa, are the traditional famine zones of the country. The disaster of the 1960s was more prolonged, more damaging to life and property, and more exhausting to the peasantry. While the traditional famine areas were the main victims of the disaster, areas in the south-west also experienced starvation following a prolonged drought in 1965-66. The last famine, the worst tragedy to have occurred during the Old Regime, became a world event partly because of the scale of the suffering involved but, more importantly, because of the attempt made by government officials to cover it up. Peasants in large parts of the north-east bore the brunt of the disaster; however, rural areas in the east and the south were also badly battered.

These three famines (there may have been some more localized disasters) took a heavy toll of life and property, making the rural world even more fragile and more vulnerable. It is customary in this country to attribute famine to natural causes the failure of the rains, pest infestation, locust invasion, etc. however, natural disaster is only the last straw that triggers the forces of destruction already latent in society. Famine is a measure of the vulnerability of the peasant world as well as of its resilience, a reflection of the nature of class relations as well as of the relations between State and peasantry. Famines do not occur if a peasant economy is robust, if the popular classes in the rural areas have a tradition of social assertiveness and resistance, or if the state is in some manner accountable to the people.

The increasing vulnerability of the peasantry, particularly in the central highlands, and the gradual opening up of seasonal job opportunities gave rise to the migration of peasants to the southern, south-eastern and south-western parts of the country. Population relocation had been going on for many decades prior to the Haile Selassie era, but it was in the 1940s and later that the movement of peasants outside their place of origin became quite significant. Here, we shall be concerned with rural-to-rural and not rural-to-urban migration.

Rural-to-Rural Migration

Wood (1977, 1982), whose work is perhaps the most thorough, distinguishes between long-distance and short-distance migration. Most of the migration between 1941-74 is of the latter kind, and it involved, typically, peasants moving to the lowland areas adjacent to their homes. In this way a large part of culturally marginal land has been brought under cultivation since the 1940s. Long-distance migration and settlement took place on a smaller scale and gradually over time. Three main periods of long-distance migration may be distinguished : the first in the early 1940s, soon after the end of the Italian invasion, when only a small number of peasants were involved. The second in the latter half of the 1950s, when, due to greater vulnerability and intense population pressure in the northern highlands, a large number of peasants went to settle in the Arssi-Bale plains and in the south-western provinces. The last period was the mid-1960s and after; attracted by employment opportunities opened up by the coffee boom of half a decade earlier, and by large-scale agricultural and agro-industrial enterprises, a large number of peasants flocked to the Awash and Rift Valleys, to the north-western lowlands (the Setit Basin) and to the coffee-growing areas, notably western Kaffa. Table 2 is a summary of peasant migration in our period.

Table 2: Redistribution of Peasantry 1940-70

Migrants	Areas of Migration
Wollo Peasants	Awash Valley; Setit; Mettekel area (Gojam); W. Kaffa; South-west; Goffa area.
Tigraian Peasants	W. Tigrai lowlands; Setit; Awash Valley; Rift Valley; South-west; W. Kaffa.
Shoa Peasants	Arssi/Bale; South-west; Kaffa.
Begemdir & Gojam	Setit; South-west; Goffa area.

Source: Author's own field notes; Wood; Lexander; Knutsson.

Some of the migrants were temporary job seekers, returning home after a stint of employment, but many settled for extended periods, some even permanently, farming either as small owners or share-croppers. The number of seasonal or settler migrants is hard to determine, but some estimate of seasonal migration is possible from the existing fragmentary evidence

(Dessalegn 1986). Up to 0.25 million peasants may have been beneficiaries of seasonal employment in the various plantations, commercial farms and agro-industrial schemes in the Awash and Rift Valleys and in the Setit Basin; if we add to this the considerable number of peasant migrants who travelled to the coffee areas every year, the total number of seasonal migrants is quite impressive.

Peasant agriculture was operating in difficult circumstances partly for the reasons given above, and partly because it was burdened by a variety of State and landlord exactions. Agricultural taxationconsisted of the land tax, cattle tax (applicable mainly in pastoral areas), and agricultural income tax which was introduced in 1967 to replace the old tax in lieu of tithe.[9] The land tax, to be paid by the landowner, was often passed on to the tenant; while it was not burdensome, it was complicated, since it was based on whether the land was measured or unmeasured (a higher tax applied if measured), its fertility, and the province in which it was located. Agricultural income tax was assessed on annual income levels, and for many peasants it was E$6.50 or less. There were also the education and health taxes, both of which were levied on the same basis as the land tax and collected at the same time. The total tax obligation of a peasant owner-operator working one to two hectares of land would be between E$4.00 and E$10.00 depending on his annual income; peasants paid 20 birr in taxes during the military regime. The point, however, was that the iniquitous nature of tax assessment and payment was a source of irritation among many peasants. Through a variety of loopholes and corruption almost all large landlords, and many smaller ones, ended up paying no taxes at all on their property. The tax was often passed on to the tenantry which had no choice on the matter.

Of all the peasant groups, the tenantry was burdened the most. Apart from the various taxes they had to pay the State, tenant farmers had a number of obligations to the landlord, of which land rent was the most onerous. Customary practices, which differed from region to region, set rent at one-third to one-half of the harvest, but it was not uncommon in some areas for landlords to demand more. Tenants had neither written contracts nor guarantees that the land they were working would not be rented to someone else at short notice. While abrupt termination of rental arrangements was not widespread, tenants nonetheless laboured in an uncertain environment, in which security of tenure and produce was never assured. Many tenants therefore attempted to overcome this by staying on good terms with their landlords, which often meant providing them with additional labour services and 'gifts' of various kinds on special occasions.

As noted earlier, the agricultural data in various official documents are almost worthless, since they were based on guesswork, or collected through questionable methods. In the area of revenue, trade and import/exports, there is more reliable information. Agriculture was a significant source of State revenue (though not the most significant), contributing in the early 1970s between 15% and 18% of the total revenue. Moreover, its potential as a future source of additional taxes did not pass unnoticed by decision-makers at the time (World Bank 1973, Vol. III, Annex 13).

Virtually all the country's exports consisted of agricultural goods, some 90% of which originated from the peasant sector. Some oilseeds, pulses and livestock products were all that modern agriculture contributed to the export drive. Coffee, the country's main export, accounting for up to 60% of export earnings in the 1960s, was mostly a peasant product, even though most of what was exported was not actually grown by the peasants themselves. There were three main 'systems' of coffee production. Forest production, accounting for about 60% of the coffee marketed, was by far the largest; this was coffee which grew in the wild in large forest areas, but was mostly harvested and brought to the market by the peasantry. Peasant coffee groves, maintained by rural households in Sidamo and Harrar provinces mainly, accounted for between 30% and 35% of the crop marketed. The rest came from modern or quasi-modern coffee plantations owned and managed by private entrepreneurs. In the early 1970s, coffee share of export earnings fell below 50%, while those of legumes and oilseeds rose appreciably. By 1974, gross earnings from all exports had reached US$238 million. Table 3 shows the composition of the country's exports in 1972, which seems to have been an average year, and 1952.

Table 3: Exports by Value 1972, 1952

	1972 % of total exports		1952 % of total exports
Coffee	48	Coffee	51.8
Oil Seeds	14	Oil Seeds	11.7
Hides/Skins	12	Hides/Skins	14.8
Livestock Prod.	8	Cereals	14.9
Legumes/Veg.	8	Other	6.8
Other	10		
Total	100		100

Source: CSO, 1975; USDA, 1956.

Policies, Plans and Prospects

The distinctive aspect of the country's agricultural policies during the Old Regime was that they were outward oriented, in two senses. First, international donor agencies, the World Bank and USAID (the US Agency for International Development) in particular, had considerable influence on policy formulation. The major objectives and programmes of development were freely borrowed from them and, to a lesser extent, other members of the donor community. It is true that planners became increasingly conscious of the complexities of development problems and policy planning over the years, nevertheless, most of the ideas incorporated into the major policy programmes came from outside the country.

Secondly, development policy relied heavily on financial and technical support from the donor community. In the early years of the Old Regime, in the 1950s and early 1960s, the aim of policy was to improve agricultural export potential and boost foreign earnings. The idea that agricultural growth should also bring about improvements in the rural population's nutritional and living standards came later; the goal of social equity through expanded employment and redistribution of wealth emerged in full only on the eve of the fall of the Old Regime, at the time the fourth development plan was being drafted. It should also be noted that agricultural policy was inconsistent and, until the last quarter of the Old Regime, decidedly biased against the peasant.

The idea of extension services to support agriculture came from USAID, and the first extension programme was started in 1954 through the agency's initiative as part of its agricultural training and assistance programme. The extension service, which was based at Alemaya College, was transferred to the Ministry of Agriculture in 1963, and by 1965 its staff numbered a mere 100 (Siira 1965). At the close of the decade, the service had not expanded appreciably; the field personnel had grown to 125 regulars and 75 specialists deployed in coffee growing areas. At this time too, the Ministry of National Community Development fielded rural agents responsible for a variety of community development activities; these numbered about 350. In comparison, at the beginning of the 1960s, Tanganyika, as it was then called, had an extension staff of over 1,000. On the other hand, the Extension and Project Implementation Department (EPID) of the MoA, which became responsible for all extension work, employed a total of 1,020 field agents in 1974. If we add to this the considerable number of extension personnel deployed by what were called the comprehensive projects, such as CADU, WADU, etc., it is evident that the 1970s and the changes in extension policy introduced by the end of the 1960s brought about a dramatic development in extension services. The peasant was now actively being sought by the 'development' State.

In the 1950s, agriculture was not considered important by decisionmakers, and State budgetary allocations to the Ministry of Agriculture remained woefully low. In this decade too, extension services were limited in scope:

the aim was to provide advice and information to the farming community, and the focus was mainly on livestock production (FAO/Huffnagel 1961). Sheep breeding, cattle raising and poultry were emphasized with the goal of raising exports of wool, hides and skins and poultry products. In imitation of American farm experience, considerable effort was made to organize in the rural areas Farmers' Youth Clubs whose main responsibility was to promote poultry production; by 1964, some 140 such clubs were formed throughout the country (see USOM/E annual reports; Siira 1965). It was only in the latter part of the 1960s, when extension services were revamped, that the focus of activity shifted to crop production and land use (thanks mainly to FAO and the World Bank). The idea that extension work should involve the distribution of yield-improving inputs to peasants and, along with this, improved farming practices a shift away from the oral discussion of the previous period was accepted and became part of government policy in 1967 (World Bank 1973, Vol. II).

There is no better way to examine the evolution of agricultural policy than through the various Five-Year Development Plans, which were the main instruments of development effort. In them, one can discern three main 'doctrines' which came to play a significant role in shaping agricultural policy. The first may be described as benign neglect of peasant agriculture, the second as alienating it and the active promotion of large-scale commercial farms, and the third, a swing in favour of small farms and peasant enterprises.

The Five-Year Plans

The First Five-Year Development Plan, to run from 1957 to 1961 (IEG 1956), laid heavy emphasis on building up the country's infrastructure. Priorities in investment were given to transport, communication and energy; service posts and education also got considerable support. Agriculture in general was at the lowest end of the scale of priorities. It was believed, though without solid evidence, that growth in food production had kept slightly above population growth in the first half of the 1950s, and was expected to do the same in the plan period without much support. The main stumbling block here was that peasant agriculture was an unknown quantity, since no serious attempt had been made to conduct field surveys and to collect useful information. Some support was offered in the area of coffee production and livestock breeding with the aim of improving the country's foreign exchange earnings.

In each of the three plans the agricultural sector received the least investment in comparison with the other major sectors In the First Plan it received 8%, in the Second 17% and in the Third 11% of total investment allocations. The lion's share in all cases went to transport, communications, energy and utilities. The manufacturing sector fared much better in relative terms, receiving investment allocations of 11%, 22% and 20% respectively in each of the Plans.

The Second Five-Year Development Plan (1963-67) is distinctive because it was here that the decisive turn in favour of agricultural modernization was made (IEG 1962). This shift away from smallholder agriculture and in favour of mechanization was to be the guiding doctrine for the next decade. The argument at the time was that modernization was necessary to achieve higher rates of growth; but modernization was also seen as providing a strong stimulus to peasant agriculture. The modern sector of agriculture was to be responsible for producing industrial crops, but was also to serve as the centre for the 'demonstration and dissemination' of efficient methods of farming to the peasantry. The goals for peasant agriculture remained modest, namely, to increase cereal production for domestic consumption and to improve production of exportable commodities such as coffee and livestock. Of the total monetary investment earmarked for agriculture in the plan period, the peasant sector received only 10%, commercial agriculture 53%, and manpower and resource inventory, the rest. Moreover, agriculture as a whole received less investment allocation than each of the major economic sectors, although, in relative terms, the investment allocated to it was higher than in the previous plan. Here the 'propulsive sectors', as they were called, were identified as mining, manufacturing and power.

Where precisely the idea of agricultural modernization originated and how it came to be so strongly endorsed by policy makers is an interesting question. It is evident that the chief influence was US advisors who were involved in a variety of programmes which later shaped government thinking. Certainly, the early staff reports of Alemaya College reflect a strong bias in favour of mechanization and large-scale enterprise, and of American methods of farm management (USOM/E 1955, 1956). Most mission and evaluation reports commissioned by USAID in the 1960s were quite positive about the prospects of commercial agriculture (SRI 1969d; USDA 1969). In support of earlier USAID positions, the SRI report insisted there were few alternatives to agricultural modernization, and recommended that policy should strongly support what it called a 'corporate development' strategy which would offer priority to commercial agriculture and agro-industrial enterprises, and to medium to small farms that produced mainly for the export market. The World Bank was equally positive about the policy of modernization (World Bank 1967), calling it an 'effective strategy' and a 'sound approach to development' (World Bank 1970, Vol. II), and later recommending greater investments in mechanization and modernization (1972).

The Third Five-Year Plan (1968-74), the last to be implemented during the Old Regime, is significant for two main reasons (IEG 1968). First, partly as a result of the strong donor support it had received, partly due to some successes in the plantation and agro-industrial schemes in the Awash Valley, the plan enthusiastically endorsed commercial agriculture. Modernization was seen as the catalyst which would accelerate agricultural growth, which in turn would rapidly improve the country's export performance; it was also felt that the impact of commercial agriculture on the economy as a whole would be immediate and effective. The case of mechanization, which was strengthened as pessimism about peasant agriculture reached a high point in the late 1960s. As in previous plans, agriculture received the lowest investment allocation in relation to the other major sectors, but once again the distribution of investment within agriculture itself was heavily weighted in favour of commercial farms, which received 58% of development allocations while the peasant sector had only 10%. Secondly, the Plan made concessions to the peasant sector and approved a programme of extended support to smallholder production. This came to be known as the package programme, and first consisted of the comprehensive or integrated package approach, and later, of the minimum package service.

The most dramatic reversal of government thinking on agricultural development occurred, first quietly and tentatively in 1971, then boldly and aggressively in 1973, at the time the Fourth Five-Year Development Plan was being drafted. In a short paper in 1971, the planners broached the idea of reversing the order of priorities accorded to the modern and peasant sectors of agriculture (IEG 1971). The document went so far as to suggest that smallholder agriculture ought to be given as much support as large-scale agriculture. But it was in 1973 that the re-ordering of priorities was placed on the agenda. There was widespread consensus (how that consensus was arrived at is not clear) among policy planners that the goal of development should not be merely quantitative growth but must also involve the improvement of living standards and the equitable distribution of wealth. The objective of the Fourth Plan (which was not completed) was to ensure 'that the benefits of social and economic development were more equitably distributed among the population' (PCO 1973a:I.8). The most important policy on the agricultural development strategy was to entail a twofold innovation: a) There was to be a greater emphasis on the development of smallholder agriculture as commercial agriculture was relegated to a less significant status; and b) an integrated rural development programme was to be set up in the framework of awraja self-administration. The legislation for local administration at the awraja level was approved in 1966, although no practical steps were taken to set up the necessary institutions.

Integrated Rural Development

The idea of integrated rural development came first from the International Labour Office (ILO), which had been asked to advise the government on projects for rural employment, and which strongly recommended integrated rural development schemes as a solution to rural unemployment (ILO 1970; Blaug 1974). The ILO's arguments were deceptively simple, and the solution it proposed appeared at least affordable. It estimated that the rural labour force would grow by a high rate, and rural unemployment would soar even if employment opportunities were opened up rapidly in the modern sector of the economy, which it saw as unlikely. Blaug, the head of the second ILO Employment Mission which came to advise the government in 1972-73, strongly argued that the reduction of 'rural unemployment by agricultural development rather than by the development of manufacturing in urban centres has become a prime policy objective in most developing countries'.[10] Integrated rural development programmes were the only solution to provide employment opportunities to the rural population on a sufficiently large scale. Such programmes would take advantage of the minimum package services, promote local participation by incorporating peasant self-help schemes, and enhance the development of local resources.

The new strategy, which was set out in series of documents distributed for discussion in 1973 (PCO 1973a, 1973b) recognized that although inefficient by 'modern standards', peasant agriculture was nonetheless the most significant sector of the rural economy and held better prospects in the long run than modern agriculture. There is sufficient evidence, planners argued, that small farmers 'utilize their cropped areas more intensively and frequently realize higher yield per hectare' (PCO 1973a:III-11) than large-scale farmers. With greater extension support, more reliance on green technology, and expanded credit services, smallholder agriculture could become the main force in rural development. The added advantage here, it was believed, was that peasant agriculture would absorb a high percentage of the rural labour force which would otherwise remain outside the development process. Not only was large-scale agriculture NOT offering comparable employment opportunities; it was displacing tenants and poor peasants and thereby compounding the unemployment problem. The key concept for the forthcoming Fourth Plan was thus greater emphasis on small farms development, and greater assistance to the peasant sector (PCO 1973b: Annex II).

The master strategy for invigorating smallholder agriculture was to be integrated rural development, which was to consist of four broad programmes: a) spreading the seed-fertilizer technology through the accelerated expansion of MPP; b) mass adult education aimed at extending literacy/numeracy, and agricultural and vocational training; c) labour-intensive rural public works to develop infrastructure, and provide rural employment; and d) expansion of basic health services to the peasantry. The new policy was not only strongly peasant-oriented but also sought to 'penalize' commercial agriculture, the darling of the two earlier plans. It recommended the abolition of tax exemptions and fiscal incentives from which owners and operators of large farms had benefited since the mid-1960s. It recommended that new civil infrastructure projects in the rural areas be constructed to serve in the main smallholder enterprises (1973a: Ch. III).

The Package Programmes

The comprehensive package approach refers to large, multi-purpose and integrated development operations such as the Chilalo Agricultural Development Unit (CADU), which was started in 1967 with Swedish aid, and the Wollaita Agricultural Development Unit (WADU) which was set up in 1970 with IDA/World Bank assistance. A third comprehensive project, the Ada District Development Project (ADDP), was launched with USAID support in 1972. Other multi-purpose programmes included HADP (Humera Agricultural Development Project), TAHADU (Tach Adiabo and Hadekti Agricultural Development Unit) in Tigrai, and SORADEP (Southern Regional Agricultural Development Project)serving the central Rift Valley areas. There were also several low-profile integrated programmes run by government agencies other than MoA in several parts of the country. The main objectives of the programmes were the following: to provide peasants easy access to modern inputs; to promote better farming techniques and farm implements; to organize peasants into co-operatives that would offer them better access to credit; to expand normal extension services; to improve marketing facilities and prices for peasant produce; and to build rural public works such as feeder roads, water projects and environmental protection schemes. Let us briefly examine CADU, the most successful of all the comprehensive programmes (on WADU see MoA 1973, esp. Vol. I).

CADU

It is worth noting that the South-east Asian experience in integrated rural development served as a model for CADU. The 'intensive agricultural district' programmes in India, and more importantly the Comilla multi-purpose project in what was then East Pakistan (now Bangladesh), were the main inspiration behind the project when it was being prepared by its Swedish planners. Later, some CADU staff visited both programmes and returned with favourable impressions (SIDA 1966; CADU 1969). At the time the project was being put together, the World Bank and FAO were preparing to put before the Ethiopian authorities an integrated approach to rural development based on the widespread use of green revolution innovations, and SIDA planners freely borrowed some of their ideas (SIDA 1966:111). It is thus not an exaggeration to say that CADU was designed and launched without a serious investigation of local peasant experiences, agricultural needs and development priorities. In fact, until the project document was completed the planners did not know where the project was to be located; it was then that the government offered the Swedish International Development Agency (SIDA) half a dozen or so project sites in different agro-ecological zones to choose from.

Most evaluations of CADU show that the programme was on the whole a success, even though the extent of success remains a bone of contention.[11] Nevertheless, the all-round impact of the project on the Chilalo peasantry has not, to my knowledge, been fully investigated. Instead, CADU and SIDA officials on the one hand, and outside investigators on the other, were eager to demonstrate the benefits of the project in terms solely of income and productivity improvements. However, as there was no reliable base value of incomes, production or yield in Chilalo before the project was launched, and as the various surveys on these issues were conducted in different localities, thus making comparison difficult, measuring economic improvements came to involve a good amount of speculation and guess-work.

The project office estimated in the early 1970s that average peasant income in the project area grew by E$75 annually since 1968 (CADU 1971a:4). Holmberg (1973), who made a serious effort to measure income and consumption levels in the area, came to the conclusion that mean annual income in Etheya, a relatively well-endowed and prosperous area which was a beneficiary of CADU from the very beginning, was about E$1,618 in 1971-72, and that the median income of peasants here had doubled in the four years of CADU activity (1979:88-89). Cohen (1974), on the other hand, suggests that a participating household in Chilalo working about 6 hectares of farm land may have increased its income annually by E$ 200 to 300, while Tesfai Tecle (1975) argues that the average income of a 'middle peasant' in Chilalo increased from E$314 in 1966 to E$883 in 1971 (:56). Despite these seeming improvements in income, however, EPID noted that the amount of rural tax collected from Chilalo awraja (i.e., land, income, health and other taxes) declined annually between 1967 and 1971; similarly, tax assessment also showed a decline in these years (EPID 1974b:82). In contrast, there is strong evidence that the number of overall beneficiaries grew considerably over the years reaching its peak in the mid-1970s, and that a good deal of rural infrastructure was constructed in the area.

Let us now consider the project's main areas of failure. It is my opinion that CADU failed to promote innovative farming practices that were not dependent on costly modern inputs. Its effort to popularize new technical equipment like the moldboard plough, the harrow and the ox-cart was by and large unsuccessful (vid. Gill 1976). The most serious failure of the project lay in the social consequences of its activities in Chilalo. In the first place, the main beneficiaries were the more prosperous peasants and those with secure tenure arrangements. The poor and a majority of the tenantry benefitted the least. The issue of social equity came to weigh heavily on the main donor, SIDA, which exerted considerable efforts to have the government pass legislation to relieve the burden of those with insecure tenures who were unable to benefit from CADU programmes. Secondly, considerable peasant evictions from the land took place in the area particularly in the period when CADU was most active and its programmes were beginning to pay off. Thirdly, the package of innovations offered to the participating peasantry was highly dependent on external economies and consequently, from a cost-benefit point of view, what was achieved would not in the long-run be worth the cost or sustainable.

The second strategy of rural development promoted by the government in the period 1968-74 was the Minimum Package Programme (MPP)designed to reach a greater number of peasants, and which eventually was believed to lead to agricultural transformation. The idea of the MPP came from the World Bank (with support from FAO) towards the end of the 1960s (World Bank 1970, Vol. II). FAO's Freedom from Hunger Campaign had been conducting fertilizer trials in various parts of the country since 1965, and the results were said to be very encouraging. Moreover, both donors were of the opinion, even from the start, that the comprehensive programmes were far too costly to be extended to the mass of the peasantry and to serve as a viable vehicle for rural development on a large scale. These were the main reasons for the concept behind the MPP. The Bank seems to have had no difficulty convincing Ethiopian agricultural experts and officials to try it on a limited scale. The objective was to provide peasants a select number of 'proven innovations' (such as fertilizers, high-yield seeds, etc.) which were believed to possess high impact capability. These innovations were to be introduced first in high potential areas and, with greater success and peasant participation, to other areas eventually. It was believed that these innovations would have immediate results in the form of high output, high yield and increased income for peasants. This was the green revolution dressed up in Ethiopian garb. The World Bank was quite enthusiastic about the prospects, believing that a real agricultural transformation was possible in the framework of smallholder production and at a modest and affordable cost to the country (World Bank 1973, Vol. II).

The Minimum Package Programme, administered through EPID, a unit within the Ministry of Agriculture, became operational in the latter part of

1971. FAO's fertilizer programme was integrated into the MPP soon after EPID was established. EPID's task from the very beginning was ambitious. It was responsible for the distribution of modern inputs (fertilizers, improved seeds, crop-protecting chemicals), the dissemination of technical innovations and better methods of crop management and the organization of co-operatives for credit and purchasing services. The methods employed for the dissemination of innovations were rather conventional, and were borrowed from the Asian experience. They consisted in demonstrating to farmers new techniques and inputs, selection of what were called model farmers to spearhead the adoption process and advice and verbal exhortation by dedicated but inexperienced extension agents in the field.[12] Field agents worked in what were called extension areas, five of which made up a Minimum Package Programme Area or MPPA, which catered on the average for about 10,000 peasant beneficiaries. In the nature of things, almost all the extension areas (some 250 had been set up by 1974) were located in communities served by the major road networks. The input approach for such was the Ethiopian style of green revolution was heavily dependent on modern transport services. Moreover, until 1975, EPID relied on fertilizer as its main innovation and, for a variety of reasons, it was unable to provide high-yield seeds or crop-protection chemicals.

By 1974, EPID had reached only 50,000 beneficiaries. Total fertilizer sales increased from 946 metric tons in 1970-71 to 6,724 metric tons in 1973-74; improved seed sales rose from 22 metric tons to 123 metric tons in the same period (EPID 1975b:14). At the end of 1974, extension work in all its forms (i.e., MPP, the comprehensive approach and others) had reached about 16% of the estimated farming population. In the second phase of EPID, i.e., 1975-80, the aim was to extend the programme to involve about 25% of peasant households in the country; by the end of this period, namely, after ten years of operations, the average income of participating households was expected to increase by 25 to 40%.

EPID and the integrated programmes did register some significant successes; for example, promising improvements in output and productivity were observed and a dynamic peasant sector began to emerge as a consequence in Arssi, and southern and south-western Shoa where the new programmes had been tried out the longest. Cohen, who earlier was a critic of the programmes (1975), but later became an enthusiastic supporter of the integrated approach, has ranked CADU among the best known development projects in the world, comparable to the famous models in Mexico and India (1987:14-15). This is an exaggeration. The government itself rejected the CADU approach in the end, saying it was too costly to replicate elsewhere.

EPID and the MPP approach had inherent limitations. The input approach, as it came to be practised, did not employ novel methods and did not take into account the experience of the peasant, the farming system in use, or the property structure in force. It did not attempt to introduce a more dynamic and more resilient farming system; the modernization of peasant agriculture was to consist solely of supplying modern inputs, in practice, mostly fertilizer. The modern, in other words, was to be grafted on the traditional. When drought struck in the third year of the programme, MPP beneficiaries as well as non-beneficiaries became equally vulnerable, and EPID, unable to meet the challenge in a novel way, turned itself into a relief agency through the initiative of FAO and other donors (EPID 1974a, 1975a). Secondly, the input approach inevitably led to greater dependence on external economies, on the one hand, and growing government subsidies on the other. By 1974, EPID came to realize that there was an urgent need to diversify its extension package in the light of sharply rising fertilizer costs. More non-chemical inputs and improved farming practices were some of the options it began to consider seriously (EPID 1974c:6). The most significant shortcoming of the programme had to do with the effectiveness of the innovations themselves on the one hand, and the distortions caused by the existing property system on the other.

From the very beginning, the impact of fertilizers and improved seeds was considerably exaggerated and what the World Bank called 'proven innovations' were proven not really in the context of peasant practices in Ethiopia but elsewhere in the Third World. The green revolution requires a variety of basic infrastructure (including water management and irrigation schemes), very few of which were in place during the implementation of the new programmes. High-yield seeds, for example, perform better under irrigation, but Ethiopia is water-deficient, and its surface and underground water sources are either insufficient for large-scale irrigated agriculture or the investment needed to promote such a venture is prohibitive.

EPID's own evaluation of the impact of fertilizer on crop yield revealed some surprising results (EPID 1974b:20). Except for maize, fertilized fields showed a yield difference of between 30% and 40%, which was too small to make a significant difference in income, taking into account the cost of the input, the time and trouble of obtaining, transporting and storing it by the peasant. CADU's experience is similar: the difference in crop yield between fields using green revolution and traditional inputs is 50% or less (CADU 1972, 1975a). It has been shown elsewhere in this country, including WADU trials in the 1970s, that a yield response of less than 60 to 70% cannot be physically seen in the field by the average peasant; and peasants are more willing to try fertilizers if the yield response is 100% or more and if the economic returns are significantly good (Dessalegn 1990b:37-38). EPID's conclusion was that, for peasants growing small-stalk crops, using fertilizer was not of great benefit. Table 4 presents comparative figures for crop yield from EPID and CADU surveys.

Moreover, the incremental income obtained from fertilizer was dependent not just on the rate of crop yield but also on the price of the input itself. EPID argued that higher fertilizer prices to farmers would negate productivity gains, and advised the government to be prepared to offer price subsidies on fertilizers to support MPP beneficiaries. Without such subsidies, or exceptionally high grain prices, the use of green technology inputs would be unprofitable to all classes of farmers (EPID 1974b:22-25).

Judged from the standpoint of social equity, the package programmes were clearly a failure. The 'proven' innovations went mostly to small landlords and owner-cultivators while poor peasants and tenant farmers were largely left out. According to EPID (1974b:71), some 85% of input sales went to owners, and only 5% to tenants. The CADU experience is also similar: more landowners benefitted from its services than share-croppers or poor peasants (CADU 1971). The method of input distribution in fact favoured owners and discriminated against tenants, who were obliged to show written contracts from their landlords to be eligible for credit and other services a practice which was discontinued in 1974 following concerted complaints by donors and technical advisors. The co-operatives that were the main channel of credit and related services were often dominated by small landowners and 'rich' peasants. The co-operative movement in any event was slow: from 1966, when the co-operative legislation was approved, to 1974 not more than one co-operative society managed to obtain registration. The average peasant was not quite aware of the benefits of co-operatives and lacked the skills to set them up to the satisfaction of the authorities.

Table 4: Yield Figures for Selected Crops with and without Modern Inputs (quintals per hectare)

Crops	Not Fertilized		Fertilized	
	EPID	CADU	EPID	CADU
Barely	10.1	16.5	13.3	20.51
Teff	8.0	12.1	10.9	16.0
Sorghum	19.0	-	23.0	-
Maize	43.8	27.1	64.8	32.5
Wheat	10.6	16.2	14.9	22.61

Source: EPID, 1974b; CADU, 1975.

Note 1: High-yield varieties were used; all the rest are local varieties in both CADU and EPID trials.

Moreover, both the MPP and the comprehensive programmes gave rise to peasant evictions on a large scale. Landlords who adopted the new innovations, or wished to turn their land into commercial enterprises removed the tenantry on their property at short notice. The experience was similar in Arssi, the Ada area, and the south-western parts of the country.

The input approach discriminated against all peasants who did not live close to the road network. An extension area was where the inputs and the agents were and such areas had to be in a location served by a road; it was designed to reach peasants along the road and ten to fifteen kilometres on each side of it. Thus extension touched only those peasants on or within a short radius of an all-weather road; all others who were only accessible by animal transport were left out (see Map 2). In the early 1970s some 70% of rural households were not accessible by road.

Finally, EPID was a bureaucratic organization, and it suffered all the attendant ills of such an outfit. It also had insufficient trained manpower, and was hurt by delays and inefficiencies in operations. The cost of the agency was also high: some 50% of the EPID budget was spent on staff salaries and office expenses. This may be considered reasonable in comparison with the other comprehensive programmes such as WADU, where staff and office expenses ate up 90% of the agency's budget.

The package programmes were not a resounding success, but they were not total failures either. They did raise the problem of rural development in a way different from earlier doctrines, and focused attention on peasant producers, their potentials and limitations. I believe this, more than anything else, is their success story. Indeed, in some areas and among some peasant groups the green revolution did show considerable potential. In the first half of the 1970s, for example, successful peasants involved in the CADU programme had an average cereal yield of 20 quintals per hectare or more, which was equal to or better than yield levels achieved by the average south Asian peasant in the same period and for the same category of crops (FAO 1987:17-18). The green revolution, we should note, had a much longer history in Asia than in Ethiopia.

The programmes, however, aroused considerable controversy. In particular, advisors from Sweden, the country which contributed heavily both to EPID and CADU, took a very critical position, while others were on the whole quite positive (see Dessalegn 1986 for some of the literature). One of the most persistent critics of the programme was Michael Stahl (1973, 1974) who argued that the package approach benefited the rich and not the poor, led to the eviction of tenants, and strengthened the position of the landed classes in the rural areas. He does, however, admit, somewhat grudgingly, that the programme was beneficial to some needy peasants who managed to participate in it long enough. Quite the opposite view was taken by Tesfai Teckle, an Ethiopian specialist who evaluated the programme on the eve of the revolution (1975). His verdict was that the MPP was a success, while the integrated projects were too expensive to sustain or duplicate elsewhere in the country. The MPP, he thought, recorded major achievements in the first phase of its operation. Many experts believe, he pointed out, 'that Ethiopia has so far been fortunate in developing a rather simple technological package ... that is widely applicable' (1975:90).

The World Bank, on the other hand, was over-enthusiastic about the success of the inputbased approach implemented by EPID (World Bank 1975a:41-42). The application of fertilizers, it noted in one of its policy papers, has been so successful as to convince Ethiopian peasants of their usefulness without much persuasion by extension personnel. It attributed the rapid adoption of modern inputs to the following factors: a) a first class technical package offered to peasants; b) sufficiently respected community people prepared to act as model farmers without payment; c) a 'land tenure system which does not discourage production above subsistence level'; and d) a loose system of credit. It suggested, moreover, that the MPP was uniquely suited to Ethiopian conditions. There are, it pointed out, 'few examples of this type of national program, despite its considerable advantage for countries with limited resources and massive rural poverty. Social and economic stratification in many South Asian countries, for example, would seem to preclude widespread application of the minimum package approach'. Needless to say, the Bank's enthusiasm was not fully supported by the evidence that both EPID and the older comprehensive programmes had accumulated over the years.

Plans and Achievements

How much was accomplished and what advances were made in nearly two decades of development planning? This is a difficult question to answer, and the conclusions I offer are my own and subject to debate.

In the area of agricultural production in general, the achievements were quite modest. Measured in quantitative terms employing conventional indices (such as output, productivity, etc), or in terms of food security and nutritional adequacy, the agricultural record of the Old Regime is more than disappointing. Assessments provided in official documents point out that agricultural growth fell below the targets set for it, and were often below population growth in each of the three plan periods; outside the MPP areas productivity was either stagnant or growing at unsatisfactory rates, and that the structural impediments to improved production grew more burdensome, not less (Ministry of Planning 1967b; PCO 1973b).

There are, however, some bright spots in the general picture, namely, that agriculture would have fared even worse had it not received the modest level of support it did in the years since the early 1960s. Perhaps of greater significance is the fact that a considerable number of rural producers became increasingly aware that modern inputs and new forms of cultivation could improve their output and their income, and that the road to 'modernization' did not necessarily lead to the tractor, the harvester and the displacement of the poor. Those peasants who were fortunate enough to benefit from the package programmes (rich peasants and small landowners, mostly) were setting a pace which would have given rise to a dynamic peasant sector with great potential if it had become widespread.

It should be noted that, viewed in regional terms, the south benefited more than the north from the various agricultural programmes implemented during the Old Regime. For reasons which we do not have space to discuss here, policy planners favoured the south more than the north. By the close of the Old Regime, regional disparities had a distinctive north/south profile, though there were some significant exceptions i.e., economic regions which did not fit into this scheme. The involutionary process noted at the outset of this chapter was more evident in the northern provinces of Wollo, Tigrai, Eritrea and eastern Begemdir. In contrast, the areas showing good prospects and undergoing considerable improvements were Arssi province, and the south-central and south-western regions where the package programmes were heavily concentrated and where resource endowments were generally better (see Map 2 above).

If we were to point to one critical bottleneck which impeded the successful implementation of the three plans it would have to be the structure of landholding which gave the agrarian order of the time an inflexible character (Dessalegn 1984, Ch. 2 for a brief discussion). In the Second, but more so the Third Plan, a strong case was made for far-reaching land reform, without which, it was argued, progress in all sectors of the agrarian economy would be blocked. But no such reform was ever attempted, and the half-hearted tenancy reform which the government finally managed to submit to Parliament in the early 1970s never made it into the law books. It may be worth noting in this connection that, of the two major donors involved in the country's agriculture, USAID was not convinced of the need for land reform (Miller 1963) while the World Bank was lukewarm about it (World Bank 1975b).

Indeed, while policy planners and political activists were demanding radical land redistribution, the Ministry of Land Reform and Administration (MLRA), which was set up in 1966, was quietly promoting resettlement(or land settlement as it was then called) as a viable alternative (see Dessalegn 1989 for details). The major assumption within MLRA and its expatriate advisors was that vast and unutilized resources as much as 12 million hectares according to some estimates were held by the government in the form of State domain land. These resources could easily be distributed to land-hungry peasants and those with insecure holdings. Land settlement had a double-edged objective: it was seen as relieving the population pressure in the northern provinces and as a means of distributing under-utilized land to the poor and the landless. It was, in other words, a resettlement programme as well as a land reform measure and, in this latter guise, was meant to reassure the landed classes that their property and economic power in the rural areas was not in danger.

By the time the Old Regime was overthrown, however, resettlement had been tried on a limited scale with mixed results. On the other hand, the landed classes must have come to regret, specially on the eve of the revolution, their stubborn resistance to the land and tenancy reform initiatives proposed in the past, many of which were mild enough not to have threatened their power and property, which the revolution duly swept away without anyone shedding a tear.

Conclusion: Involution or Evolution

Why did peasant agriculture in the Old Regime fail to make a decisive turnaround, to transform itself (or be transformed) into a dynamic system of production? How do we explain the agricultural stagnation of the country, and the involution of peasant production in most parts of the central and northern highlands? What were the odds favouring capitalist development, either smallholder or large-scale, in the rural economy?

A brief review of the literature may help us place these questions in perspective. In the general debate on the economic and social backwardness of Ethiopia, the earliest and the most common explanation was cultural and socio-psychological. Highland Ethiopian culture, it was argued, is a confining one, resistant to change and even reactionary. Social and inter-personal relations are based on strong traditional values which promote unquestioned acceptance of authority and hierarchic order on the one hand, and inter-personal rivalry on the other. Individuals are wont to seek their own short-term self-interest, and success is based on manipulation of others rather than personal achievement. Secretiveness and withholding of information is said to be customary. Ethiopian culture, we are told, is defined by the wax-and-gold syndrome, i.e., by ambiguity and equivocation, and is opposed to the rationalist ethos of modern societies (Levine 1965; Korten 1972). The weight of tradition inhibits the search for new ideas or new methods of work; indeed, tradition as codified in religious practice, often defines the conditions of labour and the forms of employment.

In my view, such cultural theses are seriously flawed, for at the heart of their argument is the highly subjective proposition that all cultures which are not informed by western values are backward (for example Japan is the so-called 'Asian tiger', etc.).

More relevant to us may be what I call the single-factor explanation of backwardness. The factors which are often singled out are insufficiency of modern infrastructure in the rural areas, market dependency, peasant inadequacy (ignorance, backward farming methods, etc.), and the land tenure system. The World Bank has been the most persistent advocate of heavy investment in rural transport. The lack of adequate transport services, it is believed, has been a principal constraint in the movement of food grain from surplus to deficit areas and has contributed to the food supply deficiency in the country (Fekadu and Phillips 1972). More significantly, the restricted movement of agricultural produce and of people has underdeveloped the rural market system, making it play a less vigorous role in peasant production than it would have played if the opposite was the case. The greater the market integration of the peasant, it is argued, the greater the chances for a shift from a subsistence economy, which now defines the logic of peasant production to a market (i.e., capitalist) economy.

Until the beginning of the 1970s, policy planners blamed peasant inadequacy for the lack of progress in agriculture. Cohen's political-economy approach links together peasant inadequacy, the land system and other factors to explain agricultural stagnation (1987:45-46). He argues that, without significant reforms, the rural sector will continue to be an impediment to development, but serious reforms were blocked by the alliance of urban elites and the landed classes. Modernization was thus frustrated by a combination of class forces on the one hand, and an exploitative property arrangement on the other.

Then there are the neo-Malthusians, whose explanation of long-term agricultural decline shifts the argument to demography and technology. The simplest neo-Malthusian position sees accelerated population growth and declining land resources as being responsible for pushing the already vulnerable agrarian sector to the brink of disaster (Robinson and Yamazaki 1986). A more nuanced approach is that taken by James McCann (1988). Following LeRoy Ladurie, McCann attempts to apply elements of the Malthusian model to Ethiopian agrarian history. LeRoy Ladurie's secular Malthusianism (1974) was set in the framework of an agrarian cycle corresponding to significant swings in demography. A sharp demographic expansion leads to a decline in land productivity, to technological stagnation and the pauperization of the masses. This is accompanied by widespread famines and epidemics which decimate the population and bring the decline of agriculture to its lowest point. The agrarian cycle begins again with gradual prosperity after the 'biological' disaster since the population density is low and land resources are once again abundant. McCann's agrarian model is not exactly cyclical, but he traces the impact of demography, climate, technology, cropping and property systems (and also political factors) on agriculture, and examines their contribution to productivity decline and stagnation. As with LeRoy Ladurie, he sees a demographic explosion as being responsible for triggering the chain of events; the existing technological stagnation and the ever-decreasing resource base give rise to greater impoverishment and to more environmentally damaging farming practices. What we have here is a vicious circle, not an agrarian cycle.

McCann's arguments may be criticized on three counts: he overstates the impact of the demographic factor; he gives very little credit for the considerable technological advances initiated by peasants themselves; and he underplays the sociological factors and the impact of class relations. McCann's work is mostly about the agricultural history of north-east Ethiopia, a region dominated by cereal cultivation and a rugged environment. The agrarian history of the regions defined by the *ensete* culture, which McCann did not study, provides some interesting contrasts, of which the following are noteworthy: a) it is possible to contain the demographic pressure or minimize its impact by such adaptive mechanisms as intensive cultivation, more and better use of resilient crops, and by planting cultivars that promote economy of land use; and b) high population pressure is not incompatible with environmentally responsible farming practices (Dessalegn 1990b, 1992; Jackson 1970; and Jackson et al. 1969). The *ensete* zone has managed to sustain a much higher density of population than the cereal zone, and has had fewer famine experiences.

For a fresh approach, we need to turn from political economy and demography to sociology and class relations. If we leave aside for the moment the inchoate capitalist farmer of the late 1960s and early 1970s (see below), we may say that the agrarian class structure of Ethiopia has remained unchanged for perhaps a century. No intermediate class or social strata appeared between the lord and the peasant, both of whom were 'frozen' within the existing system; they were content, in other words, to maintain the existing social and economic relations. One strong piece of evidence for this is the dearth of peasant uprisings, which are often taken as indicators of the nature of class relations and of class tensions at a given time. Moreover, as noted above, neither lord nor peasant actively sought technological changes or changes in the methods of production. Technology, it should be stressed, does not change unless there is a class or social force which needs better technology and is able to use it profitably. In brief, we are referring to social stagnation as a critical factor in agricultural involution.

Tied to this is a second factor, namely, that the land system and the ensemble of social relations built on it further discouraged innovative endeavour or the emergence of innovative elements. With the exceptions noted below, peasant society was and remained undifferentiated. I believe differentiation would have had a healthy impact on the agrarian economy. A third factor is that peasant society was insufficiently integrated into the international market or the world system. I am not, of course, arguing that population pressure, and/or resource insufficiency were irrelevant to the questions under discussion; they have had a significant impact, but the primacy accorded them by the neo-Malthusians and others is, I believe, misplaced. Let me deal with this last point first.

As indicated earlier, the peasant sector was the main source of export earnings, contributing four-fifths or more of the country's exports. This dominant position remained unchanged all through the Old Regime. It would be an exaggeration to say that, for this reason, the peasantry was integrated into the world market. Peasant products were channelled to European or American markets mainly through the agency of the export merchant. For the majority of peasants, the local market was far more significant than the world market, and the logic of peasant production centred around self-sustenance and the preservation of existing standards of life. The few industrial goods the peasant purchased from the market were either mostly produced in-country, could easily be substituted with products of the indigenous craft industry, or were insignificant in so far as the world market was concerned. Then, as well as today, salt, sugar, cheap textile products, edible oil and kerosene were mostly what peasants bought from the local market.

Relations between the landed classes and the subordinate peasantry remained for the most part traditional all through the Old Regime. The chief method of surplus extraction, such as rent in kind and labour services, was neither suitable for capital accumulation nor conducive to improved production. The absence of long-term contractual arrangements between the lord and the tenant, which was the norm, discouraged investments on the land or experiments on new methods of production. Though the evidence is lacking, there is good reason to believe that tenant holdings may have grown smaller from the end of the 1950s. Plot consolidation and enlarged operations were closed to rest holders in the north and owner-operators in the south due to the system of partible inheritance in which a father divided up his property among all his children at the time of his death. Subsistence agriculture is essentially polyculture, a practice which again encourages land fragmentation and discourages crop specialization. In contrast to the landlords of pre-modern Europe who were closely involved in the agrarian economy, the landed classes in this country showed little interest in agricultural production and land management.

The package programmes, and certain forms of export agriculture, invigorated a good number of small to medium operators. These elements came from the strata of small landowners, owner-operators and those who worked their own land as well as land rented from others. It is interesting to note that commercial agriculture attracted not only farmers employing modern machinery but those using the ox-drawn plough. In areas like Ada district, and in the Rift Valley regions, small owners participated vigorously in the new agriculture, often evicting their tenants and operating their farms with traditional equipment. Small operators played just as significant a role as large capitalist farmers in the rapid development of the Setit-Humera region. Some 42% of the cultivated area in the region was operated by ox-ploughing farmers and the rest by tractor operators in the early 1970s (Dessalegn 1986). In the period 1970-73, AID Bank, which was the main source of credit for rural enterprises, made loans to commercial farmers worth E$18.9 million. In the same period, its loans to farmers' co-operatives totalled E$15.3 million, of which 92% was taken out by Humera small farmers' co-operatives (AID Bank 1974).

Owner-operators and owner-tenants were a force in the rural economy, although we have no hard evidence to measure it. The latter peasants are specially interesting. While the evidence is patchy, one is tempted to view these peasants as enterprising spirits who acquired tenancy rights to earn more income even though their own plots do not seem to have been small (MoA, 1975:61-68). Whether these two rural elements would have eventually emerged as the energetic force bearing the seeds of capitalism is, of course, an intriguing question, but in the given circumstances, and in the face particularly of the existing property structure, the prospects of such a development would not have been easy.

To complete the discussion of agrarian class relations, a few words on commercial agriculture are in order. In the early 1970s, commercial agriculture, concentrated in the Awash Valley, the Rift Valley, Arssi and Bale provinces, the Setit lowlands and western Ethiopia, operated about 3% of the agricultural area of the country and contributed some 7% to the gross value of agricultural production. Its contribution to the country's export earnings was modest but had been increasing considerably since the 1960s. By far the largest operations outside Setit Humera were State and foreign-owned; on the other hand, many of the private enterprises were small to medium operations struggling to survive. In the field of employment creation, commercial agriculture played a contradictory role: it provided considerable off-season jobs to peasants particularly in the Awash Valley and the Setit basin, but evicted a large number of peasants from their fields and threatened small operators in other areas. Commercial enterprises practised a form of agriculture which was environmentally damaging; soil management techniques were frequently poor and occasionally irresponsible. The urge to recoup one's investments and enjoy the profits quickly made farm operators unconcerned about the long-term environmental consequences. Indeed, even under the best conditions, peasant techniques of controlling soil erosion were frequently superior to those employed by commercial farmers (Ware-Austin 1970).

The capitalist farmer, who briefly held the limelight on the stage, appeared, as it were, when the play was about to come to a crashing end. This is perhaps in keeping with its birth, which was just as unconventional and precipitate as its end. The commercial farmer was, by and large, the urban petty bourgeois turned rural capitalist and was active only in the last six or so years of the Old Regime. The most active entrepreneurs were high and middle-level civil servants, professionals, businessmen and, on occasions, senior military officials. As in other African countries, it was the prospects opened up by the green revolution that attracted commercial investment in agriculture (Goody 1980). For the majority of entrepreneurs involved, especially the urban-based ones, it was the contract arrangement which provided access to land and, on occasions, to farm machinery. The capitalist farmer was typically a transient farmer with all the worst attributes that go with such a profession. The system of transient cultivation was one in which the farmer was frequently not a farmer by profession:

> ... *did not reside in the vicinity of his farm and was solely interested in extracting as much profit as possible and within the shortest time. Because of the hostile environment, the insecurity of tenure and uncertain future prospects ... the transient cultivator was not primarily concerned with the development of the land, with long-term investments or amicable relations with the surrounding peasantry. He was basically a 'moon-lighter', out to make a quick buck.... He appeared on his farm only occasionally, made the most minimal improvements on his holdings and defaulted on his debt payments as often as he thought he could get away with it* (Dessalegn 1986:85).

Table 5 shows the social or class background of commercial farmers registered with the Ethiopian Chamber of Commerce and operating in selected parts of the country. In 1973, there were a total of 1,500 registered commercial farm operations.

It is interesting to note that, among the landed classes, the local gentry were by far the largest group. Further, indigenous farm operators, i.e., farmers residing in the locality of their farms, mostly local landlords and local petty bourgeois elements, were not insignificant. In Arssi, for example, indigenous operators made up 25% of all the commercial farmers; they were located in the Hitossa and Koffele areas. In Bale, the figure was 17% and 37% in Harrar. Indigenous farmers in Kaffa, mostly coffee growers around the Sokorou area (some 80 km east of Jimma), made up 20% of all farmers while in Wollega the figure was 33%.

Table 5: Class Background of Select Commercial Farmers

Region	Petty bourgeoisie	Percentage of farmers Landed class	Other/unknown
Arssi	73	17	10
Bale	69	25	6
Kaffa	66	23	11
S. Shoa	72	19	9

Source: Compiled from Directory of Ethiopian Chamber of Commerce.
Note: 'Landed class' includes nobility and local gentry.

It is tempting to argue that commercial agriculture represented the 'propulsive force' (to use a favourite phrase of the early planners) which was poised to transform the agricultural economy of the country. But a careful examination suggests that the route to capitalist development would have been more complex, and less dependent on the 'transient' rural capitalist. Already, in the last years of the Old Regime, commercial agriculture was showing signs of old age, having lost its earlier robustness due, among other things, to the oscillations of the world grain market, declining productivity and higher prices of imported machinery and spare parts. It was indeed becoming clearer that improving peasant farm practices would bring more benefits, at least as far as food crops were concerned, than bringing new land under mechanized cultivation, mainly because the land available for such purposes would have required heavy investment. Moreover, the route to capitalist development via commercial agriculture would have involved massive evictions of peasants from the land, the consequences of which would have been profound rural discontent and maybe even violent disorder. In contrast, transformation through the agency of the smallholder-turned-capitalist 'kulak' would have involved less social pain, and would have been more sustainable in the longrun.

All this is speculation, however, and no one will really know what the nature of the changes would have been if the Old Regime had not been so rudely dismantled and if the political process had allowed a peaceful transition. I would like to end this chapter with the following words of Ann Lambton, a distinguished specialist in agrarian studies (1971):

> *The quality of the Ethiopian peasants is one of the assets of Ethiopia. They are, in general, industrious and independent. The aim of any agrarian policy should be to help them to realize their potentiality and to treat them as an asset and not a liability.*

Notes

1. The temptation to compare the record of the Old Regime and that of the military government may be great; our intention here, however, is to examine the subject at hand in its own context. The Old Regime refers to the Imperial Ethiopian Government (IEG). The present breakdown of the administrative boundaries of the country, and the names of the administrative units, which were introduced in 1986, are confusing, to say the least. We shall stick to the boundaries and names as they were used in the early 1970s (see Map 1).
2. See the agricultural section in CSO's Statistical Abstracts of the 1960s and early 1970s. See also Abraham, 1972 for an extended discussion. The first micro-level survey was conducted in 1957-58. CSO's first and second round surveys appeared in the 1960s and early 1970s.
3. Many of the ideas and programmes of the two institutions are available in the annual reports submitted to the Ethiopian government by the American staff; see USOM/E, 1955-65, Vols. 2-12. The earliest report is IECAMA, 1953. Some aspects of the content of the instructions offered by the American instructors may be gleaned from *Experiment Station Bulletin* (a research forum published at Alemaya College), Nos. 1, 1955 to 60, 1969. For a short history of American involvement in Ethiopian agriculture, see Adams, 1970.
4. The dearth of studies by Ethiopians is evident in some of the major bibliographies; see Alula and Dessalegn, 1986: Ch. V; Abbink, 1991:IX.
5. I do not include here the works of anthropologists (such as Brooke, 1956 and Messing, 1957) many of which are unpublished dissertations and are not easily accessible to the general reader.
6. See MoA, 1962; Ministry of Planning 1967A; IEG, 1968. 'The Ethiopian peasant farmer', two Ethiopian economists point out, 'pursues farming practices which are very much in the biblical tradition of his forefathers' (Assefa and Eshetu, 1969:112).
7. While irrigation, mainly using flood-management techniques, and terracing are known to have been employed by Sub-Saharan African cultivators in pre-colonial times, the animal-drawn plough was virtually absent here (Sutton, 1989). In contrast, Ethiopian peasants in various parts of the country, at least at one time in the past, made use of furrow-irrigation and other water management techniques, contoured-ridge construction and various biological conservation methods.

8. I have dealt with the land resources of the country and the politics of its assessment in the 1960s and early 1970s in Dessalegn, 1989. In the early 1970s foreign advisors reported to the MLRA that the country possessed between 10 and 12 million hectares of underutilized land that could easily be granted to the landless and the needy; the total land under cultivation then was between 6 to 7 million hectares.
9. For the tax and other agricultural legislation, see The Consolidated Laws of Ethiopia, Vols. I and II.
10. The ILO employment Policy Mission, which was in the country in 1972-73, held a national workshop in July 1973 at which, according to Blaug, the Mission's findings and recommendations were fully discussed; the national authorities subsequently undertook to give due consideration to both the recommendations of the Mission and the conclusions of the workshop in preparing the Fourth Five-Year Plan (p.117 footnote). The earlier Mission (ILO 1970), whose recommendations were similar to this one, was also sympathetically received by the national authorities.
11 CADU has been extensively evaluated, and the following are some of the major works of academic interest: Cohen, Holmberg, 1973; Stahl, 1974; Tesfai Tecle, 1975.
12. The discussion of EPID is based on the following primary sources: EPID, 1970, 1972, 1974b and 1974c. See also Schulz, 1976; Stahl, 1973; and Tesfai Tecle, 1975. An early project document defined the goal of MPP as follows (EPID, 1972:12). The programme will: 'offer farmers an integrated "minimum" of services. Extension agents, assisted by "model farmers" will advise farmers on what inputs to use and how to use them. Inputs will be made available through marketing centres to be established under the Project. A credit system will operate in the areas to ensure that credit is available to enable eligible farmers to implement the advice given to them'.

For a detailed discussion of the MPP strategy and the administration of the programme (EPID 1972); for a critical in-house evaluation (EPID 1974b).

References

A. Primary Sources

Agri-Service, Ethiopia, 1974, 'Living Standards and Productive Activities in Some Rural Areas of South-western Ethiopia', Socio-Economic Section Paper No. 3, Addis Ababa.

AID Bank, 1974, *Management Report*, Addis Ababa.

Central Statistical Office (CSO), 1968, National Sample Survey; First Round (1963-67), Addis Ababa.

------------, 1963-75, Statistical Abstracts (Annual), Addis Ababa.

------------, 1975b, Report of the National Sample Survey, Second Round; Vol. V, Land Area and Utilization, Addis Ababa.

Chillalo Agricultural Development Unit (CADU), 1968, General Agricultural Survey of the Project Area, CADU Pub. No. 14. Addis Ababa.

------------, 1969, Tentative CADU Programme, 1970-72, CADU Pub. no. 26, Addis Ababa.

------------, 1971a, CADU Annual Report 1970-71, CADU Pub. no. 65. NPP.

------------, 1971b, CADU Evaluation Studies: General Agricultural Survey 1970, CADU Pub. No. 71, Assela.

------------, 1972, Case Studies on Farm Households in the Assela Area, No. 78. Assela.

------------, 1975, Crop Sampling Survey 1973-74, CADU Pub. No. 108, Assela.

Ethiopian Chamber of Commerce, 1973,*Directory of Agriculture*, Commercial Farms and Agri-Business Firms 1973-1974, December, Addis Ababa.
EPID, 1970, A Master Plan for Extension and Project Implementation Department, EPID, Pub. No. 1, Addis Ababa.
------------, 1971, Plan of Operations for the Extension and Project Implementation Department, No. 3, Addis Ababa.
------------, 1972, Minimum Package Project Programme, Loan Application to IBRD/SIDA, EPID, Pub. No. 6, Addis Ababa.
------------, 1974a, Short-Term Recovery Programme for Drought Stricken Provinces of Ethiopia, EPID, Pub. No. 16, Addis Ababa.
------------, 1974b, EPID Phase II - Proposals for the Extension of EPID during 1974-75 - 1979-80 and for Support by SIDA, EPID, Pub. No. 21, Addis Ababa.
------------, 1974c, Annual Report for 1973/74 Financial Year, EPID Pub No. 24, Addis Ababa.
------------, 1975a, Report on the Short-Term Recovery Programme of Drought Stricken Areas in Ethiopia, EPID, Pub. No. 30, Addis Ababa.
------------, 1975b, The Second Phase of the Agricultural Minimum Package Program for the Period 1976-77 - 1979-80- A Project Proposal, Pub. No. Addis Ababa.
FAO, 1983, *Food Aid in Figures*, FAO, Rome.
------------, 1987, *1984-1985 World Crop and Livestock Statistics* FAO, Rome.
------------, 1988, A Summary of the Agricultural Ecology of Ethiopia. Main Report, FAO, Rome.
FAO/Huffnagel, 1961,*Agriculture in Ethiopia*, Compiled by H.P. Huffnagel, FAO, Rome.
FAO/UNDP, 1984, Assistance to Land-Use Planning, Ethiopia,*Technical Report Series* 1 to 8. Prepared for the Ethiopian Government, FAO, Rome.
Haile Selassie University, 1972,*Consolidated Laws of Ethiopia*, Vols. I and II, Prepared by the Faculty of Law. Addis Ababa.
IBRD: See World Bank.
Imperial Ethiopian College of Agriculture and Mechanical Arts (IECAMA), 1953, (*First Annual Report*), NPP.
------------, 1955-1969, *Experiment Station Bulletin*, Nos. 1 to 60, Dire Dawa.
Imperial Ethiopian Government (IEG), 1956, *First Five-Year Development Plan* 1957-1961, Addis Ababa.
------------, 1962, *Second Five-Year Development Plan* 1963-1967, Addis Ababa.
------------, 1968, *Third Five-Year Development Plan* 1968-1973, Addis Ababa.
------------, 1971, 'A Statement of Development Strategy and Policies Presented to the First Meeting of the Consultative Group for Ethiopia', April, Addis Ababa.
ILO, 1970, 'Report to the Government of Ethiopia on Integrated Rural Development' ILO, Geneva.
Ministry of Agriculture (MoA), 1953, Agriculture in Ethiopia, Addis Ababa.
------------, 1962, *Second Five-Year Development Plan* 1962-1967, Addis Ababa.
------------, 1973, Ethiopia, Wolamo Agricultural Development Unit Program, Phase II Project Proposal, Vols. I, II, Addis Ababa, June.
------------, 1975, *Agricultural Sample Survey 1974-75* (Report), Vols. I and II, Addis Ababa.
MoA/FAO, 1984-85,*Ethiopian Highlands Reclamation Studies*(Various reports), Addis Ababa.
Ministry of Planning and Development, 1967a,*Regional Aspects of National Planning* Parts I and II, Addis Ababa.

------------, 1967b, *Implementation Report of the Second Five-Year Development Plan,* Addis Ababa.

SIDA, 1966, Report No. I: On the Establishment of a Regional Development Project in Ethiopia. Part I - General Report. Project Preparation Team. NPP, October.

Planning Commission Office, 1973a, (PCO), Strategy Outline for the Fourth Five-Year Plan, April, Addis Ababa.

------------, 1973b, *The Third Five-Year Plan: An Assessment and Implementation* Report, Vol. II, Annex I-VII, October, Addis Ababa.

UNDP, 1974, *Report on Development Assistance to Ethiopia,* April, Addis Ababa.

USA Operations Mission to Ethiopia (USOM/E), 1955-65, *The Agriculture of Ethiopia.* Report of the Staff of Imperial Ethiopian College of Agriculture and Mechanical Arts, and Agricultural Technical School, Jimma and Alemaya.

United States Department of Agriculture (USDA), 1956, The Agricultural Economy of Ethiopia. Prepared by Henrietta Holm, FAS-M-13, Washington, DC.

------------, 1969, *A Survey of Agriculture in Ethiopia,* by O.Sabatini and Louise N.Samuel, ERS-Foreign 254, Washington, DC.

World Bank, 1967, *The World Bank Group in Ethiopia,* World Bank, Washington, DC.

------------, 1970, *Economic Growth and Prospects in Ethiopia* (in five volumes). Report No. AE-9, World Bank, Washington, DC.

------------, 1972, *Agricultural Sector Review,* Ethiopia (in three volumes), Vol. I, II, III, Report No. PA-143, World Bank, Washington, DC.

------------, 1973, *Agricultural Sector Review,* Ethiopia (in three volumes), Vol. I, II, III, Report No. PA-143a, World Bank, Washington DC.

------------, 1975a, *Rural Development,* Sector Policy Paper, World Bank, Washington, DC.

------------, 1975b, Land Reform. Sector Policy Paper, World Bank, Washington, DC.

B. Secondary Sources

Abbink, J, 1991, *Ethiopian Society and History. A Bibliography of Ethiopian Studies 1957-1990,* African Studies Centre, Leiden.

Abraham, W.I., 1972, *Ethiopia's Estimates of Cereal Production: How Good Are They?,* Staff Report No. 3, Addis Ababa, Central Statistical Office.

Adams, Dale, 1970, 'Agricultural Development Strategies in Ethiopia 1950-1970', Unpublished paper, USAID, Addis Ababa, September.

Alula Hidaru and Dessalegn Rahmato, 1976, *A Short Guide to the Study of Ethiopia: A General Bibliography,* Greenwood Press, Westport.

Assefa Bequele and Eshetu Chole, 1969, *A Profile of the Ethiopian Economy.* Oxford University Press, Addis Ababa.

Bahru Zewde, 1986, 'A Bibliographical Prelude to the Agrarian History of Pre-Revolution Ethiopia', *In Proceedings of the Third Annual Seminar of the Department of History* Addis Ababa University.

Bauer, Dan, 1973, 'Land, Leadership and Legitimacy among the Tigray of Ethiopia', Ph.D. Dissertation, University of Rochester.

------------, 1977, *Household and Society in Ethiopia,* Michigan State University Press, East Lansing.

Blaug, Mark, 1974, 'Employment and Unemployment in Ethiopia', *International Labour Review,* 110, 2:117-43.

Bloch, Marc, 1966, *French Rural History,* University of California Press, Berkeley.

Braudel, F, 1985, *Civilization and Capitalism 15th-18th Century. Vol. III, The Perspective of the World,* S Reynolds. Harper & Row, New York.

Brooke, C, H, 1956, 'Settlement of the Eastern Galla, Hararge Province, Ethiopia', PhD Dissertation, University of Nebraska.

Bunting, A H, 1963, 'A Plan for Agricultural Research and Specialist Services in Ethiopia'. Prepared for IEG, Ministry of Agriculture], Reading, England.

Chambers, J.D. and G.E. Mingay, 1966,*The Agricultural Revolution 1750- 1880* Schoken Books, New York.

Cohen, John, 1974, 'Rural Change in Ethiopia: The Chilalo Agricultural Development Unit', *Economic Development and Cultural Change*, 22, 4: 580-614.

------------, 1975, 'Effects of Green Revolution Strategies on Tenants and Small-scale Landowners in the Chillalo Region of Ethiopia',*Journal of Developing Areas*, 9,3.

------------, 1987, *Integrated Rural Development, The Ethiopian Experience and the Debate*, SIAS, Uppsala.

Collins, E.J.T, 1969a, 'Labour Supply and Demand in European Agriculture 1800-1880', In Jones and Woolf (eds.), 1969, Agrarian Change and Economic Development, Methuen, London, pp. 61-94.

------------, 1969b; 'Harvest Technology and Labour Supply in Britain, 1979-1870', *The Economic History Review*, 2nd Ser., XXII, 3:453-73.

Cossins, Noel and Bekele Yemerou, 1974, 'Still Sleep the Highlands: A Study of Farm and Livestock Systems in the Central Highlands of Ethiopia', Livestock and Meat Board, Addis Ababa.

Damon, E G, 1962, 'The Cultivated Sorghums of Ethiopia',*Experiment Station Bulletin*, No. 6, Dire Dawa.

Dessalegn Rahmato, 1984,*Agrarian Reform in Ethiopia*, SIAS, Uppsala.

------------, 1986, 'Moral Crusaders and Incipient Capitalists: Mechanized Agriculture and Its Critics in Ethiopia', in *Proceedings of the Third Annual Seminar of the Department of History*, Addis Ababa University.

------------, 1989, 'Rural Resettlement in Post-Revolution Ethiopia: Problems and Prospects', in Conference on Population Issues in Ethiopia's National Development, *Report on Conference Proceedings*, Vol. II, ONCCP, Addis Ababa.

------------, 1990a, 'Famine in Peasant Consciousness: Aspects of Symbolic Culture in Rural Ethiopia', in *Proceedings of Fifth Seminar of the Department of History*, Addis Ababa University.

------------, 1990b, 'A Resource Flow Systems Analysis of Rural Bolosso (Wollaita)', a Report prepared for Redd Barna-Ethiopia, Addis Ababa, Redd Barna-Ethiopia.

------------, 1992, 'The Dynamics of Rural Poverty: Case Studies from a District in Southern Ethiopia', CODESRIA Monograph 2/92, CODESRIA, Dakar.

Eichberger, W G, 1968, 'Food Production and Consumption in Ethiopia', unpublished Paper, USAID Office, Addis Ababa.

Ethiopia Observer, 1957, Special Issue on Agriculture, 1,10.

Experience Inc, 1972, Report No. I: The Feasibility of Producing Pulse Crops for Export Markets. Report No. II: The Feasibility of Producing Cereal Grain Crops for Export. Report No. III: An Implementation Plan for a Seed Improvement Program in Ethiopia. Report No. IV: The Transportation, Processing and Storage of Ethiopian Grain and Pulses for Domestic and Export Markets, prepared for the Ministry of Agriculture under Contract to USAID. Minneapolis, Minnesota.

Fekadu Ebba and R Phillips, 1972, 'Supply and Demand Projections for Food Grains in Ethiopia 1970-1980', Food and Feed Grain Institute, Kansas State University.

Geertz, C, 1963, Agricultural Involution, University of California Press, Berkeley.

Getachew T Medhin and Tilahun Makonnen, 1974, 'Socio-Economic Characteristics of Peasant Farms in the Central Highlands of Ethiopia- Ada Wereda', College of Agriculture, Debre Zeit.
Gill, G, J, 1976, 'Farm Technology Pilot Survey',*IDR Research Report*, No. 23, Institute of Development Research, Addis Ababa University.
Goody, Jack, 1980, 'Rice-burning and the Green Revolution in Northern Ghana',*The Journal of Development Studies*, 16, 2:136-55.
Greene, D, A, 1974, 'Ethiopia: An Economic Analysis of Technological Change in Four Agricultural Production Systems', African Studies Center, East Lansing.
Gryseels, G and A M Anderson, 1983, 'Research on Farm and Livestock Productivity in the Central Highlands', *Research Report* No. 4, ILCA, Addis Ababa.
Hoben, Allan, 1975, *Land Tenure among the Amhara of Ethiopia* University of Chicago Press, Chicago.
Holmberg, J, 'Survey of Consumption Patterns in Etheya Extension Area', CADU, Pub. No. 90, Addis Ababa, CADU, 1973.
Humphreys, C, 1974, Ada Baseline Survey, Part I: Farm Characteristics of the Ada Wereda, IDR Paper No. 10, Addis Ababa.
Jackson, R T, 1970, 'Land Use and Settlement in Gamu Goffa, Ethiopia', Occasional Paper No. 17, Department of Geography, Makerere University, Kampala.
Jackson, R, T, *et al.*, (eds), 1969, 'Report of the Oxford University Expedition to the Gamu Highlands', Department of Geography, University of Oxford.
Jones, E, L, 1965, 'Agriculture and Economic Growth in England, 1600-1750', *Journal of Economic History*, XXV, 1:1-18.
Jones, E, L, and S, J, Woolf, (eds), 1969,*Agrarian Change and Economic Development* The Historical Problems, Methuen, London.
Jutzi, S, and G, Gryseels, 1984, 'Farmers Switch to Oats in the Ethiopian Highlands', ILCA Newsletter, 3,3:3-5.
Knutsson, K, 1969, Ploughland and Swidden: A Dual System of Agriculture in Western Ethiopia, unpublished paper, Addis Ababa.
Lambton, Ann, 1971, Ethiopia: An Approach to Land Reform,*Bulletin of the School of Oriental and African Studies*, XXXIV, 2:221-40.
LeRoy Ladurie, E, 1974,*The Peasants of Languedoc*, University of Illinois Press, Urbana.
Levine, D, 1965, *Wax and Gold: Tradition and Innovation in Ethiopian Culture* University of Chicago Press, Chicago.
Lexander, A, 1970, 'Land Ownership, Tenancy and Social Organization in the Wajji Area', CADU, Pub. No. 7, Assela, CADU.
McCann, James, 1988, 'A Great Agrarian Cycle? A History of Agricultural Productivity and Demographic Change in Highland Ethiopia 1900-1987', Working Paper No. 131, African Studies Center, Boston University.
Mesfin, Kinfu, 1974,*A Bibliography on Land Tenure, Land Reform and Rural Land Use in Ethiopia*, MLRA, Addis Ababa.
Mesfin Wolde Mariam, 1984,*Rural Vulnerability to Famine in Ethiopia 1958-77. Vikas* New Delhi.
Messing, S, 1957, 'The Highland-Plateau Amhara of Ethiopia', Ph.D. dissertation, University of Pennsylvania.
Miller, Leonard, 1963, 'Developing Ethiopian Agriculture',*Experiment Station Bulletin*, No. 22, Dire Dawa.
Miller, L, F, and Telahun Makonnen, 1965, 'Organization and Operation of Three Ethiopian Case Farms', *Experimental Station Bulletin*, No. 35, Dire Dawa.

Murphy, H, F, 1963, 'Fertility and Other Data on Some Ethiopian Soils', *Experiment Station Bulletin*, No. 4, Dire Dawa.

----------, 1968, 'A Report on the Fertility Status and Other Data on Some Soils of Ethiopia', *Experiment Station Bulletin*, No. 44, Dire Dawa.

Pankhurst, S, 1957, 'Imperial Ethiopian College of Agriculture and Mechanical Arts', Ethiopia Observer, 1.10:312-17.

----------, 1959, 'Agricultural Extension Services', Ethiopia Observer, III, 2:55-56.

Robinson, W, and F, Yamazaki, 1986, 'Agriculture, Population and Economic Planning in Ethiopia 1953-80', *Journal of Developing Areas*, 20,2:327-48.

Schulz, M, 1976, Organizing Extension Services in Ethiopia Before and After Revolution. Heft 17. Saarbrucken, Verlag der SSIP-Schriften Breitenback.

Shepherd, Jack, 1975, *The Politics of Starvation*, Carnegie Endowment, New York.

Simoon, F, J, 1960, *North-west Ethiopia: Peoples and Economy*, University of Wisconsin Press, Madison.

Siira, E, 1965, Present 'Status and Problems of the Agricultural Extension Department and Recommendations', unpublished Report, USAID, Addis Ababa, January.

Stahl, Michael, 1973, Contradictions in Agricultural Development, a Study of Three Minimum Package Projects in Ethiopia, Report No. 14, Scandinavian Institute of African Studies.

----------, 1974, *Ethiopia: Political Contradiction in Agricultural Development*, Raben, Stockholm.

Standford Research Institute (SRI), 1968, Ethiopian Agriculture Study, Vol. I, prepared for IEG under contract to USAID, Menlo Park, Calif.

----------, 1969a, The Resources and Economy of Ethiopia, prepared for IEG under contract to USAID, by Kifle-Mariam Zerom. Menlo Park, Calif.

----------, 1969b, A Development Program for the Ada District, Based on a Socio-Economic Survey, prepared for IEG under contract to USAID, Menlo Park, Calif.

----------, 1969c, Production of Grains and Pulses in Ethiopia. Prepared for IEG under contract to USAID, Menlo Park, Calif.

----------, 1969d, Marketing of Grain and Pulses in Ethiopia. Prepared for IEG under contract to USAID, by A. R. Thodey, Menlo Park, Calif.

----------, 1969e, Development of Agriculture and Agro-Industry in Ethiopia. Strategy and Program, prepared for IEG under contract to USAID, by C. Miller *et al.* Menlo Park, Calif.

Stavis, B, 1977, Social Soundness Analysis of Ethiopia's Minimum Package Program II, a Report to USAID, Addis Ababa and Ithaca, NY, July.

Stokes, E, 1978, *The Peasant and the Raj*, Studies in Agrarian Society and Peasant Rebellion in Colonial India, Cambridge University Press, Cambridge.

Sutton, J, E, G, (ed), 1989, 'History of African Technology and Field Systems', Special Volume of Contributions in Azania, *Journal of the British Institute in Eastern Africa*, XXIV.

Tesfai Tecle, 1975, The Evolution of Alternative Rural Development Strategies in Ethiopia, *African Rural Employment Paper* No. 12, Department of Agricultural Economics, Michigan State University, East Lansing.

Thompson, F M L, 1968, The Second Agricultural Revolution, 1815-80, *Economic History Review*, 2nd Ser., XXI, 1:62-77.

Tigrai Rural Development Study, Main Report and Annexes 1-12, a Study Commissioned by the Ministry of Overseas Development (UK) for RRC and carried out by Hunting Technical Services, Boreham Wood, England.

Ware-Austin, W, D, 1970, *Soil Erosion in Ethiopia*, Institute of Agricultural Research, Addis Ababa.

Warriner, Doreen, A Report on Land Reform in Ethiopia. Prepared for the Ministry of Land Reform, Addis Ababa, 1971.

Watt, Ian, 1988, 'Regional Patterns of Cereal Production and Consumption', in Zein Ahmed Zein and H. Kloos (eds), *The Ecology of Health and Disease in Ethiopia*, Ministry of Health, Addis Ababa.

Westphal, E, 1974, *Pulses in Ethiopia*, CAPD, Wageningen.

------------, 1975, The Agriculture of Ethiopia, CAPD, Wageningen.

Wood, A, P, 1977, 'Resettlement in Illubabor Province, Ethiopia'; Ph.D. dissertation, University of Liverpool.

------------, 1982, 'Spontaneous Agricultural Resettlement in Ethiopia 1950-74', in J. Clarke and L. Kosinski (eds), *Redistribution of Population in Africa*, London, Heinemann.

4. Running to Keep in the Same Place: Industrialization 1941-74

Eshetu Chole

Alice looked round her in great surprise. 'Why, I do believe we've been under this tree the whole time! Everything's just as it was!'

'Of course it is', said the Queen. 'What would you have it?'

'Well, in our country', said Alice, still panting a little, 'you'd generally get to somewhere else if you ran very fast for a long time as we've been doing'.

'A slow sort of country!' said the Queen. 'Now, here, you see, it takes all the running you can do to keep in the same place. If you want to get somewhere else, you must run at least twice as fast as that!'

Lewis Caroll, Through the Looking-Glass

The period 1941-74 represents both continuity and change in the structure of the Ethiopian economy. This can be grasped best by examining the first three-quarters of the Twentieth Century in three phases: from the beginning of the century to the Italian invasion of 1936; the period of the Italian occupation; and finally the period of our prime interest, i.e., 1941-74.

Phase one was decisive in defining the major contours of the country's subsequent political economy (Addis Hiwet 1975:58). To begin with, the political boundaries of the Empire State were already well established towards the end of the Menelik era, which falls within this period. A concomitant development was the emergence of the landed aristocracy to the position of undisputed ruling class, a situation which was terminated only after the 1974 revolution. There is little of substance that took place in this regard after the Italian occupation. These two developments between them defined the nature of the Ethiopian State and hence the possibilities open to it, as well as the limitations within which it was to operate. It was also this period that witnessed the completion of the Addis-Djibouti railway and the growth of Addis Ababa and other towns.

The period of Italian occupation (1936-41) registered some industrial advance,[1] although not as significant as is usually believed. This was partly because it was so short-lived, but more importantly, because of Italy's basic strategic interest in Ethiopia. The Italians were essentially not interested in promoting autonomous industrial development in Ethiopia; their interest was rather in creating a colonial economy on the basis of large-scale agricultural farms. The only manufacturing enterprises that they set up, and these largely in Eritrea, were small-scale factories producing consumer goods such as soap and textiles. In fact, from the perspective of long-term industrial development, the most enduring contribution of this period is not the setting up of these enterprises but the construction of over 6,000 kms of roads.

It is thus no wonder that the structure of the Ethiopian economy in 1941 was little different from what it was in the pre-occupation period. One can go even farther and argue that, in one sense, the post-war period hardly represents a radical break with the periods preceding it, particularly with respect to the magnitude and role of the industrial sector. If industrialization is understood as a transformation in the structure of output and employment, it is difficult to speak of such a transformation. For, even at the end of this period agriculture loomed large in the structure of output, and even more in the structure of employment. It is in this sense that we can speak of the post-war period as representing continuity with the past.

Yet, it would be highly misleading to suggest that little of importance was achieved in this period as far as the country's industrial development was concerned. In fact, it is generally recognized that whatever measure of industrialization Ethiopia can claim owes its genesis to the post-war era. The country's industrial development was bound to be fragile because of a large number of inherent limitations. However, to any extent that we can talk of industrialization at all, we can do so legitimately only of the post-1941 era.

In dealing with this era, we run into the familiar problem of historical periodization. The historian, depending on the major focus of investigation, can divide the period between the restoration and the revolution in so many different ways. For our purposes, however, the practical criterion of convenience will suffice. We have accordingly divided the 1941-74 period into three.[2]

Phase 1: 1941-52: This period of reconstruction saw very little industrial development relative to subsequent periods and can therefore be treated as a homogeneous historical phase. The terminal date is especially apposite because it represents the establishment of the federation of Eritrea with Ethiopia. The discussion of this period makes no reference to Eritrea. But it may be noted that 'Eritrea's manufacturing activities date mainly from 1936' and that 'a new wave of industrial expansion set in after 1943' (United Nations 1950:14).

Phase 2: 1953-61: The origins of Ethiopian industrialization can be placed within this period. The terminal year is chosen because it coincides with the completion of the First Five-Year Plan.[3]

Phase 3: 1962-74: This is the period of the Second and Third Five-Year Plans and perhaps the most eventful phase of industrialization. It takes us up to the fall of the old order.

1941-52: Restoration and Reconstruction

It is useful to begin our account of this period with a review of the situation that Emperor Haile Selassie encountered upon restoration. Politically, the situation was far from auspicious, for at least two reasons. First, there were problems of internal security.

Large areas of south and south-west Ethiopia remained disaffected and outside Addis Ababa's authority; London controlled the Ogaden and various reserved areas; there was trouble brewing in the north and the imperial army was thoroughly dependent, as was the Emperor, on a small British military mission for supplies and leadership (Marcus 1983:18).

Secondly, and related to this, the British imposed on the emperor 'a master-client relationship' (Addis Hiwet 1975:87), a situation which he naturally found unacceptable. As Marcus (1983:9) points out, the Emperor's return was a bitter-sweet moment: he was home, an emperor in a palace, but he was neither authoritative nor apparent sovereign. The British were everywhere and acting as if Ethiopia was a colony'. It is for this reason that Spencer (1984:99) was led to observe that even as late as the end of 1943 'Ethiopia was for all practical purposes a British protectorate'.

In these circumstances, therefore, Haile Selassie's major preoccupations were to reclaim full sovereignty for Ethiopia and to consolidate his rule by centralizing and modernizing the government. These concerns were bound to influence the substance of his economic policies.

On the economic front, the situation was somewhat mixed. According to one report (State Bank of Ethiopia, 1949b:12), 'the surrender of the Italian forces in 1941 left Ethiopia in a very confused condition'. It continues:

The whole administrative and economic structure of the Empire had to be rebuilt from nothing. The Campaign, by which the Italian occupation of Ethiopia was brought to an end, was hardly complete and distant provinces were still in an unsettled condition. Lines of communication had been destroyed as a result of the operations.

The traditional trade channels of Ethiopia had been dislocated by five years of enemy occupation, during which the economy of the country had been distorted to meet the exigencies of the Fascist regime. New trade connections were established by the Allies, designed to provide for the imperative needs of the outside world, still at war. The exportation of important commodities was monopolized and, generally speaking, exports and imports were subjected to control by allied authorities.

The monetary situation of Ethiopia was no less confused. Three different kinds of currency were in use, namely, the Italian Lira, the East African Shilling and the Maria Theresa Thaler. The Italian Lira was soon eliminated as a result of steps taken by the government but the East African Shilling and the Maria Theresa Thaler continued for nearly four years as legal tender of the country.

Further, and as pointed out earlier, the Italian legacy was not much in terms of providing a leverage for economic development.

The Italians initiated over a 1,000 industrial establishments during the period of occupation, but only few had been completed at the time of their withdrawal from the country. Many were designed to serve specific Italian needs but only a handful were of permanent value to the country (Lipsky 1962:262).

At the same time, however, and particularly with respect to the prospects of industrial development, the Italian period was not without its positive effects.

The fascist government introduced money wages and encouraged production of food crops to satisfy settler requirements. A protoconsuming society more or less emerged, particularly among those who had collaborated with the Italians in government and commerce. While traditional demand for cotton, salt, kerosene and the like strengthened, new needs appeared for tools, machinery, technical equipment, trucks, spare parts and petroleum products. Generally, however, demand for capital goods was only characteristic of Ethiopia's few urban, political-administrative, market centers, whereas the countryside merely adopted modern money to fulfill traditional needs. In other words, the Italians spurred Ethiopia's growth along lines already evident before their occupation. When the emperor and his followers returned, they found a familiar but more complex, larger, and better organized economy to exploit for the satisfaction of high wartime demand for Ethiopia's produce (Marcus 1983:44-5).

Whatever one's assessment of the Italian economic legacy may be, the international economic environment facing Ethiopia immediately after liberation is generally judged to have been favourable. It must be noted in this connection that while the war was over for Ethiopia, it was still raging in the rest of the world. And this proved a boon for Ethiopia, essentially because of the buoyant world market for primary products. In addition to a lucrative grain trade, there were also profitable outlets for the country's traditional exports. Coffee, hides, beeswax were finding quick markets, particularly in the adjacent Middle East. The elasticity of supply was high owing to the Italian-built road system. Even with worn-out transport, the exchange of goods between the interior and the capital 'speeded up enormously'. Anonymous backers financed newly opened Indian and Arab firms, and everyone profited, including, for the first time, 'a number of Ethiopians, many of the upper classes, who have now turned to trade' (Marcus 1983:44).

According to the same source, this favourable situation lasted through 1945, but we have it on the authority of a State Bank report (1949a:1) that, already, by the end of 1948 the 'post-war boom conditions (had) ceased'. However, favourable as the export situation may have been in the immediate post-war years, one should be wary of exaggerating its long-term consequences. At the very least it should not blind us to the fact that the Ethiopian economy in that period was very backward and that its agriculture, which was then and remains to this day its backbone, was as primitive as any to be found elsewhere. As such, it was in no position to generate the kind of surplus needed to finance accelerated industrialization. Therefore, the major economic problem faced by the post-war government was one of generating the funds requisite for modernizing and centralizing the bureaucracy. Confronted with the reality of meagre resources for undertaking this task, it is no wonder that it had to turn to foreign benefactors, first the British and then the Americans.

As in the political arena, Anglo-Ethiopian relations were full of tensions in the economic sector. On 31 January 1942 Ethiopia and Britain signed an agreement under which the former obtained a four-year subvention of £3,250,000 from the latter. But the subvention had its costs. The agreement gave Britain 'control over currency and foreign exchange and exports and imports, which had to be authorized by the Cairo-based Middle East Supply Centre' (Marcus 1983:13). It is significant that Ethiopia was not to have its own currency until 1945. More specifically:

The British East African shilling was made the official monetary unit. Ethiopia's currency board was set up in London rather than in Addis Ababa and two of its three members were designated by the British government. The currency was backed by currency reserves in London in the form of consols. Imports and exports were controlled from London and the foreign exchange generated by exports went to British currency reserves (Spencer 1984:99).

Naturally, the Ethiopian government was not pleased with this state of affairs. Its sentiments were expressed by John Spencer, the American advisor, in the following terms:

Specifically, their (the Ethiopians') grievances relate to exchange control, the attempt to force ... sterling ... upon the country, the refusal to allow the minting of coins or the printing of currency and the requirement that all dollar exchange be converted before being brought into Ethiopia. It is felt that such policies impose an entirely unwarranted restriction upon Ethiopia's economy and industry (Marcus 1983:25).

This agreement was terminated on 25 August 1944. It was followed by the Anglo-Ethiopian Agreement of 19 December 1944 which, though politically significant, had very little economic content apart from the fact that Britain conceded control of the AddisDjibouti railway to Ethiopia. By this time British influence in Ethiopia was clearly on the wane. The two subsequent agreements (those of 24 August 1948 and 29 November 1954) gave legal form to this fact, especially the latter having provided for 'a return of the Haud and the Reserved Area to Ethiopian administration in fact and in law' (Spencer 1984:276).

The decline of British influence went hand in hand with the growth of relations between Ethiopia and the United States, relations which were to be economically more meaningful over the long haul. In this connection it is significant that as early as 11 June 1943, President Roosevelt had written to Emperor Haile Selassie agreeing 'to supply such articles, services, and information as we may be in a position to furnish for the defence of Ethiopia, and, through other means as may be possible, to render all practical assistance in the rehabilitation of your country' (Marcus 1983:21). This was followed by the signing of the Mutual Aid Agreement of 9 August 1943.

In June of that year the Ethiopian government asked for a United States technical mission to be sent to Ethiopia to investigate the country's resources and its economic problems and to draw up an aid package for its development. In addition to agricultural development, mineral exploitation and the development of transportation and communications, Ethiopia also sought:

The ability to semifinish raw hides and skins, which, because of the shortage of shipping, were deteriorating and going to waste. Again, stressing the future, Yilma (Yilma Deressa, the leader of the Ethiopian delegation to the United States) suggested that Ethiopia's leathers would find a great post-war market. Altogether, the Ethiopian official asked for a total of 286 experts and technicians, among them doctors, teachers, nurses and engineers, and fifty-four master blacksmiths, tanners, carpenters, masons, plumbers, and shoemakers to train Ethiopian youth in needed trades (Marcus 1983:19-20).

Based on Yilma's request, the United States sent a technical mission to Ethiopia, which arrived in May 1944. It was 'composed of experts in transportation, agriculture, public health, animal husbandry, mining and engineering' (Marcus 1983:27). It is noteworthy that no experts in industry were included.

Unfortunately, the mission's efforts did not bear much fruit, for reasons that had nothing to do with the mission itself. It had indeed produced 'a multi-volumed recommendation of projects worth ninety-one million dollars', but these were rejected by the US government as 'out of proportion to Ethiopia's capacity to finance' (Marcus 1983:58-9).

The mission's programme was revised in 1947 by the US Department of Commerce and this revision bore the kernel of subsequent Ethio-US economic relations. According to Marcus (1983:59), the US planners saw Ethiopia's major problems as '1) repairing and maintaining the Italian-built communications network; 2) building modern social, educational, and economic infrastructures; and 3) increasing agricultural production and industrial output'.

With respect to industrial development, the recommendation was for implementing a strategy of what one would have called import substitution. The revised programme emphasized projects which could either add to foreign exchange or diminish external spending: 'In this manner, an orderly process of expansion, development and technological modernization can be accomplished'. The planners, however, did not intend to restrict Ethiopia's foreign trade but to change its composition: 'To the extent that imports of cotton textiles, salt, sugar, and gunny sacks are reduced or eliminated, Ethiopia will be enabled to purchase machinery, fuels, and other goods abroad in larger quantities than heretofore' (Marcus 1983:59-60).[4]

More specifically, the revised development scheme recommended:

A three-year $11,740,000 program to establish three industries: six meat-processing centers, each containing slaughter-houses, canneries, and by-product plants; six associated tanneries to process hides; and a cotton textile complex capable of producing ten million pounds of cloth annually. Although initial foreign exchange requirements would be high, Ethiopia would soon garner valuable hard currency by exporting hides and packed and canned meats and by supplying half of its own textile requirements (Marcus 1983:61).

It was further envisaged that, on the basis of the foreign exchange generated in this manner, additional industries, including a cement mill, a machine shop, a tire-recapping plant, a potash plant, a chemical factory, etc., would be set up (Marcus 1983:61-2).

However, little was to materialize out of this scheme. Basing largely on the work of the technical mission, the Ethiopian government put in a request for a loan of $130,088,870 in January 1948, of which more than 83% was for infrastructure and the remaining $21,588,870 for industrial development

(Marcus 1983:64). The industrial package included 'meat packing and related undertakings, sugar and alcohol production, textiles, logging and lumber, vegetable oils and soaps, salt, chemicals, leather and tanning, glass, cement and bricks and batteries manufacture and related repair' (Marcus 1983:64-5).

But the request did not fall on responsive ears. Surprisingly, textiles manufacturing was dropped because 'it may be cheaper for Ethiopia to continue to buy textiles on the world market, than to develop an industry which would require imports of cotton, technicians, training a labour force, and securing spare parts and spindles'. Instead, Ethiopia ought to concentrate on small-scale meat-packing and leather industries, since both products would find immediate markets and 'provide sufficient foreign exchange to enable Ethiopia to service a loan far in excess of the one (considered) here'. (Marcus 1983:66-7).

The review concluded by stating that 'Ethiopia would have to be satisfied with a five million-dollar loan, rigidly supervised by US or International Bank officials' (Marcus 1983:67). In other words, Ethiopia was granted less than 4% of its requests. This attitude of the American government was to persist until the outbreak of the Korean crisis and Ethiopia's involvement in it on the side of the United States. In fact, 'it was not until the Suez crisis of 1956 that the United States finally provided Ethiopia with the type, if not the amount, of American assistance the Emperor really wanted' (Marcus 1983:5).

That the government placed much hope on the contribution of foreign capital is evident from the fact that one of its first measures in the area of economic policy was the issuance, in 1950, of a 'Notice for the Encouragement of Foreign Capital Investment'. At the time this Notice was issued, the country had very little industry to speak of, and whatever existed was largely owned and operated by expatriates. The major objective of the notice was to attract capital and technology from abroad through direct foreign investment. As is evident from its title, its concern was with foreign not indigenous investment.

It was designed exclusively for the benefit of foreign investors, to whom it accorded special facilities and incentives in the form of exemptions from profit tax for five years, guarantees regarding the remittance of a fixed proportion of earned profit and duty-free importation of necessary machinery. Moreover, foreign technology suppliers were given complete freedom with respect to the acquisition of equity holdings in firms and, where local participation was considered necessary, it was understood that such participation in equity and management would in most instances take the form of only a minority interest. Though the Notice provided incentives and guarantees for foreign investors similar incentives were not available either to existing or potential domestic investors and the situation remained unchanged until the enactment, 13 years later, of the Investment Decree of 1963 (Faruqi and O'Brien 1976:27). There is no evidence, however, to suggest that the Notice was successful in attracting foreign investment.

In such circumstances, therefore, it is hardly surprising that no significant level of industrial activity could commence in the immediate post-war period.[5] Faced with enormous tasks of economic reconstruction and development on the one hand, and meagre domestic resources and niggardly foreign assistance on the other, the government had little scope for bold initiatives in the area of industrial development, even assuming it had the requisite will to embark on such initiatives. It was not until the late 1950s that there was any visible sign of industrial activity (Table 1).

This is corroborated by the available statistical evidence, even though it is patchy, contradictory, and therefore of dubious reliability. One problem is related to the items included under the rubric of manufacturing. In addition to manufacturing proper, some sources include cleaning, hulling and grading of coffee, cleaning grain and oilseeds, flour milling, sawing, mining and electricity. On top of this, figures are seldom comprehensive and not always recorded on a consistent basis. They should therefore be used to indicate broad orders of magnitude, and not taken as exact representations of the situation. With these caveats, we can now turn to look at the available statistics.

A census of industries undertaken in 1949-50 [Ministry of Commerce and Industry (MCI 1951:202-3) provides information on a number of establishments, employment and investment, summarized in Table 1. According to this source, there were 83 establishments in that year, although this must be an exaggeration. This is because ten of these were flour mills, five were 'lumber' (probably meaning sawmills), and five were establishments producing electric light and power. Taking these out would reduce the number to 63. The same figure seems to apply to 1952 as well (MCI 1955:101; Pankhurst 1957:54).

Total capital invested in the 63 enterprises amounted to more than E$16.4 million, which does not tally with the statement that in 1950 'the total amount of investment in manufacturing was not more than E$5 million or probably less' (Faruqi and O'Brien 1976:42). Employees in these enterprises numbered 5,765, of which 5,621 were Ethiopians and 144 foreigners. It seems this figure had risen to 8,450 by 1952 (Pankhurst 1957:154).

According to the Ministry of Commerce and Industry (Table 2), the 1952 value of production in manufacturing industry was E$ 25.1 million in gross terms (excluding flour mills, sawmills and carpentry shops).[6] Not unexpectedly, textiles were the most important sub-sector.

Table 1: Manufacturing Industries in Ethiopia (1949-50)

Industries	Number of establishment	Employees Ethiopian	Foreign	Capital invested (birr)
Alcohol	4	285	11	1,080,000
Beer	1	60	5	1,500,000
Bricks, tiles and cement pipes	3	160	6	150,000
Buttons	1	16	-	15,000
Canned tomatoes	1	250	-	200,000
Cement	1	650	15	400,000
Cigarettes	1	150	1	300,000
Cotton yarn and grey sheeting	1	1070	21	2,500,000
Cotton yarn no.4 and 6	1	711	1	800,000
Eau de Cologne rose water essential oils	1	12	-	15,000
Felt hats	1	5	-	8,000
Flour	10	300	20	3,500,000
Glassware	2	140	2	650,000
Gunny bags and rope	1	330	5	500,000
Hydrogen and Oxygen	1			80,000
Knitted wear, rain coats and carpets	2	89	3	125,000
Leather and shoes	6	280	14	1,085,000
Lumber	12	1,200	15	400,000
Oil, vegetable	8	250	32	4,915,000
Pharmaceuticals	1	4	1	3,000
Plywood	1	90	3	300,000
Shoeheels and lasts	1	5	1	10,000
Sodawater, lemonade and mineral water	2	75	1	130,000
Soap	8	180	3	590,000
Vaccines and serums	2	16	6	80,000
Wheat paste and biscuits	2	171	7	853,850
Wines	3	22	6	120,000
Electric light and power	5	430	90	5,132,690

Source: Ministry of Commerce and Industry 1951, pp.202-3.

Therefore, regardless of some undeniable progress, the role of manufacturing industry in the economy remained negligible. Thus, we are informed, in 1950 for example, it constituted only 1% of the Net National Product (First Five-Year Plan: 48).[7] In 1952, the terminal year for this period, industry, handicrafts, construction and transport between them accounted for less than 8% of the national income (Pankhurst 1957:153).

This does not mean that the period was devoid of developments which had an impact on industrial growth. Examples are advances in education (the opening of several secondary schools and a technical school) as well as expansion in trade, whose contributions to the development of industry, however limited, need not be ignored. Even taking these into account, however, our fundamental conclusion must be that the 1940s were an uneventful period in the history of Ethiopia's industrialization.

Table 2: Gross and Net Values of Production of Manufacturing Industry in Ethiopia, 1951-53 (excluding Eritrea E$1,000)

	Gross value of production			Net value of production		
	1951	1952	1953	1951	1952	1953
Textiles	4,013	11,614	10,416	1,513	5,935	3,834
Flour mills	4,814	4,326	4,841	819	409	718
Oil mills and soap factories	4,634	3,873	6,547	975	742	2,156
Tobacco and cement	2,625	4,200	2,225	1,267	1,688	1,449
Leather tanning and shoes	1,319	1,852	2,151	487	658	1,050
Sawmills and carpentry shops	1,552	1,312	2,149	-	-	1,393
Alcohol distilleries	1,354	1,656	807	-	-	349
Beers, wines, lemonades, etc.	1,632	1,907	2,494	940	1,135	1,607
Printing and publishing	-	-	686	-	-	449
Bricks	-	-	116	-	-	-
Miscellaneous	284	406	299	-	-	180
Total manufacturing industries	22,227	31,146	32,731	7,000	11,600	13,204

Source: Ministry of Commerce and Industry 1955.

1953-61: The Origins of Ethiopian Industrialization

If any period deserves to be designated as having represented the commencement of industrialization in Ethiopia, that period is without doubt 1953-61. Writing in 1967, a World Bank mission noted that, of the manufacturing establishments in existence at the time, more than 60% were established after 1957 (IBRD/IDA 1967:12). For convenience we will divide this period into two: 1953-57 and 1958-61.

1953-57:

The period 1953-57 was one of significant development in manufacturing industry. As indicated in Table 3, the index of manufacturing production (excluding Eritrea) rose from 163 to 308 (1950=100), corroborating Lipsky's claim that the gross value of industrial output nearly doubled; he also claims that net value increased by 2.5 times and that industrial employment increased by 40% (Lipsky 1962:259). In general economic terms, however, the period seems to have been characterized by ups and downs. Thus, while 1953 was called 'a good year for Ethiopia', 'in sharp contrast, 1954 was a disappointment, since Brazilian coffee glutted the market' (Marcus 1983:96).

Table 3: Index Numbers of Industrial Production (1950=100) (excluding Eritrea)

Industrial Group	1951	1953	1955	1957
Manufactured foods	104	119	223	286
Beverages and Tobacco	121	188	199	227
Textiles	72	267	395	507
Leather goods	113	197	213	357
Building materials, etc	102	114	221	201
Miscellaneous	113	126	161	111
Total, Manufacturing	101	163	249	308

Source: Stanley and Karsten 1965, p.10

It is reported that eight manufacturing enterprises were established in Ethiopia (excluding Eritrea) during 1952-54 (First Five-Year Plan: 99). This number is not particularly impressive; what is noteworthy, however, is the types of establishments set up. Most prominent among these was the Wonji sugar factory, which was officially inaugurated on 20 March 1954, the agreement for which was concluded in 1951. The significance of this undertaking lies both in the scale of operations involved as well as in the participation of foreign capital which it entailed. Already, by 1955 the factory was producing 17,000 tons of sugar; in 1956 the plantation and refinery between them employed 4,900 Ethiopians (Pankhurst 1957:148). The Wonji Sugar Estate was a joint operation between the Ethiopian government and the Dutch firm N.V. Handelsvereeniging (HVA), the latter providing the bulk of the initial investment of E$25.9 million (Pankhurst 1957:148). This enterprise was destined to play an important role in the country's industrial history.

Also established during the 1952-54 period were 'a new textile factory in Addis Ababa, two new wood-processing plants and three leather and footwear factories' (First Five-Year Plan: 99). By 1954, the total number of manufacturing establishments (excluding cleaning plants for coffee and cereals) in the country (including Eritrea) had reached 154, of which 83, or nearly 54%, were in Eritrea (First Five-Year Plan: 99). These enterprises were entirely engaged in the production of consumer goods for domestic consumption, the most prominent of which were beverages, timber, oil, soap, textiles and flour.

Again, in the 1952-54 period, new investments in manufacturing industry (excluding Eritrea) totalled nearly E$20 million, and 'the greater part of these investments went into the construction of the sugar plant, the textile factory and the leather and footwear factory' (First Five-Year Plan: 100).

By the end of 1957, the gross value of output of manufacturing industry had reached E$81.8 million, with almost 80% of this being accounted for by food processing and beverages (62.7%), and textiles (15.9%) (First Five-Year Plan: 114).

It must be noted that whatever industrial development took place during this period did so in the absence of an articulated policy framework. As already pointed out, the only relevant policy document was the 1950 'Notice for the Encouragement of Foreign Capital Investment', which did not play an effective role in attracting foreign investment. It can be said that whatever industrial activity took place in this period was entirely spontaneous and did not benefit from a conscious State policy with respect to industrialization.

1957-61: The First Five-Year Plan
The significance of the next phase is that, for the first time in Ethiopian history, we witness an attempt to consciously plan the course of economic development. Although the First Five-Year Plan (FFYP) was launched in 1957, it was actually prepared in 1954-55 with the help of Yugoslav experts. The decision to plan, as well as the involvement of Yugoslavs in the drawing up of the plan, had nothing whatsoever to do with ideology. It was rather dictated by purely pragmatic considerations.

To appreciate this fact one must take a quick glance at the general Ethiopian socio-economic setting of the time. Even though there was a measure of involvement of Ethiopian capital in trade and other services, there was virtually no indigenous participation in the field of industry The FFYP, after stating the importance of capital mobilization and noting that 'commercial capital, which is of exceptional importance in the present phase of the country's economic development, is predominantly of foreign origin', proceeded to draw the implications of this fact:

One of the consequences of this is that there is not much evidence of commercial capital being invested in industry. This type of capital which is in the hands of foreigners tends to remain in the field of commerce, while, in the main, savings and profits are remitted abroad. The problem is all the more intensified by the fact that a national middle class has yet not developed to enter the field of commerce and invest capital in productive enterprises (First Five-Year Plan: 15).

It is therefore not surprising that even in those days the government had begun to assume considerable responsibilities for investment. As indicated in the FFYP, 'in recent years about half of total investments were financed by government. This type of investment must undoubtedly play an increasingly important role in the country's economic development' (First Five-Year Plan: 16). The nature and extent of government involvement was thus a matter of necessity, reflecting the low level of domestic entrepreneurship, and not a matter of ideological predilection.

In fact, the plan is quite clear on the relative roles of different types of capital: private and public, domestic and foreign. Among the 'principles of economic policy' enunciated in the document, the first three deal explicitly with this question and deserve to be quoted in full:

1) The Government should play an active role in the development of the country, particularly in creating basic facilities required for speedy development, such as transport, communications, power, public services, education, health, etc. The Government should also be active in those sectors where public interest requires it, as well as where private enterprise does not show sufficient initiative or efficacy. To play its part successfully the Government should be supported by an administration and other public services capable of carrying out their functions efficiently.

2) Private initiative should be further fostered and developed by various measures of economic policy. The economic activity of private persons should also be co-ordinated with the principal aims of the plan. Investments in productive activities should be encouraged by various policy measures and by developing basic facilities such as transport and power, etc.

3) Private and public foreign investments in various branches of the economy should be further encouraged by creating favourable conditions. A better basis for foreign capital investment would be achieved by developing natural resources and basic facilities, by expanding the domestic market and by maintaining a favourable balance of payments (First Five-Year Plan: 144).

That the plan was intended to be indicative rather than obligatory was also clearly articulated, especially with respect to the industrial sector.

Since ... future industrial development will depend mainly on private initiative the programme for industrialization is both a prognosis and a programme of development, including main targets and measures of industrial policy. The Plan has a firm and obligatory character only in so far as it refers to the development of the public sector and the financing of industry from public sources (First Five-Year Plan: 102).

This was the policy setting within which the planning exercise was attempted. What can be said about the state of the economy on the eve of the FFYP? A short and accurate answer is that, although some measure of industrialization had taken place since the immediate post-war years, there was no discernible change in the structure of the economy, in the standard of living of the people, and more germane for our purpose in the tempo of industrialization.

Manufacturing Industry in the First Five-Year Plan

What, then, was the strategy for industrialization incorporated into the FFYP? This strategy was entirely anchored on the development of light consumer goods industries catering for the domestic market.

In existing circumstances industrial development must concentrate on the processing industries making full use of existing supplies of agricultural raw materials. It is important that extensive processing of agricultural products should be undertaken and that some imported commodities be replaced by domestic production.

In the forefront of these are the textile industries making cotton products and sacks, both of which are consumed on a large scale and could be produced from locally-grown crops. Next in importance is the food processing industry. It has, on the one hand, to supply the growing domestic market, and on the other, to develop part of its production for export.

In this respect, there are favourable prospects for increased export of livestock and meat products, as well as for the establishment of factories for meat processing, sugar refining and oil pressing. It would be desirable

> to encourage leather tanning, footwear manufacture, timber processing and furniture production, etc., in order to improve the supply to the domestic market and reduce the need for imports in all cases where available raw materials would make this profitable. There is also a need for a metal processing industry to produce and repair agricultural tools and implements. Having in view an extensive building programme, new enterprises are needed for the production of building materials such as cement, bricks, glass, etc. Conditions for this development are available as raw materials are plentiful and the demand for these products is increasing.
>
> The growth of industrial production should be accompanied by the development of cottage industries and handicrafts which deserve encouragement since they provide employment and income for a considerable number of the population and supply useful goods for the home market (First Five-Year Plan: 234].

In other words, although the phrase was not used, the strategy was to be one of import substitution, based on light consumer goods, with a view to the domestic market and with no export horizon for manufactured goods.

What role was envisaged for manufacturing in the general scheme of the plan and what targets were set out for it? The pride of place in the FFYP was accorded to the development of infrastructure, followed by manufacturing industry. Thus, of the total monetary investments planned for 1957-61, transport and communications were allotted 45% and manufacturing industry 10.7% (First Five-Year Plan: 34). The manufacturing sub-sectors which were given the highest priorities were textiles and food processing, these two between them accounting for nearly 70% of planned investment in manufacturing, the rationale being 'very favourable natural and market conditions for these two industrial branches which have the most favourable prospects for development' (First Five-Year Plan: 104).

It is interesting to note that, of the total investment of E$57.1 million planned for manufacturing, 65% was expected to be generated locally while the remaining 35% was anticipated to take the form of direct private foreign investment, excluding another E$7 million, or 13%, which represented war reparations (First Five-Year Plan: 104). This means that nearly half of the total investment in manufacturing was expected to be financed by external resources. In contrast, the share of private domestic investment was only 14%, the other sources being bank credits (28%), budgetary funds (10.5%) and public enterprises (0.9%) (First Five-Year Plan: 105).

In terms of production, the value of manufacturing output was planned to rise from E$81.8 million to E$175.5 million during the plan period, and manufacturing employment was expected to reach 28,000 by 1961 (First Five-Year Plan: 114-5).

Industrialization During the First Five-Year Plan Period [8]
The index of manufacturing production increased from 208 in 1957 to 455 in 1961 (1950=1000) (Stanley and Karsten 1965:10). But the achievements of the FFYP, with respect to industrialization, fell short of target. The Second FiveYear Plan (SFYP) provides a succinct summary:

The development of manufacturing industry in the past period shows two important facts: first, that industry has begun to penetrate the structure of national economy, and second, that the economy was not yet sufficiently penetrated by industrialization. The results achieved so far are encouraging but modest; they do not exceed an initial stage of the development of industry. Gross industrial output grew from E$73 million to E$116 million over the past five years, but the contribution of manufacturing industry to the national income remained small (Second Five-Year Plan: 47).

It is interesting to note that actual manufacturing output fell short of target in spite of the fact that investment in this sector had overshot the plan figure to reach E$80 million (Second Five-Year Plan: 48). The official explanation given was that 'several industrial projects of great importance to the national economy were started but not completed during the period' and that 'many industrial projects which had been foreseen by the Plan were not erected for various reasons (Second Five-Year Plan: 48). Significantly, those that were not started at all were the metal, chemical and leather industries (Second Five-Year Plan: 182).

There was also very little change in the structure of industry. In fact, the share of food processing and textiles had risen to more than 80%. Although 'building material and other non-metallic mineral products showed a visible increase', we are told that 'other branches which existed at the beginning of the planned period increased rather slowly' and that 'few new commodities have been added to the previous production (SFYP: 48).

The achievements of the FFYP, with respect to manufacturing employment, were close to target but still modest. In 1961 there were 27,600 people employed in manufacturing (SFYP: 194), representing an average increase in annual employment of about 1,800. Not surprisingly, the structure of employment was dominated by the food and textiles sub-sectors, which between them accounted for nearly 74% of the jobs.

We conclude, therefore, that as Ethiopia was entering the 1960s, it was doing so with a weak industrial base. This weakness manifested itself in the size and structure of the manufacturing sector, in its capacity to generate employment, and in its low level of technology. It is against this background that the Second Five-Year Plan was launched.

1962-74: The Limits of Industrialization in a Stagnant Economy

This period was destined to be the most eventful one in Ethiopian history. In political terms, the country was to emerge out of its seclusion and participate more actively in international affairs, especially in the African arena, as its leading role in the Organization of African Unity was to demonstrate. Internally, however, this was to be a period of crises. The abortive coup d'etat of 1960 was only the beginning of a period that was to witness the birth and full-scale development of the war in Eritrea, peasant unrest in other regions of the country, and growing opposition to the regime among students and intellectuals, climaxing in the fall of Haile Selassie, the one person who had towered over Ethiopian affairs during the entire period of our study.

In the economic field the planning effort continued and, before the end of our period, two more five-year plans were to see the light of day, with a fourth already in the wings when the Old Regime collapsed. Planning or no planning, however, economic growth tended to be sluggish and uneven, largely on account of an agrarian framework that was generally considered to be an impediment to development, including industrial development. A major departure of this phase was the emergence and rather brisk development of commercial agriculture, which was, however, destined to be short-lived.

In the manufacturing industry, ownership and management continued to be concentrated in foreign hands as whatever indigenous capital existed largely found outlets in trade and housing. The rates of growth of manufacturing during this period were consistently faster than those recorded for agriculture. But the country's industrial base remained low and its capacity to generate employment unimpressive.

Industrial Policy

In discussing industrial development during this period an important point to underscore is the central and steadily increasing role played by the government. This took the form of actual government investment in manufacturing, providing mechanisms for the financing of industrial investment by private enterprise, and creating an environment of incentives to attract private capital into manufacturing.

With respect to direct government investment, the Third Five-Year Plan (TFYP) identified three broad areas for government involvement.

a) Basic manufacturing enterprises which are particularly vital to the overall growth of the economy, and to the ability of the industrial sector to meet the objectives of the plan;

b) Commercial manufacturing enterprises, essentially of the types that attract private investment (and) also considered particularly vital to the growth of the economy, as well the ability of the industrial sector to meet the objectives of the plan [after ascertaining 'within a reasonable period' that private investment is not forthcoming];

c) Small factory manufacturing enterprises which face initial growth problems, and which, by providing seed beds for the development of Ethiopian entrepreneurship and management, justify government investment (TFYP: 222-3).

Accordingly, 60% of the investment planned for manufacturing was expected to come from public sources.

With respect to industrial financing, the government created a variety of financial institutions to promote lending to private investors: first the Development Bank and then the Investment Corporation, which were later merged to form the Agricultural and Industrial Development Bank.

The extensive role of government in manufacturing may in part be seen as a corollary of the shortage of private capital. But the government went to great lengths to attract capital, especially capital of foreign extraction It will be recalled that as far back as 1950 it had issued a Notice designed for this purpose. Subsequently, an Investment Decree was issued in 1963, followed by a more elaborate Investment Proclamation in 1966 The 1963 law:

First, consolidated under one heading all the relevant earlier legislative instruments dealing with investments, importation of machinery and capital equipment and foreign exchange and fiscal regulations; second, created a formal institutional machinery which had hitherto been lacking; and third, for the first time extended the system of incentives to cover both domestic and foreign investment (Faruqi and O'Brien 1976:27).

Although it 'represented an improvement over the situation in the 1950s', it did not represent a basic departure in government policy.

There was little evidence of any shift in the basic premise underlying government policy. It still did not prescribe any explicit measures for encouraging domestic investment or entrepreneurship, nor did it incorporate any obligations to be fulfilled by foreign technology suppliers. Its object was simply to offer incentives and guarantees (Faruqi and O'Brien 1976:27-8).

The highlights of the 1966 law, which were to apply to agricultural, industrial, mining, transport and tourist enterprises, included provisions for the following incentives: a) relief from payment of income tax for five years for investment of no less than E$200,000 (and for a further three years in the case of an extension of investment); b) relief from payment of import duties on agricultural and industrial machines as well as on building and construction materials; c) relief from payment of export duties and transaction tax on exported manufactured goods; d) tariff protection for infant industries; and e) generous provisions for remittance of profits.[9] As a study by the Stanford Research Institute (SRI) (1968:3) pointed out, the incentives provided to the foreign investor were liberal

> *The investment climate of Ethiopia may generally be viewed as favourable in terms of those conditions of importance to potential investors ... The IEG (Imperial Ethiopian Government) considers increased investment of foreign and domestic private capital vital to the growth and development of the country's economy and welcomes foreign private investment. Its policy toward stimulating domestic and foreign investment is supported by liberal investment incentives.*

This statement, although generally true, needs to be qualified. Thus:

> *Although the IEG has taken steps to attract private investment, the potential foreign investor is left largely on his own to determine the opportunities that exist, the incentives that are available and the procedural rules that must be followed. There is no government agency in Ethiopia whose function is to assist the investor with respect to these problems* (Stanford Research Institute 1968:7).

In addition, the law was unlikely to be of much relevance to Ethiopian investors because the E$200 million investment required to qualify for the various incentives was bound to be too high for local capital. As the study (SRI 1968:20) concluded:

> *Considering the size of the Ethiopian economy, the acquisition of a sum such as E$100,000 from almost any domestic source of group of sources is a prodigious task. The acquisition of twice that sum is limited to an even smaller group, which would be largely composed of only the smallest caste of the already wealthy and at the pinnacle of the social and economic structure.*

The 'strategy' of industrialization, if one can use such a term, continued to be one of import substitution, a process which was already beginning to experience difficulties.[10] However, it is interesting to note that, beginning with the SFYP, one observes an articulation of a 'longer view' of industrialization, characterized by a move from exclusive reliance on industries producing consumer goods.

> Conceived as the initial phase of the twenty-year development programme, the Second Five-Year Development Plan has to create the preconditions for faster industrialization. With this in view, the Second Plan's industrial programme envisages preparatory work and construction of the iron and steel combination which is to be erected in the country. The combination will consist of iron mines, power plants and iron and steel works, with a final capacity of 80,000 tons of steel per annum. Steel production is anticipated for the beginning of the Third Five-Year Plan, so that the newly established metal processing industry will be supplied with raw materials, partly by the Akaki Steel Plant and partly from imports. Meanwhile, prospecting for iron ore and coal in other promising regions is also foreseen by the Second Plan in order to find out possibilities of erecting new steel plants to supply other regions of the country. The building up of the chemical industry, which is to be started during the Second Plan, is also of a long-term development nature. Based on mineral raw materials and wood, as well as on the by-products of the oil-refinery, the chemical industry will have to play an important role in overall economic development (SFYP: 71-72).

This was conceived as part of a broader strategy of structural transformation. It is against this background that the specific targets set out for the manufacturing sector must be examined.

The Second Five-Year Plan and its Achievements

The SFYP gave priority to the development of agriculture (essentially commercial agriculture), manufacturing and transport, whose relative shares of planned investment were 20.9%, 18.8% and 16.8%, respectively (SFYP: 102).

Within manufacturing, which was allotted a total investment of E$318.5 million, first priority was given to chemicals (30.3%), followed by food and beverages (23.6%), steel and metals (16%), and textiles (10.2%). The relative change of emphasis between textiles on the one hand, and steel and metals on the other, is interesting.

No less interesting is the projected financing of these investments. Of the investment in manufacturing, 62% was expected to be financed from abroad, the rationale given being that 'big and expensive industrial projects will be built with a predominant participation of equipment which must nearly all be imported' (SFYP: 192). Whatever the logic, one observes growing dependence of the manufacturing sector on foreign capital, in both intent and practice.

With respect to employment, which was not one of the strongest aspects of the manufacturing sector, the SFYP anticipated that jobs in this sector would increase by 30,000 during the five-year period, raising the employment figure to 57,900 by 1967 (SFYP: 194). Of the planned increase, almost one-third was expected to be accounted for by the textile industry.

These were the intentions, but the achievements, on the whole, fell short of target. Although output grew at the respectable annual rate of 16%, it was far too little compared to the planned rate of 27%. Actual investment (E$306 million) was also short of that intended (E$318 million). The only thing we are told about employment is that it 'increased at a slightly faster rate than that expected in the plan, if the agricultural workers on the sugar estates were included' (TFYP: 217-8).

We will now turn to a more detailed examination of the record. In doing so we will not follow strictly the plan years, which are themselves not particularly consistent, but historical periods which are more convenient to deal with because of the readily available data. Accordingly, we will begin with a review of the first half of the 1960s.[11] Between 1960 and 1965, manufacturing output valued at current prices more than doubled, but when valued at constant prices, this rate went down to between 16 and 18% per annum (Anonymous, 1967: 6).

The structure of output is again dominated by food and textiles, which in 1965 accounted for 58% of the manufacturing output; adding beverages raises the figure to 64%. It is interesting to note, however, that the relative role of the first two had been declining over the five-year period; that of food from 39% to 29% and that of textiles from 34% to 29%. On the contrary, the share of beverages doubled from 8% to 16%. But this is hardly evidence of structural change, because the overwhelming dominance of consumer goods continued unchallenged. This happened in spite of the fact that the share of what one might call 'heavy industry', i.e., steel, electrical machinery, metallic and non-metallic products, chemicals, etc., had risen from 6% to 13% 'admittedly a notable development, but involving only small magnitudes' (Anonymous, 1967:8). What is even more significant is that the share of manufacturing in GDP continued to be small, having reached only 2.8% in 1965 (Anonymous 1967:8).

With respect to investment, we have to rely on less solid data. Measured in current prices, investment in manufacturing rose from about E$32 million in 1961 to E$74.5 in 1965, but it is difficult to tell what this means in real terms (Anonymous 1967:9). Not surprisingly, of the total investment in manufacturing during 1961-65 (E$223.2 million), the bulk went to textiles (24.8%), food (21.1%), and beverages (10%). A figure of 21.3% is reported for chemicals, but we are told this figure 'is not beyond doubt', even given the fact that 'the oil refinery at Assab has absorbed a considerable amount of development expenditure' (Anonymous 1967:10-1).

Employment in the manufacturing industry is reported to have increased from less than 28,000 in 1961 to more than 48,000 in 1965 (the figures including both permanent and temporary workers). This works out to a rate of 15% per year, which is fairly high. But, 'whether this is *high enough* for an economy like that of Ethiopia can only be judged in terms of the structural change it induces' (Anonymous 1967:2).

The evidence demonstrates that structural change had not materialized, because 'the structure of employment in (1961) was, on the whole, similar to that of 1965 and the two branches of manufacturing that provided about 3/4 of total employment in 1961 (food and textiles) still accounted for 72% in 1965' (Anonymous 1967:4). The only qualification to this pattern is that there had been a modest increase in the relative shares of chemicals, steel, metals and electrical machinery.

The output of the manufacturing sector was, for the most part, locally consumed, but there were also some developments in the area of exports From E$10 million in 1961 the value of manufactured exports in current prices had risen to E$18 million in 1965. While this achievement is not insignificant when viewed in absolute terms, 'it ceases to impress' when viewed in a comparative perspective. In 1965 the share of manufactures in total export value was only 7.2%, hardly a performance deserving celebration. 'In 1965, as in 1961, products of the food processing industry represented by far the largest portion of manufactured and semi-manufactured articles' (Anonymous 1967:13). It should be noted in this connection that a process of import substitution had taken place, with regard to some commodities (such as cotton yarn, cotton fabrics, beverages and building materials). But there was still plenty of scope for further import substitution (Anonymous 1967:17-8).

In concluding our review of the record for 1961-65, we note that there were a number of positive developments in manufacturing: growth in output, investment, employment and exports. However, in terms of structural change, both within manufacturing and with respect to the role of manufacturing in the economy, there was no significant departure. In other words, there were changes, but these changes cumulatively did not have enough impact to alter the nature of the manufacturing sector and the character of the Ethiopian economy.

Industrialization During the Third Five-Year Plan Period [12]

The major departure of the TFYP was that it recognized in more explicit form than ever before the crucial role of agriculture in Ethiopia's development. In particular, it gave considerable emphasis to commercial agriculture, on the assumption that its development would be a spur both to peasant agriculture and to the nonagricultural sectors.

Gross output in manufacturing at current prices was expected to double (from E$350 million to E$700 million) or to grow at an annual rate of 14.9%, while value added was expected to rise from E$140 million to E$280 million during the plan period (TFYP: 227). Most of the growth was expected from the traditional industries, namely 'food processing, textiles, and, to some extent, leather and shoe-making industries' (TFYP: 45). But this did not deter the planners from once again talking about structural change:

> *The pattern of industrialization of Ethiopia is expected to undergo a change during the third plan period. Steel and metal products, leather and shoes, and chemicals will record large increases in production and emerge as major industries. Electrical industries will make a good start and substantially meet consumer demand for many products* (TFYP: 227).

It seems that they were not sobered by the contradiction between their vision of structural change, on the one hand, and the stubborn reality of a manufacturing sector that had constantly failed to register it, on the other.

The plan also anticipated a rapid increase in exports of manufactures; at current prices these were expected to rise from E$23 million in 1968 to E$60 million in 1973, the items on which hope was placed being meat and meat products, and leather and shoes (TFYP: 228).

The planned investment for manufacturing was E$515 million, of which E$350 million, or 68%, was expected to be financed from external sources (TFYP: 229). It is remarkable that, in the face of a disappointing inflow of foreign capital into the manufacturing sector, the government persisted in its hope of attracting resources from abroad.

Employment in the manufacturing sector (both permanent and seasonal) was expected to rise from 66,000 in 1968 to 110,000 in 1973, it being anticipated that, by 1973, the dominant sub-sectors would be textiles (31%), food (21%), and leather and shoes (15%). A notable departure is that non-metallic mineral products were expected to account for 9% of manufacturing employment (TFYP: 236).

These were the salient components of the TFYP as far as manufacturing was concerned. What, then, were the actual accomplishments? We note, to begin with, that the aggregate performance of the economy left much to be desired:

> *The Ethiopian economy has continued to grow very slowly from a low per capita income base. The overall growth rate of the economy during the TFYP period was disappointing both in terms of the TFYP targets, which were recognized as overly optimistic, and in comparison with the moderate growth rate during the First and Second Plan periods. The*

growth rates of all major sectors were lower than forecast in the Plan. Second, the growth rate of GDP fell even further in the last three years despite an export boom from 1972 to 1974 (World Bank 1975:2).

Of the factors that accounted for this state of affairs, the major ones were the drought of 1973, inadequate domestic resource mobilization and a lower-than-expected inflow of external resources leading to a low investment effort, and a 'failure to introduce badly needed institutional reforms', especially in the area of land tenure (World Bank 1975:2). As the Bank (1975:3) concludes, 'recent economic trends have done little to change the poverty and underdevelopment of the Ethiopian economy'.

The state of manufacturing was obviously affected by this state of affairs. One observes a tendency for the pace of industrial growth to slacken during this period. Gross value of manufacturing output rose from E$467 million in 1968-69 to E$890.6 million in 1973-74 (Table 4). In constant prices, however, the increase was from E$114.1 to E$173.3 (Table 5), or a growth rate of about 8%, which compares rather unfavourably with the corresponding figure for 1960-61 and 1967-68, which was 14.5% (World Bank 1975:15). It is especially revealing that manufacturing output in constant prices declined from 1972-73 to 1973-74, further confirming a tendency for output to slacken towards the end of our period. Moreover, the value of fixed capital assets, which stood at E$385.3 million in 1968-69, declined steadily during the following years, reaching E$361 million in 1971-72. There was, however, a recovery in the next two years.

Between 1968-69 and 1973-74, employment in manufacturing rose from 47,332 to 57,320, an average annual increase of less than 2,000, which again compares unfavourably with the record for 1961-65. It also compares unfavourably with the growth in output. Thus, while real manufacturing output grew by an average of 10.4% during this period, employment grew by only 4.2%. Growth in employment therefore lagged considerably behind growth in output, demonstrating the very weak capacity of the manufacturing sector to create jobs.

Even more disappointing was the record of investment in manufacturing From E$62.4 million in 1968-69, investment in this sector declined steadily in 1971-72, reaching its lowest level in ten years. There was a significant recovery in 1972-73, only to be followed by a decline in the following year.

The disappointing performance of the manufacturing sector was due to a wide variety of factors, including the sorry performance of agriculture, with its attendant consequences on the growth of income and resource mobilization, and the limited room left for further import substitution in consumer goods. Further:

Table 4: Performance of Manufacturing Industry

	1961-62	1962-63	1963-64	1964-65	1965-66	1966-67	1968-69	1969-70	1970-71	1971-72	1972-73	1973-74
Number of establishments				272	273	395	442	479	401	420	421	436
Number of employees	27,000	31,500	36,300	46,205	47,343	44,349	47,332	48,903	51,588	53,319	54,818	57,320
Fixed capital assets (E$000)					243,665	342,365	385,319	369,221	368,519	361,061	389,954	425,149
Gross value of production (E$000)	116,350	148,805	176,500	215,061	269,822	357,110	467,039	542,645	625,936	689,462	772,535	890,637
Wages and salaries (E$000)				32,965	41,567	48,888	57,907	61,824	69,648	73,685	80,086	87,994
Capital expenditure (E$000)		31,965	49,000	67,605	74,941	52,391	62,355	44,204	36,333	31,204	43,991	36,264

Notes: No data is shown for 1967-68 because of incomplete coverage of the industrial survey for that year. Only establishments employing more than ten persons are included.

Sources: *Statistical Abstract*, issues for 1969-1972, 1975-76, pp. 59, 54, 54, 51, 58, 54, respectively.

The disappointing performance has also been attributed to high internal transport costs, to unforeseen consequences on international transport costs following the closure of the Suez Canal, and to an uncertain investment climate for foreign capital. Few large industrial investments were undertaken during the TFYP period; most investment in the sector was for expansion of existing firms. The shortfall in industrial investment can be partly attributed to the lower-than-anticipated inflow of foreign capital for manufacturing (only half the amount forecast in the Plan), but the initial investment target was undoubtedly over-ambitious and there were also shortfalls in domestic investment by both the public and the private sectors (World Bank 1975:15).

For all these reasons, industrialization on the eve of the revolution was, if not grinding to a halt, at least settling down to a slow pace.

Table 5: Manufacturing Output at Constant (1960-61) Factor Cost

Year	E$ million	as % of GDP
1964·65	72.0	2.6
1965·66	83.4	2.9
1966·67	94.4	3.1
1967·68	103.2	3.3
1968·69	114.1	3.5
1969·70	139.9	4.1
1970·71	158.3	4.4
1971·72	164.0	4.3
1972·73	175.2	4.5
1973·74	173.3	4.4

Source: Central Statistical Office, Statistical Abstract issues for 1971, 1972, 1975, 1976, pp. 126, 125, 137, 140.

Summing Up: Through the Looking-Glass

We are now in a position to summarize the salient features of industrialization in Ethiopia during the period 1941-74. One could say that in 1941 the manufacturing sector was starting almost from scratch. In fact, as mentioned earlier, even as late as 1950 this sector contributed barely 1% of the national income and in 1952 it provided only 8,450 jobs. Notable developments did subsequently take place. Between 1954 and 1969, for example, there was 'a sixfold rise in value added in the modern manufacturing sector; a 2.3 times rise in employment in that sector and an increase of some 2.6 times in labour productivity in modern manufacturing' (Faruqi and O'Brien 1976:24). By the end of our period, the number of industrial enterprises had grown considerably (to 436), the share of the sector in GDP had increased to 5.2% at current factor cost (although only to 4.4% at constant factor cost) (Statistical Abstract 1976:140-134), and employment had risen to 57,320.

These achievements need not be gainsaid, but neither do they give cause for celebration; as a record of one-third of a century they are simply inadequate. At the end of our period, the role of the manufacturing sector in the economy was marginal in all the major aspects. As pointed out earlier, at the end of our period its contribution to national income in real terms was less than 5%; employment fell short of 60,000, out of a population then estimated at 27 million; its contribution to gross fixed capital formation was less than 8% (Statistical Abstract 1976:138) and it accounted for less than 5% of total export earnings (Statistical Abstract 1976:103). Although its rates of growth had consistently far outpaced those of agriculture, they had failed to transform the structure of the economy. Thus, in 1964-65, manufacturing accounted for 2.6% of the GDP at constant factor cost; by 1973-74 this figure had reached only 4.4%, i.e., a mere 1.8% increase over an entire decade. It should also be noted that the manufacturing rates of growth should be viewed against the very low base with which comparisons are made. Moreover, outperforming the agricultural sector is hardly a matter of distinction, for the record of this sector was generally dismal.

This, in the final analysis, was the major constraint with which the manufacturing sector had to reckon. Put simply, the chain of causation led from a stagnant agriculture to a slow rate of aggregate economic growth, to a low level of income, which in turn meant not only low savings and investment but also low purchasing power, thereby denying industry the extensive market without which its dynamic growth is unthinkable. Thus, the manufacturing sector had to operate within the straitjacket of a stagnant economy, a fact that explains not only its marginal role but also its deceleration towards the end of our period.

Another feature of the industrialization of the period was its almost exclusive reliance on light consumer goods. At the end of our period (1973-74), textiles accounted for 30.9% of the gross value of production, 41% of employment and 45.1% of investment in manufacturing industry. Adding food and beverages raises the figures to 59.4%, 66.4% and 63.8% respectively. In contrast, the share of steel, metal and electrical industries was only 5.6%, 3.4% and 1.3% respectively (Table 6). It is also worth noting that, with respect to the production of consumer goods, there was relative neglect of small-scale industries, in spite of their recognized capacity to generate employment and other positive characteristics (Woldu 1983:346-7; Eshetu 1986:33-40).

Table 6: Structure of Manufacturing Industry (1973-74) (%)

Sub-Sector	Gross value of production	Employment	Investment
Food	18.6	20.3	16.1
Beverages	9.9	5.1	2.6
Tobacco	3.3	0.8	5.9
Textiles	30.9	41.0	45.1
Leather and shoes	4.1	4.8	11.9
Wood	2.4	7.4	0.9
Non-metallic mineral products	2.9	7.1	2.7
Printing	1.6	2.6	0.7
Chemical	20.7	7.5	12.8
Steel, metal and Electrical	5.6	3.4	1.3

Source: Statistical Abstract 1976, p.55.

It should be pointed out that much had been achieved in the way of import substitution, especially in such areas as textiles, food and footwear. Thus, 'by 1970 substantial import substitution had occurred in the consumer goods sector where imports fell from 73% to 30% of the total domestic supply over the period (1954-70)' (Faruqi and O'Brien 1976:26). Thus, already in 1972, Guisinger (1972:15) was led to conclude that:

The first stage of the IS (import substitution) process is drawing to a close. Some efficient import-replacing opportunities still exist but the value added from new IS activities will only make a modest contribution to the future rate of industrial growth.

But the manufacturing sector in our period was stuck in this early phase of import substitution, unable to venture meaningfully into export or, as pointed out earlier, into the production of the needed inputs locally. It is especially true that it lacked a base for capital goods, thereby making the industrial structure fragile. Again, to quote Guisinger (1972:15):

Substantial scope for further IS does remain in the intermediate and capital goods sectors, but in both of these sectors the minimum efficient scale of plant is typically much larger than the volume of goods which the Ethiopian market can absorb in the near future; and if import substitution is brought about by high protection, the result will most likely be inefficient high cost industries which will place a drag on the long-term economic growth of the economy. For the most part, exports of manufactured goods have failed to develop, except in those industries which treat exports as a vent for the surplus between domestic capacity and domestic demand of those which provide only a minimum elaboration of agricultural products.

It should also be noted that whatever import substitution took place was characterized by considerable inefficiency, with obvious consequences for the economy and society. There is unanimous expert opinion that the manufacturing sector was excessively protected (Guisinger 1972; Barac 1975). In the first place, the tariffs granted were much higher than necessary for the objective of protecting new industries. This was true of nominal tariff rates, but even more of effective protective rates, which were higher than the nominal ones in almost every important case. Table 7 illustrates this point.

Table 7: Nominal and Effective Rates of Protection for Selected Manufacturing Industries in Ethiopia

Product	Nominal Tariff	Effective Rate
Synthetic textiles	140	522
Cotton yarn	53	502
Galvanized iron sheets	49	435
Cotton cloth	93	388
Shoes	110	280
Ceramic tiles	68	188
Men's suits	88	165
Soaps	43	126
Jute and sisal bags	70	90

Source: Guisinger, 1972.

Secondly, once tariff protection was granted for certain commodities, it tended to perpetuate itself, regardless of whether a specific industry had improved or not improved its efficiency over time. This is a clear violation of the spirit of the infant industry argument, whose basic premise is that new industries should enjoy protection only until such time as they become competitive enough not to require protection any longer. In the Ethiopian case, however, 'tariffs were never revised downward, which resulted in parasitic features in many sectors of manufacturing industry' (Barac 1975:5). This happened in spite of repeated expert recommendations for the downward revision of tariffs. In fact, the establishment of a committee for revising tariffs periodically had been included in the TFYP, but the committee never saw the light of day. Even more curiously, 'instead of decreasing tariffs, the government did the opposite' (Barac 1975:6-7). This had an adverse effect on consumer prices (and hence on consumer welfare) as well as on production.

Another factor militating against efficiency in the manufacturing sector was the very limited extent of competition among producers 'The domination of a few firms in various production lines resulted in prices which tended to be as high as tariff protection permitted it' (Barac 1975:9-10). Barac summarizes the picture for 1969-70, on the basis of 37 industries:

A quarter of the branches have one company each accounting for more than 50% of sectoral output. In 13 cases sectors are dominated by duopolies. In 34 of the branches the top three firms accounted for more than 50% of sectoral output, in 26 of them the proportion rose to over two-thirds, and in 15 cases (more than two-fifths of the branches) the top three companies accounted for 90 or more per cent of the output in the particular sector. Only in three branches, 'grain milling and baking', 'sawmills' and 'other non-metallic minerals' did the top three companies account for less than half of the sector's production(1975:12).

One other factor contributing to inefficiency was the widespread existence of capacity under-utilization in many manufacturing enterprises largely due to problems related with ensuring a steady supply of raw materials, shortage of spare parts, and limited demand.

A third major point to note is that whatever growth took place during this period represented dependent industrialization This dependence manifested itself in at least two ways: dependence on foreign capital and dependence on foreign inputs. As pointed out repeatedly throughout this chapter, the bulk of the investment in manufacturing, especially in the larger enterprises, was foreign. For example, a 1967 survey showed that most of the 489 commercial and industrial establishments with a paid-up capital of at least E$10,000,385 were owned and managed by non-Ethiopians (IBRD/IDA 1970:6). And in 1969-70, out of a total paid-up capital of E$323 million in manufacturing, E$138 million, or 60%, was foreign (Czvis 1972:3). Another source corroborates this point as follows:

Foreign equity holding had a dominant position (i.e. more than 50% equity holding) in as many as 23 of the 34 branches. In fact, in ten manufacturing branches foreign participation accounted for as much as 80-100%; in nine it was between 60 and 79 and in four it ranged between 50 and 59%... Foreign capital and technology seemed to have concentrated mainly in modern manufacturing, particularly in those branches which were among the more dynamic and technology-intensive in the sector, e.g. fabricated metal products, basic metal industries, textiles (the largest single branch in manufacturing in Ethiopia), food products, and several branches of the chemical industry. By contrast the majority of branches where Ethiopian capital was dominant were among the more 'traditional' ones in the sector. At least six of the eleven branches were of this kind tobacco, beverages, paper products, printing, cement, and grain milling. Of the remaining five which corresponded to 'modern' manufacturing, Ethiopians had a marginal majority in three and a significant majority in only two branches (Faruqi and O'Brien 1976:30-2).

The extent of foreign dominance was actually even more pronounced than the foregoing statistics suggest. The study cited above identified 51 firms which made the 'hard core' of Ethiopian manufacturing at the time (accounting for 80% of paid-up capital, over 76% of value added and 69% of employment in the sector as a whole) and reached the following conclusions:

> The characteristics of ownership of the 51 major firms may be summarized as follows. First, in 29 firms foreigners had an outright majority of the equity (i.e. 51% or more), in another four they had 50%, and in five firms foreign participation was below 50%. Even in those cases where foreign equity holding was less than 50%, there may still have been effective control by foreigners because foreign equity represented a single block vote and such shareholding was always combined with management contracts. In brief, 38 of the 51 major firms in manufacturing in Ethiopia were either foreign-owned or foreign-managed, or both; these firms, moreover, accounted for 75% of the value added by the sample firms and for 57% of the value added in the whole of manufacturing in Ethiopia. Secondly, only ten of the 51 firms were wholly Ethiopian and of these eight were in the public sector. In view of the particular manufacturing branches in which they operated, these firms had substantially lower ratios of value added to paid-up capital than firms with foreign participation. When these Ethiopian firms were weighted in terms of their share in paid-up capital they accounted for 30%, although their share in value added was only 15%. Thus, measures of foreign control based on paid-up capital alone tended to exaggerate the importance of wholly Ethiopian enterprises in modern manufacturing (Faruqi and O'Brien 1976:32-3).

One important aspect of dependence on foreign capital is over-invoicing of imported inputs. One study estimates the over-invoicing of intermediate imports for the manufacturing sector in 1969-70 at E$32 million, although another one reduces the figure by half (Barac 1975:20). Barac also gives a figure of E$5 million for under-invoiced exports. He even goes farther and concludes that the contribution of foreign companies to the development of

Ethiopian manufacturing was negative in the sense that value added was smaller than the cost of imported inputs (Barac 1975:21). Therefore, it is:

safe to conclude that direct foreign investment with foreign control combined with tax holidays which mostly favoured big foreign companies and other privileges resulted in a total deadlock and made a negligible contribution to the real development of Ethiopian manufacturing industry (Barac 1975:23).

From this the author draws the questionable and drastic conclusion that 'foreign capital participation in Ethiopian manufacturing industry should not be continued or revived' (Barac 1975:24). Without denying the adverse consequences of foreign investment, it must be stated that such an extreme and dogmatic position is neither desirable nor feasible. In fact, this view stands out as a singular exception. Thus, according to the Stanford Research Institute (1968:91), the incentives granted to foreign investment 'were necessary for the investments to take place', it being presumed that the effect of such investments was beneficial on balance. And, according to another view, 'the major problem that the nation has (sic) today is not the result of exploitation by foreign capital but the failure to exploit such foreign capital' (Befekadu 1980:122).

Whatever the net effect of foreign investment may have been, there is an interesting paradox to contemplate here: manufacturing was foreign-dominated, but the government wanted still more foreign capital; but and here is the rub not enough of it was forthcoming. In fact, its annual inflow was declining in the last years of our period. The manufacturing sector was thus locked in this contradiction and hence its capacity for autonomous development was virtually nil.

The sector was also heavily dependent on imported inputs, including technology. True, many of the industries (for example textiles and food processing) utilized a lot of local inputs. But it is equally true that, even for raw materials, a number of enterprises were highly dependent on imports Especially noteworthy in this regard are iron and steel, paper and printing, electricals, metal products and chemicals. In 1969-70, for example, the import content of raw materials was 15% for food and beverages, 27% for textiles and apparel, 92% for the chemical industry, and 57% for other sub-sectors (basic metal and non-metallic industries, leather and shoe, tobacco, wood, printing, etc.) (Czivis 1972:4). Some details on the nature of such imports are given as follows:

Textiles are dependent up to 27% of the total value of raw materials in imported cotton and man-made fibres. Other products are following the same pattern; for example, tobacco is still largely dependent on imported raw tobacco, fibre bags use substantially imported jute and matches are based on imported woodsticks. Canned meat, vegetables and fruit have a high import dependence because of imported cans. The beer industry has to rely on imported malt, (the) paper factory on imported pulp, etc.

In 1971-72, imported raw materials accounted for 41% of total raw materials used in manufacturing, the figure reaching 91%, 89% and 74% in the chemical, basic and fabricated metal producing industries respectively (Barac 1975:27). And as far as intermediate and capital goods are concerned the import dependence of the sector was almost total. With respect to technology, the following observations are in order. First, the extent of technological dependence:

Import substitution in modern manufacturing depended on the application of technology new to Ethiopia and that technology was obtained from abroad. The dependence on foreign supplies was most striking in the machinery and transport equipment sector where, in the period 1966-69, imports accounted for 91% of the total investment. Technology imports in the form of know-how mainly came under the rubric of technical assistance. Between 1964-65 and 1968-69 total technical assistance to Ethiopia amounted to E$421 million, that is 56% of the value of imported capital goods over the same period (Faruqi and O'Brien 1976:26).

The most important sources of technology and management were Holland, Japan, India and Italy, which in 1969-70 between them accounted for 84% of the value added of a sample of firms surveyed (Faruqi and O'Brien 1976:33).

The available evidence further suggests that the conditions under which technology was transferred were not favorable to Ethiopia. To begin with, a good deal of the machinery operating in manufacturing enterprises was brought into the country in the 1950s and 1960s, most of it second hand, and thus created serious problems of maintenance towards the close of our period. As such, it hardly represented the stuff by which dynamic industrialization is propelled.

The major modality for technology transfer was the management contract, which in most cases gave management far-reaching control over the appointment of the managing director, the employment of technical and professional staff, and training. It also included tie-in clauses involving purchase of intermediate inputs from the source country. Further:

many of the management contractors in Ethiopia appear to have maintained their initial bargaining advantages through contracts of long duration. Of the 12 contracts on which information was available, only one contract was for three years; in contrast, nine were for ten years or more. In fact, in two cases, contractors who had entered into long contracts in the first place negotiated their contracts before the terminal date for further long periods to perpetuate their control over management decisions in exchange for some concessions on training, sales and imports. None of the contractors seemed to show any interest in training Ethiopians to take over such key managerial and technical functions (Faruqi and O'Brien 1976:35).

It is also known that some firms engaged in the practice of overpricing technology initially imported in connection with new operations (Faruqi and O'Brien 1976:39). The upshot of all this is that since Ethiopian manufacturing was highly import-dependent, it had very limited linkages with the rest of the economy. This seriously limited its capacity for acting as an agent of structural transformation, which was the historical mission of the industrial sector in advanced countries.

Finally, the benefits of industrialization, skimpy as they were, were very unevenly distributed in regional terms The country's industrial establishments tended to be concentrated in Addis Ababa, along the Addis Ababa-Nazareth axis, in Asmara and Dire Dawa. Thus, of the manufacturing establishments covered by the 1970-71 survey of industries, 92% were located in Shoa, Eritrea and Hararge and these regions accounted for 91% of the labour force in manufacturing (Barac 1975:4). In the specific circumstances of industrial development in Ethiopia, this was perhaps inevitable. But it is also true that it tended to give the regional pattern of industrialization a lop-sided character which was not always desirable.

These, then, were the characteristics of industrialization in Ethiopia in the period between the Italian occupation and the eve of the revolution. To give the matter a wider perspective, it should be pointed out that they were not characteristics unique to Ethiopia or even to pre-revolution Ethiopia.[13] They represented the essential character of industrialization in the context of economic stagnation. Indeed, such is the nature of underdevelopment that, as the Queen in *Through the Looking-Glass* aptly observed, 'it takes all the running you can do to keep in the same place [and] if you want to get somewhere else, you must run at least twice as fast as that!'

Notes
1. Industry in its broad sense includes manufacturing, mining and quarrying, construction, and the utilities. In this chapter, however, it has been used in its narrow sense of manufacturing.
2. There are overlaps in the historical periods, a situation made unavoidable by the form in which data were available. Although such overlaps may offend those with a penchant for neat categorization, they do not affect our conclusions one way or the other.

3. Strictly speaking, the First Five-Year Plan was not concluded in 1961 but in 1962, as it had to be extended to the end of the Ethiopian fiscal year. But, for our purposes, this is a fact of minor importance.
4. The statements in quotation marks are quoted by Marcus from the original United States document.
5. The only major industrial undertaking of this period was the setting up of the Cotton Company of Dire Dawa in 1943.
6. Another example of contradictory data presented by a single source is the following. The Ministry of Commerce and Industry (MCI 1955:79-102) gives the following two sets of figures for the value of industrial production:

	Value of Production (E$ million)	
Year	(1)	(2)
1951	27.7	22.2
1952	37.2	31.1
1953	39.7	32.7

The figures under (1) refer to the gross value of industrial production (excluding mining and construction) while those under (2) refer to the gross value of manufacturing industry. One finds no obvious explanation for the differences in the figures.
7. This document is henceforth cited as FFYP.
8. Our information on the achievements of the FFYP is derived from the Imperial Ethiopian Government's, *Second Five Year Development Plan 1955-1959 E.C. 1963-1967 G.C.* (Addis Ababa: October 1962). This document is henceforth cited as SFYP.
9. Further, one study (Stanley and Karsten, 1965:94) points out that 'the Emperor and the Government officials stress on every occasion again and again that the expropriation of foreigners is not intended and could never take place without full compensation'. Given the extensive nationalizations that were to take place in 1975, this statement must be taken as a revealing commentary on the permanence of policy in an environment of political fluidity.
10. For a general treatment, see Guisinger, 1972; Mead, 1971; Schmidt, 1968. For a specific examination of the textile industry, see Eshetu, 1973.
11. For 1960-65 we have relied on an anonymous paper entitled 'Industrial Development in Ethiopia (1954-58, E.C.) - Part A: A General Assessment', 17 March 1967, mimeographed. References to this chapter will appear as Anonymous.
12. As originally conceived, the TFYP was to cover the period 1968-73. However, during the course of its implementation (in 1971), 'the Government decided to extend the period of the Plan by one year and to revise several plan targets downward. The principal reasons given for the revisions were that the economy had been adversely affected by the closure of the Suez Canal and the fall of coffee prices, and that more time was needed to implement planned policy measures and institutional reforms' (World Bank 1975:1). In other words, the TFYP period was extended to fiscal year 1973-74, which takes us more or less to the end of our period. Therefore, even if not strictly accurate, in our discussion the TFYP period and 1966-74 are taken as roughly coterminous.
13. For a picture of the post-1974 period, see Eshetu, 1986-87.

References

Addis, Hiwet, 1975, *Ethiopia: From Autocracy to Revolution*, Merlin Press, London.

Anonymous, 1967, Industrial Development in Ethiopia (1954-1958 E.C.) - Part A: A General Assessment, Addis Ababa.

Assefa Bequele and Eshetu Chole, 1969, *A Profile of the Ethiopian Economy*, Oxford University Press, Nairobi.

Barac, Stevan, 1975, Some Problems of Development in Ethiopian Manufacturing Industry, in Commercial Bank of Ethiopia, *Market Report*, May-June 1975.

Befekadu, Degefe, 1980, Industrialization, Investment Policy and Foreign Capital in Ethiopia 1950-74, in Institute of Development Research, Addis Ababa University, *Proceedings of the Seminar on Industrial Transformation in Ethiopia*, Nazareth, 18-20 January 1980.

Bekure, W, Semait, 1984, Industrial Development in Addis Ababa Area (A Miniature Capitalist Penetration), *Journal of Ethiopian Studies*, 17.

Central Statistical Office, Results of Survey of Manufacturing Establishments, various issues, Addis Ababa.

------------, *Statistical Abstract*, various issues, Addis Ababa.

------------, 1977, Indices of Manufacturing Production, Sales and Output of Electricity, *Statistical Bulletin No. 14*, Addis Ababa.

Commercial Bank of Ethiopia, 1974, Growth and Structural Change of Ethiopian Manufacturing Industry, *Market Report*, March-April 1974, Addis Ababa.

------------, Import-Substitution in Ethiopia - Some Reflections, *Market Report*, September-October 1974, Addis Ababa.

Czivis, O, 1972, Ethiopia: Country Brief and Draft Proposal of Country Programme for Industrial Sector, Addis Ababa.

Duri, Mohamed, 1969, Private Foreign Investment in Ethiopia, 1950-68, *Journal of Ethiopian Studies*, 7, 2.

Eshetu, Chole, 1973, Import Substitution in Practice: The Case of the Ethiopian Textile Industry, unpublished Ph.D. Dissertation, Syracuse University.

------------, 1986, The Impact of Industrial Development on Employment Generation in Ethiopia, paper presented to the First National Symposium on Industrial Development in Ethiopia, Addis Ababa.

------------, 1987, Constraints on Industrial Development in Ethiopia, *Mondes en Developpement*. This paper also appears in *Eastern Africa Social Science Research Review*, 3, 2 and in *Proceedings of the Ninth International Conference of Ethiopian Studies*, Nauka Publishers, Moscow.

Faruqi, Rumman and O'Brien, Peter, 1976, Foreign Technology in the Growth of the Modern Manufacturing Sector in Ethiopia 1950-70, *Africa Development*, 1, 2.

Imperial Ethiopian Government (IEG), 1950, Statement of Policy for the Encouragement of Foreign Capital Investment in Ethiopia, Addis Ababa.

------------, 1954, A Proclamation to Encourage Agricultural and Industrial Expansion in Our Empire, Addis Ababa.

------------, n.d., First Five-Year Development Plan, 1957-61, Addis Ababa.

------------, 1962, Second Five-Year Development Plan 1955-59 E.C. 1963-67 G.C., Addis Ababa.

------------, 1963, Investment Decree, 1963.

------------, 1966, A Proclamation to Provide for the Encouragement of Capital Investment in Ethiopia, Addis Ababa.

------------, 1968, Third Five-Year Development Plan, Addis Ababa.

International Bank for Reconstruction and Development/ International Development Association, 1967, The Economy of Ethiopia (in five volumes) - Volume I: Main Report, World Bank, Washington, DC.

------------, 1970, Economic Growth and Prospects in Ethiopia (in five volumes) - Volume II, World Bank, Washington, DC.

Lipsky, George, A, 1962, *Ethiopia: Its People, Its Society, Its Culture*, Haraf Press, New Haven.

Marcus, Harold, 1983, *Ethiopia, Great Britain and the United States 1941-74: The Politics of Empire*. Berkeley, Los Angeles, University of California Press, London.

Mead, Donald C, 1971, Import Substitution and Production for Export in the Industrial Sector, mimeo, Addis Ababa.

Ministry of Commerce and Industry, 1951, *Economic Handbook of Ethiopia*, Berhanena Selam, Printing Press, Addis Ababa.

------------, 1955, *Economic Progress of Ethiopia*, Nairobi.

Pankhurst, Richard, 1957, The Industrialization of Ethiopia, *Ethiopia Observer*, 5.

Pankhurst, Sylvia, 1957, Ethiopia's Industrial Progress, *Ethiopia Observer*, 5.

Schmidt, Wilson, 1968, An Analysis of Tariff Protection for Industry in Ethiopia, mimeo, Addis Ababa.

Spencer, John, 1984, *Ethiopia at Bay: A Personal Account of the Haile Selassie Years*, Algonac, Reference Publications, Michigan.

Stanford Research Institute, 1968, *Industrial Investment Climate in Ethiopia*

Stanley, S, and Karsten, D, 1965, Industrial Development of Ethiopia, A Report Prepared for the United Nations, New York, Addis Ababa.

State Bank of Ethiopia, 1949a, *Monthly Letter*, 1, 3.

------------, 1949b, *Monthly Letter*, 1, 4.

United Nations, 1950, Report of the United Nations Commission for Eritrea, General Assembly Official Records: Fifth Session Supplement No.8 (A/1285), Lake Success, New York.

Woldu, G, Michael, 1983, A Review of Industrial Development Policies in Ethiopia, in Institute of Development Research, Addis Ababa University, *Proceedings of the Seminar on Industrial Transformation in Ethiopia*, Nazareth, 18-20 January 1980.

The World Bank, 1975, Ethiopia-Recent Economic Developments and Current Prospects (in two volumes) - Volume II: Recent Economic Developments, World Bank, Washington, DC.

5. The Development of Money, Monetary Institutions and Monetary Policy 1941-75

Befekadu Degefe

On 1 January, 1975, the Provisional Military Administrative Council (PMAC) nationalized privately-owned financial institutions, including three commercial banks, thirteen insurance companies and two non-bank financial intermediaries.[1] On 21 September, 1976 this same government recreated the National Bank of Ethiopia (NBE), an institution established in 1963, as the nation's central bank,[2] and articulated its responsibilities and granted it commensurate powers.

The goals of NBE were defined as the provision of stable monetary environment conducive to the attainment of national economic goals including high levels of economic growth and employment, with stable prices and a healthy balance of payment.[3]

Among its powers the most visible are a) the exclusive right to issue legal tender currency, b) regulating the supply and availability of money and credit as well as applicable interest rates; c) establishing, consolidating, or dissolving banks and other financial institutions as well as supervising, controlling, defining and modifying their operations and functions; and d) determining the exchange rate and managing the international reserves of the country.[4]

By the time the military government came to power in 1974 and nationalized financial institutions and recreated the central bank, the national currency was well established, financial institutions and particularly commercial banks well diffused and the tradition and culture of banking fast spreading in the urban centres.

In 1941 when the country was liberated from the brief Italian occupation it had neither a national currency nor a financial institution. Their non-existence was, however, not for lack of want or attempt. As early as 1893, Emperor Menelik minted and issued silver dollars and silver and copper coins. The intention behind issuing this currency had less to do with economics and was more an assertion of political independence, since a national currency was expected to confer and confirm such an identity.[5] Between 1896 and 1928 the Ethiopian government continued to issue these currencies but they failed to enjoy wide circulation. Paper currency was introduced into the economy by the Bank of Abyssinia in 1914 but it failed to make a significant impact on the society (Pankhurst 1968:491). The failure was not surprising in a country where coins were the more popular stores of value in relation to paper currency on account of durability. In 1932 the Bank of Ethiopia started issuing new currencies in notes and coins until it was interrupted by the Italian occupation in 1936 (Pankhurst 1968:492; Perham 1969:212). During the Italian occupation, the Lire and Maria Theresa Thaler (dollar) served as mediums of exchange. Italian attempts to limit the role of medium of exchange to the lire was not successful.

The Maria Theresa Thaler or dollar (MTD), has had a long history in Ethiopia and left important imprints on the monetary scene of the country. The coin was first minted in Vienna in 1751 to commemorate the coronation of Maria Theresa as Empress of Austria. The remarkable thing about this silver coin was that it was never used as legal tender currency in its country of origin (for the history of MTD, see Pankhurst 1967 and 1968).

The MTD was introduced into Ethiopia by traders at the end of the Eighteenth or beginning of the Nineteenth century. It was widely accepted and enjoyed extensive circulation. Attempts to replace it by other currencies proved unsuccessful until 1945.[6]

The MTD, despite its popularity, suffered from a number of weaknesses. First was its weight, which made its transportation very difficult. One MTD weighed 28.5 grams so that 3,500 MTD had a weight of one quintal.[7] The second problem was that it lacked lower denominations, thus limiting transaction to whole MTDs.

Perhaps its most conspicuous weakness and ironically its source of popularity was that it was a commodity currency. The value of the coin was not derived from its face value (which it did not have) but the value of silver from which it was made. Thus, when the price of silver increased its value also increased and vice versa. In turn the instability in its value was transferred to the price of goods.

In addition to these major weaknesses, and what aggravated the problem of instability in its value in the domestic market, was the incapacity of the government to control the volume circulating in the country, since it was a foreign currency. The amount floating in the economy at any time depended on how much was brought in by traders, how much was hoarded, the quantity converted to ornaments and how much was taken out by traders, making the government a passive audience. When the price of silver increased, people tended to melt the MTD and sell it as bullion, exacerbating its supply and therefore the price of goods. The only option the government had to ensure that sufficient quantity of MTD circulated in the economy was to find ways to increase their inward flow and minimize their outflow. This was attempted by the government of the day without apparent success.[8]

During the occupation banking services were provided by branches of the Banco d'Italia, Banco Nazionale de Lavoro, Banco di Roma and Banco di Napoli, among others.

While banking services under the Italians was widespread with branches in all the important urban centres, it was, nevertheless, not a novel institution to Ethiopia. The first bank in the country, the Bank of Abyssinia, was established in 1905, and its shares traded in the important international capital markets including London, Paris, Rome, Berlin, Vienna and New York. The initial offering was oversubscribed and less than 10% of the potential buyers were able to purchase shares.[9] In 1908 a development bank, Société Nationale d'Ethiopie Pour le Développement de l'Agriculture et du Commerce, was established and in 1915 two foreign banks, the Banque de l'Indochine and the Compagnie de l'Afrique Orientale opened a branch and an agency respectively (Pankhurst 1968:498).

The Bank of Abyssinia was, overall, a successful venture paying dividends of 3% during the early years and 4% in the later years of its operation. However, it was heavily criticized for being foreign owned, in pursuit of profit and exploiting its monopoly position. In 1931 the Ethiopian government purchased the bank, rechristened it the Bank of Ethiopia and created the first nationally-owned bank on the African continent. Although the bank was closed by the Italians in 1936, and ceased to exist, the Ethiopian government never acknowledged its liquidation. This bank was in existence until 1964 when the Ethiopian government finally liquidated it.[10]

At liberation in 1941, the currency situation was confused and chaotic. In addition to the MTD and the Italian lire, the Egyptian pound, the South African rand, the Indian rupee, the Yemeni rupee and the East African shilling were circulating, the first two as the legacies of the past and last five representing the powers and realities of the times. Such a bewildering monetary environment needed clearing up and attempts at doing so got under way immediately, initially by the British and then by the Ethiopian government.

This is where we pick up the story of how the Imperial Ethiopian Government initiated and developed the financial system that the military regime nationalized three decades later. To structure the chapter, the following section outlines the development of central banking from 1942 to 1974. The powers and duties the central bank had at nationalization defines the framework for subsequent sections. The next section deals with the exclusive power of the central bank to issue legal tender currency, followed by a section on the control of money, credit and interest rates. The last two sections examine the central bank's responsibility of managing the nation's foreign assets, and take a cursory look at the arrangements for the financing of economic development.

The Evolution of Banking

Although the banking system made important imprints on economy and society, Ethiopia failed to create a national currency before the Italian occupation in 1935. Following the restoration of independence in 1941, the monetary scene was chaotic with the Italian lire, the MTD, the East African shilling (EAS), the Indian rupee and the Egyptian pound circulating as mediums of exchange. While the lire was a relic of the Italian occupation and the MTD a carry-over from earlier periods, the rest of the currencies were introduced by the British military forces who helped liberate the country and assumed responsibility for its administration.

The Anglo-Ethiopian Agreement of 1942

After liberation, the Ethiopian government set about establishing its authority over the length and breadth of the country. Perhaps as one means of consolidating its power, it had as a priority the creation of a national legal tender currency and the restoration of banking institutions to clear up the confusing financial environment. The major stumbling block against the immediate realization of these goals was the plan the British Government, and in particular the War Office, had in store for the future of the country. The British military establishment considered and treated Ethiopia as an Occupied Enemy Territory (OET) and assumed the responsibility for its administration 'until its status should be decided by the Peace Conference' following the end of the War (Perham 1969:391). This position of the War Office was, however, contrary to the understanding and aspirations of the Imperial Ethiopian Government (IEG) as well as the attitude and sentiments of the British Foreign Office, whose considered opinion was that the country was more of an ally than an OET.[11]

Among the first laws enacted by the British Military Administration in April 1941 was the definition of legal tender currencies comprising the Maria Theresa dollar, the East African shilling, the Egyptian pound and the Indian rupee (Barclay's Bank 1948:63-64). The lire was also circulating freely in spite of its exclusion from this list.[12]

At the same time, the Barclay's Bank (Dominion, Colonial and Overseas) was invited by the British Government to open a branch in Addis Ababa 'to facilitate financial arrangements of the (British) Military forces by providing banking services and serving as a medium for the introduction of a currency'. It was in business from 1 July 1941 to 15 April 1943.

A compromise between the Foreign and War Offices of the British Government must have been arrived at sometime in late 1941, resulting in a draft 'Agreement' between the two governments. The draft was completed in London and despatched for ratification to Addis Ababa in October 1941. Attempts by Ethiopia to negotiate the 'Agreement' and suggested amendments were rebuffed by the British who used all possible pressure for its immediate adoption. The Emperor finally gave in and signed the Anglo-Ethiopian Agreement on 31 January 1942, following which the Ethiopian Government was officially reinstated on 1 February 1942.[13]

While the agreement officially recognized the nation's independence and British military forces and administrators were moved to Harar, it nonetheless conferred on the British the right to have the final say on all important issues. To monitor the situation and ensure that the Ethiopian Government remained within the ambit of the agreement, the British Government assigned 'advisors' to all ministries, including a financial advisor to the Emperor and judges in the high courts. These 'advisors' were, needless to say, an extension of British Government, whose 'advice' originated in their respective ministries in London and were in turn apprised of the intentions and deeds of the Ethiopian Government. It was near to impossible to say or do anything without London knowing about it.

The part of the Agreement relevant to the subject at hand is Article VI(d) which in part reads 'in all matters relating to currency in Ethiopia, the Government of the United Kingdom shall be consulted and that arrangements concerning it shall be made only with the concurrence of that government' (Perham 1969:464-69). Analogous to the other parts of the 'Agreement', this article was found unacceptable to the Ethiopian Government which suggested an amendment to the effect that 'all matters relating to currency in Ethiopia shall be the subject of consultation between the two governments'.[14] Not surprisingly, this was rejected since in essence it required Ethiopia to consult and not be bound to obtain Britain's agreement.

It was under these obvious constraints that the creation of financial institutions and the national currency were initiated in 1942.

The State Bank of Ethiopia, 1943-63
The first major step taken by the Ethiopian Government in the area of currency and banking was the establishment of the State Bank of Ethiopia (SBE) on 26 August 1942.[15] The legislation establishing the bank had only three articles the first identifying the proclamation as 'State Bank Proclamation of 1942', the second confirming the establishment of the State Bank and the third defining its capital at one million MTD. This is a strange way of establishing a bank since neither the proclamation nor any accompanying legislation detailed its powers, duties and responsibilities.

Furthermore, while the bank was established in late August, C S Collier, a Canadian, was appointed Governor in late July.[16]

As a matter of fact, the Charter which defined its powers, duties and responsibilities had been prepared and was to be issued concurrently with the establishment proclamation, had it not been for the strong British opposition to the setting up of the bank. Fortunately, the British did not foresee the possibility of the natives establishing a bank and so did not include limitations and/or conditions governing the establishment of such an institution in the 1942 agreement. In the circumstances the best they could do was limited to discouraging the government from establishing the bank and making an orderly operation difficult if not impossible in case they proved recalcitrant.

The British 'discovered' the Emperor's intention to establish a bank (at first understood the institution either as a central bank or reviving the Bank of Ethiopia) under the governorship of Collier as early as February 1942. The Foreign Office had no objection to its establishment and the presumed governor because the bank was an idea that was close to the Emperor and, once established, it could easily be brought under strong British influence. Collier was also endorsed by the Foreign Office because, in addition to being very close to the Emperor, he had been very useful to them in the past and could be relied upon to do so in the future.[17] But the British Treasury had strong objections to the establishment of the bank and advised the Ambassador to Addis Ababa to approach the Emperor and members of the government and kill the offending idea on the following grounds:

a) A central bank was not required in a country like Ethiopia where the credit machinery was primitive;

b) Credit facilities provided by a commercial bank such as Barclay's were dangerous;

c) Arrangements for currency issue were better performed by the Currency Board;

d) A central bank would be very expensive to run. It would need capital of its own which was available neither from the Emperor nor the British. Furthermore, the British Government would not give facilities for the raising of such capital in the London capital market. The Currency Board, on the other hand, was expected to be self-supporting and earn profit after the initial expenditure on the production of notes and coins;

e) There was a likelihood that it could be misused by the Emperor. The doctrine of the independence of a central bank from the government would not be respected and the Emperor might use it as a convenient source of credit or revenue to supplement his own resources.

To blunt the Ethiopian attempt at establishing a bank, the Treasury expedited its effort at finalizing the details of the Currency Board while the Bank of England made sure that no equity participation nor credit would be made available to the new bank from international capital markets. The Foreign Office was informed of the establishment of the Bank on 23 July 1942 (a month before the official announcement) with the qualification that it was nothing other than a State treasury and for internal purposes only.[18]

It was under such a heavy-handed constraint that the Ethiopian Government established the SBE. While this was an affront to the British, at the same time they did not want to go too far and issue the Charter of the State Bank which defined its powers, duties and responsibilities, along with the management structure for fear of reprisal. In April 1943 (almost a year after its establishment) the State Bank of Ethiopia opened its door for business in Addis Ababa with branches in Dire Dawa (May), Dessie (August) the same year while a seven-man Board of Directors was appointed to administer its affairs on 30 June 1943.[19] The SBE started operation without any law vesting it with authority to do so.

The problem of clearing the legal vacuum in which the SBE functioned was consummated when its Charter was issued in November 1943 (although it was dated 30 August 1942).[20] A year later the government issued additional legislation once again reiterating the effective date of the Charter as 30 August 1942.[21] An additional legislation backdating the authority and capacity of the SBE was needed to dilute any doubt about the legality of its operation (lending, accepting deposits, etc.) with no law investing it with such powers prior to the issue of the Charter.

The Charter endowed the SBE with legal personality (Article I), recognized it as the banker to the government (Article II), invested it with full powers to perform commercial banking in Ethiopia and abroad (Article III) and provided it with a seven-man Board of Directors for its administration (Article IV) along with rules and regulations governing its affairs (Article V). The Charter also underlined the fact that the SBE was under the Ministry of Finance which was mandated to inspect its accounts as well as the proceedings and minutes of its Board. Furthermore, the Board was required to submit financial statements and annual reports to the Minister of Finance.

This extraordinary and remarkable strategy of establishing the bank paid off handsomely. The British could not have taken measures against its establishment in 1942 since they did not know what it was supposed to do.

Then the Bank started operation without any inkling about its duties and responsibilities. By the time this was disclosed through the publication of the Charter, it was too late, since the Bank had already been in business with branches in all the important trading centres in the country. The best they could have done thereafter was to control it from inside. Their attempt to place Britons on the Board was spurned and the Canadian governor was removed and replaced by an American, George A. Blowers, in November 1943.[22] The leadership of the SBE was to remain under the Americans until 1959 when the first Ethiopian governor took over.[23]

On 23 July 1945 the government issued the new national currency. Consequently, the functions of the SBE were expanded to include central banking in the already successful commercial banking. For this purpose the SBE was divided into two major departments the issue department to take care of the central banking functions and the banking department for the commercial banking business.

In 1949 the SBE expanded to include exchange control among its functions for which purpose it established an Exchange Control Department as one of its major operational divisions.

By 1950, through learning by doing and learning to deal effectively with monetary and balance of payment problems, the SBE had in place all the powers and responsibilities of a central bank, although it was never honoured with the emblem. It was the source of currency, banker to the government, manager of the nation's foreign assets in addition to controlling money, credit and interest rates. By the mere fact that the banking department of SBE was the only commercial bank in the country, the powers of its central banking function were exercised in and through its sister department the Banking Department.

Such institutional arrangements for commercial and central banking remained in place until 31 December 1963 when the SBE was dissolved in favour of apportioning its responsibilities between the National Bank of Ethiopia (the central bank) and the Commercial Bank of Ethiopia In consequence the issue department was elevated to the status of central bank while the banking department evolved into the Commercial Bank.[24]

Although the SBE was by far the most dominant and important financial institution it was, nevertheless, not the only bank in the country. The Banque de l'Indochine established a branch in Addis Ababa in 1943, although it was never authorized to accept deposits. Its operations were limited to channelling credit to exporters and importers from external and particularly French financial institutions.

When Eritrea was federated with Ethiopia in 1952 and incorporated into the nation a decade later, two Italian branch banks, Banco di Roma and

Banco di Napoli, continued to function. Although these two commercial banks exposed the SBE to its first competitive challenge in mobilizing and allocating financial resources, the contest was easily contained because of the fact that the Italians limited their operation to the Eritrean economic space.

The Development Bank of Ethiopia was another financial institution operating independently of the SBE and providing medium and long-term credit for industrial and agricultural development. The Development Bank had a long gestation and was preceded by two institutions. In 1945 the government established an Agricultural Bank for the purpose of assisting small holders whose cattle were ravaged during the Italian occupation. In 1949 this bank was converted into an Agricultural and Commercial Bank but was overtaken by events before it could start operating seriously.

In 1950, the World Bank agreed to provide US$2 million to finance the foreign exchange costs of development projects. Among the conditions attached to the financial support was the establishment of a development bank which was to be managed by IBRD. The Ethiopian Government decided to convert the newly established Agricultural and Commercial Bank into the Development Bank of Ethiopia. The DBE started business in May 1951.[25]

Two other financial institutions were established in the early 1960s. The Imperial Home Ownership and Savings Association was established in 1962 as a building society with assistance from the USAID and the Ethiopian Government. The association competed for deposit with the SBE matching its interest rate of 4% per annum on saving deposits but expanding the interest-earning deposit from the SBE's E$10,000 to E$25,000.

The Investment Bank of Ethiopia was established in 1963 as a holding company for government investment with the objective of developing entrepreneurship in the country through equity participation, underwriting and sale of stocks (shares).

The Era of Central Banking 1964-74

At midnight on 31 December 1963, the SBE ceased to exist and its responsibilities were divided between the newly established National Bank of Ethiopia and the Commercial Bank of Ethiopia. The termination of SBE and the emergence of these two institutions in its stead were the logical consequences of the process which started two decades ago. At the beginning of the 1960s, the national currency was firmly established, banking services reasonably diffused throughout the major towns and cities and banking culture well inculcated among the urban population.

There had also been important structural shifts in the economy. An economy that was purely agricultural in the 1940s was diversified to include industry, albeit as a junior partner. The growth of urban centres brought about important population flows from rural areas into towns and cities. The opening up of the country's inaccessible regions through road construction and the expanded domestic services of Ethiopian Airlines introduced trade to the remotest corners of the nation.

Given the demands on banking services occasioned by changes in the economic structure and people's behaviour, it was axiomatic that the SBE needed to undergo extensive reformulation and reorganization.

The National Bank (NBE) and the Commercial Bank of Ethiopia (CBE) were natural outgrowths of the SBE. The former inherited the central banking function, and the latter, the operations of the Banking Department. Thus, the two institutions and the nation at large benefitted from this development since the accumulated experience in their respective ambits over the previous two decades enhanced their capacity to meet the challenges of their assignments. Apart from the different management, they continued to do what their respective departments were doing under the SBE.

The CBE was turned into a share company and registered as a commercial bank with the traditional powers and responsibilities accorded to such institutions. It was wholly government-owned, with its shares subscribed by the Ministry of Finance and four State-owned enterprises.

The NBE was established by a national Charter and had its powers and duties defined in the Monetary and Banking Proclamation The Charter was divided into five chapters, the first of which defined its name, purpose and legal status; the second articulated its powers and functions, the third its capital, reserves and financial statements, the fourth its organization and administration. The fifth chapter annulled all previous laws and regulations, which were inconsistent, and defined the mechanism for the transfer of the relevant assets and liabilities of the SBE to the NBE.

The Monetary and Banking Proclamation set out the classical functions of central banking. Its six chapters defined its powers and duties, the monetary unit and the legal tender, its relation with the government, banks and other financial institutions, licensing and supervision of banks. The final chapter included transitory and general provisions.

The NBE was first and foremost required to pursue and operate in ways that would optimize the national interest. If in the course of doing so it incurred losses, the government was to make up for any shortfall and maintain its capital intact (Article 13(3) of the Charter). Secondly, the NBE was to enjoy complete operational autonomy by virtue of Article 2 of the Charter which established: 'the purpose of the Bank, by which it shall be guided in all its actions, is to foster monetary stability and such credit and exchange conditions as are conducive to the balanced growth of the economy'.

The functions, powers and duties of the NBE, as addressed both in the Charter and the Proclamation, included:

a) The exclusive right to mint, print and issue legal tender currency (Article 8 of the Charter);

b) Regulating the supply, availability and cost of money and credit (Article 2 (a) of the Proclamation);

c) Managing and administering the nation's international reserves (Article 2(b) of the Proclamation);

d) Licensing and supervision of banks (Article 2(c) of the Proclamation); and

e) Performing such other functions as central banks customarily performed (Article 2 (d) of the Proclamation).

These powers and duties established the framework within which the Central Bank operated until 31 December 1974 when the nationalization of banks and other financial institutions, in combination with the shifts in the political and ideological environment, transformed the economic milieu in which it was operating. Henceforth, financial institutions were to be State-owned and resources allocated through central planning rather than the market. In consequence, the Central Bank was re-established on 21 September 1976 with responsibilities and functions expedient to extent conditions and intentions.

Issuing Legal Tender Currency

The confused monetary environment, following the expulsion of the Italians in 1941 and emanating from the multiplicity of legal tender currencies, needed clearing up and attempts at doing so were started immediately by both the British and Ethiopians. While there was concurrence on the need between the two governments, there was divergence on the nature and appropriate mechanism for the making and issue of the new currency. The two approaches will be dealt with in tandem.

The Making of the National Currency 1941-45 [26]

The British Plan

The Anglo-Ethiopian Agreement signed in 1942 was ceremonial as far as the British were concerned. First, they were in a position to exploit the financial, political and military weakness of the Emperor and enforce their will. Secondly, most of the ideas contained in the 'Agreement' were on the drawing board even before the agreement was signed. This was particularly true of the currency plan which was prepared by the British Treasury and circulated for comments at the Bank of England and the Foreign Office as early as May 1941.[27]

This plan was nothing but an extension of the Sterling Exchange System in operation in its colonies in West and East Africa. The operational elements of the system were simple and analogous to the gold standard. A Currency Board, made up of representatives from the British Treasury, the Bank of England and the Territory, was designated as the monetary authority and charged with exchanging sterling for local currency and vice versa on demand.

The salient points of the Currency Plan submitted to the Ethiopian Government for immediate ratification indicated that:[28]

a) The currency would be called the Ethiopian pound and would be in parity with the Pound sterling, with millesimal subsidiary coins of which the principal would be a silver shilling;

b) A Currency Board would sit in London and would be composed of three people made up of the Ethiopian Ambassador, and two Britons, one nominated by the British Treasury, the other by the Bank of England, and both to be appointed by the Ethiopian Government;

c) The responsibilities of the Currency Board would be:

Manufacturing of the Currency. The notes would be of 1, 5, 10, and 50 pound denominations. If the Ethiopian Government agrees, existing plates of the Bank of Ethiopia's notes with suitable changes in wording could be used. If this is not acceptable, the government is to make its suggestions known as soon as possible, on the basis of which new plates would be prepared. The subsidiary coins would be of 1, 2, 10, and 50 mils, the latter equal to one shilling. The exact composition and design would be decided by the Board and presented to the Ethiopian Government for approval.

Issue of New Currency. Notes and coins are to be issued in Addis Ababa initially in exchange for circulating currencies (EAS, Egyptian pound, Indian rupees) other than MTD and the Italian lire and against payment of sterling. However, MTD could be swapped for the new currency not through the Board but through banks and exchange dealers. Later issues would be in exchange for hard currencies earned through the export of goods and services.

Management of the Currency. Full reserve against notes and coins issued would be held in sterling or sterling-denominated securities to ensure convertibility of the Currency.

The Ethiopian Initiative
Upon receipt of the British proposal, the Ethiopian Government lodged its objections and suggested amendments. The Ethiopian Government's rejection of the Currency Plan, as submitted by the British, was based on and derived from sound economics.

The weaknesses of the Currency Board were serious and well known. Among these were:

a) The determination of the money supply by the balance of payment. How much money floats in the economy is a function of the current account balance and foreign investment and not domestic parameters;

b) Such a monetary arrangement has a built-in destabilizing effect. The quantity of money could increase or decrease when the economy can least afford such expansion simply because the current account happens to be in surplus or deficit. Since local authorities have no means to sterilize such impact, the result could be violent inflation and deflation;

c) Monetary authorities have limited degrees of freedom to pursue policies conducive to and supportive of economic development. Credit is limited both in volume and time to the short term to accommodate possible withdrawal of money from the economy in case of deficit in the current account;

d) The 100% sterling reserve limits foreign exchange availability for the importation of developmental factors such as capital goods and other essential goods and services.

These conspicuous economic constraints were bolstered by political factors. Ethiopia had always been suspicious of British intentions over the country. Given the total control over policy through their advisors and their heavy military presence, the currency plan must have been perceived as the final touch on the complete absorption of the country into the British Empire as a 'protectorate', if not as a colony.

The Ethiopian counter-proposal was to have the Board sit in Addis Ababa and its size increased from three to five, the two Britons to be joined by two others representing the Ethiopian interest and the fifth to be a neutral member in the person of the US Ambassador to London. The Board was also to make decisions in consultation with and not independent of the Ethiopian Government. The currency reserve was also to be expanded to include gold (to be supplied from domestic mines), silver (to be made available through the demonetization of MTD), and the government instrument of debt. These amendments to the Currency Plan were, not surprisingly, rejected. Acceptance would have destroyed the Currency Board as it existed and operated in the British Territories i.e. (Befekadu 1992).

The Ethiopian Government had the choice of implementing the British Plan or pursuing the difficult option of developing an alternative arrangement independently to clear up the chaotic monetary environment. What made this option hard was Britain's determination to have Ethiopia join the sterling monetary zone 'for the benefit of surrounding territories'.[29] To force compliance, the British were starving the country of a medium of exchange by withdrawing the currency reserves and/or refusing to supply divisionary East African Shilling (EAS) coinage.[30]

Despite (or because of) the relentless and brutal pressure, the Ethiopian Government opted for the rejection of the British Plan and began exploring possibilities for an alternative arrangement without, however, disclosing their intention of doing so. Consequently, the search for the new scheme needed to be conducted in secret. This proved a difficult task since, as pointed out earlier, transport and communications were under the complete control of the British and, with advisors in all key places, there was nothing both in deeds and intentions they did not discover sooner or later.

The breakthrough came when the American Councillor in Eritrea, led by E.Talbot Smith, visited Addis Ababa in September 1942. The Ethiopian Government took advantage of this opportunity to brief the American on British behaviour and intentions and used him as an envoy to convey Ethiopia's desire for a closer relationship with the US (Marcus 1983:12-13). The American was sympathetic and his report to the State Department convinced the US Government to free Ethiopia from British control as 'the first of the allied countries to be freed' (Marcus 1983:15). In August 1943, the Ethiopian Government was invited to attend the World Food Conference. The conference was more of a cover, since the real intention of the two governments was the signing of a Mutual Aid Agreement and finalization of arrangements for the manufacturing of the new currency. The US Government agreed to provide 5.4 million ounces of silver on a lend-lease basis to be minted into half dollars and swapped for the MTD.[31]

By 1944, the new currency was ready for issue but two subsidiary problems forced a delay. The first was the 1942 Anglo-Ethiopian Agreement which was still in force and required the consent of the British Government in anything relating to the currency. With their Currency Plan still on offer, it was clear that they would not have consented to the making and issue of the new currency. The agreement was renegotiated and a new convention governing the relationship between the two countries was signed on 19 December 1944. The new agreement restored full and complete sovereignty to Ethiopia.

The second problem, although a minor one, concerned the payment of US$200,000 to cover the cost of manufacturing the currency to the National City Bank of New York. The problem was not that Ethiopia lacked the foreign exchange as much as it needed Britain's exchange control clearance for payments outside the sterling zone, a condition imposed on the country since November 1942.[32] Where payment needed to be made outside the sterling zone, the Ethiopian Government was required to lodge an application to the British Embassy in Addis Ababa. If the Embassy established the legitimacy of the request and was satisfied that the reason for payment was acceptable and the proposed amount reasonable etc., it recommended release of the requested sum to the Foreign Office in London which would in turn request the Bank of England through the Treasury to release the foreign exchange. It was obvious that the Ethiopian Government could not have applied for the use of US$200,000 by disclosing the true purpose. Not only would this have been rejected, it could also have given away a closely and successfully kept secret and thus jeopardize the project.

Instead, the Ethiopian Government applied for the use of US$350,000 for the purchase of textile, a commodity hard to get from the sterling zone then, on account of Second World War, from the United States. The permission was granted and the fund was transferred to the National City Bank of New York. The cost of engraving, minting and printing the new currency was paid out of this fund.[33]

Issuing the Legal Tender Currency

By any standard, the creation and successful launching of the legal tender currency was not only the most revolutionary initiative but also among the crowning achievements of the Imperial Regime. Prior attempts at endowing the country with a national medium of exchange proved futile for various reasons. While these failures were sobering in themselves, there was the determined British factor of including Ethiopia in its currency zone. Given the high stakes involved, success required careful and meticulous planning and execution, and the Ethiopian Government could not have done any better.

Although the British had been informed of the Ethiopian Government's attempt at creating a national currency independently of their plan as early as mid-1943, they could not have taken any measures against it because they believed that nothing was going to come out of it. When the Ethiopian Government made the issue of the legal tender currency public in May 1945, the British were banking on its failure and were confident of the resurrection of their plan sooner than later.

By May 1945, the Ethiopian Government had finalized all the ground work for the currency to be released. The necessary legislation was promulgated and the SBE reorganized to include an issue department among its operating divisions.

The currency proclamation started by defining the monetary unit of the country as the Ethiopian dollar (E$) with a value of 5.52 grains (equivalent to 0.355745 grams) of fine gold.[34] This link with gold was in accord with the new monetary system established by the Breton Woods Agreement of 1944, which, *inter alia*, created the International Monetary Fund (IMF) and the International Bank for Reconstruction and Development (IBRD, also known as the World Bank) of which Ethiopia was signatory and founding member. Such linkage between the national currency and gold automatically established the exchange rate between it and other currencies with the same arrangement. Accordingly the exchange rate between the Ethiopian dollar and the US dollar was US$0.4025 and sterling 2/ per Ethiopian dollar.

The new currency was made up of notes of 1, 5, 10, 50, 100 and 500 dollar denominations and coins of 1, 5, 10, 25 copper and the 50 cents of silver.[35] The notes were in different sizes (the one dollar being the smallest and the 500 the largest) and of different colours, a differentiation that would prove of value in a predominantly illiterate society with physical impairment (blindness) as a means of easily identifying the different denominations. Similarly, the 1, 5, 10 and 25-cent copper coins came in different sizes of ascending order. The 50c coin was silver-coloured, reflecting the metal from which it was made. However, the sizes of the 25c and 50c were identical, a point that was to generate problems at issue.

The proclamation identified the SBE as an agent of the government and vested it with exclusive powers to issue the paper currency, for which purpose it was to organize an issue department.[36] The issue of coins was retained by the Ministry of Finance. Consequently the SBE, established in 1942 and operating as the sole commercial bank since April 1943, was henceforth, to also serve as the central bank of the country, thus combining the two functions.

The proclamation identified the new currency as the only legal tender in the country. For this purpose, it immediately demonetized the MTD which was to be treated as silver bullion with a price of one Ethiopian dollar per MTD.[37] The East African shilling was given a sixmonth lease of life as legal tender currency, which was later extended by an additional four months.[38]

The new legal tender currency was ready for issue. But two interrelated problems need to be dealt with before we pick up the story. One is the principle and the second the mechanism of issuing the legal tender currency, both of which have important implications for the conduct of monetary policy.

The basis on which banks issued legal tender currency had been a subject of debate. The origin of the controversy was the innocuous and common sense principle that, for anything to serve as money, it must be acceptable, which implied that people should have confidence in its value and secondly, it must be available in sufficient quantity to satisfy the liquidity needs of the community. While no one would have any quarrel with such self-evident truth, the problem could arise because these two requirements could generate mutual conflict, i.e., attempts to increase liquidity could undermine confidence and vice versa. The controversy proceeds between those who favour confidence more than liquidity and those who favour the latter without undermining the former. Historically, the position of those favouring confidence have been grouped under the 'currency school' and those of liquidity the 'banking school' (for an insight into this debate, see Schumpeter 1986: Part III, Chapter 7).

The position of the currency school was that banks should issue legal tender currency in exchange for precious metals (gold and silver) of equal value to be redeemed on demand. Such an arrangement would render the danger of over-issue impossible and give people confidence since they could change their token currency holdings into precious metals of equal value whenever they felt like doing so. The banking school was opposed to this on the grounds that such an arrangement would fail to provide the necessary liquidity since the money floating in the economy would be determined not by the needs of the society but by the flow of precious metals into the banking system. They argued that when the economy was buoyant and needed a larger volume of money, the money supply could actually decrease because of the outflow of precious metals, generating depression and vice versa. This meant that the monetary authorities should be in a position to satisfy the liquidity needs of the economy. While the obvious advantage of this principle was that the money supply would be elastic, there was the danger of over-issue which undermined confidence. The issue had never been resolved satisfactorily and countries operated on the cardinal principle of balancing these two essential requirements of monetary management.

Over the last three decades, Ethiopia has gradually moved from the currency school to the banking school. In 1945 the primary focus was on generating confidence in the new currency. In the previous decades attempts by Menelik, Haile Selassie, the Italians and British to supplant the MTD with their own currencies failed because people had complete confidence in the silver coin.

Consequently, the State Bank was required to back all notes it issued to the extent of 100% of which 75% should be in gold, silver and foreign assets and the remaining 25% in Imperial Treasury obligations. The reserve fund was to be held separate from all other assets and used for the sole purpose of currency redemption.[39]

The mechanism of issue follows automatically once the principle is established, since the State Bank was to release notes in exchange for gold, silver and foreign currencies while fiduciary issue was to be limited to 25% of notes issued. The gold sold to it by the government was obtained from domestic mines. The MTD was immediately demonetized and purchased by the SBE on a one to one basis as silver bullion. The foreign currency was initially obtained from the East African Shilling and later export earnings.

When the currency was issued on 23 July 1945, it was received enthusiastically. The timing was also perfect, in being far from the harvest and export season when the demand for medium of exchange would have been at the highest possible level, and by which time the currency would have been well established. Although both the notes and coinage won unexpectedly rapid acceptance there was a notable preference for coins in the rural areas since the peasant was attracted more by durability than convenience.

There is no better testimony of the success of the new currency than one grudgingly made by a British official, in his report to the Foreign Office: 'The new currency is in fact a success and, in retrospect, it seems a great pity that the (British) Treasury were so intransigent in the 1942-44 wrangle'.[40] A minor problem encountered immediately after issue but soon rectified was due to the more or less equal size of the 25c copper coin and the 50c silver coin. These two coins were easily distinguishable on the basis of colour one being brownish and the other silverish. This was the situation until some enterprising people dipped 'the copper quarters in a nickel solution' and passed them off as half dollars. The problem was resolved when the 'quarter coins' were taken to the Orma Garage where a crude gear-cutting machine incised equally crude 'tooth marks' around the circumference of each coin' (Spencer 1987:109).

The principle of the currency school followed by the SBE as a mechanism of note issue was a success in engendering confidence. However, it did impose major constraints on government borrowing and imports. Fiduciary issue under the arrangement established in 1945 was not on a need basis but automatically adjustable to the gold, silver and foreign exchange holdings of the bank. To illustrate this point, if the gold, etc., holdings of the issues department of SBE increased by E$7.5 million, the SBE could issue E$10 million in notes of various denominations of which E$2.5 million originated from government treasury obligations. On the other hand, if the gold, etc., holdings of SBE decreased by E$10 million, the government had to pay back the E$2.5 million it borrowed from the SBE regardless of its fiscal position. The second and more important drawback of the system of issue was the tying up of a large amount of foreign exchange as currency reserve. As a result the country was unable to use this foreign exchange to finance imports of developmental factors of production such as capital goods. Thirdly, the system was inherently inflationary and deflationary, depending on the balance of payment position. When the BOP was in surplus, the SBE released and when in deficit absorbed notes of equal value. Since the SBE lacked the means to sterilize the potentially negative impact of the expansion and contraction of the money supply occasioned by changes in foreign assets, the economy was obliged to adjust to these shocks through changes in prices.

Five years later, the Ethiopian Government decided to lower the gold, silver and foreign exchange currency reserve in favour of government treasury obligations. Consequently the fiduciary issue was raised from 25% to 70% and the precious metals and foreign asset backing declined from 75% to 30% of the notes issued.[41] This arrangement remained in force until 1964 when the international reserve fund was to include only gold and foreign exchange and the proportion reduced to 25% of notes issued and the sight liabilities of the National Bank of Ethiopia.[42] In addition to this rearrangement, the issue of coins, hitherto the responsibility of the Ministry of Finance, was transferred to the NBE.[43] The issue of currency was managed and operated under this arrangement until 1976.

Control of Money, Credit and Interest Rates

Although the responsibility of controlling money, credit and the interest rate was explicitly assigned to the Central Bank upon its formation in 1964, the State Bank of Ethiopia exercised this power until its demise on 31 December 1963. Prior to and after the establishment of NBE, the major determinants of money and credit were foreign assets and domestic credit, although their relative importance has undergone significant change with time. To properly appreciate these developments, the analysis of the behaviour of money, credit and interest rates needs to be partitioned into four periods the years prior to the currency reform (1941-45), the early years of the national currency (1945-50), the middle years (1950-63), and the final years (1963-74).

Prior to the Currency Reform: 1941-45

The Money Supply

These were the years when the nation did not have its own legal tender and the moneys floating in the economy were the different foreign currencies.

While the overriding goal was the creation of a national currency, immediate attention focused on ways to rationalize the chaotic monetary situation. Consequently, the Ethiopian Government favoured and used the MTD as its official currency while the British insisted on the adoption of the Currency Plan and use of the EAS in the interim. To ensure compliance the British withdrew MTD from circulation and starved the economy of coins of lower denomination. The result of the British policy was to decrease the medium of exchange i.e., the money supply.

On the other hand, it was the obligation of the Ethiopian Government to ensure availability of money in quantities adequate to satisfy the transaction and store of value needs of the society. Given the heavy-handed British intervention, the option the Ethiopian Government had was to prohibit the outflow of MTD by travellers, particularly traders. To this effect it enacted a law in September 1942 prohibiting outflow of MTD without the express approval of the Ministry of Finance. Contravention of the provision was to result in the confiscation of the MTD if any attempt was made to take it out of the country, heavy fines and imprisonment.[44] Further to this, the government defined the MTD and EAS as the legal tender currencies with the lire to be demonetized after three months.[45]

In 1942 the government introduced exchange controls.[46] The purpose had less to do with conservation of foreign exchange than ensuring that sufficient quantity of the legal currencies floated in the economy.

Despite these measures, the quantity of MTD floating in the economy continued to decline. Farmers refused to sell their products for anything but the MTD, which was then hoarded. Traders exported the MTD not only because it served as a medium of exchange in the countries of the Middle East but also because the price of silver increased in these markets. Consequently, the exchange rate of the EAS relative to the MTD deteriorated. The market exchange rate increased to EAS 3:MTD, while the official exchange rate moved from EAS 1.875 to EAS 2 per MTD where it stayed until 1945.

The exchange rate instability between the two legal tender currencies had unpleasant economic and welfare consequences. Exports, mainly agricultural, were constrained with negative impact on imports. Employees were paid their wages and salaries in the EAS and saw their real income declining since they had to make purchases in the market in the more expensive MTD.

Implementing the sterling based Currency Plan would have been the easy way out, since the British were willing to supply the economy with sufficient MTD to stabilize the market exchange rate. But this plan was anathema to the Ethiopian Government, which persisted in holding out against the unsavoury British pressure while refining and promoting the new national currency. However, its intransigence was proving costly to the economy. Prices denominated in EAS kept on rising, reflecting the exchange rate between itself and an ever-dwindling MTD. The young SBE suffered from the outflow of MTD which never came back to it in deposits. Any attempt on its part to purchase MTD in the free market would have aggravated the exchange rate instability. It therefore pursued the policy of releasing EAS and conserving its limited MTD reserves.

Despite these constraints, the SBE proved its resilience and recorded success. The only deposit services it provided was current account so that there was no interest cost on deposits. The performance of the SBE for the three years is shown in Table 1. Deposits (predominantly in EAS) registered increases of 15% and 25% in 1944 and 1945 respectively.

Table 1: Conditions of SBE (end of year, 000 MTD)

Assets	1943	1944	1945
Cash	9894	5913	10748
Balances abroad	1553	4420	5306
Investments			13
Loans and Advances	754	2048	2177
Accounts receivable	255	120	135
Others	708	3717	2391
Total	13,164	16,218	20,770
Liability	1943	1944	1945
Capital	1,000	1,000	1,000
Deposits	11372	13086	16324
Reserves		3	33
Others	792	2129	3413
Total	13,164	16,218	20,7700

Source: Adopted from SBE, Monthly Letter, Vol. I, No. 4.

Credit and Interest Rates

The Bank maintained a strong cash position amounting to 87%, 37% and 66% of deposits in 1943, 1944 and 1945 respectively on account of the highly conservative credit policy it pursued. Productive utilization of the resources mobilized was limited by the chaotic monetary and economic environment. Mortgage loans were stymied by the difficulty of obtaining clear property titles. The demand for loans by the indigenous population was very low, most probably on account of cultural and traditional factors which discouraged debt. Consequently, bank credit was directed more to merchandise which were hypothecated to the bank. Unfortunately, the interest rate the bank charged for the different lines of credit cannot be traced. The average interest rate (obtained by dividing interest and discount earned by advances and loans at end of the years) averaged 6%. The SBE registered its first and only loss in 1943. Thereafter, the Bank continued to enjoy an increasing amount of profit.

The Early Years of the National Currency 1945-50

Issue of Legal Tender Currency

The quantity of money floating in the economy and the volume of credit extended by SBE were intimately tied to the amount of currency issued. While the issue of coins was the exclusive ambit of the Ministry of Finance, for which it provided a 100% backing, the issue of notes was reserved for the issue department (the central banking wing) of SBE with the proviso of 100% backing, 75% of which was to be in the form of precious metals (gold and silver) and foreign assets, while the balance was to be provided by the Government. Consequently, the major determinant of the quantity of notes issued was the balance of payments position of the country, with gold and silver coming a distant second and fiduciary issue, third.

Issue of notes increased from E$23.6 million at the end of 1945 to E$49.7 as of May 1950, posting an average annual growth rate of 19%. The first two years should be considered as periods for replacing the existing currencies of MTD and the EAS which formed the entire backing for the notes issued except for the insignificant amount of fiduciary issue. As from 1947, the proportion of foreign assets was gradually reduced while gold, silver and fiduciary issue grew in prominence.

The SBE pursued a highly conservative policy of note issue during the initial years. There was on average unutilized reserves of gold, silver and foreign assets equivalent to E$8 million between December 1945 and May 1950; although these reserves covered a declining proportion of notes issued (from 100% in 1945 to 75.1% in May 1950), it nevertheless averaged 88% during the period. On the other hand, fiduciary issue increased from E$0.6 million in 1946 to E$9.3 million in December 1949. This volume of issue complemented the conservative policy of the SBE. The government could have increased the volume of fiduciary issue from E$5.9 million in 1946 to E$12.4 million in May 1950.

The issue of coins underwent a phenomenal increase from E$6.6 million to E$29.9 million worth between 1946 and 1950. At an average of 36% of the total currency issued, the volume of coins is high, but this is explained in the preference for coins, particularly the half-dollar silver coin, by the overwhelming majority of the people who happened to be rural residents

Table 2: Relationship Between Issue of Notes and Backing: 1945-50
(E$ million)

	Notes issued	Gold	Silver	Foreign assets	Total	Required	Excess	Government Section	Coins Coins
Dec. 1945	23.6	-	-	23.6	23.6	17.7	5.9	-	6.6
Dec. 1946	39.19	-	2.1	36.0	38.1	28.6	9.5	0.6	14.5
Dec. 1947	37.4	1.5	5.7	27.5	34.7	26.0	8.7	2.8	27.8
Dec. 1948	42.4	4.3	5.4	27.0	36.7	27.5	9.2	5.8	28.8
Dec. 1949	40.4	6.2	9.2	15.1	30.5	22.9	7.6	9.3	26.4
May 1950	49.7	7.4	12.2	17.7	37.3	30.0	7.3	9.3	29.9

Source: SBE, *Monthly Letter*, various issues.

Money Supply and Credit

Money supply was a function of the balance of payment (reflected in the volume of currency issued) and domestic credit. The balance of payment will be discussed in detail in the next section but one should nevertheless note its impact on the currency issued.

The volume of domestic credit extended by the SBE was also limited partly because of low demand, coupled with its conservative policy. Although the SBE was designated as the banker to the government, it was a recipient of deposit and was never a lender. First, the circumstances, conditions and size of credit to be extended to the government was never articulated. Second, and more importantly, the government was running a budget surplus during this period as a result of which the issue never arose.

Private credit was limited to trade, particularly external trade, since security was guaranteed through the hypothecation of the merchandise. The mortgage business was limited because of the scarce provision for clear titles. Credits for other uses, such as working capital for manufacturing industries, were virtually nil since there were very few of these establishments in the country. Consumer credit was also unknown. Consequently, the credit market and its impact on the money supply remained small. For example, the ratio of money supply to currency issued (i.e. what one may take to be the closest to the money multiplier) declined from 1:43 in 1946 to 1:12 in May 1950 averaging 1:21 for the early years of the new currency.

Broad money (M_2) came to the scene in 1946 following the introduction of saving deposit. Again this monetary aggregate started with a relatively high ratio of 1:46 to currency issued and experienced distinct variability, averaging 1:35 for the period.

The rate of growth of money supply, seems to be inordinately high with 17.3% compared to the moderate 8.8% for broad money during the 1945-50 period. This is explained by the substitution of new money during the early years, particularly 1945 and 1946, and thereafter, the demand for money was sustained by increased monetization of the economy, a factor that was to become more important in the coming years. However, the point that needs to be kept in mind is that money supply during the period was determined less by domestic needs and more by exogenous factors.

While the direct impact of changes in external asset was obvious with respect to the volume of currency issued, it was also the determining factor, with the quantity of credit and therefore the money supply extended by the SBE. For a dependent economy like Ethiopia, an increase in credit was more likely to decrease the foreign exchange holdings of the central bank, leading to monetary contraction. The credit extended by SBE was, of necessity,

Table 3: Money Supply: 1945-50
(E$ million)

	CI[1]	COB[2]	Demand deposit	Time deposit	Money supply M₁	Money supply M₂	Rate of growth M₁	Rate of growth M₂	Ratios M¹/C¹	Ratios M¹/C¹
1945	30.2	20.3	23.3	-	43.3	-	-	-	1:43	-
1946	54.4	42.2	26.2	10.4	68.9	79.3	59.1	-	1:27	1:46
1947	65.2	55.4	21.0	7.8	76.4	84.2	10.9	6.2	1:17	1:29
1948	71.2	62.6	18.4	11.6	81.0	92.6	6.0	10.0	1:14	1:30
1949	69.8	62.6	17.7	12.0	80.3	91.9	-0.1	-0.1	1:15	1:32
May 1950	79.5	74.6	21.3	20.4	89.0	109.4	10.8	19.0	1:12	1:38

Source: SBE, *Monthly Letter*, various issues.
[1] CI = Currency issue
[2] COB = Currency outside banks

limited to the short term given the nature of the deposits it mobilized from its clients. Under the circumstances, credit was overwhelmingly weighted in favour of international trade. Consequently, an increase in credit would decrease foreign reserves. This would be all the more so since credit-financing exports would increase income, thereby resulting in higher demand for imports, while credit extended to finance imports directly decreases the foreign exchange holdings of the Bank. Hence, the volume of credit was closely tied to the foreign reserves position of the country. The decrease in foreign assets had two negative impacts on the economy. First, it placed the country in a precarious balance of payment position. On the domestic front, the money supply would contract since the SBE took in notes it issued in exchange for foreign currency.

Loans and advances to deposit averaged 59% during the period under review. There was an inverse relationship between credit and the foreign exchange holdings of the banking department with a one-year lag. Thus, the depletion of foreign exchange in the banking department in 1947, for example, was followed by falling loans and advances in 1948 and so on.

Table 4: Deposits, Loans and Advances and Ratio: 1945-50 (E$ million)

	Deposits	Loans and advances	Loans and advances as % of deposits	Foreign exchange holdings of the banking department
1945	23.3	8.9	38.7	5.3
1946	36.6	17.5	47.8	7.5
1947	28.8	19.6	68.1	2.4
1948	30.0	17.9	59.7	6.8
1949	29.8	24.7	82.3	3.9
May 1950	41.9	24.2	57.8	8.6

Source: SBE, Monthly Letter, various issues.

With the introduction of saving and time deposit services in January 1946, the SBE began paying interest on these lines of deposit. From January 1946 to June 1949, saving deposits earned an annual interest rate of 3%. Fixed deposits for six months were paid 1% per annum while longer deposits earned 2%. These rates were revised as from June 1949. Savings deposits were to earn 4% while interest rates on fixed deposit both for short and longer term increased by one percentage point to 2% and 3% respectively.[47] Average interest rate charged however, remained steady between 5% and 6%.

The Middle Years: 1950-63

Issue of Notes

By 1950, the currency was well established. The decision of the government not to devalue the currency, following the British devaluation of September 1949, was made in the interest of maintaining public confidence in the new currency. Instead, the government reduced the gold, silver and foreign exchange component of the currency reserve in favour of fiduciary issue in May 1950. Consequently, the precious metals and foreign asset currency reserve was reduced from 75% of the total note issue to 30%. The 70% of fiduciary issue was to be backed by government treasury obligations equal to 110% of the notes issued.[48]

The potential impact of such a change was to render the money supply expansionary. At the end of May 1950, the gold, silver and foreign exchange reserve amounted to E$37.3 million to back the issue of notes equivalent to E$49.7 million. As a result of the change in backing, these reserves were reduced to E$11.2 million, thus releasing E$26.1 million to the banking department.

The expansionary impact of the decrease in the currency backing on the money supply, however, remained illusive. This was due to the conditions attached to the use of the fund released from the currency reserves as well as the conservative practice of the SBE. While the advantages of such rearrangement increased the degrees of freedom of the monetary authorities in the management of the monetary affairs of the country, this nevertheless was attenuated by the government's decision not to decrease the foreign exchange component of the backing. In effect, what happened was to shift the basis of the currency backing from *de jure* to *de facto* obligation.

On decreasing the precious metals and foreign asset backing the government was to transfer these to the SBE in exchange for domestic currency. Furthermore, the financial resources so obtained by the government were to be used to finance capital expenditure only. For this purpose, a committee was established to oversee, approve and direct its use. Secondly, the SBE was to release the excess foreign exchange to its banking department to finance imports.

Despite the increase in domestic and external resources, the quantity of notes issued actually remained low. The government was slow in first initiating the use of the funds made available to it and was even slower in its appropriation. In the SBE conservation and caution ruled its operations. Foreign assets held by the bank for the exclusive purpose of redemption remained significantly higher than warranted by law, as evidenced by Table 5. Up to the mid-1950s the excess precious metals and foreign exchange currency reserves averaged 25% of notes issued. In other words, the SBE could have increased the issue of notes by 25% per annum or the banking department could have financed more imports. But that was not the case.

Money and Credit

The balance of payment and domestic credit remained the determinants of money supply, with the impact of the latter enhanced at the cost of the former. In addition to fiduciary issue being now responsible for up to 70% of the notes issued, the domestic credit market was strengthened by advances in economic development. Credit relationships between the SBE and the government were also articulated during this period.

Government Credit

The government was in a position to borrow both from the SBE as well as from the non-banking public to finance its deficits.

Table 5: Notes Issued and Currency Reserves: 1950-63
(E$ million)

	1950	1951	1955	1957	1960	1961	1962	1963
Notes issued	52.9	75.6	126.4	134.5	134.7	147.6	156.4	168.5
Currency reserves								
Required	15.9	22.7	37.9	40.4	40.4	44.3	46.9	50.6
Actual	31.2	40.6	64.4	47.4	47.7	56.6	65.5	74.1
Gold and silver	22.6	23.0	25.0	25.1	13.1	14.0	13.1	6.0
Foreign assets	8.6	17.6	39.4	22.3	34.6	42.6	52.4	68.1
Excess reserves	15.9	17.9	26.5	3.4	7.3	12.3	18.6	23.5
Government treasury obligations	21.3	35.0	62.0	87.0	87.0	91.0	91.0	91.0
Excess reserves as % of notes issued	40.3	46.3	49.1	64.7	64.6	61.7	58.2	54.0

Source: SBE, Report on Economic Conditions and Market Trends, various issues.

Proclamation 112 of 1950, in addition to lowering the precious metals and foreign assets currency reserve components, also defined the maximum the government could borrow from the SBE. Accordingly, the central government, its subsidiaries, corporations and associations in which the State had majority or controlling interest were not to be indebted to SBE in excess of E$5 million, of which E$3 million was to be in direct and the balance in indirect obligations.

This limitation was the beginning of an important tradition. Given the fact that the SBE was owned by the State, operated under the auspices of the Ministry of Finance and managed by a Board of Directors appointed by and serving at the pleasure of the government, it needed to have specific definitions of what it was expected to do in cases where the State needed to tap into the financial resources it had mobilized. In addition to protecting itself from the vagaries of the policy makers, it also helped to impose fiscal prudence on the government.

Where the financing needs of the government were beyond these limits, an alternative means of mobilizing financial resources was necessary. In the 1950s there was no need to mobilize resources to finance government deficit since it succeeded in holding its increasing expenditure below its revenue. The lean years were made up for from the savings it accumulated during the fat years.

Towards the end of the 1950s, the gap between revenue and expenditure continued to rise, requiring an increased source of financing. The government, rather than borrowing from the SBE, developed an alternative mechanism through the issue of bonds. This type of mobilizing resources to finance government deficit had the added advantage of boosting the nascent capital market.

Proclamation 172 of 1961 authorized the Ministry of Finance to issue government bearer bonds, the total value of which was not to exceed E$30 million, maturing in a maximum of ten years and carrying interest rates of up to 6% per annum.[49] The first government bonds with a value of E$4 million, carrying interest rates of 4% per annum and maturing in five years, were issued in July 1963.[50]

Private Credit

The demand for credit by the private sector was also on the increase as a result of growing economic activity. Trade was expanding into all the corners of the country following improved transportation and communication. Manufacturing industries were mushrooming. The demand for housing was also increasing at a fast rate, boosting the construction industry. The consequence of these developments was an increase in the demand for credit.

The SBE was, however, not in the a position to satisfy the increased demand because of the negative impact domestic credit could have on the balance of payment. Despite such restraint the volume of domestic credit in 1963 was five times more than it was in 1950.

Domestic credit therefore came to play a more important role in determining the money supply than the balance of payments had in the earlier years. As a result, the money supply recorded high growth in the 1950s and early 1960s.

Table 6: Currency, Money and Credit: 1950-63
(Period Averages, E$ million)

	Currency issued	COB[1]	Demand deposit	Quasi money[2]	Narrow money	Broad money	Loans and advance	as £ of total deposits
1950	81.6	70.4	21.7	20.7	92.1	112.8	21.7	51.2
1951	108.1	88.6	19.2	26.2	107.8	134.0	11.5	25.3
1952	117.9	91.5	25.0	34.5	116.5	151.0	19.0	31.9
1953	134.0	111.2	26.9	63.7	138.1	201.8	19.9	22.0
1954	161.0	124.2	24.2	12.8	148.4	161.2	18.9	51.1
1955	164.2	129.3	28.6	14.6	157.9	172.5	30.8	71.3
1956	165.9	134.5	34.0	21.1	168.5	189.6	47.5	86.2
1957	178.6	148.7	40.4	21.3	189.1	210.4	57.5	93.2
1958	162.6	139.2	54.3	16.9	193.5	210.4	56.7	79.6
1959	165.3	145.9	53.9	21.5	199.8	221.3	59.1	78.4
1960	174.1	155.7	65.4	24.6	221.1	245.7	73.3	81.4
1961	187.4	167.2	69.7	30.0	236.9	266.9	84.3	84.6
1962	197.4	180.7	72.2	38.0	252.9	290.9	99.9	90.7
1963	211.5	193.0	80.2	43.7	273.2	316.9	109.7	88.5

Source: SBE, Report on Economic Conditions and Market Trends, various issues.

Note: 1) COB = Currency outside banks
2) Includes government deposits to 1953.

Another impetus for the high monetary expansion both in terms of currency issued, and the money supply came from the federation with Eritrea. With effect from 1952, the Ethiopian currency started replacing the East African shilling which was the medium of exchange until then. The process of supplanting the EAS was completed in 1955, after which the growth rate started to slow down.

The fall in the volume of currency issued as from 1958 was due to the precipitous decline in foreign reserves resulting from the unfavourable balance of payment position. This was also reflected in the volume of loans and advances provided by the banking system, since, as pointed out above, the credit policy of the banking system was closely tied to the foreign exchange position of the country.

Interest Rates
The interest rate both on deposit and credit were administratively determined by the SBE rather than market. Since the SBE provided current account services until January 1946, there were no interest rates on deposits. When the SBE expanded its deposit services to include time and saving deposits, it started paying interest. However, interest-bearing deposits were limited to E$5,000. In doing so, it meant to minimize its cost on deposits exceeding this sum. In this instance, it is useful to keep in mind that the more prominent policy objective of SBE was the sustainability of the balance of payment rather than mobilization of financial resources and the expansion of domestic credit. The ceiling on interest-earning deposit remained in force until 1960 when it was raised to E$10,000.

Interest rates on deposit changed slowly. Saving deposits earned 3%, time deposits for less than six months were paid 1% and longer periods 2% per annum beginning in 1946. In 1949, these rates were raised to 4%, 2% and 3% respectively. In 1958, there was a 4% increase in saving deposits.[51]

Interest rates on loans were relatively high. Up to 1955 the lending rate ranged between 7% (merchandise loans) and 9% (personal guarantee loans). To commemorate Emperor Haile Selassie's Silver Coronation Jubilee, interest rates on all loans were reduced by one percentage point in 1955.[52]

The Final Years: 1964-75
The most important event and one that delineated the pre- and post-1964 period was the establishment of a central bank in the country. As pointed out earlier, the creation of a central bank was the logical outcome of developments initiated two decades earlier. The SBE had successfully combined the functions of central and commercial banking. The new central bank was made necessary by the expanding responsibilities of the SBE which could not have been handled efficiently within its existing structure.

The new Central Bank assumed the responsibilities of the issue department of SBE. Except for the widening and deepening of its functions, there was nothing radically new in terms of its responsibilities. The new bank assumed the functions of issuing legal tender currency, managing the foreign assets of the nation, serving as a banker to the government and licensing and supervising commercial banks. In its role as the exclusive source of legal tender currency, it was granted the additional power to issue coins, a function that was performed until then by the Ministry of Finance.

As a banker to the government, the Central Bank extensively expanded the nature and volume of credit it was to make available to the former. The government was to borrow in the form of direct advances from the NBE a maximum of 15% of the ordinary revenue it collected during the previous fiscal year, repayable within six months in the following fiscal year. Repayment was set as an unwavering precondition for new credit from the NBE; direct advances were subject to a minimum of 3% interest, the exact amount of which was to be arrived at through negotiation between the Central Bank and the Ministry of Finance.[53]

The right of the government to mobilize financial resources through two instruments, bonds and treasury bills, was also recognized. Bond maturity was not to exceed ten years and one year for treasury obligations. The maximum that the Central Bank was to hold of these instruments of government debt through purchase in the open market or in securities and reserves of commercial banks was not to exceed four times the sum of its capital and general reserve fund in the case of bonds and 50% of this sum in the case of treasury bills.[54]

In 1969 the amount of money the government could borrow from and through the Central Bank was revised. Direct advance was increased to 20% from the 15% of the ordinary revenue of the government. The maximum in bond holdings of the NBE was not to exceed three times the capital and the general reserve fund plus E$82 million. The value of treasury bills to be held by the bank was not to exceed 12% of the ordinary revenue collected by the government during the previous fiscal year.[55]

The NBE was also given the power and responsibility to license and supervise commercial banks. Proclamation 206 of 1953 permitted the establishment of private commercial banks with the sole requirement that 51% of their capital was to be owned by Ethiopian nationals.[56] Although the minimum capital requirement was not defined in the Proclamation, this was rectified by a regulation issued by the NBE in 1964. All commercial banks needed to be capitalized at a minimum of E$2 million, the total amount of which was to be paid up at the time of establishment.[57] By the time financial institutions were nationalized by the Military Regime on 1 January 1975 there were four commercial banks the Commercial Bank of Ethiopia (wholly government-owned), the Addis Ababa Bank, Banco di Roma and

Banco di Napoli. The authority of the NBE over the commercial banks included the supervision of their operation as well as inspection and auditing of their books.

The operational relationship between the Central Bank and the Commercial Bank started with the identification of the former as their banker accepting deposits and extending credit at interest rates determined by it. The NBE was also to set the interest rate they paid on deposits and charged on different lines of credit. The right to impose variable reserve requirements on the different lines of deposit was also recognized as the power of the Central Bank.

Following its establishment, the NBE issued a series of rules and regulations specifying its relationship with the commercial banks and defining its code of conduct. The reserve requirements were established at 5% for saving and time deposits, 10% for demand deposit and liquidity requirement was set at 25% of each commercial bank's short-term liabilities.[58]

Among the credit policies, commercial banks were forbidden to lend to the central government, except for the purchase of treasury bills, and were not to lend to or invest in foreign government nationals and organizations. They could not own land other than their office premises or extend credit on the security of its shares and set the limit of a maximum of 10% of the sum of its paid-in capital, general reserve and surplus to any single borrower.[59]

The NBE set out its interest rate policy by first establishing its own interest and discount rates on eligible papers. The NBE was to discount papers and provide advances to commercial banks at the rate of 4% on exports and treasury bills and 5% on all other eligible papers.[60] Commercial banks were to charge not less than 1% above these standard discount and advance rates if what each bank was to charge above this minimum was to be set by the market.[61]

Following this regulation, the banks set their own individual rates on different lines of credit. However, all the commercial banks took their lead from the Commercial Bank of Ethiopia which was by far the most dominant in the country. These rates varied from a minimum of 6% (on exports) to 9% (for personal guaranteed loans).[62] Interest rates on deposits were also defined by the NBE at 4% on saving deposits of up to E$10,000. Time deposits were to earn 3% for 30 days to 6 months, 3% for six to 12 months and 4% for deposits exceeding one year.

As of September 1966 the NBE raised its discount and advance rates by half percentage points. In August 1970 the discount rate on treasury bills were raised from 5.5% to 6% while those on other eligible papers were increased by one percentage point from 5.5% to 6.5%. Commercial banks followed suit with the interest they paid on deposits and charged on loans. As of February 1966 interest on savings deposit increased from 4.5% to 5% and again in August 1970 to 6% per annum. The corresponding rates on time deposits were 4% and 5% on deposits held for 6-12 months and 5% and 6% on deposits for periods longer than 12 months. The rate on time deposits for 30 days to 6 months was increased from the 3% set in 1964 to 4% in August 1970.[63]

Lending rates were also changed following the increase on deposits. Export credit (the most favoured of the different lines of credit) changed from 6% to 9% in 1964 to 7%-9% in September 1966 and again to 7.5% to 9.5% in August 1970. Credit for all other purposes changed from 7% to 9% in 1964 to 8.5%-11% in December 1971.[64]

Money Supply and Domestic Credit

The money supply increased from E$259.6 on 31 December 1963 to E$694.3 million on 31 December 1974. The volume of money (M2) was even more impressive, increasing from E$306.6 million to E$1075.0 million respectively.

Table 7: Money Supply and Determinants: 1963-74
(end of year, E$ million)

	1963	1965	1968	1971	1974
Foreign assets	160.7	214.3	170.6	117.7	611.2
Domestic credit	150.2	240.0	383.9	557.0	634.6
Government	20.3	47.1	96.5	108.6	64.8
Private	129.9	192.9	287.4	448.4	569.8
Quasi money	47.0	71.4	125.2	214.6	380.7
Other items	- 4.3	- 32.8	- 45.6	- 51.5	- 170.8
Money supply (1+2-3+4)^1	259.6	350.1	383.7	408.6	694.3
Volume of Money (5+3)^2	306.6	42.5	508.9	623.2	1075.0

Source: NBE, *Quarterly Bulletin*, (various issues)

Note: 1) Money supply is narrow money or M_1. 2) Volume of money is M_2

The major impetus behind the expansion in money supply was domestic credit with foreign asset playing a secondary role. The increase in money supply was tempered by growth in quasi money (saving and time deposit).

The expansion in domestic credit was mainly due to the private sector. Government credit from the banking system (made up of direct advance bonds and treasury bills holdings) was very modest as a result of the conservative and prudent fiscal policy of the government.

Managing Foreign Assets

The management of foreign assets of the nation was recognized as one of the responsibilities of the National Bank of Ethiopia (NBE) upon its formation in 1964. This was a function performed by the State Bank of Ethiopia since 1942.

The foreign asset of Ethiopia had always attracted the attention of its policy makers because of its supreme importance. From 1945 to 1976, the international reserve of the country served the dual purpose of anchoring the issue of domestic currency as well as financing current transactions. While the overall responsibility of managing the external reserve of the country was the function of the Central Bank (the issue department of SBE from 23 July 1945 to 31 December 1963 and the NBE thereafter), there was nevertheless a division of labour between itself and the commercial banks (the banking department of SBE up to 31 December 1963). The Central Bank assumed the direct responsibility of managing that part of the foreign exchange held as currency reserve while the commercial banks were delegated the authority to manage and finance current international transactions. This operational arrangement was more a result of an institutional division of responsibilities. The central bank is a banker to banks and the central government and does not deal with the non-banking public, which is the exclusive domain of commercial banks and other financial institutions. Consequently, the private sector dealt with commercial banks for all its foreign currency needs as well as other services.

The supreme importance of foreign assets stems from these dual roles. Whatever happens to the foreign assets is reflected in the economy through corresponding changes in the money supply. Since the amount of currency the Central Bank was to issue depended significantly on the availability of foreign exchange, managing the domestic money supply in effect meant managing the foreign assets. The smaller the foreign currency reserve the smaller would be the volume of currency issued and, given the negative impact of domestic credit on foreign reserve, the smaller would be the domestic money supply. The second and equally important aspect of foreign asset stems from the traditional balance of payment considerations and again its impact on domestic money supply. A deterioration in the balance of payment would not only decrease the import capacity but also the money supply, since domestic currency is absorbed into the banking system in exchange for foreign currency and vice versa.

The central problem of monetary policy in Ethiopia, particularly until the early 1960s, was the Central Bank's incapacity to sterilize the impact of external factors on the domestic economy through the money supply. Since the money supply was determined by foreign assets, domestic monetary policy was therefore anchored to it. As will be made clear, the credit policy of the SBE was closely tied to the foreign asset position. An increase in credit was likely to erode the foreign asset. As a consequence of these factors, the Ethiopian monetary policy rested in effect on the management of the foreign assets.

Through the years, the monetary authorities had taken measures to attenuate the impact of the external sector on domestic money supply and, through it, the economy. These measures included decreasing the foreign exchange backing of the currency in favour of fiduciary issue, increasing the supply of domestic credit, and open market operation through the capital and money market.

Despite these measures, domestic monetary policy was not fully disengaged from the vagaries of the country's external position. This is understandable given the fixed exchange rate system whose par value was never changed. As such, the Ethiopian currency seems to hold the record in maintaining its original par value to this date.

The monetary authorities shied away from using the exchange rate as an internal and external balancing instrument not because the need did not arise but because the benefit was perceived to be less than the cost.

Between 1945, when the new currency was issued, and 1974, the exchange rate came under serious threat three times. The first was in 1949 following the devaluation of the pound sterling by about one-third. Against all expectations, the government decided not to devalue the currency.[65] There were very good reasons behind this decision. First, the balance of payment position of the country did not require such means of adjustment, although with the revival of European agriculture, the value and quantity of exports were not increasing at the rate registered during the earlier years whereas imports increased considerably. While the Ethiopian authorities were aware of the comparative disadvantage resulting from the decision against devaluation, they were nonetheless confident that this negative impact could be made up for by such means as upgrading the quality and increasing the quantity of the exportables and improving domestic transportation to decrease costs.

The second and perhaps the more important rationale for not devaluing was the possible negative impact such a decision could have had on people's confidence in the new currency. Had the government devalued the currency, it could have undermined confidence, thereby giving rise to falling demand for money and the development of a black market for foreign exchange.

The second time the exchange rate came under pressure was in 1958 when the country was plunged into a serious balance of payments crisis. Although foreign reserves were depleted again the government decided against devaluation. The final and the most serious challenge came during the

1971-73 period, following the devaluation of the US dollar to which the Ethiopian dollar was pegged. Again, the monetary authorities decided against devaluation as a result of which the Ethiopian dollar was revalued by 7.9% in 1971 and 10% in 1973 against the US dollar.[66]

The basic justification against devaluation had been the same throughout the different years of crisis. Since Ethiopia was a price taker in the world market, there was no advantage in devaluation. If the currency were devalued, it would increase the domestic currency price of imported consumer goods, raw materials and capital goods. On the other side of the balance sheet, exporters would have higher income in domestic currency for the same quantity of exports. The combined effect of higher import cost and higher income of exporters would be higher demand resulting in higher prices. On the other hand, output both in the short and long run were presumed to decrease in the short-run because the higher cost of importing raw materials for agriculture (fertilizers and chemicals) and industry would decrease the capacity as well as interest of producers to purchase inputs and thus result in lower capacity utilization. The fall in output would most probably result in higher prices which could be of advantage to producers at the cost of consumers. Long-run growth was also expected to be negatively affected because the higher costs of capital goods were likely to constrain investment.

On the other hand, exporters could be encouraged to expand their output and upgrade the quality of their exportables and so improve their competitiveness in the world market. To this end, the government eliminated tax on non-traditional exports while reducing it on others with the exception of coffee. At the same time, it assumed quality control of exportables by establishing the Ethiopian Grain Board and the Coffee Board to license exporters and assure the highest possible quality of the exportables.

On the import side, the government imposed higher taxes on consumer goods, minimized duties on raw materials and capital goods while inputs such as fertilizer and fuel enjoyed government subsidies. With the elimination of the exchange rate as one possible instrument of monetary and balance of payment adjustment, the government depended on administrative control. These were of three types exchange control, credit restraint and prior deposit on imports.

Exchange Control
Legal exchange control goes as far back as 1942 when the government introduced authorization from the Ministry of Finance to own, hold and export foreign exchange.[67] Proclamation 31 of 1942 was amended by Proclamation 99 of 1948 which, among others, transferred the implementing authority from the Ministry of Finance to the State Bank of Ethiopia.[68] Both

proclamations were, however, not implemented since they were not accompanied or followed by regulations defining the method and procedure for their enforcement. This problem was rectified in 1949 through Legal Notice No. 127 which established the details of how the foreign exchange control was to be implemented.[69]

The exchange control system can be described as quantitative restriction. All exporters were required to surrender their foreign exchange earnings to the SBE and later to NBE in exchange for local currencies. Importers had to obtain payment licences. The SBE established the Exchange Control Department to implement the system. With the exception of the growth of activity the same procedure was continued under NBE.

The Exchange Control System operated fairly successfully, supplemented by other instruments. As a rule, foreign exchange for current transactions was readily available during the entire period under review. However, there was stringent control on capital account and whatever leakages there were in foreign exchange must have been to service this need.

Credit Policy

The Credit Policy of the SBE and later the NBE was used as an instrument for managing foreign assets. When the balance of payment position of the country was strong, the banking system expanded credit and vice versa.

The idea behind the use of credit as a balance of payment instrument was simple, by virtue of the presumption that it had direct or indirect impact on foreign exchange holdings of the banking system. If credit is provided to finance imports, then this decreased the foreign exchange directly. On the other hand, credit extended for domestic economic activity would have decreased the foreign reserves by increasing the demand for imports. For example, if the SBE had granted credit for the purpose of financing construction, its foreign exchange balance would have been affected since the utilization of the fund required imported materials. In addition to the general credit squeeze, the SBE denied credit for the importation of certain goods on the grounds that they were either luxuries or were domestically produced.

The credit crunch designed to conserve foreign exchange did have a negative impact on the economy. But the government did not have any other option, given the link between foreign asset and the issue of domestic currency under the fixed exchange rate regime. If the credit policy were liberal when the balance of payment was under strain, the money supply would be squeezed. The government could have made use of interest rate as a means of curtailing demand for credit but again this was ruled out. In the circumstances, tight credit policy was considered the lesser of the evils and was vigorously pursued whenever the balance of payment, and through it, the foreign asset position came under threat.

Prior Deposit
Tight credit policy was effective to the extent that importers had to finance their purchases from abroad through bank loans. But it was possible that importers could finance their purchases either from their own fund or resources mobilized from outside the banking system.

In order to deter importers, the government made extensive use of prior deposit varying between 75% and 150% of the value of imports, depending on the nature of the product. These funds were impounded for as long as it took for the goods to arrive in the country. Such practices were expected to increase the cost of imported commodities, thereby consequently deterring the importer. Prior deposits were instruments of last resort and were used when all other measures failed to curb the volume of imports. They were used from August 1959 to April 1962 and again from 1968 through 1971. These measures were supplemented by travel and remittance controls.

The instruments for the management of foreign assets did serve the nation well from the point of view of conserving the foreign reserves, although the economy suffered from it. Throughout the period 1971-75, the balance of payment was maintained at a sustainable position. Debts and other obligations were paid on schedule. On 31 December 1974 when the Military Regime nationalized banks and other financial institutions, the country had accumulated more than US$350 million in foreign assets, a very comfortable position indeed.

Financing Economic Development
The Banking Department of SBE and the Commercial Bank of Ethiopia thereafter were the most dominant financial institutions in the country. With extensive branches, their mobilization capacity was very intensive. As of 31 December 1974 the Commercial Bank of Ethiopia held more than 80% of the deposits in the banking system while the balance was accounted for by the Addis Ababa Bank, Banco di Roma and Banco di Napoli. During earlier periods the proportion of the financial resources of the State Bank and later the Commercial Bank was even larger on account of the fact that either it was the only such institution in the country (up to 1952 when Eritrea was federated with Ethiopia) or the operations of the other commercial banks were localized (as in the case of Banco d'Roma and Banco d'Napoli in the province of Eritrea) or were too small to enable the latter to seriously compete with it (after 1964 when, in addition to the two Italian banks, the Addis Ababa Bank was established).

In 1964 the total financial resources mobilized by the financial institutions (excluding the Central Bank) from their deposit clients was E$165.1 million which, by 1974, had increased to E$575 million.[70]

These financial resources were unfortunately not available to finance development projects. The limitations, in addition to the externally-oriented credit policy, were inherent in the nature of commercial banks. The commercial banks were mobilizing on a short-term basis from the saving units while development projects required long-term financing. The longest period for which the Commercial Bank of Ethiopia extended credit was five years. All other credits were of shorter term duration.

The inability of commercial banks to finance development projects of long gestation and duration was apparently clear to the Ethiopia government from the outset. Consequently, it sought to develop alternative sources and modes of financing long-term investment. During the entire span of the period 1941-75, the government pursued an inward-looking development policy and an outward-looking financing mechanism. To this end, and as from 1945, the government offered liberal incentives to foreign (and later national) investors in all sectors of the economy and provided adequate shelters from external competition through high tariff and non-tariff barriers (Befekadu Degefe 1981).

Domestically, the government, with the advice and support of the World Bank, converted the newly created Agricultural and Commercial Bank into the Development Bank of Ethiopia in 1951.[71] The Bank was established with a capital of E$13 million (US$5.2 million) of which E$11 million was paid up. The World Bank provided a credit of US$2 million to cover the external cost of the Bank's credit. Management was to be agreed upon by the Ethiopian Government and the World Bank. The Bank was granted special privileges such as exemption from all taxes and duties as well as independence from the control and supervision of the Central Bank.[72]

The Development Bank of Ethiopia (DBE) was in operation from 1951 to 1970. During its active life it provided credit and equity financing to the agricultural and industrial sectors of the economy. The major problem DBE faced was resource constraint. In 1969, the last year of its working life, its working capital was made up of E$11 million of the paid-in capital and E$6.5 million in long-term loans. Consequently, it was forced to depend on repayment of past loans to finance new credit. It is apparent from the annual reports of the Bank that the demands for loans were much higher than its capacity. For example, in 1969, there were 709 applications valued at E$23.1 million of which 118 loans valued at E$4.3 million were approved while the balance was turned down mainly for lack of funds.[73]

Despite attempts by the government at encouraging domestic and foreign capital to invest in productive activities, the result was not satisfactory. Hence, the government was forced to invest in productive activities either on its own or in partnership with foreign capital. To encourage private sector investment, the government supported the development of capital and money markets.

The capital and money market in Ethiopia was initiated by private enterprises as far back as 1956. The first company to offer shares valued at E$1 million to the general public was Ethiopian Abattoirs. Thereafter, other companies including the Bottling Company of Ethiopia (producers of Coca Cola) and Indo-Ethiopian Textiles entered the market. The total shares offered to the Ethiopian public during the 1956-58 period was E$3.1million.

However, the real breakthrough came in 1959 when the State Bank of Ethiopia, an owner of a large chunk of shares floated earlier, offered to act as an agent and provide the public with facilities to purchase and sell shares. The first company to float its shares through the SBE was HVA (Ethiopia) which made available E$5.6 million (20% of its capital) worth of shares to the new market. Of this sum E$2.5 million was purchased by the public and the balance was held by the SBE.

The SBE subsequently established the Share Exchange Department to manage and direct the market. The Department remained active until 1965 when its responsibilities were transferred to the newly established Share Dealing Group, an association of local banks made up of NBE, Commercial Bank of Ethiopia, Addis Ababa Bank, Banco di Roma, Ethiopian Investment Corporation and the Development Bank of Ethiopia. The Ethiopian Investment Corporation (established in 1963 as the Investment Bank of Ethiopia) was a holding company for government-owned enterprises with the objectives of supporting investment through credit, underwriting and sale of shares. The rationale for the establishment of Share Dealing Group (SDG) in 1965 was the growth of the market beyond the support and facilities provided by the SBE (until 1963) and the NBE thereafter. Upon formation the SDG was offering over-the-counter market. The market was governed by Rules and Regulations of the SDG which defined the purpose and established the code of conduct.

The market gradually expanded through new share companies and government securities (bonds and treasury bills). The clients included banks, insurance companies and, most importantly, small savers.

By the time the Military Regime nationalized banks, financial institutions and industries, there were 20 companies whose shares were traded with capitalization exceeding E$100 million. Unfortunately, this was brought to an end by the Military Regime.

Another significant development in long-term financing took place in 1970 when the government amalgamated the Development Bank of Ethiopiaand the Investment Corporation to create the Agricultural and Industrial Bank of Ethiopia (AID Bank) with an enhanced capital of E$100 million. Its ambit included investment in agriculture, industry through credit and equity participation.

The Commercial Bank of Ethiopia established the Mortgage Corporation as a subsidiary in 1965 to invest funds mainly in the construction and real estate sectors of the economy on a long-term basis. The Mortgage Corporation, along with the Imperial Savings and Home Ownership Association a public company established in 1961 with the objective of mobilizing and financing low to medium-cost housing— eased the acute housing shortage in the capital. These attempts at creating a medium for the financing of economic development had a positive impact until they were emasculated by the Military Regime.

Prices

It would be remiss for one to exclude the development in prices when discussing money. However, the link between money and prices during the period 1941-75 was very thin, if any. Prices in Ethiopia were more sensitive to the weather, which affected agricultural output and therefore food prices and the price of imports. As a result of a combination of these two factors, the general price index increased to 159.7 in December 1974 from its base year of 1963, averaging a respectable 5% per annum.[74]

The absence of correlation between money and prices is obvious from the more or less tight money environment pursued by the central banks, coupled with the relatively high rate of economic growth.

Notes

1. Ministry of Information, *Ethiopian Herald* Volume XXX, No. 1225, January 2, 1975. The Commercial Banks were Addis Ababa Bank, Banco di Roma and Banco Di Napoli. The insurance companies were African Solidarity, Ethio-American Life, Blue Nile, Ethiopian General, Imperial, Afro-Continental, Pan-African, Union, Ras, Ethiopian Life and Rasai. The non-bank financial intermediaries were The Imperial Savings and Home Ownership Public Association and the Mortgage Corporation.
2. Provisional Military Administrative Council (PMAC) 'Monetary and Banking Proclamation', Proclamation No. 99 of 1976). The NBE was established in 1963 by a Charter and its powers and duties were defined in a Proclamation. Imperial Ethiopian Government (IEG), 'National Bank of Ethiopia Charter' (Order No. 30 of 1963) and IEG Monetary and Banking Proclamation (Proclamation No. 206 of 1963).
3. Proclamation 99 of 1976, Article 6.
4. *Ibid.*, Articles 7, 8, 9.
5. Between 1893 and 1896, 20,200 silver dollars and 51,200 dollars worth of silver and copper coins were issued, (Pankhurst 1968:478-493).
6. Both Emperors Menelik and Haile Selassie as well as Italians during their period of occupation (1936-41) and the British (1941-45) attempted to supplant the MTD with their own currencies but were unable to do so.
7. Perham gives the weight of an ounce per coin, (1969:212).
8. See for example IEG, 'Proclamation to Prohibit the Export of Maria Theresa Dollars' Proclamation No. 23 of 1942.

274 An Economic History of Modern Ethiopia

9. The Bank was established and managed by the British through the National Bank of Egypt. It was granted monopoly for 50 years. (See Pankhurst 1968:494-498).
10. Liquidators were appointed in 1945 and 1956. See Legal Notices No. 81 of 1945 and No. 201 of 1956 respectively. According to Ato Tafara Degefe, the first General Manager of the Commercial Bank of Ethiopia and the Second Governor of NBE, the Bank of Ethiopia was finally put to rest in 1964 (interviewed 20 January, 1992).
11. The position of the Foreign Office was unequivocally established on 4 February, 1941 by Mr Anthony Eden, the Secretary of State for Foreign Affairs in the House of Commons. (for the full statement, see Perham 1969:463).
12. Barclay's Bank, 1948:57. For the full story of the bank's activity in Ethiopia, see pp. 54-74.
13. FO/371/31597 Mitchell to War Office, February 2, 1942.
14. FO/371/31597 Mitchell to War office, 30 December 1941.
15. IEG, State Bank Proclamation (Proclamation No. 21 of 1942).
16. IEG, General Notice No. 7 of 1942. Mr C.S. Collier, a Canadian, had a long history in Ethiopia. He was the Governor of the Bank of Abyssinia from 1919 to 1931 and Deputy President of the Bank of Ethiopia from 1931 to 1935. (See Pankhurst, 1968:497).
17. FO/371/31596 Row Dutton to Mackereth, 20 February 1941 and FO/371/31596 Mackereth to Howe, 28 February 1942. Mr Howe was appointed HIM Minister in Ethiopia on 3 February 1942.
18. FO/371/31596 Howe to Mackereth 23 July 1942.
19. State Bank of Ethiopia, *Monthly Letter*, Vol. I, No. 4, p. 2. The first Board Members were Tsehafe Tezaze Wolde Giorgis (President), Mr. C.S. Collier, Negadras Gebre Egziabher, Ato Makonnen Desta, Lij Yilma Deressa, Dr. Ambaye Wolde Mariam and Ato Aklilu Habte Wold. IEG, General Notice No. 14 of 1943.
20. IEG, 'Charter of the State Bank of Ethiopia' General Notice No. 18 of 1943. Although the date of issue is given as August 30, 1943, the Charter must have been promulgated in November since both General Notice No. 17 and 19 were dated so.
21. IEG 'Interpretation of Certain Powers Granted in the Charter of SBE' General Notice No. 29 of 1944.
22. C.S. Stafford, the financial advisor to the Emperor, made a number of requests to be permitted a seat on the Board first to the British Government and later to the Ethiopian Government. He was refused permission by his government earlier (FO/371/31596 Mackereth to Howe, 23 August 1942). When his government granted him permission to his incessant request, the Ethiopian Government refused to allocate him a seat on the Board (FO/371/31596, Stafford to Howe, 31 August 1942). C.S. Collier was appointed Auditor General while he was travelling in the Middle East and India on Bank business on 14 November 1943 and George Albert Blowers was the first American appointed Governor of SBE (IEG, General Notice No. 17 of 1943 and FO/371/35613. Howe to Gilbert, 6 December 1943).
23. Ato Menasse Lemma was appointed Acting Governor in 1959 and Governor in 1961.
24. IEG, 'Charter of the National Bank of Ethiopia' Order No. 30 of 1963 and Commercial Bank of Ethiopia, Articles of Association (December 1963, Addis Ababa).
25. IEG, 'Development Bank of Ethiopia Establishment Proclamation' Proclamation No. 116 of 1951 and SBE, *Review of Economic Conditions and Market Trends*, No. 42, May 1959, pp. 4-11.
26. This section summarizes the details of the making of the Ethiopian currency dealt with in another paper; see Befekadu Degefe, 1992.
27. FO/371/31596 Memorandum on Currency Plan for Ethiopia, HIM Treasury, 1 May 1941.

The Development of Money, Monetary Institutions and Monetary Policy 275

28. The final version of the Currency Plan was prepared at an interdepartmental meeting in which the Treasury, Colonial War and Foreign Offices were represented on 2 January 1942 (FO/371/31597. Mackereth to Malkin, 3 January 1942). The finalized currency plan was dispatched to Addis for ratification by the Ethiopian Government in April 1942 (FO.371/35614. Mackereth to Howe, 15 April 1942.
29. FO.371/35613; Mackereth to Row-Dutton, 21 July 1943.
30. British pressure on the Ethiopian Government to force compliance started in mid-1942 when the MTD reserve was moved to Harar with their army. Thereafter, the British either refused or were slow in providing small denomination East African shilling coinage. For details, see Befekadu, 1992.
31. The Ethiopian Government was not entirely successful in its attempt to keep the process of creating the new currency a secret from the British. The first breakthrough came from their Ambassador in Washington as early as July 1943 (FO/371/35613; Washington to Foreign Office, 5 July 1943) with latter follow-ups. This information was sent to Addis Ababa for confirmation. Because the Ethiopians guarded their secret successfully from their end, the British could not confirm and therefore failed to discover the goings-on. The British finally broke the Ethiopian secrecy veil in December 1944 (FO/371/41475; Howe to Mackereth, 15 December 1944).
32. FO/371/35612, Foreign Office to Addis Ababa, November 1942.
33. FO.371/41475, Howe to Mackereth, 15 December 1944.
34. IEG, Currency and Legal Tender Proclamation, Proclamation No. 76 of 1945, Article 2.
35. *Ibid.*, Article 1 of Schedule A. The Article includes a twenty-dollar note which was not part of the original consignment. In fact the E$20 note was not released until 1963.
36. *Ibid.*
37. *Ibid.*, Schedule C Article 4.
38. *Ibid.*, Article 2 and IEG Legal Notice No. 90 of 1945 for the extension.
39. IEG, Proclamation No. 76 of 1945 Article 4.
40. FO/371/46048, D.M.H. Richie to Foreign Office 10 October 1945. See also FO/371/46048, Sarrel to Foreign Office, 2 October 1945.
41. IEG, Currency (Amendment) Proclamation, Proclamation No. 112 of 1950, Article 4.
42. IEG, Monetary and Banking Proclamation, Proclamation No. 206 of 1963, Article 8.
43. IEG, National Bank of Ethiopia Charter, Order No. 30 of 1963, Article 8.
44. IEG, Prohibition of Export of Maria Theresa Dollars, Proclamation No. 23 of 1942. See also Legal Notice No. 32 of 1943 which limited travellers out of Ethiopia to take with them a maximum of £15. Any amount in excess required special licence from the Ministry of Finance.
45. IEG, Legal Tender Proclamation, Proclamation No. 32 of 1942.
46. IEG, Currency Proclamation, Proclamation No. 31 of 1942.
47. State Bank of Ethiopia, *Monthly Letter*, Vol. I, No. 9, July 1949, p. 8.
48. IEG, Currency Amendment Proclamation, Proclamation No. 12 of 1950.
49. IEG, Government Banks Proclamation, Proclamation No. 172 of 1961.
50. Ministry of Finance, Premium Bonds Regulation, Legal Notice No. 274 of 1973.
51. SBE, *Reports on Economic Conditions and Market Trends*, No. 38, May 1958, p. 11.
52. SBE, *Report on Economic Conditions and Market Trend* No. 32, May 1956, pp. 5-6.
53. IEG, Proclamation 206 of 1963 Article 13(3).
54. *Ibid.*, Article 13(4) - (8).
55. IEG, Monetary and Banking Proclamation (Amendment) Decree, Decree No. 54 of 1969.
56. IEG, Proclamation 206, Chapter 5, Article 32(1).
57. NBE, Supervisory Regulation - NBE/SU/C Minimum Capital Requirements, 29 April 1964.

58. NBE, Credit Regulation - NBE/CR/D Reserve Balance Requirements, 29 April 1964 and Supervisory Regulation - NBE/SU/F, Liquidity Ratio of Banks, April 29, 1964.
59. NBE, Credit Regulation - NBE/CR/E Credit and Purchase Transactions of Banks and Other Designated Financial Institutions, April 29, 1964.
60. NBE, Credit Regulation - NBE/CR/A Standard Rates of Interest Charged by the National Bank of Ethiopia, April 29, 1964.
61. NBE, Credit Regulation - NBE/CRB Interest Charged on Loans by Banks and Other Designated Financial Institutions, April 29, 1964.
62. NBE, *Quarterly Bulletin* No 33(91), March 1972, Table 21, p. 77.
63. NBE, *Quarterly Bulletin* No. 33(91), March 1972, Table 21, p. 77.
64. *Ibid.*
65. SBE, 'The Ethiopian Economy Since the Sterling Devaluation and the Introduction of Foreign Exchange Control' *Monthly Letter*, Volume I, No. 14, December 1949, pp. 1-5.
66. NBE, *Annual Report*, July 1974 - June 1975, pp. 29-32.
67. IEG, Currency Proclamation, Proclamation No. 31 of 1942.
68. IEG, Currency Amendment Proclamation, Proclamation No. 99 of 1948.
69. Ministry of Finance, Foreign Exchange Regulation, Legal Notice No. 127 of 1949.
70. NBE, 'Statement of Condition of Commercial Banks in Ethiopia' *Quarterly Bulletin* (various issues).
71. The Precursors of the Development Bank of Ethiopia date from 1945 when the government established the Agricultural Development Bank with the objective of providing loans to small farmers whose cattle were destroyed by the Italians during their occupation. In 1949, this bank was converted into the Agricultural and Commercial Bank. This institution was converted into the Development Bank before it started operating. (IEG, Proclamation to Provide for Establishment of the Development Bank of Ethiopia, Proclamation No. 15 and 116 of 1950).
72. SBE, *Monthly Report on Economic Conditions and Market Trends*, Vol 2, No. 8, pp. 1-2.
73. Development Bank of Ethiopia,*Annual Report for the Year 1969*(Addis Ababa 1970).
74. CSO, *Retail Price Index for Addis Ababa*, (various issues). This was and still remains the only index of consumer price index in the country.

References

Barclay's Bank, 1948, 'A Bank in Battledress',*Cape Times*, for private circulation.
Bafekadu Degefe, 1981, 'Indigenization of the Ethiopian Economy', in Adebayo Adedeji, (ed), 1981, *Indigenization of African Economies*, Hutchinson, London.
------------, 1992, 'The Making of the Ethiopian Currency: 1941-1945', Institute of Development Research.
Marcus, H, G, 1983, *Ethiopia, Great Britain and the United States*, University of California Press, London.
Pankhurst, Richard, 1967,*Primitive Money, Money and Banking in Ethiopia*, Commercial Bank of Ethiopia, Addis Ababa.
------------, 1968, *The Economic History of Ethiopia*, HSIU Press, Addis Ababa.
------------, 'The Marie Theresa Dollar in Pre-War Ethiopia',*Journal of Ethiopian Studies*, Vol. 1, No. 1.
Perham, Margery, 1969, *The Government of Ethiopia*, Faber, London.
Schumpeter, J, A, 1986,*History of Economic Analysis*, Oxford University Press, New York.
Spencer, J, H, 1987, *Ethiopia at Bay: A Personal Account of the Haile Selassie Years*, Reference Publications, Michigan.

6. Demography, Migration and Urbanization in Modern Ethiopia

Alula Abate

Anyone who has undertaken research in Ethiopia will be aware of its peculiar difficulties. The problem is perhaps more acutely felt in social and economic planning and urban studies which need a tolerably accurate demographic data base. Until recently information on the Ethiopian population has been primarily speculative. Prior to the 1960s, data on aspects of the Ethiopian population were acquired from guesses and estimates made by foreign travellers, organizations and local government offices. Population guesses are available for some parts of Northern Ethiopia since the middle of the last century, but national estimates are only of recent origin, dating back to the beginning of the Twentieth Century. According to estimates made by several travellers and advisors, the population of Ethiopia at the turn of the Twentieth Century could probably have been in the range of 11 and 13 million and increasing at the rate of about 2% per annum (Pankhurst 1961:147-48). Early estimates, particularly those made during the Nineteenth Century, are of dubious merit. A few have considered taxation figures and number of soldiers to estimate population size, but most of them merely relied on very limited observation. One of the factors that may account for the under-estimation is that the most populous districts are not located along the frequented travellers' routes.

Available estimates from different sources for the 1920s and 1930s put the population of Ethiopia between 4 and 15 million. The Italian occupation forces, who had better facilities or generally were in a much better position, gave a very low estimate of about 7.5 million for 1938. This was in line with the declared colonial policy of settling a large number of poor Italians from over-populated regions. It was aimed at convincing world opinion that Ethiopia was under-populated and it needed over-crowded Italy to expand its 'Lebensraum' in Africa.

After the brief Italian occupation ended in 1941, the attempt to modernize the administration and economy of the country necessitated a whole range of data that dealt with population and other socio-economic affairs. A population estimate, which for the first time was not based on some wild guess, was carried out in 1956 by the Ministry of Interior to determine the number of constituencies and the size of the population eligible to vote in the first parliamentary election of 1957 (CSA 1988:2). According to this partially carried out enumeration (covering only 87% of the population), the population of the country stood at about 22,108,000. Although the data varied in coverage and quality, these early estimates have remained a useful point of reference.

During the 1950s when the First Five-Year Development Plan was being drafted, the absence of any reliable information on the size, composition, rate of growth and spatial distribution of population and other data relevant to socio-economic planning was acutely felt. Urgent actions were taken to remedy these lacunae. The Planning Board, basing on the estimates of the Gotha Almanak, UN Demographic Yearbook (1951), Taverna and Zervos and the Ministry of Interior, estimated the population in 1956 at 19,500,000. It is not altogether clear why this figure is significantly lower than those given by the Ministry of Interior and Taverna and Zervos. However, it is interesting to note that the Planning Board used its estimate to project the population of the country and its rates of growth both backward to 1950 and forward to 1966 (Table 1).

Table 1: Estimation of Population and Annual Growth Rate by the Planning Board (1950-66)

Year	Size of Population (million)	Annual growth rate
1950	17.8	1.5
1954	18.9	1.5
1956	19.5	1.5
1957	19.8	1.5
1961	21.0	1.5

Source: R. Pankhurst, 1961:149.

Two estimations carried out by Mesfin Wolde Mariam (1961:15-18) during the same period put the population figures for 1957, 1961 and 1965 at 23.2, 24.6 and 25-30 million respectively. In the light of the recent census, these estimates, which at the time were considered too high, appear to have been based on a much firmer evidence than most other sources.

With the establishment of the CSO and the initiation of a series of national sample surveys and other ad hoc sub-national surveys in the 1960s, a new era was ushered in with regard to the collection of reliable demographic and other socio-economic data. Two rounds of National Sample Surveys were conducted between 1964-67 and 1968-71. Because of differences in area coverage and the sample design used, comparison of the two periods has turned out to be a difficult task (Mitik Beyene 1988:21). The first round survey covered 83% of rural areas in 12 administrative regions and 195 urban centres of various sizes, whereas the second round surveys covered 82.2% of rural areas in all the regions (except in Eritrea and some nomadic areas) and in 91 towns. While both surveys employed stratified sampling techniques, the first round depended on a three-stage and the second round on a two-stage sampling. Since the surveys did not cover the entire country, estimates of population size had to be supplemented from other sources. While many of these surveys continue to serve as major sources of population, economic and social information, the documentation on some of these is rather sketchy. Nevertheless, although the data generated through these attempts were not of a high quality, given the dearth of information obtaining at the time, the contribution made by these surveys was quite significant.

Among the urban centres of Ethiopia, the earliest census took place in Addis Ababa in 1961 and was repeated in 1963 and 1967. After the region was federated with Ethiopia, the first census in Asmara was carried out in 1968. In the 1970s several important surveys were conducted, the first of which was the Addis Ababa Manpower and Housing Survey that took place in 1976. Two years later, a Demographic Survey for Addis Ababa, a Manpower and Housing Survey for Seventeen Major Towns and a Population Sample Survey for Asmara were carried out.

Although there is still great room for improvement, the country has shown significant progress in the field of data collection since 1980. As part of a rural integrated household survey programme, a Rural Demographic Survey, Rural Labour Force and Rural Health and Rural Nutrition Survey were carried out between 1981 and 1983. Since these surveys covered only rural areas, data generated by them are of limited direct application to urban studies. However, in the absence of a census, the 1978 Survey of the Population and Housing Characteristics of 17 Towns is one good source of migration data, although for some unknown reason, information on a very important town, Nazareth, is missing.

A characteristic of the available data on urbanization in Ethiopia is that they are limited in coverage and suffer from inconsistency and incomparability. Since no strict criteria were followed, definitions employed on what is 'urban' and methods adopted to collect data varied temporarily. Even between various agencies and ministries there appears little unanimity on what 'urban' constitutes. During the First Round Survey an urban centre was defined largely on the basis of administrative functions; in the Second Round an attempt was made to be more comprehensive by including service and market functions. With the introduction of a minimum size criterion of 2,000 inhabitants in the 1971 survey, though still far from being satisfactory, certain inconsistencies and confusions which existed in previous surveys were partly eliminated.

The National Population and Housing Census of 1984, although it covers only 85% of the population, presents a milestone by providing comprehensive socio-economic and demographic data for the entire country. Although not all the variables included in the census about 35 in all are yet to be made available one can now form a more reliable demographic picture of the country by putting together the most recent information with the ten surveys and partial censuses undertaken since 1960.

Characteristics of the Population

Population Size and Growth

Given the disparate nature of the various sources, it is a daunting task to estimate with any degree of accuracy the past size and growth pattern of the Ethiopian population. Basing on the different population estimates for the period 1956-84, Tesfa-Yesus (1990:110) calculated the implied growth rates to range between 2.2 and 4.8% per annum for the period 1957-84 and 1981-84 respectively. Two important observations can be made regarding these estimates and the growth rates they imply. First, the implied growth rates for both the first round National Sample Survey (1967-84, 3.6%) and the second round (1970-84, 4%) are unbelievably high compared to the rate from the recent census. This indicates that the sample surveys suffer from a large under-count. Secondly, despite the widely differing population basis used, on the whole, the results from the various estimates clearly indicate an increasing rate of growth.

According to the 1984 Population and Housing Census, the population of Ethiopia stood at 42,185,000, a result based on about 85% enumeration and 15% estimation. The census report indicates that the population was increasing yearly at the rate of 2.97%. In order to understand the growth pattern of the population, an attempt was made by the CSA to reconstruct the data and, using the 1984 census result as a base, a reverse population projection was made to go back to 1900. While annual population growth rates for 1950-85 have been reconstructed on the basis of more robust data, those for 1900-50 were highly hypothetical and speculative. Table 2 shows the reconstructed annual rates of growth, estimates of population size and the expected doubling time of the population.

It is assumed that the population was growing at less than one per cent per annum between 1900 and 1920, and 30 years later in 1950, it reached two per cent. After 1950, the population was growing at an average of 2.2% annually during 1950-70 and 2.7% during 1970-84. The growth of the Ethiopian population has quickened tremendously and has more than quadrupled since 1900 and almost tripled since 1950. The years before the 1940s were characterized by a notable increase, but its pace was negligible compared to growth since the middle of the 1970s. If the 1980-84 growth rate continues, there will be more than 65 million people by the end of this century, rocketing to more than 250 million within 50 years from now (CSA 1988:25). Since the growth rate itself continues to rise without showing any sign of reaching a plateau in the near future, these figures may in the end be rendered too conservative.

Table 2: Population, Reconstructed Annual Growth Rates and Expected Doubling Time

Year	Population	Growth rate %	Population doubling time
1950	19,182.0	2.0	35
1955	21,197.1	2.1	33
1960	25,550.0	2.2	32
1965	26,281.8	2.3	30
1970	29,488.2	2.3	30
1975	33,058.8	2.6	27
1980	37,684.7	2.8	25
1984	42,185.0	3.0	24
1990	50,973.9	3.5	20

Source: Based on CSA, 1988.

Age-sex Structure
Age and sex are important attributes useful to the appraisal of the present and future situation of a given population. It is an important source of information for the estimation of parameters such as the dependency burden, labour supply, reproduction potential, food supply and social services needed. Since the reported age data from the earlier sources were either incomplete or altogether unreliable, the CSA blended the results of the 1980-81 rural demographic and the 1978 Urban Manpower and Housing Surveys with those of the 1984 census to project the 1985 age-sex structure. This forms the basis for the age-sex structure of the national and regional populations subsequently projected on a yearly basis for a period of 10 years.

According to the age-sex structure presented in Table 3, in 1988 almost 47% of the population were under 15 years of age whereas 45% were between 15 and 54. Those 55 years old and above account for about 9%. This gives a very high dependency burden of 124%, which means that every 100 active persons will have to support or provide for 124 individuals in addition to themselves. By contrast, the aging index (10.6) is low, indicating a young population with a low average life expectancy.

The reported sex ratios for the different age-groups are very irregular, ranging from 80 to 136 for the 25-29 and 70-74 age groups respectively. Over-enumeration of males, under-counting of females, misreporting of ages, irregular sexual mortality and other aberrant behaviour could be attributed to this disproportionate sex ratio. The available evidence suggests that the aggregate estimated sex-ratio appears to have declined over the years. It stood at 102.8 in 1967, 99.5 in 1984 and 98.8 in 1988 (CSO 1970, 1974a; OPHCC 1987; CSA 1988b). The sex-ratios for most urban centres have consistently exceeded those of the rural areas primarily because female selectivity among most urban migrants has been quite a consistent feature of Ethiopian urbanization over the last three decades (Alula Abate 1985:257).

The age-sex distribution reveals a structure which is typical of developing countries. The population pyramid of Ethiopia shows the characteristic broad base resulting from high birth rates associated with a declining death rate. It is also far more squat than those for developed countries because the proportion of the population attaining 65 years and over is very small, containing only slightly more than 4%. This population shape, together with limited or no birth control, positive attitudes towards large family size and early marriage, creates a situation of high reproductive potential and increasing growth rate for some time to come.

Fertility: Levels and Trends

Until recently, the only sources available for the estimation of fertility levels and trends in the country were the two National Sample Surveys (First Round 1964-67 and Second Round 1968-71), the 1981 Demographic Survey and the surveys of major towns conducted since 1960. Lately an increasing number of studies on fertility have become available, although most of them do not cover the whole population. They either deal with an aspect of fertility of the rural population (Abate Mamo and Morgan 1986), compare and contrast fertility levels between selected administrative regions (Kebede 1986; Genet Mengistu 1987; Alemtsehay 1988; Assefa 1991), estimate fertility levels in selected famine-affected regions (Asmerom Kidane and Assefa 1988), or study patterns of fertility in Addis Ababa (Van Kesteren 1989; Van Kesteren and Markos Ezra 1989; Alemseghed Gebre 1989 and Groenewold, Swanhilde and Araya Demissie 1989). However, there are a few exceptions that have attempted a study of fertility on a more or less country-wide basis (Abdulahi 1979 and CSO 1984).

Since the margin of error for the National Sample Survey round one (1967) is wide, only figures for 1970 and 1981 will be considered here. Table 4 shows the crude birth rate (CBR) and total fertility rate (TFR) for 1970 and 1981. The CBR is easy to compute and understand, but it can be a deceptive measure where births are incompletely recorded. The TFR is also subject to the same kind of inaccuracies and uncertainties. With this caveat in mind, we shall now compare the figures for 1970 and 1981. For 1970, there are hardly any differences between rural and urban areas in terms of CBR and TFR. However, significant differences are observed in 1981. There is an increase of 22.5% in the CBR and 24.2% in the TFR. Both the CBR and TFR totals increased between 1970 and 1981, while an 8.3% decline is recorded for urban areas during the same period. The general tendency for fertility levels measured by CBR, TFR, CWR and GRR has been consistently higher in rural areas and, with the exception of Addis Ababa, steadily increasing in rural as well as urban areas between 1964 and 1981 (CSO 1984:8, 1985b:7).

Table 3: Estimated Age-sex Composition of Population, Ethiopia:1988

Age	Male %	Female %	Both estimated %	ASSR
0-4	17.63	17.81	17.72	98.84
5-9	16.32	16.08	16.20	101.27
10-14	13.06	12.15	12.61	107.36
15-19	9.36	8.76	9.06	106.58
20-24	6.88	7.54	7.21	91.05
25-29	5.76	7.19	6.48	80.08
30-34	5.39	6.36	5.88	84.66
35-39	4.96	5.46	5.21	90.79
45-49	3.64	3.58	3.61	101.69
50-54	3.04	2.82	2.93	107.86
55-59	2.54	2.20	2.37	115.61
60-64	2.18	1.81	1.99	120.70
65-69	1.63	0.89	1.06	136.40
70-74	1.21	0.89	1.06	136.40
75-79	0.81	0.61	0.80	133.08
80+	1.31	0.86	0.99	131.20
Total	100	100	100	98.81

Source: Computed from OPHCC, 1985:170.

Table 4: Fertility levels in Ethiopia: 1970 and 1981

Locality	Crude birth rate 1970	1981	Total fertility 1970	1981
Rural	42.8	48.5	5.8	7.7
Urban	42.9	39.6	5.7	6.2
Total	42.8	47.6	5.8	7.5

Source: CSO, 1974 and 1985.

Recent studies conducted in a few administrative regions indicate marked differences in level of fertility. For the period 1968-71, the reported total fertility rates ranged from 3.3 (Illubabor) to 6.2 (Gamo Gofa and Harerge) and in 1981 it ranged from 6.0 (Shewa) to 9.4 (Bale) (Hadgu 1978: 68 and CSO 1986). The considerable variation in total fertility rates between the two periods is largely attributed to improvements in quality of data rather than changes in actual levels of fertility. A comparative study of fertility using both Brass and Coale and Trussel methods between Gonder and Harerge shows that while their reported total fertility rates are different (higher for Harerge), the adjusted total fertility rates are similar for both regions (8.0) (Genet 1987:70). In the case of Illubabor and Wello, Alemtsehay (1988:28) reports an identical situation where adjusted fertility rates were of similar levels for both regions. However, both studies report statistically significant differences in average parity between these two pairs of regions. Furthermore, there are strong indications that differences in levels of fertility in rural Ethiopia are mainly influenced by ethnicity, religion, literacy and marital status (Seleshi 1986; Genet 1987 and Alemtsehay 1988).

Mortality: Levels and Trends

Mortality levels can be measured by various indices, depending on the purpose and type of study. We shall use only the crude death rate(CDR) and infant mortality rate (IMR) as shown in Table 5. As can be inferred from the figures given in this table, mortality measured by the CDR and the IMR, though still very high, has been declining in the period under consideration. Although the data from the 1967 sample survey are unreliable, there are strong indications that, due to improvements in health services, a perceptible declining trend started in the 1960s. In the period 1970-81 the level of mortality was consistently higher in rural areas than in urban areas. The difference in CDR in 1970, between rural and urban areas, was 20.1%, and this figure subsequently went down to 17.5% in 1981. However, during the same period rural areas registered a higher rate of decline (12.2%) than urban areas (9.7%).

Table 5: Mortality Rates for Ethiopia: 1970 and 1981

Locality	Crude Death Rate 1970	1981	Infant Mortality Rate 1970	1981
Rural	20.3	18.1	155	141
Urban	16.9	15.4	134	117
Total	20	17.9	153	139

Source: CSO, 1974 and 1975

Compared to the CDR, the IMR is a far more revealing measure of the level of mortality in a population. Not only did rural infants have a higher incidence of mortality in 1970 than urban infants (higher by 15.7%), the gap further widened (20.5%), so that relatively, infants born in rural areas were exposed to greater risks than was the case in urban areas.

A pattern of variation similar to that of fertility applies to the estimated national level of infant and child mortality and the crude death rate. In 1980-81 seven administrative regions had a CDR greater than the average and ranged from 15.4 in Wellega to 22.5 in Bale (CSO 1984:15). On the basis of the 1978 Ministry of Health data the United Nations Fund for Population Activities (UNFPA) also reported a high child mortality of 247 per thousand children under the age of five (UN 1980:8, 50). All available sources suggest that in rural Ethiopia, mortality is relatively heavy during infancy and early childhood, so that at present about one-half of all deaths in the country is made up of children under the age of five.

Mortality in the country decreased by almost 12 percentage points in only ten years, namely from 20 per thousand population in 1970 to 17.9 per thousand population in 1981. These changes can be attributed largely to successes in reducing infant and child mortality. These decreases have resulted in an increased life expectancy at birth and will continue to do so in the future as further reductions in mortality levels are expected. A consistent downward trend in mortality rates since the 1960s and fertility that has maintained not only a sustained high level but has also experienced increases have combined to ensure rapid population growth in the country.

Within the space of less than two decades the country suffered at least two major catastrophic famines and large parts have witnessed protracted and devastating insurgencies. To what extent these cataclysmic events have influenced Ethiopia's demography, in particular in slowing down the growth rate, will have to await a comprehensive study and analysis. However, a recent study of the 1984-85 famine refugees indicates an exceptionally high death rate and a drop of 26% in the total fertility rate among this group between 1981 and 1985 (Asmerom Kidane, 1989:518, 521).

The crude rate of natural increase went up in rural Ethiopia, from 2.25% in 1970 to 3.04% in 1981, whereas in urban areas it declined from 2.6% to 2.4% during the same period (Table 6). The CSA has projected the population of the country under different fertility level assumptions over a 50-year period beginning in 1985 (CSA 1988b). Even if one is to assume a rapid decline in fertility, (say a drop of 60%) a situation which is highly unlikely the population would still increase to 165 million by the year 2035. However, the current age structure of the population, which has a high inbuilt potential for rapid population growth, will lead to a greater population size than is suggested here (CSA 1988b:10).

Table 6: Crude Rate of Natural Increase 1970 and 1981

Locality	1970	1981
Rural	2.25	3.04
Urban	2.60	2.41
Total	2.28	2.97

Source: Computed from Tables 4 and 5.

Population Distribution

Patterns of Population Distribution

A cursory look at a population map of Ethiopia will show that people are not evenly distributed throughout the nation. There are disparities between administrative regions, *awraja* and *wereda*, the North and the South, the highlands and the lowlands, *enset*, coffee and cereal-growing regions, town and country. Variation in population size and uneven distribution are the most common features.

It is common practice to divide the country into attitudinal zones because economic activities, ways of living, temperature, rainfall and health etc., are closely tied up with the 'national divisions on a vertical plane'. The highlands of Ethiopia, mostly surrounded by hot and dry lands, provide excellent conditions for settlement, which is clearly reflected in the distribution of population. However, the use of diverse data bases, level of aggregation and the varied altitudes used to demarcate physiographic zones, have led to different estimates. Whatever data and unit of analysis used, one fact stands out clearly: the *Woina Dega*, together with the lower portion of the *Dega* zones sustains the bulk of the country's population.

Table 7 shows the vertical distribution of population in different attitudinal zones. Although it accounts for only about 31% of the total areas, a little over 67% of the population live between 1800-2600 metres, a zone which roughly corresponds to what is commonly referred to as the *Woina Dega* but also includes the lower part of the *Dega*. However, the maximum concentration is observed in the altitudes between 2,200 and 2,600 metres, where nearly 40% are crowded into only 12% of the land area. On the other hand, while two-thirds of the land lies below 1,800 metres, it only accounts for about one fifth of the population. Compared to the land located below 1,800 metres, the mountainous regions above 2,600 metres have roughly ten times less living space and yet support half the size of population found below 1,800 metres.

Table 7: Size of Attitudinal Zones, Population and Annual Mean Temperature

Altitude (metres)	Area (000 km²)	%	Population 1984 (millions)	%	Mean annual temperature	Average density persons per km²
Above 2,600	70.3	5.8	4,352162	10.4	<16	45,0
2,200 - 2,600	144.7	11.8	16,458509	39.2	16 - 18	78.0
1,800 - 2,200	237.9	19.4	11,717297	27.9	18.22	36.0
1,400 - 1,800	344.1	28.11	4,858919	11.5	22 - 24	12.5
1,000 - 1,400	163.4	13.4	3,452498	8.2	24 - 26	16.4
Below 1000	263.1	21.5	1,180023	2.8	26	4.0
Total	1223.5	100.0	42,019418	100.0	-	34.3

Source: Based on Aynalem Adugna, 1984:63, 64.

Of some 42 million people in 1984, by far the largest number were found in Shewa administrative region. Table 8 indicates that over 9 million, or about 23% of the country's population were concentrated here, whereas nearly the same number of people were distributed in seven administrative regions, i.e. Arsi, Bale, Gamo Gofa, Illubabor, Keffa, Tigray and Asseb. Harerge with nearly 10% and Illubabor (i.e. if we leave out Asseb as a unique case) with a little over 2% of the total, make up respectively the second most and the least populous regions. Out of the 15 regions, the populations in 11 regions ranged between 1 and 4.2 million, and of the remaining, three had less and one had more than this range.

More than the absolute size, the population density exhibits greater spatial variation as the unit of analysis descends the administrative hierarchy from the region down to the *wereda* level. But on the whole, the range in the size and density of population increases and becomes greatest at the *wereda* level.

The crude density for Ethiopia in 1984 was about 34 persons per square kilometre of land. At the regional level, the highest human-land ratio was recorded for Shewa (118.8 persons/km²) and the lowest for Bale (7.9 persons/km²), i.e., discounting Asseb as being not a fully-fledged administrative region (Table 8). Close to 53% of the *awrajas* had over 50 persons per square kilometre, and of these about 65% fell within the range of 50-100 persons per square kilometre, and only slightly more than 3% registered more than 200 persons per square kilometre.

These ratios are convenient in terms of ease of reference but their informative value is limited in a large country such as Ethiopia, whose land mass is vast and which has marked environmental differentiation. An altogether different picture, which can be more revealing, would emerge if one were to relate the rural population to the size of cultivated land. It is difficult to get reliable data on the amount of cultivated land in the country. Estimates of the land area under cultivation vary between 10% in the 1960s and 14.8% of the country in the 1980s (World Bank 1970:3; Nelson and Kaplan 1981:147, PMGSE 1984:34-38 and MOA 1984:vol. 1-32).

In 1983-84, the Ministry of Agriculture carried out a wide-ranging survey in the country to provide information on the agricultural sector and the population whose livelihood depends on it (MOA 1984). Given the general under-reporting of land holding by peasants and the problem of converting local land measurement units into metric equivalents, it is quite a risky exercise to calculate agricultural density. Agricultural densities calculated for the administrative regions are given in Table 8 and ratios for the *wereda* are given below. However, these figures can be taken at best as being in the order of magnitude.

At the *wereda* level, agricultural densities range between 74 persons per square kilometre in Debark (Semien *Awraja*) and 3459 persons per square kilometre in Offa (Welayta *Awraja*). Most of the *wereda*s with very high agricultural densities are found in Welayta, Sidama and Jemjem *Awrajas* (located in Northern Sidamo), but a few other densely settled areas are also situated in Kembata and Hadiya, Chebo and Gurage *Awraja* (in Shewa) and Genale *Awraja* (in Bale). A striking feature of these *wereda*s is that they are all predominantly enset growing areas.

A committee recently formed by the Council of Ministers to study the problem of land fragmentation and consolidation indicated that there are about 3.4 peasants per hectare, or about 344 persons per square kilometre and that about 22.5% of the population live below 1,500 metres altitude, of which less than half can be considered as pure nomadic herders (PDRE Council of Ministers 1982:72-73). If this population group were to be excluded, then the average agricultural density for the whole country would go down to about 288 persons per square kilometre.

Although the proportion of the population living in urban areas is comparatively still small, it shows a steady growth in absolute terms. In 1970 about one-tenth of the total population was estimated to live in urban areas. This proportion increased to 10.9% in 1970 and 11.3% in 1984. In general, an urbanization rate of 1.7% for the period 1967-1984 implies a slow rate of change in the degree of urbanization (Alula Abate 1989:621).

Table 8: Population, Area and Density by Administrative Region: 1988

Administrative Region	Area km²	%	Population	%	Crude density	Agricul. density[1]
Arsi	23,675	1.9	1,662,232	3.9	70.2	308
Asseb	27,465	2.2	89,299	0.2	3.3	-
Bale	127,053	10.2	1,006,490	2.4	7.9	744
Eritrea	93,679	7.5	2,614,699	6.2	27.9	N.A.
Gamo Gofa	40,348	3.2	1,248,033	3.0	30.9	792
Gojam	61,224	4.9	3,244,881	7.7	53.0	324
Gonder	79,565	6.3	2,921,124	6.9	36.7	441
Harerge	272,637	21.8	4,161,167	9.9	15.3	1,102
Illubabor	46,367	3.7	963,954	2.3	20.8	572
Keffa	56,634	4.3	2,450,368	5.8	43.3	733
Shewa	85,094	6.8	9,503.140	22.5	111.7	407
(without	84,854	-	8,090,563	19,0	95,3	346
Sidamo	119,760	9.6	3,790,578	9.0	31.7	883
Tigrai	64,921	5.2	2,409,699	5.7	37.1	N.A.
Wellega	70,481	5.6	2,477,276	5.9	35.1	425
Wello	82,144	6.6	3,642,013	8.6	44.3	412
Total	251,282	100.0	42,184,952	100.0	33.7	

Source: Central Statistical Office, *Census Supplement 1*, Dec. 1985, Central Statistical Office, *Statistical Abstract*, 1984.

Note: 1) Agricultural density is *Agricultural Population* per km² of cultivated land.

Striking spatial variations exist among the regions of the country in terms of both the proportion of population living in urban places and number of urban centres. The relative share of the administrative regions in the overall urban population in the country ranged between 1.2% in Illubabor and 46.8% in Shewa in 1984. Shewa and Eritria accounted for 64.4% of the country's urban population, but this proportion declined to 56.2% in 1984 (Alula Abate 1989:633). On the other hand, six regions together accounted for only 11.9% of the total urban population in 1984.

Wide variations are also observed in the distribution of urban centres and their relative growth. In 1984, Shewa with 20.2% of the urban places in the country stood first, followed by Sidamo (10.1%), Tigrai (9.09%) and Harerge (8.4%). The percentage share of urban centres in Eritrea, Gamo Gofa, Shewa and Harerge declined between 1967 and 1984, whereas Gojam, Gonder, Wellega and Keffa registered increases between 1.2 and 1.7% (Alula Abate

1989:636). Out of the 12 towns with 50,000 or more inhabitants, five were in the north, four in the central, two in the eastern and one in the southern parts of the country. Altitudinal variation in the distribution of towns is manifested by the fact that about 95% of the towns are located in the highlands, in the *Woina Dega* and *Dega* zones i.e., above 1,500 metres (Abdurahman 1987:25 and Galperin 1981:78).

Factors Affecting Population Distribution
Although the factors that affect population distribution in Ethiopia are many, encompassing a wide range of physical, socio-economic, political, cultural and technological factors, the influence of a good number of them are not known with any degree of certainty. The interrelationships between the population on the one hand and the natural and human environments on the other are neither simple nor static; they are modified whenever there are changes in the population or in any one variable or a combination of the physical and socio-cultural variables.

More than anything else, the distribution of population in Ethiopia is a function of two variables: altitude and nature of the terrain. These factors control climate, i.e. rainfall and temperature, and these in turn strongly influence population distribution. The Ethiopian highlands are mostly open plateaux with good soils, warm to cool temperatures and sufficient precipitation for agriculture. Accordingly, high population size and densities are found in the highlands, in the *Woina Dega* and lower *Dega* zones.

Because the highlands are much more convenient to live in than the lowlands, except the Somali, the Afar, the Nilotic and the Omotic groups on the western and south-west borderlands, the majority of the other ethnic groups, speaking over 70 languages, inhabit the highlands. The early development of mixed farming, which depended on the plough, became the predominant base of economic activity so that, today, in the sedentary agricultural areas a direct correlation between size of cultivated land and size of population is observed. A correlation of these two variables computed for 383 *weredas* gave a high positive correlation co-efficient ($r = 0.75$) (Aynalem Adugna 1987:37). It is clear that in rural Ethiopia population increases as the size of the cultivated land increases and that the intensity of agriculture significantly determines population density, as the *enset*-growing areas strongly indicate. As the demand for food increases with growing population and a concurrent degradation of the land, more and more people are being forced to live above and below the attitudinal optimum belt of habitation. In more recent times industrialization and modern economic development have attracted migratory flows from rural hinterlands to agro-industrial zones, development corridors and growing urban centres.

The rugged topography served as an impregnable fortress and place of refuge for the development of a highland-based civilization with important historic centres which at one time or another became seats of kingdoms and dynasties. The fact that most of the urban centres, much of the communication, transport and other modern facilities are located in the highlands can also be explained in terms of the past.

Population Mobility

Migration Studies in Ethiopia

The very few migration studies that have been undertaken so far, are mostly general in scope and limited in their data-base. Several studies (Bondestam 1972; McCann 1987, 1988; CSA 1991) identify in a general manner the historical movement of population from north to south, highlands to lowlands over short and long distances and migration from areas of relatively fast agricultural development where population density is moderate or big, to unknown destinations. Other works (Ponsi 1982; Kloos and Aynalem Adugna 1989) assess the level and pattern of migration at the national level, using the little available data. The aim is to find the degree of population concentration and indicate the regions which experience net gains and losses of population through migration.

Another group attempted to study migration to specific areas, regions or urban centres (Prost-Toiurnier 1974; Alula Abate 1972; Palen 1975; Bjeren 1984; Kloos 1982; Bekure W/Semait 1984; Beyene Dolicho 1985; Wood 1983; Hadgu Bariagaber and Asmerom Kidane 1985; Arkebe Asgedom 1985; Baker 1986; Almaz Amine 1990). Some of these studies deal with labour migrations to the Awash Valley and coffee-growing areas in terms of aggregate flow patterns, ethnic groups involved, some demographic characteristics and regions of out-migration. However, only one of these studies (Beyene 1985) attempts to lock into the spatial and temporal patterns and assess some of the causes and consequences of the migration with reference to the labour supply areas.

Studies of migration to specific towns and their regions are limited to Addis Ababa, Nazareth and a few other small and medium-sized towns in the Harerge and Gonder highlands and Shashemene in the south. Most of the studies in this group try to identify the people who migrate, particularly with respect to industrial labour (Bekure 1984), and analyze the factors that motivate them to move. (Arkebe 1985; Kebede Mammo 1991). Works on the smaller towns are concerned with the growth of these centres and the origin of the migrants (Mullenbach 1976).

Spontaneous Rural-rural Migration

The available historical evidence strongly suggests that there were large inter-regional movements of people from the areas of relatively dense population and low economic opportunity to areas of less density and greater opportunity. Although there are no comprehensive data or historical studies for all regions, the general direction of population movement resulted in a net movement of permanent migrants from the northern regions to the south. For the earlier historical period, information on demographic variation across the highlands and over time is primarily qualitative in nature. It is clear that people had been distributing themselves, temporarily and permanently, voluntarily and under pressure. Mobility included pioneer colonization of uninhabited areas and the redistribution of population between inhabited areas. There were also movements upslope, which pushed the upper limit of cultivation to the frost line, and downslope into lowlands and the edge of the lowlands which had been primarily pastoral grazing areas.

The major causes of out-migration from the northern highlands frequently cited are push factors, among which exponential population growth stands out prominently. Population growth in and of itself would not necessarily have led to major population moves. It is the conjuncture between increasing population, finite amount of agricultural land, long adaptive delays in technology and inherent instability which suppressed both gross product and per capita production and thus led to both localized and long-range migration and the expansion of cultivation. The interplay between demographic expansion and limited resources led, according to McCann (1988:2), to 'a cycle of progressive squeezing of production capacity of the agrarian economy in a north-to-south and east-to-west pattern'.

Recent studies suggest the existence of strong elements of continuity in mobility patterns from the past to the present (Wood 1982:160; CAS 1991). Following mobility patterns of the past, much population redistribution has continued in all administrative regions resulting from the close links between population growth, migration and declining productivity (Almaz Amine 1990). Much of population redistribution has been taking place within already settled regions, but there is also a trend to move into less productive and more risky lowland areas. It is difficult to determine the volume of mobility from the northern, central and eastern highlands prior to the post-war years, but in the period 1950-74 it is conservatively estimated that the newly settled areas increased land under cultivation by about 25% and more than one million people were involved in the move (Wood 1982:157).

Rural-to-rural mobility is dominated by subsistence farmers, but with the growth of commercial farming since the mid-1960s, circulating migration became increasingly important (Kloos 1982; Beyene Dolicho 1985). Redistribution of the highland population occurred mostly through the movement over relatively short distances, but in cases when serious natural calamities struck, or when information regarding a particularly attractive farming area was available, some longer distance movement was undertaken.

Three types of land which are chosen by peasants to settle and cultivate or to provide seasonal labour have been identified (Wood 1988:160). One type of land of colonization which probably received the greatest numbers of settlers and represents a continuation of a long-term historical process, is found along the eastern escarpment of the northern and central highlands. Similarly, downslope movement had been taking place along the southern edges of the northern highlands (the rift valley) and the southern highlands (the Ogaden) and to the west to the Setit Humera lowlands. These areas have traditionally been used by pastoralists as grazing lands.

The second type of lands which attracted immigrants were the little used grasslands and woodlands along the western edge of the northern highlands and major gorges and river valleys found within the highlands. For a long time these areas were avoided by settlers because they are drought-prone, infested with malaria and human and animal trypanosomiasis and generally of low agricultural potential.

Until the recent government-sponsored resettlement drive for famine victims from drought-affected areas of the northern regions, the forested areas of the south-western part of the northern highlands received the lowest number of settlers. Following the devastating drought/famine of 1984-85, the government decided to move about 0.5 million people from Tigray, Wello, northern Shewa and Kembata and Hadiya and settle them in this region. Within the northern and, to a lesser extent, eastern highlands upslope, there has been a long-standing movement and most of the Ethiopian highlands have been cleared for cultivation.

The type of movement which has attracted greater attention is the circulatory movement of labour associated with the coffee-producing areas of south-west Ethiopia and the emergent mechanized commercial agriculture. The flow of seasonal migrants to the coffee regions was estimated for the early 1970s at over 50,000, which increased the size of the local population by between 5 and 10% (Wood 1983:55). These temporary labourers, who mostly came from as far away as Gonder, Gojam and Wello, followed a pattern that was established by historic links and information flow. The movement also included itinerant traders and bar girls who made a living during the coffee harvest season. The Land Proclamation of 1975, which nationalized all rural lands, forbade the hiring of labourers by individual farmers and this brought to an abrupt end the possibility for many peasants to supplement their otherwise insufficient farm income.

The most important areas of commercial agriculture to which both labourers and peasant farmers flocked were the Awash Valley, the Rift Valley south of the Awash river, the Setit-Humera lowlands in north-western Ethiopia and the plains of Jijiga. Although these commercial farms produced mostly cash crops destined for export and raw materials for local industries, farmers and labourers engaged in this sector were fewer in number and land brought under cultivation was probably less than 25% of the area which subsistence farmers colonized.

Farm labour (both permanent and seasonal) engaged in 16 irrigation schemes in the Awash Valley in 1976 totalled about 150,000, of which 100,000 were alien migrants from the overcrowded highlands (Kloos 182: 139). The labourers were mostly from the small densely settled areas of Kembata, Hadiya, Wolaita, northern Shewa, Wello and Tigray. No data are available regarding the number of settled farmers and seasonal labourers engaged in such areas as Setit-Humera, Abderafi, Gode, Jijiga and the Lakes region of the Rift Valley but, taken together, their numbers would certainly be more than those in the Awash Valley. Before the 1940s northern Ethiopians were also able to participate in wage labour in the colonial economies of Eritrea and the Sudan, both in agriculture and construction. There were also large numbers of migrants who were engaged in trade and services in towns and others who served as soldiers in the Italian army in Eritrea and Libya (McCann 1987:187-189). Since 1974, as a result of the internal strife, large numbers of people, mostly from the north and variously estimated at between 300,000 and 500,000, have fled the country and taken refuge in Sudan alone.

Planned Rural-rural Mobility
Relatively little planned resettlement was carried out before the revolution, because the government was largely committed to using, for estate agriculture and political purposes, land under its jurisdiction which it distributed as grant to regime supporters. In spite of this, some relocation of population was achieved through the creation of more than 6,500 new farm units under 21 schemes (Wood 1985:87, 92). In contrast to the rural population that undertook resettlement spontaneously, the planned resettlement schemes involved not more than 0.2% of the rural households at that time (Wood 1985:87, 92). By the late 1960s a number of reports commissioned by the Ministry of Land Reform recommended that planned and spontaneous resettlement schemes should be used as a development

measure for reducing poverty, increasing agricultural production and rehabilitating and protecting the country's natural resources. Through this Ministry tentative steps were taken in 1972 towards the development of a policy on population redistribution. Although there was no concrete plan of implementation, the suggestion was to move some 700,000 households from the overcrowded and eroded highlands to the under-utilized lower altitude areas and to create resettlement opportunities for the annual increment of new households (Wood 1985:94).

The implementation of this bold plan was impeded by several factors, some of the biggest obstacles being the land tenure system and the high costs involved (Eshetu and Teshome 1988:178). Since the revolution, the pace of resettlement has accelerated so that in the first decade alone it increased six-fold. The nationalization of rural land, the need to find a lasting solution to the recurrent famines that affected large sections of the population and the delegation of authority to the RRC, are all aspects of resettlement that helped to facilitate the implementation of the programme. It thus became possible to resettle about 46,000 families comprising 142,000 people by 1984 (Pankhurst 1988:15).

Following the second devastating famine to hit the country within a decade, a new phase of resettlement programmes was started in 1984 (Dessalegn Rahmato 1989). In eighteen months the Workers Party of Ethiopia moved about 600,000 settlers from Wello, Shewa, and Tigray to mainly Wellega, Illubabor, Gojam and Kefa. Once the emergency and the crisis abated, the government created a new settlement authority with expanded duties and powers to complete the task of resettling the original target of 1.5 million people.

Urbanward Migration

There were two types of movement of people to Ethiopia's urban centres: rural-urban and urban-urban. Information based on the 1984 census, recently released by the CSA (1991) on both types of migration streams, was aggregated with other forms of mobility so that its analytical usefulness is limited. Only after changes in the administration and political structure took place in the late Nineteenth and early Twentieth Centuries and after the Italian occupation in the 1930s, did one witness a period of rapid urban development and diffusion (Alula 1985). Table 9 shows the share of migrant population out of the total population of selected urban centres in 1967 and 1978.

Table 9 shows that in 1967, in eight centres out of 13 towns, migrants constituted a larger proportion of the population. By 1978, this number had increased to ten. In urban centres like Addis Ababa, Jima, Bahir Dar, Akaki (there was a considerable decline in the proportion of migrants), in Nekemte and Debre Zeit the proportion of the migrant population declined in 1978, while in Desse, Asssela, Debre Birhan, Harar, Gonder, Mekele and Dire Dawa, it increased during the same period.

Although these figures do not indicate whether or not these migrants came directly from rural areas, it is clear that changes in the direction of mobility have been taking place in Ethiopia in recent years. There is no hard evidence as to why such changes took place. One possible reason could be that the opportunities that were imagined to exist in the attraction points of the 1960s, such as Addis Ababa and Akaki, were no longer strong enough to attract distant migrants. The introduction of a pass system, which helped to control movement and residence and housing shortages in the regional centres may be cited as the major causes of these changes (especially as a result of the expansion of bureaucracy).

Except for Addis Ababa, there is a preponderance of female migrants over male migrants for both 1967 and 1978. This proportion is significantly high for Bahir Dar, Desse, Gonder and Mekele. Addis Ababa had slightly more male migrants in 1967 but the situation was reversed in 1978.

With the exception of Addis Ababa, there are no data as to the origin of migrants destined to specific urban centres. The patchy information suggests that areas of considerable land pressure, such as southern Shewa, areas of environmental problems, (especially northern Ethiopia) and many of the southern regions, where tenancy had been dominant, were possible places of origin for rural-to-urban migrants.

There are strong indications that large numbers of urban migrants had lived in at least one other town before moving on to a larger town (Bjeren 1984). Circulatory or seasonal migration to towns is known to occur widely, but unfortunately, few studies have been done on this topic (Baker 1986; Shack 1966; Fekadu Gedamu 1966). Data on places of birth are given in Table 10 for selected towns to indicate the prevalence of step-wise-migration. While about 70% of the migrants were born in rural areas, the population of urban-born migrants who moved to these towns ranged between 10.2% in Bahir Dar to 50.5% in Dire Dawa. Urban centres such as Dire Dawa, Harar, Mettu, Nekemte and Jima had more than one-third of their migrant population coming from other urban centres, while in towns such as Bahir Dar, Debre Birhan, Akaki, Desse, Assela and Goba most of the migrants came directly from rural areas. In terms of birth place, there appears some degree of variation in the sex composition of the migrant population. Except in Bahir Dar, female migrants were mostly urban-born but in Mettu and Awassa migrants were mostly male and rural-born.

Table 9: Percentage Distribution of Urban Population Classified by Migrants and Non-migrants for Selected Urban Centres, 1967 and 1978

	1967						1978					
	Non-migrants			Migrants			Non-migrants			Migrants		
	Female	Male	Total	Female	Male	Total	Female	Male	Total	Female	Male	Total
Addis Ababa	21.1	23.2	44.3[a]	28.2	27.5	55.7	22.6	24.7	47.3[c]	24.8	27.9	52.7
Asmara	25.6	25.9	51.5[b]	20.6	27.9	48.5	-	-	-	-	-	-
Dire Dawa	23.0	26.1	49.1	24.6	26.3	50.9	23.8	24.1	47.9	23.2	28.9	52.1
Jima	23.1	26.8	49.9	24.6	25.5	50.1	25.8	26.3	52.1	22.8	25.1	47.9
Desse	23.9	27.5	51.4	19.4	29.2	48.6	23.1	22.3	45.4	22.0	32.6	54.6
Bahir Dar	13.4	15.6	29	27.8	43.2	71.0	20.7	18.9	36.6	24.1	36.3	60.4
Assela	17.4	24.0	44.1	24.3	24.5	58.8	17.2	18.4	35.6	31.0	33.4	64.4
Akaki1	12.5	14.4	26.9	35.0	38.1	73.1	19.1	21.8	40.9	26.5	32.6	59.1
Debre Berhan	19.3	24.6	43.9	21.2	34.9	56.1	20.4	21.6	42.0	22.4	35.6	58.0
Harar	27.5	32.3	59.8	18.4	21.8	40.2	27.2	28.9	56.1	18.4	25.5	43.9
Gonder	25.1	31.2	56.3	17.4	26.3	43.7	21.2	25.3	46.5	19.9	33.6	53.5
Mekele	26.5	32.4	58.9	15.6	25.5	41.1	21.0	23.0	44.0	22.6	33.4	56.0
Debre Zeit	16.5	20.3	36.8	26.5	36.7	63.2	22.1	22.7	44.8	25.0	31.1	56.1

Source: [a]The 1967 estimates are taken from the *Addis Ababa Population Sample Survey of October 1967*, CSO, July 1972, Statistical Bulletin No. 8.
[b]Figures for Asmara for 1968 are obtained from CSO, 1974, *Results of the 1968 Population and Housing Census, Population and Housing Characteristics of Asmara*
[c]The 1978 estimates for Addis Ababa are obtained from CSO, 1978, *Report on the Analysis of the Addis Ababa Demographic Survey*, Sept, 1978. CSO: Statistical Bulletin No. 27, 1980.

Net migration to urban areas increased in the 1960s to reach an annual rate of about 3.8% (assuming an annual rate of natural increase of 2.5%). Using length of residence criteria, in 1971 about half the population of towns of 20,000 and more were in-migrants (CSO 1975). But by 1984 net migration to towns slowed down to an average annual rate only slightly above 1%. An analysis of the growth rates of 33 of the largest towns in 1967-84 showed a wide variation in growth rates among individual urban centres (Kloos and Aynalem Adugna 1989:43).

Preliminary data on migration between administrative regions are now available, thanks to the 1984 census. The information on in, out and net migration is presented in Table 11. However, it should be noted that a completely different pattern would emerge if the actual figure of those dragooned to move and the regions of destinations were made public.

Table 10: Percentage of Population by Place of Birth for Selected Towns (1978)

	Urban-born			Rural-born		
	Male	Female	Total	Male	Female	Total
Addis Ababa	-	-	-	-	-	-
Bahir Dar	5.3	4.9	10.2	34.6	55.2	89.8
Debre Berhan	9.6	13.1	22.7	29.0	48.3	77.3
Debre Zeit	10.2	13.7	23.9	34.3	41.8	76.1
Nekemte	15.3	18.8	34.1	29.5	36.4	65.9
Mettu	18.6	23.5	42.1	30.5	27.4	47.9
Awassa	15.3	16.4	31.7	35.2	33.1	68.3
Goba	7.9	8.9	16.8	34.6	48.6	83.2
Assela	5.3	7.9	13.2	42.9	43.9	86.5
Gonder	10.4	13.2	23.6	26.9	49.5	76.4
Mekele	12.8	15.4	28.2	27.6	44.2	71.8
Desse		8.9	16.6	32.6	50.8	83.4
Akaki	8.4	10.1	18.5	36.5	45.0	81.5
Arbaminch	12.2	15.8	28.0	38.4	33.6	72.0
Harar	19.5	29.2	48.7	22.4	28.9	51.3

Source: CSO, *Statistical Bulletin 27*, 1980. AAMPP, 1985; CSO, *Report on the Analysis of the Addis Ababa Demographic Survey*, September 1978.

In 1984, of the seven administrative regions which showed negative net migration, i.e., more out than in-migration, four (Eritrea, Gonder, Wello and Tigray) were from the north. Six out of eight regions which experienced net in-migration were from the south and south-western Ethiopia. According to this data, the major direction of movement in 1984 was from the north to the south. The regions which registered net out-migration may be designated as 'over populated' and suffering from either long-term environmental degradation, repeated droughts or lack of security.

If Addis Ababa and Asseb were excluded, the rate of net migration ranged from -6.7% in Wello to 5.9% in Bale. The average turnover rate for 1984, i.e., the number of persons mobile for every 100 persons, was many times higher than the rate recorded a decade earlier. Unlike the other regions which provide data for the rural and urban populations, migration data for Addis Ababa and Asseb refer to only urban populations. The two towns are important centres of attraction for immigrants and therefore exhibit very high rates of net migration and turnover.

In the absence of comprehensive data, only the order of magnitude of urbanward migration can be assessed using information on degree of urbanization and rate of urban growth for 1938-84. Table 11 shows changes in the type of urbanization in Ethiopia between 1938 and 1984.

Table 11: In, Out and Netmigration, 1984

Region	In-migration	Out-migration	Net migration (%)	Rate of net migration (%)	Rate of turnover (%)
Arssi	142,647	0,834	61,813	3.7	13.4
Bale	83,684	37,840	45,844	5.9	15.16
Eritrea	50,662*	70,917	- 20,255	- 0.8	4.6
Gamo Gofa	27,654	40,714	- 13,060	- 1.0	5.4
Gojam	75,508	71,150	4,358	0.1	4.5
Gonder	35,544	98,720	- 63,176	- 3.2	6.8
Harerge	84,078	64,921	19,157	0.7	5.5
Illubabor	64,172	30,829	33,343	3.4	9.8
Keffa	94,207	44,116	- 5,091	2.0	5.6
Shewa	228,989	626,230	- 397,241	- 5.0	10.6
Sidamo	77,876	92,035	- 14,159	- 0.4	4.5
Tigray	14,426*	116,445	- 102,019	- 4.2	5.4
Wellega	74,150	57,213	16,937	0.7	5.3
Wello	28,107	234,185	- 206,078	0 - 6.7	8.5
Addis Ababa	643,366	72,196	571,170	40.1	50.3
Asseb	21,665	4,330	17,335	53.4	80.1

Source: CSA, 1990, Population and Housing Census, National Preliminary Analytical Report. In-migration refers to actually enumerated urban population.

During this nearly half a century period, the proportion of the population classified as urban increased significantly. From an estimated size of 657,100 in 1938, the urban population rose to 4,357,500 in 1984. Though the level of urbanization was still low, a steady growth was visible in the proportion of urban population (Figure 1). The percentage share of urban population was 5.4% in 1938 and 7.6% in 1967. In 1984, it increased to 10.3%. As the proportion of the urban population increased significantly between 1938-84 from 5.4% to 10.3%, it is now just beginning to attract attention from policy makers. Despite this increase, the present level of urbanization is still low, even by African standards. The Ethiopian society remains primarily agrarian, inadequately endowed with human and other resources essential to urban forms of life.

Net migration to urban areas seems to have reached its highest point in the 1960s, at about 3.8% (assuming an annual rate of natural increase of 2.5%). By 1984 it had slowed down to slightly more than 1%. There is no hard evidence as to why the rate of urbanward migration has noticeably declined in recent years. The results of the few available studies are not definitive but rather more suggestive. The general impression one gets is that net flow of migrants from the rural areas seems to have been fairly closely related to the country's level and rate of economic development. It is, therefore, no mere accident that average Gross Domestic Product and net urbanward migration have both shown a declining trend in the 1980s, averaging about 1 per cent per year.

Table 12: Urbanization in Ethiopia: Overall Changes (1938-84)

Year	Total population	Urban population	Urban per cent	No. of Urban localities
1938[1]	12,000,000	657,100	5.4	63
1967[2]	23,667,400	1,815,329	7.6	157
1975[3]	27,102,100	3,195,880	11.6	183
1984[4]	42,184,952	4,357,500	10.3	296

Source:
1) *Guida dell' Africa Orientale Italian*, Milano, 1938.
2) CSO, *Survey of Major towns in Ethiopia*, Statistical Bulletin No. 1, Addis Ababa, December 1968.
3) CSO, (Statistical Abstracts, 1976).
4) CSO, *Population and Housing Census Preliminary Report*, A.A., 1984.

Patterns, Trends and Processes of Urbanization

Pre-Twentieth Century Urbanization

To understand the patterns and processes of contemporary urbanization, it is essential to look into recent trends and determine to what extent they have affected the spatial, economic, social and political structure of major urban centres in Ethiopia. Prior to the Twentieth Century, the few cities that existed actually represented only transient episodes in the long and essentially rural history of the country. Much of the urban history of the country following the Axumite period was characterized by the absence of fixed urban centres resulting from the 'political nomadism' that prevailed. The tradition of 'roving' or 'wandering' political capitals prevailed in the country until Addis Ababa became the permanent seat of government 100 years ago (Akalom 1966; Horvath 1969). However, its incidence was considerably curtailed due to the weakened institution of the monarchy and the consequent rise of regional chiefs in the Nineteenth Century. In a way, the rise of regional chiefs helped to broaden the urban base because it led to the proliferation of regional capitals, though most of them were ephemeral and did not last beyond the life of the founders.

When the power and prestige of the monarchy was re-instituted in the second half of the Nineteenth Century, following the 'era of the princes', the sovereigns showed greater interest in using existing capitals as their initial bases of operation rather than creating new capitals. This condition brought about a totally different process of urbanization in the country. In earlier times Ethiopian towns were rarely formed by degrees, i.e., by the slow increment of both men and buildings. The process of urbanization, especially in the late Nineteenth Century, however, became a cumulative rather than periodically recurring phenomenon.

The Ethiopian royal or feudal military camps could be said to be the forerunners of postmedieval towns with regard to structure and form. They reflect the character of Ethiopia's court civilization and contained invariably the residence, court and administrative quarters of the king or local lord at their centres. A reception hall was erected for banquets, where the army and retainers were periodically fed and guests entertained, and nearby a church was built for religious services. Around these structures, which constituted the cores of the 'city', make-shift huts were quickly put up as dwelling units for the king's retainers and army. In the meantime, the king's military chiefs and their personal army established themselves in various parts of the city's site according to their ranks and respective positions and roles in times of combat (Akalom 1967; Alula Abate 1974).

Among a combination of physical, socio-cultural, economic and political factors that are widely acknowledged to have hampered urban development in Ethiopia, several aspects stand out prominently. Basic natural resources, such as firewood, were limited in quantity and once they were depleted they could not easily be replaced by alternative sources. Lack of engineering skills, together with the rugged topography of the land, had created obstacles to communication, hindered the exchange of goods and ideas, and generally impeded easy contact between people, thereby leading to isolation. Occupations such as the crafts, which could have triggered large-scale development of specialized skills and services, were either despised or simply ignored.

The appearance of cities presupposes the ability of rural and village communities to produce a surplus, which in turn would lead to division of labour and specialization. Successive innovations in agricultural production and in the ability to mobilize a surplus above rural subsistence were necessary prerequisites for the growth of urban settlements, a sizeable proportion of whose population were not producing foods. In pre-twentieth century Ethiopia the necessary preconditions which could have led to a permanent concentration of surplus resources and the urban transition were not met. It must be remembered that cities come into existence primarily through the mobilization, extraction and geographic concentration of significant quantities of surplus social resources.

The inefficient agricultural practices, which were often reflected in the inability of the system to raise surplus foodstuffs required by a large concentration of people who abandoned agriculture, were not conducive to the emergence of cities nor to their continued existence. The meagre appropriated surplus, rather than being invested in permanent 'forms', i.e., monuments of urban culture, largely remained dispersed and dissipated on wasteful feasts and banquets. This meant that the extracted surplus was not translated into the chain of events which led to the emergence of cities.

Furthermore, the prevalence of bloody internecine wars and general insecurity also contributed to the lack of widespread urbanization in pre-Twentieth Century Ethiopia. The urban centres that came into existence owed their origin, for the most part, to the integrative activity of the political and military power of the ruling elite, rather than to the influence of economic functions or religious activity. As a result, the chief locus of an Ethiopian urban centre was the palace and not the market or the churches (Akalom 1966). It is true that economic and religious functions often contributed to the growth of urban settlements but had not really been their cause. While there were numerous markets (some of them renowned) which on market days attracted up to 50,000 people, the majority, however, did not engender permanent forms of settlement because they were itinerant.

Early Twentieth Century Urbanization

It was only at the turn of the present century that the process of modern urbanization began to take shape in the country. This period constitutes a time of urban development and diffusion associated with important changes which occurred in administrative and political structures. It ushered in a period of stability which replaced the long period of fluid political conditions. Among the many factors which contributed to this new phase of urban development the most important were a) territorial expansion, b) the division of the country into small administrative units governed by nobles and military chiefs who were subject to the Emperor; c) centralization of bureaucracy under a ministerial system of government; d) transport and communication, which is so essential for a modern economy and urban growth, was greatly improved, i.e., construction of the Addis Ababa-Djibouti railway, introduction of motor cars, telephone and telegraph communications and postal service; e) the introduction of facilities such as banking, modern education and health facilities and f) the introduction of the exotic eucalyptus tree. These developments clearly stimulated the spread of the modern sector and greatly influenced the emergence of new urban centres and the expansion of old ones.

The rule of Menelik and Haile Selassie brought about certain fundamental changes. Innovations in the arts of warfare and administration permitted urban centres to exert a dominant influence over increasingly larger areas and developments in trade and manufactures, in time, enhanced urban pre-eminence. The domains of urban centres progressively expanded outwards from a number of spatially dispersed points and the extent of this expansion was limited only by the ability of the central authorities to maintain order in the occupied areas and the loyalty of the troops. Undoubtedly there had been territorial expansions at various points in the country's history, but these earlier attempts lacked the means of control and the organizational capacity for raising surplus resources to meet the large outlay which such efforts required. They were, and remained, mostly subject to periodic conquests and raids. However, the accumulation of raw materials and food required more than trading toeholds; it depended on the acquisition of territory.

Unlike the previous times, when campaigns were mounted, the objective was the defeat of opposing forces rather than the systematic devastation of settlement centres. The new centralized administration demanded territorial control through a permanent presence by establishing administrative and military centres to pacify the local populations and to ensure the orderly collection of surplus resources and their transfer to the central rulers.

The spread of garrisons and outposts was necessary not only for the maintenance of hegemony in newly acquired territories. They also played additional roles and served not only for defence and as staging areas for further military probes on the frontier, but also as markets. Slowly, other functional elements gravitated towards the garrisons either through a natural process or coercion, and in the end were spurred on by the introduction of modernization impulses. These centres gradually transformed themselves from military bases into urban establishments which were demographically small but quite diversified in function. In addition to the already established towns of Axum, Debre Berhan, Harar and Gondar, a number of centres appeared at end of the last century. Mekele, Asmara, Addis Ababa, Dessie, and Debre Markos were among the major towns that came into existence during this time. A large number of stations were also built along the railway line between Addis Ababa and Djibouti. These centres later grew into big multi-functional towns among which Dire Dawa, Nazareth, Debre Zeit and Akaki became prominent.

Contemporary Urbanization

The next phase in urban development, and perhaps the most significant, occurred during the Italian occupation, 1935-41 Whatever their size and complexity, urban centres in Ethiopia up to this time were essentially the result of internal economic, social and political processes. These centres were products of their societies and must therefore be viewed as one expression of a larger process of societal change. The political control exercised by the Italians introduced new forms of social and economic organization together with technological and cultural values. Italian corporate and national interests established outposts in the major centres to extract surplus resources in the form of primary products, to expand the market for Italian goods and services, and to ensure the continued subjugation of the country. Needless to say, these forms of penetration were ultimately intended to serve the single purpose of helping to maintain expanding levels of production and consumption in Italy.

During this time the process of urbanization was greatly accelerated so that, for the first time, people in Ethiopia experienced urbanization on a large scale. The country was influenced to a greater extent by the colonial intrusion than the brief occupation period might otherwise suggest. With amazing rapidity the Italians built a network of good roads and established regional administrative centres. In order to strengthen their hold on the country, they built a new type of economically-oriented urban system that superimposed rather than infused the alien elements into the traditional structure, which led to the development of dual urban systems. There are some centres where a strong pre-industrial urban tradition remains dominant and a few others built under Italian auspices in areas devoid of any previous urban experience (Mulatu 1980; Alula Abate 1985:246-247). Hotels, restaurants, bars, a variety of stores and workshops became common features of the new urban centres.

The development of transportation and communication systems and the construction of buildings and factories created workers who lived in urban areas. This in turn created a new economic class which lived by catering for the needs of the wage earners. Since the towns became the integrating nucleus of the colonial economic system, they generated an exodus of people from the rural to urban areas. This trend was supported by three interrelated factors. First, the guerilla war that continued after the collapse of the Ethiopian army and the retaliatory measures taken by the occupying forces made rural life difficult and insecure. Secondly, the war and the introduction of a new form of life led to the loosening of traditional family ties and consequently rural social structure became severely strained. Thirdly, the lure of town life and the ease and comfort imagined to exist in towns became an irresistible attraction to many. Countries at war or under occupation usually have a high proportion of males in urban centres. The attraction of many unattached women to such centres, which became inevitable at the time, has continued its momentum to the present day.

Another phase in the development of urban areas started with the end of the occupation in 1941. The period immediately after liberation was marked by an initial urban decline, brought about by destruction and dislocation during the brief war of liberation. It gathered momentum in the 1950s and 1960s and then continued at an accelerated pace. There was a great surge of rural people into the cities, attracted by the prospect of jobs in the lucrative and expanding administrative and commercial positions. The economic growth of the country's urban centres was spurred especially by capital investments extracted and transferred from rural areas and other cities within the national economy, and from net capital transfers from abroad, a trend already initiated by the Italians. The number of urban centres with a population of 2,000 and over was 157 in 1967, and increased to 297 in 1984. Of these, only four originated in the period long before the Eighteenth Century. Aksum dates as far back as 950 BC and was a prosperous city by the First Century AD. On the other hand, Debre Berhan was founded by Zera Yakob in 1454 and about a century later Harar became the capital of a Muslim Emirate. In the north, Fassiledus settled in Gondar in 1936.

Migration and Urbanization

Degree of Urbanization and Rate of Growth

Between 1938 and 1967 the number of urban centres increased from 63 to 297 in 1984. These figures suggest that the rate of entry of new towns into the Ethiopian urban system had been very fast and the trend appeared to be on the increase. Overall changes in the number of urban localities have been 371.4%.

In terms of the share of urban centres in the different size-class categories from the total numbers of urban centres, some notable changes, both positive and negative, have been recorded (Table 13). Apart from three size-classes, all the rest increased their percentage share, the most important being the 10,000-19,999 (5.8%) and the 5,000-9,999 (5.6%) size-classes. The remaining three size-classes increased their share by less than 1%. At both ends of the size-class spectrum, the percentage share of the numbers of towns declined, the highest decrease being for the 2,000-4,999 size-class (-13.1%).

While during 1965-70 the population of the smallest and largest urban centres grew relatively faster, in the 1967-84 period the situation was reversed and towns with less than 10,000 inhabitants and those above this threshold actually declined. Between 1967-84 urban population increased most rapidly in the 40,000-80,000 size class, followed by the 80,000-100,000 class.

The number of urban localities in lower size-class categories showed tremendous increases between 1938 and 1984. Whereas the number of urban centres in the 2,000-4,999 category jumped from 35 to 155, those in the category 5,000-19,999 increased from 21 to 115 and the number of localities entering the middle-sized urban categories (20,000-99,999) rose from 6 to 25 during the same period. The urban structure was dominated by a preponderance of fairly small urban localities, with less than 20,000 inhabitants. The proportion of urban localities falling in the size-class 2,000-19,000 has changed little over almost 50 years, accounting for about 89% in 1938 and 91% in 1984. While in 1938 urban centres in the 20,000-99,999 and 100,000 and over size-class categories contained only 11% of the urban localities, about 76% of the population was concentrated here (Tables 13 and 14). By 1984 the share of the urban localities and the total urban population in the two size-class categories declined to about 9% and 64% respectively.

Urban growth, especially during the 1960s and 1970s, was related to and the result of several factors. The emergence of a number of import-substitution industries, encouraged by a generous investment policy, the development of medium and large-scale commercial farming, particularly in the Rift Valley and its northern extension, the Awash Valley, and the Setit-Humera lowlands in north-western Ethiopia, as well as the general socio-economic development that prevailed in the country during this time, were primarily responsible for the emergence of new urban centres and the expansion of existing ones into major towns.

The urban population of Ethiopia grew at an average yearly rate of 3.5% between 1938 and 1967. However, this rate conceals the very rapid growth of urban population experienced during the Italian occupation. After a brief period of decline, a relatively rapid rate of urban growth took place during the 1960s and early 1970s. Between 1967 and 1975 the urban population was growing at an average annual rate of 7.1%, a rate never attained since 1938. Assuming an average annual rate of natural increase of between 2.5 and 2.7%, well over 4% of the yearly growth was attributable to migration.

Table 13: Percentage Distribution of Urban Centres By Size-Class (1938 - 1984)

Size-class	1938	1967	1975	1984
100,000 and over	1.6	1.3	1.1	0.7
20,00 - 99,999	9.5	5.7	10.4	8.4
5,000 - 19,999	33.3	27.2	48.6	38.7
2,000 - 4,999	44.6	65.8	39.9	52.2
Total	100.0	100.0	100.0	100.0

Source: Calculated from Table 12.

In order to assess the tempo of urbanization an exponential model is employed. This model measures the annual average rate of exponential change in the proportion of population in urban areas between two dates (Goldstein and Sly 1975:41). The percentage exponential rate of change in the urban centres for 1967 and 1984 is calculated and the result is shown in Table 14.

According to this computation, the tempo of urbanization at the national level was 1.7%, implying quite a slow rate of change in the degree of urbanization. The level of urbanization, i.e., urban population as a percentage of total population, was and continues to be very low even by African standards. On the other hand, it is the growth rates of urban population that are exceptionally rapid. The intriguing question is why Ethiopia has one of the lowest levels of urbanization in the continent, despite being third in terms of the size of population. This anomaly is accounted for partly by the fact that the population is essentially agrarian with a deeply ingrained rural culture, on which the forces of modernization have so far made little inroads. Italian colonialism was but a brief interlude. Also the intrusion of foreign capital was so small that the country suffered more from neglect than capitalist rape.

The annual change in the speed of urbanization ranged from -2.4% in Eritrea to 4.1% in Bale. A negative tempo of urbanization is registered in four administrative regions, i.e., Eritrea, Harerge, Tigray and Wello, indicating a decline in the level of urbanization.

In addition to differences in the rates of growth between the urban size-classes, differential growth patterns are also observed among individual centres. Population figures for 285 towns which were covered during the First and Second Round Sample Surveys are compared with figures for these same towns obtained during the 1984 census. Among those urban localities that continued to survive in 1984, the annual rate of change ranged between a -0.10% decline in Akordat (Eritrea) to 10.4% growth in Motta (Gojam). In the period under consideration, 23 urban centres showed negative growth, of which 8 were in Eritrea, four in Sidamo, three in Tigray, two in Arsi and one each in Gojam, Harerge, Illubabor, Shewa, Wellega and Wello. Another group of 15 centres disappeared from the urban system of which 8 were in Eritrea, two in Gamo Gofa and one each in Gondar, Harerge, Illubabor, Sidamo and Tigray. On the other hand, some urban centres registered significant growth. Towns such as Motta, Arba Minch, Awassa, Bahar Dar, Akaki Beseka, Shashemene, Kombolcha, and Jijiga were among the fast-growing urban areas, all of which increased in recent times at a rate of more than 8% annually.

Table 14: Annual average Rate of Exponential Change in the Proportion of Urban Population, 1967-1984

Administrative region	Urban population in per cent of total 1967	1984	Exponential change in % urban
Arssi	2.1	2.4	1.7
Bale	0.8	1.6	4.1
Gamo Gofa	1.3	1.5	0.8
Gojam	3.4	5.6	2.9
Gonder	3.5	4.7	1.7
Eritrea	13.8	9.2	- 2.4
Harege	8.0	6.6	- 1.1
Illubabor	1.1	1.4	1.4
Keffa	2.7	3.2	1.0
Shewa	45.2	45.6	0.05
Sidamo	4.7	5.3	0.7
Tigray	5.6	4.2	- 1.7
Welega	2.1	3.0	- 2.1
Wello	5.7	5.3	- 0.4
Ethiopia	8.5	11.3	1.7

Source: Goldstein and Sly, 1975:41.

Factors Contributing to the Decline of Urban Centres

Although a thorough investigation is yet to be undertaken into the factors responsible for the negative tempo of urbanization in some regions and towns since the 1970s, it is possible to tentatively suggest several causes as accounting for this decline. Political, socio-economic as well as environmental factors have combined in a complex manner by reacting on each other to bring about a decline in urbanization. The most obvious contributory factor was the fact that the population of many of the administrative regions were under-estimated during the 1967 survey. Large numbers of the centres that have showed either a declining trend or went down below the minimum population threshold of what is defined as 'urban', were generally found in regions of war and insurgency and environmentally degraded and famine-prone areas. The 1975 land reform, which prohibited the use of hired labour, affected in particular the coffee regions by stopping the large flow of migrants. Towns in these regions used to attract an influx of labourers, people seeking employment in the informal sector, petty traders and bar girls who made a living during the harvest season. It was the tighter control and restrictions on movement, the need to be physically present to stake out a claim to land, the requirement for peasants to work their own land without hired hands and the prohibition of farmers from engaging in trade to supplement their income which turned out to be more crucial in affecting rural-urban migration than ease of access to farmland *per se*.

Notwithstanding the decreasing force of the urban 'pull' factors operating in these towns, people decided to migrate anyhow, despite the constraints, and used these centres as way stations before moving on to towns which promised to offer better amenities. The generally poor performance of the economy in recent years, characterized by declining domestic savings and budgetary as well as balance of payment difficulties, have drastically reduced investment in the towns. This has resulted in severe housing shortages, limited employment opportunities and other social infrastructure in most of the major urban centres (World Bank 1987). The planned resettlement programme organized by the government since the revolution has increased at a considerable rate. No doubt, the massive movement of people to new resettlement sites partly contributed to the decline in urban growth. Left to their own devices, some of these settlers would certainly have moved to towns as the intensity of the environmental push factors increased.

Although towns such as Akakai Beseka, Bahr Dar, Asseb and Kombolcha owe their rapid growth to the presence of some industries, urbanization in Ethiopia has not been caused by industrial development. Urban growth is not being matched by sufficient economic development, industrialization and technological change to make it viable. The developed countries present a contrasting experience. As western societies industrialized and became technologically more advanced, so they became urbanized and emerged as nations of large cities. The modern process of urbanization in Ethiopia may exhibit some characteristics which relate to the stage already experienced by western societies in the Nineteenth Century, but is substantially modified by its own cultural context and by the fact that it is occurring in a radically different global framework.

Factors that Contributed to the Growth of Urban Centres

The introduction of a centralized bureaucracy by Emperor Menelik II at the end of the Nineteenth Century and its expansion resulted in the emergence and development of new regional and sub-regional centres as well as the growth and development of the existing ones. Although almost all of the towns, including the capital, Addis Ababa, came into existence largely as administrative centres, as a result of their growing importance, they later came to accumulate a range of functions in trade, commerce, religion, education and in other tertiary activities.

Developments in transport and communications have had an immediate and lasting impact on the growth and development of towns in Ethiopia since the early years of modern urbanization. They are mostly strung along the major roads and the railway line which radiate from Addis Ababa in a dendritic fashion towards the north, north-west, west, south and eastern parts of the country.

The Italian road building programme (1936-41) together with other urban promoting activities, initiated the process of modern urbanization. Since the 1950s road and air links have been extended to more remote regions and these in turn have given rise to the emergence of new urban centres and the expansion of the already existing ones. Modern urbanization in Ethiopia has not been based on industrialization and industry still plays a minor part in the urban economy as a whole. The employment structure of most urban centres reveals that the majority of economically active persons are engaged in agriculture and services. As the size of the centre increases so does the proportion of service workers and, conversely, as the towns decrease in size the proportion of the urban population engaged in agriculture increases. Because of their inadequate economic bases, many of these centres, especially those in the lower size-classes, originated and grew primarily as extensions of the rural hinterland (Alula Abate 1984:258; Berhanu Abegaz 1985:54). Yet, however small the scale may be, the contribution of industries to the growth of particular urban centres has been substantial. Table 15 indicates the relationship between degree of industrialization and size of urban population by region.

Manufacturing industries are concentrated mainly in two administrative regions, Shewa and Eritrea, with Harerge following as a poor third (Table 8). Not only do the three regions together account for 92.1% of the industrial establishments, 92.3% of the industrial workers, 95.9% of the gross value of production and 97.6% of the value added, as the share of the other regions in these categories declined between 1976 and 1984, aggravating further the problem of concentration of industrial development. Most of the manufacturing plants are located in four urbanized zones in the three administrative regions Addis Ababa with its satellite town of Akaki, Asmara, Harar, Dire Dawa and Mojo-Nazareth Wonji, of which Addis Ababa, Asmara, Dire Dawa and Nazareth are the four principal urban centres in the country.

Evidently, social, economic, and other facilities could only be provided more efficiently from settlements such as cities and towns where higher levels of human organization were found. The result was the agglomeration of industrial activities in these urban areas in their search for locational advantages.

A decade of unprecedented industrial and urban growth was experienced in Ethiopia in the 1960s and 1970s. Concomitant with the establishment of industries a process of 'tertiarization' was also taking place, expanding further the provision of urban-related economic and social activities. Thus, the hope for better access to social services and imagined employment opportunities, especially in towns with manufacturing industries, has been one of the major factors in the growth of Ethiopian towns since the 1950s.

A close relationship appears to exist between size of urban population and the extent of industrial activities. The relationship could be either causal or, as is generally the case, mutually reinforcing. Literature on Third World urbanization strongly indicates that the presence of industries and infrastructural services generally tend to increase the population-absorption capacity of towns. To test if this observation also holds true under Ethiopian conditions, an attempt was made to measure the strength of the relationships between size of urban population and number of industrial establishments. A value of 0.97 correlation coefficient (r) was obtained, suggesting a strong relationship between the two variables. The coefficient of determination (r^2) also indicated that 94% of the variation in urban growth was explained by variation in the relative level of industrialization (Alula Abate 1989).

Cash crop production and rural development projects have also contributed their share to urban growth. Coffee, the major cash crop, employs the largest number of producers in the country. The dominant position of this crop in the money economy of the country led to the emergence and growth of a large number of coffee collecting centres of varying sizes, such as Dembi

Dollo, Metu, Gore, Ghibi, Lekemt, Agaro, Jima, Dilla, Wondo, Asbe Teferi and Harar. A number of towns in the Awash Valley, the Rift Valley and the western lowlands also owed their origin and further growth to such cash crops as cotton, Sesame and horticultural products. No less significant was the contribution of rural development schemes such as CADU, WADU, ADDP (Ada District Development Project) and SORADEP (Southern Regional Development Project) (see Chapter 3 in this volume).

A number of rural-push factors, notably population pressure and famine have brought about forced migrations to towns. A substantial majority of the population (75%) of Ethiopia lives in the highlands (above 1,800 metres) on about 36% of the land. In the absence of any significant technological transformation in the agriculture sector, this has resulted in great pressures on the land, giving rise to serious land fragmentation or even outright landlessness (Fassil 1980). Lack of access to sufficient farmland together with severe environmental degradation, has been and continues to be among the major factors which force people to abandon their farms and move to towns.

The role of famine relief in urban growths in Tigray, Wello and Gonder has long been recognized (Baker, 1986:2423; Kloos and Aynalem Adugna, 1989:42). Although a substantial number of the famine victims returned to their home areas when conditions improved, some clearly remained in urban centres. Towns such as Dessie, Mekele, Wukro and Korem and a number of other smaller roadside towns grew or reversed their declining trend mainly because they became regional famine relief centres or shelter towns.

To determine the possible relationship between urban growth and population pressure on land, a correlation coefficient was calculated taking average land-holding size as an independent variable and size of urban population as dependent variable. A value of 0.45 correlation coefficient (r) was obtained and the relationship between the two variables was found to be statistically significant at 99% confidence level. The result suggests that there certainly exists a fairly strong relationship between the two variables, which confirms the fact that high pressure on land results in high urban population size and urban growth. The coefficient of determination derived from this shows that 20.2% of the variation in urban growth in Ethiopia is explained by unavailability of sufficient land for cultivation.

Furthermore, an attempt was also made to see if performance in the agricultural sector could have played any role in the rural-urban mobility of people. To measure the relationship at the *Awraja* level, urban population size and volume of agricultural production were taken as dependent and independent variables respectively. The coefficient of correlation (r) thus obtained was -0.31. The correlation was statistically significant at 99%

confidence level, thus suggesting the great significance of rural push due to failure in the agricultural sector. The coefficient of determination derived from the (r) value indicated that 9.6% of the variation in urban growth was explained by the low level of productivity in the agricultural sector (Alula Abate 1989).

Regional Patterns of Urbanization

Pre-Twentieth Century Ethiopian towns were concentrated in the highland area of the country while over much of the remainder of the country, especially the south, towns were non-existent. The towns had been linked either to the caravan trade routes or they were centres of politico-military power of the feudal elites.

In contemporary Ethiopia urbanization has, however, swept the whole of the country, with little resemblance to historic towns in terms of social, political and economic organization.

It is also important to note that all the towns which sprang up in the southern part of the country, beyond the 100 parallel, with the exception of the town of Harar, were built either at the end of the last century or during the present century. Table 16 shows the distribution of urban population and localities by regions in the past three decades.

Striking spatial varieties exist among the regions of the country in terms of both the proportion of population living in urban places and number of urban centres. The relative share of the administrative regions in the overall urban population in the country ranged between 0.8% (Bale), and 46% (Shewa). For 1984, the pattern slightly changed, the proportion of urban areas ranging from 1.2% (Illubabor) to 46.8% (Shewa). Shewa and Eritrea, the two administrative regions with the highest level of urbanization, accounted for 64.4% of the country's urban population in 1967, but this proportion declined to 56.2% in 1984. This was mainly due to the relative growth of urbanization in the other regions, but also to urban decline in Eritrea, a region of protracted insurgency. Even with the exclusion of Addis Ababa, Shewa had the highest urban concentration, accounting for 10.5% and 14.3% of the total urban population in 1967 and 1984 respectively.

On the other hand, six regions out of 14 (Arsi, Bale, Gamo Gofa, Illubabor, Wellega and Keffa) together accounted for only 10% and 11.9% of the total urban population in 1967 and 1984 respectively. While urban population was growing at an average annual rate of 7.7% in the whole country, eight regions grew at less than the national average. Despite this growth in absolute numbers, the level of urbanization in five administrative regions Eritrea, Harerge, Wello, Wellega and Tigrai actually declined in 1984, compared to the situation in 1967. Apart from Gojam (+2.0%) and Gonder (+1.1%), all the rest recorded increases of less than one per cent.

Table 15: Manufacturing Industries by Addministrative Regions
(% of Total)

	Shewa				Eritrea				Hararghe				Others			
	1	2	3	4	1	2	3	4	1	2	3	4	1	2	3	4
1976-77	61.2	61.5	59.8	64.0	20.7	18.9	25.0	20.1	5.7	10.8	8.4	9.2	12.4	8.8	6.7	6.7
1984-85	63.0	63.6	57.7	66.6	23.9	18.4	32.5	24.3	5.2	10.3	5.7	6.7	7.9	7.7	4.1	2.2

Note: 1. Establishments
2. Persons Engaged
3. Gross Value of Production
4. Census: Valuee Added

Source: CSO, Results of the Survey of Manufacturing Industries, 1976-77 and 1984-85.

The Legacy of Neglect
Implication of Rapid Population Growth
Although the influence of population changes on the socio-economic development of low-income areas is a subject that has attracted much attention in recent years, especially in the last two decades, the problem has been discussed for a long time. The problem of population, as predicted by Malthus, has not been realized in the developed countries because technological revolution in industry, agriculture and communications have led to a great increase in productivity and people have largely utilized the 'preventive checks' to control or reduce the rate of population growth. For most developing countries the problems of population are today as real and serious as they were in the days of Malthus.

It is evident that rapid population growths interact with public education, health and welfare, employment, total food supply, resources and the quality of the environment. Yet, not enough is known about the economic, social and political consequences of rapid population growth and their magnitude is uncertain. Part of the reason lies in the fact that country-specific research on the consequences of high and sometimes rising birth rates, falling mortality, differing age patterns and what a policymaker can do about these phenomena are often hard to come by. Furthermore, population growth is only one of several variables that affect living conditions. Since several variables are involved, usually working in different directions, it is impossible to isolate the effects of a single variable and blame numbers of people alone for the set of problems confronting developing countries.

Value judgements on whether rapid population growth is 'good' or 'bad' abound, but country-specific studies that determine the resulting consequences are meager, especially because the question of whether a given population is larger than one yielding maximum per capita output is very difficult to answer in any concrete situation.

Those who view rapid population growth positively reject any suggestion that population size should be limited for the purpose of achieving economic development. They argue that a large and growing population can be advantageous under certain conditions. The most common arguments usually can be summarized as follows: a big and growing population would provide a good market for products, would enable mass production techniques to be used and thus lower prices and would cause demand to rise, which would be met by increased productivity; incentive to invest would be strong and finally the burden of social cost would be spread widely. It is further held that a declining or stationary population would bring about economic stagnation.

These assumptions may conceivably be true if sufficient capital, technological skills and health services are available for people to make good use of them. It is questionable that these conditions obtain in most developing countries which, at present, have little resources to spare. The case of population limitation does not rest on apocalyptic visions of the future based on a simple, mathematical extrapolation of present rates of population growth. It is clear that available techniques of production, which largely depend on the skills the population possesses, can greatly change the simple correlation between population and resources. However, current available evidence strongly suggests that rapid population growth in developing countries has been a decided obstacle rather than an aid to economic growth and that the more rapid the rise in numbers, the greater the deterrent effects.

It is also becoming increasingly clear that rapid population growth in many developing countries poses a serious threat to development efforts. The task of providing not only food but also schools, housing, health facilities, employment, etc., for the growing numbers, which often double within a mere 20-25 years, is a staggering one. Before they can live at even the current low standard of living these populations must first eat up a portion of the present scarce supply of capital. It is this burden which defeats a nation's efforts to raise its standard of living by increasing its population. Because the degree of certainty with which one can predict both future trends and effects is improving, the assertion that rapid population growth adversely affects the society, the economy and the environment is now less frequently challenged.

A proper analysis of the relationship between the complex set of variables that affect human welfare and development in Ethiopia would require an exploration of dynamic numerical models based on a robust baseline data for both the economy and the population.

The population of Ethiopia stood at about 47.3 million in 1988 and recent CSA estimates indicate a continued high population growth of more than 3% in the 1990s. This groups Ethiopia among the high-population-growth countries in Africa. Her Gross Domestic Product (GDP) in 1988 was 8,921.4 million birr. This gives a per capita income of 189 birr or approximately US$91, which is one of the lowest in the continent.

It is indicated earlier that juvenility is a prominent characteristic of the population of Ethiopia since the proportion of population below 15 years of age is of the order of 45 to 47%. This young population is highly fecund because the unusually large increments at the base of the population pyramid, with the passing years, will expand the reproductive age-groups. This favours a continuance of high birth rates unless other factors reduce fertility.

There is a generally optimistic assessment of the natural resource potential of Ethiopia, although, contrary to popular belief, very little of this potential (in particular minerals) has materialized so far. The major known resource of the country continues to be land, where more than 80% of the population is engaged, either directly or indirectly, in agriculture and related activities. Also, the most important export commodities, both by volume and value, originate in this sector. Agricultural land, which once sufficed to support a slowly growing but much smaller population, has already been divided and subdivided beyond the limits of effective cultivation (Fassil 1980; Dessalegn Rahmato 1984; Mengistu Wobie 1986). Rapid population increase in rural areas has forced farmers to extend cropping into areas that are at best suitable only for grazing and into areas that should not even be grazed. This kind of resource pressure, as well as the pressure caused by lack of cheap fuel, has led to serious deforestation and extremely poor soil conditions in many parts of the country. The available evidence indicates that the gradually declining average farm sizes (largely due to population growth) are still getting bigger. This is raising the administrative burdens and social costs of absorbing urban arrivals, and thus diverting most, if not all, of the development resources of the country needed to improve the present miserable living conditions.

Many symptoms of stress are appearing in large parts of the country in the form of increasing rural landlessness, poverty and under-employment, food crises and famine. The cause of these problems may not be rapid population growth alone, although its impact is undeniably tremendous in countries where incomes are low and economic development is a desperate need. Taking steps to encourage some reduction in fertility, however, would go a long way to facilitate more rapid economic and social development and help to arrest or even reduce the widening gap between food requirements and production.

A recent government-commissioned study indicated that, at present, only about 0.98 hectare of land is available to a rural household, whereas at least 1.53 hectares of cultivable land are needed to meet the current requirements of a farm household of five members (PDRE Council of Ministers 1982:72 and 78). In spite of an increase in the amount of arable land and total output, per capita food production declined by over 1% per annum, while population growth stood around 3%. The growing food deficit is the result of the disappointing performance of the agricultural sector whose value added grew at an average annual rate of only 1.1% (World Bank 1987:15).

Ethiopia's increasing dependence on imported food is highlighted by the fact that cereal imports increased from only 112,000 metric tons in 1975 to 1,204,852 metric tons in 1988, almost a tenfold increase in 13 years (WFP 1989). A very striking case estimate by some western observers, including the World Bank, depicts a drastic and worsening grain problem even under optimistic assumptions. According to these estimates, some 2-2.5 million metric tons of grain deficit is foreseen for 1990s (Henze 1988:2-4).

Two to three million hectares of potentially irrigable land are believed to exist in the country but these potential resources need to be developed under schemes whose anticipated benefits have to be carefully weighed against the likely future environmental, human and economic costs. The heavy increase in Ethiopia population is likely to continue to reduce output per head unless considerable investment is made. Economists have suggested that a capital-output ratio of up to 4:1 may be needed to maintain living standards. This suggests that Ethiopia's present population growth of 3% (a rate which has not yet reached its peak) will need a net investment of 12% of the national income to even maintain the low living standards. The investment rate in the country in the 1980s has been low (average 11%) and stagnating. The volume of domestic savings (average about 3%) has been much lower than for low-income countries, and worse, it has been declining steadily. The fact that the rate of increase in production has not been able to keep pace with the rate of population increase has not only decreased savings but 'threatens the very survival of the population' (Befekadu Degefe, 1990:71).

It is clear that Ethiopia's population is already large in relation to its known resources particularly agricultural land and has a large potential for rapid further growth in the near future. With its growing population and a high proportion of dependent children the society will find it increasingly difficult to spare any of its income for savings and investment. A reduction in the present rate of population growth is highly desirable from many points of view, but it has to be made clear that such a reduction cannot be a substitute for large capital investments and massive transfers of technology. So far, there is no consistent and coherent official policy on fertility regulation, although it has tolerated privately-run family planning programmes. The present population growth rates have reached such a critical level as to require both population-responsive as well as population-influencing policies.

The Urban Predicament

In recent years the pace and magnitude of internal migration, particularly rural-to-rural migration, has picked up as a result of the government's planned resettlement programme. A combination of adverse environmental, economic and demographic problems, added to a protracted insurgency, account for this unprecedented movement of people in living memory. While it is clear that usual climatic variability has produced more than average drought years, it would be difficult to relate famine exclusively to drought. Agricultural productivity in northern Ethiopia has been declining steadily, at times even dramatically, primarily because of population pressure on land. Accelerated population growth throughout the country, including areas of high population concentration in the northern and central highlands, led to the cultivation of marginal lands which resulted in severe environmental degradation. In addition, since the urban areas are unable to absorb large rural migrations, the bulk of the increase in rural population over several decades had to be accommodated in rural areas. Yet, despite the recent apparent decline in rural-to-urban migration, the influx is still sufficiently large to overwhelm urban government. The imperial government was not sufficiently concerned about regulating the total population growth, migration and urbanization, except that it occasionally cleared the streets of the capital of vagrants and the unemployed. The *laisser-faire* policy has continued its complacent course since 1974, despite the clear writing on the wall.

In the longrun, rural-to-urban migration rates are likely to increase unless appropriate policies are designed to meet this challenge. Experience from other African countries have shown that direct population control approaches, such as relocation or closing the doors to new settlers have met with little success (Stern and White 1989). Commerce and industry are not growing fast enough to absorb the people already in the cities; the birth rates of rural-urban migrants are not spiralling downward and efforts to resettle people in frontier areas have to prove to be more than mere palliative. Clearly, more than just coercion and persuasion is called for to even out settlement patterns in the nation. Perhaps population-control measures have a role to play as tactical approaches within a total and comprehensive strategy, but they cannot by themselves resolve the urban management crisis.

Despite the very limited public cash flows, high urban unemployment and stagnant rural productivity, the government has taken a number of steps, related both to institution building and objectives, to tackle the problem. Although there were no substantial urban planning activities in the country prior to 1974, some hesitant steps were nevertheless taken in the 1960s. During this time, the Municipalities Department in the Ministry of Interior, in collaboration with an Italian firm, prepared master plans for 40 towns. With the completion of seven additional plans in the early 1970s, the number of towns with master plans increased to 47. Compared to the total number of urban centres in the country, however, the number of towns subjected to a planning exercise was indeed very small.

Ethiopia's town plans of the 1960s and early 1970s were exogenous in character and lacked local participation and support and failed to represent the problems and aspirations of their residents. Furthermore, they could not be successfully implemented due to lack of legal backing, political support and local administrative and financial capacity (Koehn and Koehn 1979:224-25).

A number of social, political and economic barriers hampered the development of a dynamic urban system even in those centres where municipalities exercised some degree of control on the administration. Squatter and slum settlements, congestion, lack of provisions, prostitution and poverty became rampant.

Since urban policies and goals were not even roughly articulated, the government has been dealing with components of the problems, such as housing, industrial location, transportation, education and health. The efforts to deal with the growth of cities and with rural areas proceeded independently. Unless and until these efforts converge, little progress can be made in understanding the problems, let alone finding solutions to them.

The preparation of master plans to guide the growth and development of urban centres was at the time part and parcel of the conventional wisdom. There was a noticeable tendency among many policy makers in Ethiopia to take a master plan as a panacea for resolving most, if not all, of the urban problems. Experience has shown that the classical master plan has not withstood the pressure of rural-urban migration. The growing gap between the realities of official plans and perspectives and the mushrooming world of the urban poor call for a more adaptive urban government.

Problems related to infrastructural development in urban areas of Ethiopia are of two types. Either they are non-existent, as is the case for most of the towns, or the services provided are so inadequate that they hardly meet the basic needs of the population.

Surveys conducted by the Central Statistical Office, the Addis Ababa Municipality and MUDH reports compiled for various towns indicate that lack of adequate basic urban services such as housing, water supply, garbage disposal, toilet and health facilities and service roads are characteristic features of the urban areas in Ethiopia.

Of the total urban areas, only 111 towns, most of which have a population of 10,000 and more, receive electricity (Asrat 1987:I-II) and only 83% of the housing units in 17 major towns have electric light (CSO, Statistical Bulletin No. 27, 1980). Overloads and frequent breakdowns are common.

To any casual observer, it is evident that most of the health problems in Ethiopian urban centres are caused by poor environment and poor personal hygiene. Available data on water supply, liquid and solid waste disposal highlight the situation of the health environment. In 1986, an estimated 8% of the rural population and 73% of the urban population had access to safe and adequate water supply. However, not all of the households that had access to improved water supply could draw water with equal ease. A study of 17 major towns made by the Ministry of Urban Development and Housing (MUDH) revealed that 36% of the housing units had direct piped water connections in the rooms or made available within their compounds, 32% drew water from public taps, 12% shared with others and 15% got water from wells and streams (MUDH and UNICEF 1983:72).

Lack of adequate and proper disposal system for liquid and solid waste has been one of the major sources of environmental pollution. Table 16 shows the woefully inadequate toilet facilities that prevail in the major urban areas of the country.

Excreta disposal which uses a modern underground sewerage system is limited to only a few towns and serves a small percentage of the population. Flush toilets (private or shared) which need to be periodically emptied by vacuum-sucking trucks cover 12% of the housing units in Addis Ababa and 3.5% in the rest of the towns. The majority of the housing units are served with dry pit latrines (57.4% Addis Ababa and 60.3% in the 17 towns), and out of these only a small proportion (about 15%) are for the explicit use of individual households. It is often difficult to vacuum-suck pit latrines because solid waste is often dumped into them and they are therefore not emptied regularly. Of the total housing units included in the survey 29.2% in Addis Ababa and 35.4% in the 17 towns do not have any toilet facility. It is also unfortunate that many public and private establishments, including schools, do not have toilets. Because of the shortage (only 52 in Addis Ababa) or total absence of public toilets, the common practice of relieving oneself in the open is not restricted to only those who have no facilities at home. Many of those who use pit latrines regularly join in as well.

A recent study conducted under a UNDP-sponsored and World Bank-financed solid waste management project for Addis Ababa showed that some 700 tons of solid waste were generated per week and only about 35% was being collected and disposed of satisfactorily (Addis Ababa City Council, 1982). Municipal collection of solid waste served only 47.4% of the housing units, whereas the rest privately disposed of their garbage in different manners but mostly threw it on any open space or into a nearby stream (Addis Ababa City Council and UNICEF 1987). Except for a few big towns, the majority did not even get this limited municipal service.

In terms of medical provision, schooling and other services, towns in Ethiopia were disproportionately served, compared to the rest of the country. Except for post-secondary education and specialized vocational schools, there is a greater concentration of educational services (Alula Abate 1985:261).

Table 16: Housing Units by Type of Toilet Facility

Urban Centres	None No.	None %	Private Flush No.	Private Flush %	Flush Shared No.	Flush Shared %	Private Pit No.	Private Pit %	Pit Shared No.	Pit Shared %	Not Stated No.	Not Stated %	Total No.	Total %
Addis Ababa	75,854	29.2	28,506	11.1	2,520	0.9	30,734	15.3	109,803	42.1	3,635	1.4	259,553	100
17 towns	53,254	34.4	3,841	2.5	1,549	1.0	23,954	15.9	66,793	44.4	1,128	0.8	150,519	100

Source: Office of the Population and Housing Census Commission: *Analytical Reports on Results for Addis Ababa*, Addis Ababa, vol. 1, No. 1, 1987.

The greatest disparities in access to health services are those particularly related to the difference between urban and rural areas. Although in recent years the government has been giving greater attention to improvement and increase in rural health services, most health facilities, including health personnel, are concentrated in Addis Ababa, Asmara, Harar and Dire Dawa. Addis Ababa alone accounts for 53.4% of the physicians, 33.2% of the health officers, 67.8% of the pharmacists, 26% of the health inspectors, 49.2% of the nurses and 17.9% of the technicians (MUDH & UNICEF 1983:73). Yet, despite this privileged position, Addis Ababa manifests similar kinds and magnitudes of health problems as the rest of the country. It suffers mostly from communicable diseases caused by unsanitary environmental conditions and personal hygiene. For instance, for the under-five age group annual diarrhoea episodes of five per child were recorded in 1984 (Elias G/Egziebeher 1987:xi). Outside the major centres, hospitals and health centres are usually understaffed, undersupplied and ill-equipped.

The issue of urban transport has never been one of the highest priorities of the government. Consequently, only three comprehensive studies have been carried out on the urban transportation problems in Addis Ababa: the Cessen Energy Study (1982), the Addis Ababa Master Plan Project Office (1985) and Roy Jorgensen Associates and Hughes Economic Planning (1983-1984) (Tesfaye Tafesse 1986:51-61). Urban public transport exists in only five centres Addis Ababa, Asmara, Dire Dawa, Harar and Jimma. Public transport is so inadequate that even in Addis Ababa up to 70% of all trips are performed on foot, mostly because of bus shortages and their inefficient deployment. Low incomes make the fares unaffordable to many and lack of proper land-use zoning are among the reasons why many business trips are made partly or wholly on foot. To alleviate the problem, an increase in the fleet of buses has been proposed together with the introduction of other mass transit vehicles such as trolley buses and operation of a better bus route network more attuned to passenger needs.

The transport technology associated with the development of most Ethiopian urban centres is rudimentary, as are their social and economic organizations. Communications depend on the pedestrian or draught animal. Thus, the urban fabric tends to be arranged so that journeys within the city can be kept relatively short. Because of the limitations of transport facilities, the functional interrelationships between the towns and the outer limits of their hinterlands are relatively poor, and tend to be distinct nuclei loosely related to a wider rural area and to other towns.

Housing is the most serious and persistent problem in urban areas, a need which the government has found difficult to meet. The rising urban population, especially in the low-income groups, and the increasingly high cost of construction materials have created a sizeable gap between housing demand and supply. The magnitude of this gap is reflected in many slum settlements, overcrowded housing units, and obsolescent units requiring replacement. Housing in Ethiopian urban centres is grossly deficient, both in quality and quantity, so that the problem has now turned to be one of the pressing national issues which cry out for immediate attention.

The problem of housing in this country is multi-faceted, with various factors such as population growth, urbanization trends and economic growth influencing housing conditions and needs.

First, the number of houses under construction are not able to meet the accumulated needs, let alone the recurrent and future needs. Secondly, those houses which were nationalized and brought under government control are becoming dilapidated due to lack of proper maintenance. Thirdly, even by Ethiopian standards, many of the housing units do not provide acceptable levels of accommodation necessary for health, privacy and development of normal family living standards.

As the survey conducted by the CSO indicates, most of the housing units in the capital where more than 30% of the country's urban population live are of low quality and, in the eyes of the middle-class observer, decrepit and dilapidated in appearance.

There is a clear relationship between economic growth and urbanization, although the nature of that relationship is the subject of intense debate. Nevertheless, development strategists of different ideological persuasions identify industrialization as the key to economic growth, and this focuses investment on the city rather than the countryside. The disagreement arises over the type of industrialization to be promoted. Whatever the type of industrial development followed, it is uncommon to find the majority of Third World urban residents incorporated into this type of employment. In Ethiopia, information gleaned from patchy sources suggests that not more than 20% of the urban labour force are engaged in the manufacturing industry. The fact that nearly 15% of the urban labour force are employed in agriculture, and that the majority are categorized as service workers, reflects the extreme backwardness of the economy and indicates that urban centres are products of the societies in which they arise. Despite some evidence of modernization, most Ethiopian urban centres could be characterized as being 'pre-industrial', trade and tribute having a predominant place in economic life. They are largely centres of consumption with a proliferation of personal services, and not centres of industry. Those economic activities contained in them, such as artisanal activities, are of lesser status, yielding little investible surplus.

As regards under-employment and mis-employment in urban areas, no attempt has ever been made to assess the magnitude. If one were to add up these three different categories, urban unemployment in Ethiopia is indeed extremely high with serious social and economic implications. The results of a survey conducted in 17 towns (Table 16) and two *kebeles* in Addis Ababa confirm the grave employment situation. The rate of participation in gainful employment for the economically active age group (ten years and above) is estimated to be around 46%, with 67% for males and 33% for females. Employment data for two *kebeles* also showed that 48% of the active population in one case and 56% of the household heads in another were either openly unemployed or underemployed (Ellias G/Egziebeher 1987:XIII; Mpyisi 1988:48).

While in the mid-1970s illiterate job seekers predominated (68%), a decade later, mainly as a result of the literacy campaign, over 50% of the unemployed had attained post-elementary education and the rate of unemployment for high-school graduates or dropouts has been increasing at an alarming pace (Hayyalu Shiferaw 1982:48; Mpyisi, 1988:49). As the proportion of the unemployed with post-primary training increases, and more and more university and technical school graduates become unemployed, there is a growing feeling that the formal school system has failed to supply the type of manpower demanded by the economy.

Urban unemployment in Ethiopia is clearly specific to age and sex. According to a survey carried out by the Ministry of Labour and Social Affairs, unemployment in the 15-34 age group was 75% in 1978 and in the 18-34 age group the rate was 64% in 1980 (Hayalu Shiferaw 1982:46). Many migrants are young and unskilled and a large proportion are unemployed. Unemployment is considerably higher for women than for men, even though many females do not actively look for work because they are aware that the opportunities open to them are severely limited.

References

Abate Mamo and S.P.Morgan, 1986, 'Childlessness in Rural Ethiopia', *Population and Development Review*, Vol. 2, No. 3.

Abdulahi Hassan, 1979, 'Fertility Levels, Patterns and Differentials in Ethiopia', in *Experts Groups Meeting on Fertility and Mortality Levels, Patterns and Their Policy Implications*, UNECA, Monrovia, pp. 163-168.

Abdurahman Mohammed, 1987, *Population Distribution and Internal Migration in Ethiopia*, Unpublished MA Thesis, ANU, Canberra.

Alemtsehay Tekle, 1988, A study of Fertility and Child Mortality in Illubabor and Wollo, rural Ethiopia, MA Thesis in demography, ANU, Canberra.

Alemseghed Gebre, 1989, *Fertility Differentials in Addis Ababa: Case Study of One Kebele*, MSc. thesis, DTRC, Addis Ababa University.

Alula Abate, 1985, 'Urbanization and Regional Development in Ethiopia'*Colloquium Geographicum*, Vol. 18, Bonn.

----------, 1989, 'Internal Migration and Urbanization in Ethiopia',*Report of Conference Proceedings, vol. II*, Conference on Population Issues in Ethiopia's National Development, ONCCP, Addis Ababa.

Asmerom Kidane and Assefa Hailemarim, 1988, 'Mortality, Fertility and Population of Famine-affected Regions of Ethiopia', IDR Resettlement Studies, Addis Ababa.

Asmerom Kidane, 1989, 'Demographic Consequences of the 1984-85 Ethiopian Famine', *Demography*, vol. 26, No. 3.

Assefa Hailemariam, 1991, 'Fertility Levels and Trends in Arsi and Shoa Regions of Central Ethiopia', *Journal of Biosocial Sciences*, Vol. 23.

Befekadu Degefe, 1990, 'Profile of the Ethiopian Economy'*The Long-term Perspective Study of Sub-Saharan Africa*, The World Bank, vol. 1, Background papers, Washington DC.

Beyene Dolocho, 1985,*The Patterns, Causes and Consequences of Labour Migrations to Metehara Estate and Neighbouring State Farms*, MA Thesis, Dept. of Geog., Addis Ababa University.

CSA, 1988a, *Population Situation in Ethiopia: Past, Present and Future*, Addis Ababa.

CSA, 1988b, *Population Projection of Ethiopia: Total and Sectoral*, Addis Ababa.

CSO, 1974a, The *Demography of Ethiopia*, Addis Ababa.

CSO, 1974b, *Population and Housing Characteristics of Asmara*, Addis Ababa.

CSO, 1985a, *Report on the results of the 1981 Demographic Surgery*, Addis Ababa.

CSO, 1984,*Study on the Levels, Patterns, Trends and Differentials of Fertility, Infant and Childhood Mortality*, Addis Ababa.

CSO, 1985b, *Population Situation in Ethiopia, 1900-1984*, Addis Ababa.

Fassil, G, Kiros, 1980, 'Agricultural land Fragmentation: A Problem of Land Distribution in Some Peasant Associations',*Ethiopian Journal of Development Research*, vol. 4, No. 2.

Genet Mengistu, 1987, 'Fertility and Child Mortality in Ethiopia: A Comparative Study of Selected Regions', Gonder and Harerge, MA thesis, in demography, ANU, Canberra.

Groenewold, G, Swanhilde, P De Jong and Araya Demissie, 1989, 'Patterns in Fertility and Contraceptive Use in Addis Ababa: Follow-up Survey Among Family Planning Acceptors', DTRC, IDR. Research Report.

Gulperin, 1981, *Ethiopia: Population, Resources and Economy*, Progress Publishers, Moscow.

Henze, Paul B, 1988, 'Ethiopia's Economic Prospects for the 1990s', Paper prepared for the Tenth International Ethiopian Studies Conference in Paris, August 22-26, 1988.

Kebede Seleshi, 1986, 'Fertility and Child Mortality in Agricultural Households of Rural Ethiopia: The Case of Arssi Administrative Region', Unpublished paper, ANU, Canberra.

Kloos, H, 1982, 'Farm Labour migrations in the Awash Valley of Ethiopia'*International Migration Review*, vol. 16, No. 1, pp. 133-169.

Mesfin, W, Mariam, 1961, 'An estimate of the population of Ethiopia'*Ethiopia Observer*, vol. 5, No. 2.

----------, 1967, 'The population of Ethiopia: An overview',*Ethiopian Geogr. Jour.* vol. 5, No. 2.

Ministry of Agriculture (MOA), 1984,*General Agricultural Survey 1983-4*, vols. 1 and 2, Addis Ababa.

Nelson, Harold, D, II and Kaplan, Irving, 1981, *Ethiopia a Country Study*, American University, Washington, DC, Foreign Area Studies. V. series.

OPHCC, 1987, *Population and Housing Census of Ethiopia Preliminary Report: Ethiopia 1984*, Addis Ababa.

OPHCC, 1985, *Census Supplement* I, CSA, Addis Ababa.

Pankhurst, Richard, 1961, 'Nineteenth and Twentieth Century Population Guesses', *Ethiopia Observer*, Vol. 5, No. 2, Addis Ababa.

------------, 1965, 'Demographic History of Ethiopian Towns and Villages', *Ethiopia Observer*, Vol. 9, No. 5, Addis Ababa.

Planning Board, 1961, 'The Ethiopian Population and Economic Planning', *Ethiopia Observer* Vol. 5, No. 2, Addis Ababa.

Provisional Military Government of Socialist Ethiopia (PMGSE), 1984, *Ten-Year Perspective Plan 1984-85 - 1993-94* Addis Ababa.

PDRE Council of Ministers, 1982 (Eth. Cal.), *Research Report on Peasant Displacement and Land Fragmentation*, Ministry of Agriculture, Addis Ababa.

UN, 1980, *Ethiopia: Report of Mission on Needs Assessment For Population Assistance*, UNFPA, New York.

Van Kesteren, Jose, 1989, *Female Labour Force Participation and Fertility in Addis Ababa, The Case of One Kebele*, IDR Research Report No. 33.

Van Kesteren, Jose, and Markos Ezra, 1989, *Female Labour Force Participation and Fertility in Addis Ababa: A Comparison of Two Communities with Different Socio-economic Status*, IDR. Research Report No. 35.

Wood, A, P, 1982, Spontaneous Agricultural Resettlement in Ethiopia: 1950-74, in Clark, J, I, and Kosinski, L, A, (eds.), *Redistribution of Population in Africa*, Heinemann, London, pp. 157-164.

World Bank, 1970, *Economic Growth and Prospects in Ethiopia* (in five volumes) vol. II, Report No. AE-9 East African Department.

------------, 1987, *Ethiopia: Recent Economic Development and Prospects for Recovery and Growth*, Washington, DC.

World Food Programme (WFP) - Unpublished data, Addis Ababa Office.

Dessalegn Rahmato, 1984, *Agrarian Reform in Ethiopia*, Uppsala, Scandinavian Institute of African Studies.

Mengistu Wubie, 1986, Problems of Land Reform Implementation in Rural Ethiopia, Ph.D. Dissertation, Uppsala University.

Index

A

Ada District Development Project (ADDP) 170
Addis Ababa Bank 40, 263, 270
Addis Ababa, land tenure 113
Administrative Reform Committee 8
Agricultural and Commercial Bank 240, 271
Agricultural and Industrial Bank of Ethiopia (AID Bank) 272
Agricultural and Industrial Development Bank 40
Agricultural Bank 240
Agricultural Exports, Committee of 147
agricultural revolution 154-5
agricultural systems 145
agricultural technology 20, 152, 155
    and social change 155-6
    See also agriculture
agriculture 10, 17, 19, 22, 317
    commercial 183, 186
    density 288
    and development 147, 156, 158, 177, 179
    extension services 165-6, 173
    Five-Year Plans 166, 168
    and GDP 21
    growth 12-13
    investment 9-10, 12, 133, 166, 168, 214
    policies 164, 166
    productivity 160, 177
    research on 144, 151
    resource base 157-8
    and society 179, 186
    taxation 163-4
    US involvement 148, 151, 167
    See also peasant agriculture, smallholder agriculture
agro-ecological regions 144
    See also agriculture
aid 50-1, 160
    See also foreign aid
air transport 11, 26
Aksum 305
Alemaya Agricultural College 147, 149
All Ethiopia Socialist Movement (AESM) (Meison) 3
Anglo-Ethiopian Agreement 199, 235-6, 245
automobiles, introduction of 130

B

balance of payments 47, 49
    See also economy
Banco di Napoli 40, 240, 264, 270
Banco di Roma 40, 239, 263, 270
Bank of Abyssinia 234
Bank of Ethiopia 234
banking system 234, 242
    See also commercial banks, name of bank
Banque de l'Indochine 234, 239
Begemder, land tenure 86-7
birth rate 282
Blowers, George A 239
Bottling Company of Ethiopia 272
Breton Woods Agreement 247
Britain
    and currency 242, 244
    and economy 198-9
    and Ethiopia 196, 198

C

capital expenditure 34
capital market 272
cereals 9, 20, 43
chemicals, investment 214
Chilalo Agricultural Development Unit (CADU) 170, 177
China, loan 51
churches, land tenure 93, 96
class structure 181-2
    and land ownership 84-5, 129, 134
    See also feudal system
coffee 311
    exports 9, 39, 41, 44, 164
Coffee Board 268
Collier, C S 237

Commercial Bank of Ethiopia (CBE) 40, 239, 241, 263, 270
commercial banks 263, 265
   See also banking system
communications
   and GDP 26, 27
   investment 9, 11, 12, 209
   See also telecommunications
Compagnie de l'Afrique Orientale 234
Conditions of the Ethiopian Peasantry (Dessalegn) 123, 125
Confederation of Ethiopian Labour Unions (CELU) 2, 3
construction 9, 25
consumption 18, 30, 159
coup, December 1960 1, 2
credit 255, 257, 259
   domestic 265
   government 259-60
   policy 269-70
   private 260, 262
   rates 252-3
currency 38, 198, 232, 234, 242, 244, 247
   1941-45 250, 253
   1945-50 253, 255, 257
   1950-63 258, 260, 262
   1964-75 262, 265
   British plan 242, 244
   confidence in 248, 250, 267
   Ethiopian initiative 244, 246
   issue of 246, 250
   notes and coins 247, 253, 258-9
   reserve 250, 258
   US involvement 245
   See also economy, money market, money supply
Czechslovakia, aid 51

D

data collection 279-80
death rate 284
Debre Berhan 305
debt 49, 53
   See also economy, foreign debt
debtera service 79
defence expenditure 33-4
demography, and famine 285
Dessalegn
   Conditions of the Ethiopian Peasantry 123, 125
   Moral Crusaders and Incipient Capitalists: Mechanized Agriculture and Its Critics in Ethiopia 125-6
devaluation 267-8
   See also economy
development 34, 54, 56, 199-200
   and agriculture 147, 156, 158, 177, 179
   industry 200, 202, 204, 206, 211
   investment 9
   rural 169-70
   See also economic development, rural development
Development Bank of Ethiopia (DBE) 40, 240, 271-72
drought 318

E

East African shilling (EAS) 247, 251, 262
   See also currency
economic development 6, 9, 19, 197, 270, 273
   See also development, economy
economy
   1941-52 196, 198
   British control 198-9
   improvements in 53
   planning 7, 9, 13, 15
   See also currency, expenditure, monetized economy, revenue, subsistence economy, taxation
education 4, 204
   investment 9, 11, 12
electricity 9, 25, 53, 221, 320
employment 24, 210, 215, 218, 325
Eritrea, federation with Ethiopia 1
Ethiopian Abattoirs 272
Ethiopian Grain Board 268
Ethiopian Investment Corporation 40, 272
Ethiopian Mortgage Share Company 40
Ethiopian Peoples' Revolutionary Party (EPRP) 3
Ethiopian Tourism and Hotels Investment Corporation 40
ethnicity, and land tenure 126
eviction 116-7
exchange
   controls 251, 268-9
   rates 247, 251-2, 267
   See also foreign exchange
expenditure 31, 36

exports 5, 9, 18, 39, 41, 47, 164, 197-8, 216-7, 268
    coffee 9, 39, 41, 44, 164
    food 159
    gold 44
    hides and skins 9, 43-4
    legumes 164
    oilseeds 42, 44, 164
    pulses 42, 44
Extension and Project Implementation Department (EPID) 165, 172, 176

F

famine 4, 160-1, 285, 312, 318
fertility rate 282, 284
feudal system 4, 14, 76
    See also class structure
Five-Year Plans
    1958-62 9-10, 166-7, 206, 211
    1963-67 10-11, 167, 213, 216
    1969-74 11-12, 168, 216, 218, 220
food 10, 221
    aid 160
    consumption 159
    exports 159
    imports 159, 317
    investment 214-5
    output 215
    production 21, 159, 317
foreign aid 49, 53
    See also aid
foreign assets 266, 268
foreign debt 51, 53
    See also debt
foreign exchange 48, 250
    See also exchange
foreign investment 2, 9-10, 12, 14, 22-23, 201-2, 209, 212-3, 224, 226
    See also investment

G

gebbar 80, 102
gebbar maret 83-84, 112
gendabal maret 83-4
Germany (Federal Republic), aid 51
Gojam, land tenure 86, 89
gold 24, 44
Gondar 305
    land tenure 92-3
    governors 97-8

Gross Domestic Product (GDP) 10, 13, 24, 316
    and agriculture 21
    and communications 26-7
    and manufacturing 221
    and services 25, 27
    and trade 25
    and transport 26-7
Gross National Product (GNP) 16-17, 19
gult 81, 96, 98
    abolition 108
    definitions 72, 76
gult gezh 97

H

Handbook of Abyssinia 96-7
Harar 305
health 320, 323
    investment 9, 11-12
hides and skins, exports 9, 43-4
Hoben, on land tenure 88-9
housing 9, 323, 324
Humera Agricultural Development Project (HADP) 170

I

Imperial Board of Telecommunications 26
Imperial Highway Authority 26
Imperial Savings and Home Ownership Association 40, 240, 273
imports 5, 9, 18, 45, 47, 53, 222, 226-7, 268
    food 159, 317
income 10, 12, 16, 19-20, 171
    See also revenue
Income Tax Proclamation 1961 2
Indo-Ethiopian Textiles 272
industrialization 129, 309
    1941-52 196, 202, 204
    1953-61 205-6
    1962-74 211-2, 214, 218, 220
    dependent 224
    and First Five-Year Plan 210-1
    geographical distribution 228
industry 1, 17, 19, 22, 25, 311
    development 200, 202, 204, 206, 211
    growth 12, 23, 24
    investment 9, 22, 24, 207-8, 212
    policy 211-2, 214
    production 9, 22

interest rates 252-3, 262, 264-5
International Bank for Reconstruction and Development (IBRD) 247
International Development Association (IDA) 50
International Labour Office (ILO) 169
International Monetary Fund (IMF) 247
investment 10, 12, 18, 28, 30, 133, 318
    agriculture 9-10, 12, 133, 166, 168, 214
    chemicals 214
    communications 9, 11-12, 209
    construction 9
    development 9
    education 9, 11-12
    electricity 9
    food 214-5
    health 9, 11-12
    housing 9
    industry 9, 22, 24, 207-8, 212
    manufacturing 9, 11-12, 209, 211-2, 214-5, 217-8
    metals 214
    mining 9
    Netherlands 206
    textiles 214-5
    tourism 9
    trade 9
    transport 9, 11-12, 209, 214
    See also foreign investment
Investment Bank of Ethiopia 240
Investment Corporation 272
Investment Decree 1963 2, 212-3
Investment Proclamation 1966 2, 212
irrigation 294
Italian occupation 194, 197, 234, 304-5
Italy, aid 51

J

Jimma Agricultural School 147, 149

L

Labour Relations Board 3
Labour Relations Proclamation 2
land
    and class 84-5, 129, 134
    conservative views 127, 129
    cultivated 288, 292, 294
    distribution 103-4
    lay holdings 94-5
    liberal views 127
    measurement 103
    nomadic 134, 138
    ownership 76-7, 80-1, 99-100
    perceptions of 122, 134
    privatization 101-2, 110, 112
    productivity 119
    radical views 122, 127
    reforms 119, 122, 178-9
    and the state 84-5, 100, 108
    taxation 109
    See also land tenure, landlessness
Land Reform and Administration, Ministry of (MLRA) 14, 178
land tenure 54, 182
    Addis Ababa 113
    Begemder 86-7
    churches 93, 96
    and ethnicity 126
    fragmentation 118, 122
    Gojam 86, 89
    Gondar 92-3
    holding size 118-9
    liberation to revolution 113, 122
    and military service 79-9, 104
    and obligation 78, 80, 118
    Shewa 81, 83
    theories of 72, 77
    Tigray 89, 91
    and tribute 81
    Wag 91-2
    See also land, landlessness, tenancy, tenant farmers
land to the tiller 122-3, 125, 126, 139
landlessness 158
    See also land, land tenure
landlords 104-5, 113, 116, 119, 122
legumes, exports 164
loans 51

M

maderiya 80-1, 105-6
manufacturing 202, 204, 206, 311
    competition 224
    and First Five-Year Plan 208, 210
    and GDP 221
    growth 12
    investment 9, 11-12, 209, 211-2, 214-5 217-8
    output 209, 215, 217-8
    under-utilization 224
Maria Theresa Thaler or dollar (MTD) 233-4, 247, 251-2

Meison
  See All Ethiopia Socialist Movement
metals 214, 221
metkaya maret 83
migration 291
  rural-rural 162, 164, 292, 295
  seasonal 293
  urban 295-6, 298, 300, 318-9
  See also resettlement
military service, and land tenure 79, 89, 104
minerals 24
  See also mining
Minimum Package Programme (MPP) 13, 172, 174, 176
  See also Package Programmes
mining 9, 24
Monetary and Banking Proclamation 241
monetized economy 5
  See also economy
money market 272
  See also currency
money supply 38, 40, 250, 252, 255, 257, 265
Moral Crusaders and Incipient Capitalists: Mechanized Agriculture and Its Critics in Ethiopia (Dessalegn) 125-6
mortality rate 284, 286
Mortgage Corporation 273
Moslems, and church obligations 93
Mutual Aid Agreement 199, 245

N

National Bank of Ethiopia (NBE) 232, 239, 242, 262, 265
National Economic Council 8
National Population and Housing Census 1984 280
National Sample Surveys 278
nationalization 232
natural resources 317
Netherlands
  aid 51
  investment 206
nomadism, definition 135

O

obligation, and land tenure 78, 80, 118
oil crisis 3
oilseeds, exports 42, 44, 164
output
  food 215
  growth of 16, 19
  manufacturing 209, 215, 217-8

P

Package Programmes 170, 175, 177, 183
  See also Minimum Package Programme
pass system 296
peasant agriculture 151, 154, 156, 158
  See also agriculture
Planning and Development, Ministry of 8
population 16, 316
  age-sex structure 281-2
  control 319
  density 152
  distribution patterns 286, 291
  early estimates 277, 280
  growth 280-1, 315, 318
  urban 300, 307, 313
potash 24
prices 41, 273
priestly land (ye-qes meret) 79
production
  food 21, 159, 317
  industry 9, 22
  tributary mode 75-6
productivity
  agriculture 160, 177
  land 119
proxy 98-9
pulses, exports 42, 44

Q

qes maret 88
quarrying 24

R

railways 130, 310
refugees 294
rents 117-8
resettlement 178-9, 293, 295, 319
  See also migration
rest 73, 75, 80-1
  absolutization of 110, 113
  and maderiya 105-6
retainers 130-1
revenue 31, 36, 164
  structure of 36, 38
  See also taxation
revolution 1974 139

roads 11, 26-7, 53, 310
rural development 169-70
See also development

S

samon maret 79, 84, 99
savings 18, 27-8, 318
security 196
Selassie, Haile, on serit 100-1
Selassie, Mahteme, on land tenure 77, 82-3
serit 78, 82, 86, 95, 138
    abolition of 100, 113
services 17, 19, 25, 27
Share Dealing Group (SDG) 272
shares 272
Shewa, land tenure 81, 83
shum-gulti 97
sisso 103
smallholder agriculture 158, 162
See also agriculture
social change, and agricultural technology 155-6
Societe Nationale d'Ethiopie Pour le Developpement de l'Agriculture et du Commerce 234
society, and agriculture 179, 186
Southern Regional Agricultural Development Project (SORADEP) 170
Soviet Union, aid 50-1
State Bank of Ethiopia (SBE) 40, 236, 240, 247, 252
steel 221
strikes 3
students 3
subsistence economy 4
See also economy
sugar 205
Sweden, aid 51
Swedish International Development Agency (SIDA) 171

T

Tach Adiabo and Hadekti Agricultural Development Unit (TAHADU) 170
tariff protection 223-4
taxation 32
    agriculture 163-4
    land 109
    See also revenue
technology 227-8
telecommunications 26, 53
    See also communications
tenancy 115-6
    See also land tenure
tenant farmers 182, 183
    See also land tenure
textiles 10, 214-5, 221
Tigray, land tenure 89, 91
tourism, investment 9
trade
    and GDP 25
    investment 9
    terms 48-9
trade unions 2-3
transport 323
    and GDP 26-7
    investment 9, 11-12, 209, 214
    See also air transport, railways, roads
tributary mode of production 75-6
tribute
    abolition 108, 110
    and land tenure 81

U

United States
    and agriculture 148, 151, 167
    aid 50-1
    currency involvement 245
    and Ethiopia 199, 201
urban planning 319, 320
urbanization 129, 279, 300
    contemporary 304-5
    decline 309-10
    early 20th century 303-4
    growth of 288, 305, 308, 310, 313
    pre-20th century 301-2
    regional patterns 313

W

Wag, land tenure 91-2
waste disposal 320-1
water supply 320
Weld, Gebre, on land tenure 77-8
wereda gendabal 83
westernization 134
Wollaita Agricultural Development Unit (WADU) 170
Wonji sugar factory 205
World Bank 50-1, 172, 177, 240, 247, 271
World Food Conference 1943 245
World Food Programme (WFP) 160

Y

ye-debtere maret 79
ye-meskel maret 79
ye-qes maret (priestly land) 79
ye-zemecha maret 89
Yugoslavia, aid 51